# At Penpoint

**A THEORY IN FORMS BOOK**
*Series Editors*
*Nancy Rose Hunt and Achille Mbembe*

# At Penpoint

African Literatures,
Postcolonial Studies,
and the Cold War

**MONICA POPESCU**

Duke University Press
Durham and London
2020

© 2020 Duke University Press
All rights reserved
Designed by Drew Sisk
Typeset in Portrait Text, Helvetica Neue, and Eurostile by Copperline Book Services

Library of Congress Cataloging-in-Publication Data
Names: Popescu, Monica, [date] author.
Title: At penpoint : African literatures, postcolonial studies, and the Cold War / Monica Popescu.
Other titles: Theory in forms.
Description: Durham : Duke University Press, 2020. | Series: A Theory in forms book | Includes bibliographical references and index.
Identifiers: LCCN 2020002233 (print) | LCCN 2020002234 (ebook)
ISBN 9781478008514 (hardcover)
ISBN 9781478009405 (paperback)
ISBN 9781478012153 (ebook)
Subjects: LCSH: African literature—20th century—History and criticism. | African literature—Soviet influences. | Cold War—Influence. | Postcolonialism—Africa. | Politics and literature—Africa. | Literature and society—Africa. | Africa—Intellectual life—20th century.
Classification: LCC PL8010 .P575 2020 (print) | LCC PL8010 (ebook) | DDC 809/.896—dc23
LC record available at https://lccn.loc.gov/2020002233
LC ebook record available at https://lccn.loc.gov/2020002234

Cover art: V. Rybakov, *For the solidarity of the women of the world!* Publishing House "Fine Art," 1973. © State Historical Museum, Moscow.

## CONTENTS

Acknowledgments  vii

Introduction  Genres of Cold War Theory: Postcolonial Studies and African Literary Criticism  1

**Part I**  African Literary History and the Cold War

1  Pens and Guns: Literary Autonomy, Artistic Commitment, and Secret Sponsorships  31

2  Aesthetic World-Systems: Mythologies of Modernism and Realism  65

**Part II**  Reading through a Cold War Lens

3  Creating Futures, Producing Theory: Strike, Revolution, and the Morning After  107

4  The Hot Cold War: Rethinking the Global Conflict through Southern Africa  145

Conclusion  From Postcolonial to World Literature Studies: The Continued Relevance of the Cold War  185

Notes  193
Bibliography  229
Index  249

## ACKNOWLEDGMENTS

"We are children of the Cold War. We came of age when it ended," states the narrator of Binyavanga Wainaina's memoir *One Day I Will Write about This Place*, and his pronouncement about his Kenyan childhood holds true for my intellectual trajectory as well.[1] It has been relatively recently that I came to understand how deeply marked my worldview has been by growing up under a soul-crushing communist regime in Romania and hearing the family stories of persecution, displacement, and survival. Escaping a detested dictatorship in 1989 only to be soon confronted with the depredations of capitalism around the world has been both a sobering experience and the seed for a comparatist perspective. Were these two inimical worlds all that different from each other, when taking into account the forms of cultural and economic imperialism they generated during the Cold War? How did people living at a distance from the metropolitan hubs of the superpowers experience the differences between the high-minded promises of each model and the often devastating reality on the ground? Getting to meet both people passionately committed to the values of Western liberal democracy and persons ardently believing in the virtues of socialism has made me curious about historical and geopolitical configurations that claimed to be radically different yet mirrored and reverse-mirrored each other. This is the seed of personal history from which this book has sprung.

It is people, though—family, friends, mentors, colleagues—who have supported and cheered me on through the various stages of this project. My editor, Elizabeth Ault, has believed in my book from day one, and her support and advice, as well as that of the team at Duke University Press (especially Kate Herman, Annie Lubinsky, Kimberly Miller, and Drew Sisk), have been invaluable. It is an honor to be part of the series Theory in Forms, edited by Nancy Rose Hunt and Achille Mbembe. I feel equally fortunate in the encouragement and discerning feedback I received from the generous anonymous readers.

Most of the funding that allowed me to travel to archives and to do what I love—research—came from the Insight Grant conferred by the Social Sciences and Humanities Research Council and, later on, the William Dawson Scholar research funds. At each archival location, wonderful staff have reeled off the much-needed threads through bureaucratic labyrinths (and kept the Minotaurs at bay), but to Andre Mohammed, Babalwa Solwandle, and Wesley Francis at the Mayibuye Archives go my most special thanks.

I have been fortunate to interact with generous communities of scholars and students who have invited me to talk about this project and served as brilliant interlocutors. Warm thanks to Jini Kim Watson and the Postcolonial, Race, and Diaspora Colloquium at New York University; Stephanie Newell and the Council on African Studies at Yale University; Magalí Armillas-Tiseyra and the Comparative Literature Department at Pennsylvania State University; Andrew van der Vlies and the Postcolonial Seminar at Queen Mary, University of London; Kerry Bystrom and the Faculty Colloquium at Bard College Berlin; Pallavi Rastogi and the Departments of English and Comparative Literature at Louisiana State University; Jean Comaroff, John Comaroff, Biodun Jeyifo, and the Harvard University African Studies Workshop; Susan Andrade, Shalini Puri, Anita Starosta, and the Humanities Center at the University of Pittsburgh; Eleni Coundouriotis, Bhakti Shringarpure, the Department of English and the Human Rights Institute at the University of Connecticut; Godwin Siundu, Alex Wanjala, and the Department of Literature at the University of Nairobi; Sarah Nuttall, Isabel Hofmeyr, and the Wits Institute for Economic Research; Heike Härting, Laura Ilea, and the explorers of "Planetary Spaces" at the Université de Montréal and the Babeş-Bolyai University; Paul Yachnin and my cohort of fellows at the Institute for the Public Life of Arts and Ideas, McGill University; and many others who listened patiently and responded graciously when this project was in its more incipient stages.

I am really fortunate to teach at McGill University, where the clichéd claim of learning from one's own students truly comes to life in spirited class debates. I have accrued knowledge along with the wonderful students in the three iterations of my Global Cold War graduate seminar. A special shout-out to Mike Britt and Zain Mian: their energetic class contributions enlivened my seminar on revolutions. My research assistants—Adriane Epprecht, Sheila Giffen, Eden Glasman, Karen Huang, Sunita Nigam, Cecelia Opatken-Ringdal, Sophie Reuss, Kasia van Schaik, and Bridget Walsh—have been the most inspiringly bright, ethical, diligent, and cheerful interlocutors, and some of them savvy travel companions to far-flung archival locations. Bridget has read and corrected this manuscript multiple times and I cannot thank her enough for her patience and thoroughness. Carolyn Ownbey's sharp eyes, maverick indexing, and intellectual camaraderie have ushered this book through the final stages to completion.

I am always amazed at and humbled by the unswerving generosity of friends and colleagues who have found the time in their very busy academic lives to read various sections of the book and give me astute and elegant suggestions. Marlene Eberhart, my Montreal mainstay, and Pallavi Rastogi, my sister from different parents, read multiple versions of the manuscript, turning up valuable feedback in record time. Both this book and I have benefited immensely from your wisdom and flair. Your sustaining love, humor, and girl talk—over prosecco or on the phone—are matchless. Susan Andrade, Sandeep Banerjee, Rita Barnard, Kerry Bystrom, Rossen Djagalov, Ioana Luca, Dan Magaziner, Bhakti Shringarpure, Cedric Tolliver, Julie Tolliver, and Katie Zien—your sharp eyes, vast knowledge, and kind spirit have markedly improved this book. With many of you I have traveled, connected, and reconnected again, shared life stories, and created precious memories. Whether chatting about the Iron Curtain or pie in the sky, Ștefan Cibian, Gaurav Desai, Alin Gâlcă Vasiliu, Shane Graham, Ken Harrow, Thomas Heise, Annu Jalais, Maggie Kilgour, Chris Lee, Andrew McGregor, Mădălina Oltean, Ara Osterweil, Lorraine Ouimet, Kevin Platt, Fiona Ritchie, Rachel Sandwell, Alanna Thain, Cristina Tipi, Liliane Weissberg, and Diana Zamfir have sustained me with their tonic friendship, academic and worldly wisdom, and joie de vivre. My extended family—wonderful cousins, aunts, and uncles—have shared love and good cheer at family events and on WhatsApp. And Ngũgĩ wa Thiong'o, who generously and wondrously visited McGill and my class in 2017, has always been an inspiration with his literary genius and his unswerving commitment to "moving the centre."

Steven Gutstein's quirky humor, zest for asking probing questions about things small and large, unwavering moral compass, and quiet and generous love have brought sunshine to my life. He is the unrivaled champion of pithy summaries for my articles, Miriam Makeba's "Qongqothwane" sing-alongs, and original ways of showing he cares. My parents, Adriana and Emil Popescu, have given me love and daily support beyond imagination. If I have succeeded thus far, it is thanks to the research and pedagogical models my thorough and brilliant father and sparklingly vivacious mother have always provided for me. Although my father is no longer with us in his physical body, his guiding presence is always with me. I am so lucky to have you in my life, and to you this book is dedicated.

I gratefully acknowledge permission to reproduce excerpts and arguments that have appeared in the following articles:

"Revolutionary Times: Mongane Wally Serote and Cold War Fiction." In *South African Writing in Transition*, edited by Rita Barnard and Andrew van der Vlies, 33–53. London: Bloomsbury Academic, 2019.

"Aesthetic Solidarities: Ngũgĩ wa Thiong'o and the Cold War." *Journal of Postcolonial Writing* 50, no. 4 (2014): 384–97.

"On the Margins of the Black Atlantic: Angola, the Eastern Bloc and the Cold War." *Research in African Literatures* 45, no. 3 (2014): 91–109.

INTRODUCTION

# Genres of Cold War Theory

## Postcolonial Studies and African Literary Criticism

"Evanston-Limuru-Yalta." This triad of locations, along with a date stamp, "October 1970–October 1975," appears at the end of Ngũgĩ wa Thiong'o's novel *Petals of Blood*. Despite its conciseness, the note provides more than the biographical information needed to understand the genesis of this novel—places where the author completed substantial parts of the work.[1] The Kenyan writer positions his birthplace, Limuru, at the center of a geopolitical equation, flanked by institutions in the United States of America (Northwestern University in Evanston, Illinois) and the Soviet Union (the Yalta residence of the Union of Soviet Writers). During a period when only the superpowers—the USA and the USSR—and their close allies had global visibility, Ngũgĩ draws attention to the determining role African culture played throughout the Cold War, while also acknowledging his cultural debts to Western literature and Eastern European writing traditions. In a process that he later called "moving the centre," this date and location stamp boldly places small-town Kenya on the cultural map of the Cold War world.[2]

This is an anecdote with synecdochic purpose. From the 1950s onward, the capitals of recently independent African nations aspired to become intellectual, educational, and political centers, cities where decolonization politics and prestige-conferring artistic programs would displace the hierarchical and oppressive cultural agendas of their former colonial overlords.[3] Whether at the first Conference of African Writers, held in 1962 at Makerere College in Kampala, Uganda; at the 1966 First World Festival of Negro Arts in Dakar, Senegal, and at its second iteration, Festac '77 in Lagos; or at their political forebear, the 1955 Asian-African Conference held in Bandung, Indonesia, intellectuals from the Third World aimed to establish systems of cultural production and circulation that were not beholden to old imperial centers like Paris and London or to the new superpower hubs in Washington and Moscow.[4] If Pascale Casanova wrote the intellectual history of world literature with paths that weave in and out of Paris, how do we do justice to the stories of Ibadan, Kampala, Freetown, Dakar, and Johannesburg, as cities where writers forged alternative aesthetics and set up cultural solidarity networks with other marginalized artists' communities?[5] African and, generally speaking, postcolonial cultural production played an important aesthetic and political role for those fighting to shake off cultural imperialism and, conversely, for the superpowers aiming to hold sway over the continent. To borrow Ngũgĩ's phrase, the writing was done "at penpoint": storming the literary metropolises of empires old and new with writing implements instead of guns, authors underlined the urgency of the project to decolonize aesthetic canons.[6] From the West and the Eastern Bloc, the superpowers and their allies deployed overt cultural diplomacy and covert sponsorship programs to conquer and harness the intellectual energy in the former colonies. This clash of aims shows that, beyond the optimism and energy of the decolonization era, the story of cultural production during the second half of the twentieth century is also a Cold War story. It is a history that has largely been presented as two separate narratives—of decolonization and of Cold War–period tribulations—which this book aims to reunite.

Postcolonial studies and Cold War scholarship treat contemporaneous cultural phenomena, yet they have seldom crossed paths.[7] Taking African literatures as an example, this book aims to rewrite their main narratives to show how cultural production in what used to be called the Third World and now is described as the Global South shaped and was shaped in turn by the cultural policies of the superpowers.[8] Whether subscribing to the ideal of socially committed writing promoted by the Eastern Bloc, or to nonaligned intellectual efforts, or to a Western belief in the autonomy of cultural production, African writers had to navigate the divided political landscapes of the Cold War era. This book historicizes the emergence of African literary studies by placing this discipline in the context of the global Cold War in order to reveal the watermark left by the Iron Curtain in fiction, essays, and memoirs penned by intellectuals from the former colonies. Combining literary history with a thematic approach, it shows that the current shapes of postcolonial and Cold War studies—their goals, methodologies, and blind spots—arise from their genealogical twining and are revealed through the juxtaposition of these two cultural scenes.

Addressing these omissions and the reasons behind them goes beyond merely filling in a gap in an already rich corpus of scholarship treating the work of canonical African writers. It means speaking to one of the blind spots of postcolonial scholarship—the relation between cultural forms of resistance to imperialism and the Cold War. It allows us to understand the roots of a dissociative approach visible in postcolonial scholarship that perplexingly separated the politics of leftist writers from their aesthetics or divided the cautious position numerous intellectuals maintained toward Eastern Bloc and Western state institutions from the literary forms and genres crystallizing their wariness.[9] These omissions highlight the paradigm within which humanities and social sciences research operated before and immediately after the fall of the Berlin Wall.

The conceptual tools that we deploy to speak about African literatures—"resistance literature," "protest poetry," "prison memoir," "national allegory," "peripheral modernisms," and the superordinate categories of "Third World literature," "postcolonial literature," and today "world literature"—have all been shaped to a greater or lesser extent by the knowledge paradigms specific to the Cold War conflict and its aftermath. "The Third World is a residual category, a grab bag for whatever happens to be left over when the supposedly significant parts of the human universe, the First and Second Worlds, have been accounted for," observes Ayi Kwei Armah in an essay from the collection *Remembering the Dismembered Continent*.[10] Published right after the end of the Cold War, "The Third World Hoax," along with the other essays in the volume, is a reminder that in cultural as in political and economic matters the countries of the African continent had to formulate their position in terms oftentimes dictated by the superpowers—the United States and the Soviet Union.

As with political concepts, so with literary theories: current understandings of the social function of the writer and modes of evaluation of literary worth are the settled shrapnel from the politico-aesthetic artillery across the Iron Curtain. Likewise, debates between African writers are the continent's scaled-down equivalent of impactful global literary transformations during the second half of the twentieth century. Therefore, attending to the superpowers' institutional, thematic, and stylistic influences substantially modifies received wisdom about African literature. Working from the continental to the global level, we can similarly rethink the genealogy of the conceptual instruments with which we work in literary studies today. Conversely, the African intellectuals' efforts to write the literature they wished to write, break aesthetic tutelages, and keep their individual voices at a time when the world became polarized between "us" and "them" show that the Cold War scholarly narrative cannot be solely concerned with the superpowers.

The study of African literature—as a discipline—was born in the crucible of the Cold War, not in the sense of a subservient form of ideological alignment, but mostly as a struggle to break free of Cold War dichotomies and to forge a participatory and determining role.[11] While rethinking the history of African literary production after World War II through a Cold War lens aims to reveal unrecognized connections and blind spots in academic scholarship, this book speaks to postcolonial cultures in other parts of the world as well. The Cold War was not only a political conflict that encompassed almost half a century but also a configuration that harnessed tremendous meaning-making machineries. It involved the production of academic and popular knowledge, a process to which literature was both participant and witness. It is with these considerations in mind that I propose a look at African cultural production as simultaneously a gauge of, material trace of, and contributor to the formation of Cold War narratives, both taking from and giving to this global discourse.

## Competing Imperialisms during the (Not So) Cold War

Popular culture, such as the James Bond movie franchise, has persuaded us that the stakes of the Cold War were high for the competing superpowers. In different yet impactful ways, the stakes were similarly high for countries from the Third World, where the hot wars and low-intensity proxy disputes unfolded, even when the celluloid world gave them just a passing nod. Jamaica, from where the fictional Dr. No plotted to destroy the U.S. space program, became, like other Caribbean nations, the target of American hemispheric influence and containment policies.[12] The superpowers' interest in controlling the resource-rich African continent, alluded to in *Diamonds Are Forever*, led to numerous military coups and the installation of puppet regimes supported by the Soviet Union or the United States.[13] The historian Odd Arne Westad has decisively exposed the false perception that the Cold War concerned only the superpowers and their close allies in the Northern Hemisphere. As the title of his pioneering study *The Global Cold War: Third World Interventions and the Making of Our Times* (2005) indicates, the conflict encompassed Asia, Africa, and Latin America, where it intersected, oftentimes with violent effects, with the struggles for decolonization. Until a decade ago, most historians and political scientists understood the Cold War as a bipolar conflict that principally concerned the USA and the USSR.[14] In these studies the Third World would garner at most a footnote on the margin of events unfolding in the Northern Hemisphere. Postcolonial polities seldom featured as qualified participants, and even destructive conflicts like those that laid waste to Angola or the Horn of Africa were treated as spin-offs of events taking place in the Northern Hemisphere or as the product of clashing local nationalisms.[15] Although marginalized in scholarship, the Third World—the nations that emerged from colonial domination after World War II—became the theater of hot conflicts, territories where absentee superpowers settled their claims to world domination. When nations with a colonial past have been mentioned in Cold War scholarship, Vietnam and Cuba are the usual candidates. Even then scholars tend to dissociatively treat either the legacy of colonial subordination to Western powers or the respective country's ideological alignment with the West or the Eastern Bloc.

While historians and political scientists have been warming up to the idea that states from the Southern Hemisphere should be integrated into the account of events, Cold War literary studies have continued to overlook the cultural output of postcolonial nations.[16] Yet creative and scholarly writing against colonialism developed concomitantly with the Cold War, when aspiring or newly independent nations were forging alliances with one of the two superpowers, or among themselves, deliberately attempting to rupture the bipolar world configurations, as in the example of the Bandung Conference and the Non-Aligned Movement. To follow Westad's formulation, writers and researchers were often enticed either by the social justice model pledged by the Eastern Bloc or by the freedom and democracy promised by Western powers.[17] Other intellectuals, whether labeling their own position as nonalignment or a "third way," attempted to either steer clear of the mainstream ideologies of capitalism and communism or create new models, such as African socialism. If previously their cultural output has been neglected in favor of a study of the Cold War in Western and Eastern Bloc literary traditions, this book is part of an emerging reorientation of the field that focuses on the contributions of countries from the Third World to the worldwide debate and the reflection of this long-lasting conflict in works from the Southern Hemisphere.

It is relatively easy to understand why the idea of the Cold War (a concept introduced by American politicians and diplomats to describe the relations between the West and the Eastern Bloc) has circumvented or marginalized the Third World. It is more difficult to grasp why the field of postcolonial studies, treating old and new types of imperialism, has not focused on the forms of domination that emerged after the collapse of the traditional colonial powers *within their obvious context*—the USA's and the USSR's scramble to augment their spheres of influence during the Cold War.[18] This second Scramble for Africa and for the rest of the Third World is not fully legible even in influential analyses of cultural imperialism. A telling example is that there are only six passing references to the Cold War in Edward Said's *Orientalism*, the book usually credited with founding the field of postcolonial studies. Despite his argument that knowledge production can be properly understood only within the imperial power structures of today and yesteryear and despite references to Russian Orientalism during the reign of the czars, in the late 1970s Said addressed only one neocolonial power, the United States, overlooking the role played by its counterpart, the Soviet Union. It is perhaps fair to object that *Orientalism* focuses on forms of imperialism from the eighteenth century to the first half of the twentieth century. Yet *Culture and Imperialism*, published in 1993, while breaking new ground with its analysis of contemporary American forms of domination, shies away from naming the Soviet Union as an imperial power co-constituting the Cold War climate.[19] Finally, until quite recently postcolonial scholars have paid insufficient attention to the events and movements initiated by Third World nations that resisted the polarization of the globe, namely, the Bandung Conference (1955) and the Non-Aligned Movement (launched in 1961).[20] This is not to say that scholars of (neo)colonialism acted disingenuously, neglecting to take a clear position in their work. The Cold War exerted pressures, the ramifications of which could not be anticipated at the time.

This dissociative approach—with postcolonial and Cold War studies following separate, largely nonintersecting paths—becomes evident when we look back at the scholarship produced during the second half of the twentieth century. Scholars of postcolonialism have treated with insight and thoroughness topics such as Ngũgĩ's condemnation of the West's continued domination of Kenya, Ousmane Sembène's criticism of neocolonialism, Nadine Gordimer's relation with Western realism and modernism, and Frantz Fanon's groundbreaking essays on the psychological effects of European racism and colonization. This axis of engagement has prioritized relations of emulation or contestation between the Third World and the West. Yet little or no attention has been paid to Sembène's training in filmmaking in the Soviet Union; Alex La Guma's extensive travels through the Eastern Bloc, his prominent role in the Afro-Asian Writers Association (AAWA), and his relocation to Cuba; or Gordimer's insightful understanding of the fault lines produced by the Iron Curtain.[21] All these cultural aspects can be properly understood only when taking into consideration the Cold War background against which they unfolded, namely, the competition between Western and Eastern Bloc forms of imperialism. Even in studies where the Iron Curtain seems to be the almost self-evident background, such as literary research on Ngũgĩ's Marxism, the two scenes are not connected.[22] Events such as Ngũgĩ's sojourn in the USSR at the invitation of the Union of Soviet Writers are left unmentioned, and the role of the Cold War unstated. In other words, essential pieces of the larger picture in postcolonial studies are still missing. It is only by restoring the Cold War as the background and shaping element of the decolonization struggles and the postindependence engagement with neocolonialism that we can grasp the full significance of the aesthetic and ideological choices made by African writers, their resistance or acquiescence to the polarization of the world, and their contributions to the global discourses informing the latter half of the twentieth century.[23]

Fragmentation, an unfortunate side effect of disciplinary boundaries, also impedes the formation of a unified picture. Political events in dialogue with each other are broken down by specialization, and so are intertextual ties. Sometimes we lose track even of overlapping and contemporaneous forms of colonialism and imperialism. For instance, there are few works of scholarship that address European colonization of distant lands side by side with the forms of imperialism developed in east-central Europe by the Russian, Ottoman, Habsburg, and Prussian Empires, or compare them to Japanese imperialism. Furthermore, the Soviet Union's imperial role has only relatively recently started to be explored in a nonpolemical manner.[24] Indirectly, the erasure or blurring of continuities and similarities between classical forms of colonialism and new forms of domination deployed by the two superpowers during the Cold War veils power interests. Making visible these connections is important for understanding the role of cultural production from the Third World in representing and challenging American and Soviet narratives.

Confusing nomenclature further complicates how the Iron Curtain cordoned off portions of writing from the former colonies. Does Rudyard Kipling's judgment that "East is East and West is West" refer only to the putative differences between Occidental and Oriental cultures, or does the East as antagonist point to the socialist bloc as well? To use Timothy Brennan's formulation, the "cuts of language" partition the East-West relation in different ways, as East can stand for the (formerly) colonized—both geographical East and Third World—as well as for the ideological enemies of the West, the countries that embraced communism.[25] As William Pietz argued, nineteenth century–style colonial rhetoric was retooled after World War II to judge Russians (and the other inhabitants of the Soviet Union) as the embodiment of irrational tendencies like despotism, which made them ontologically opposed to democratic values.[26] During the Cold War, cultural imperialism—with its marginalization of literary products that did not comfortably fit Western aesthetic principles—was sometimes directed at Third World nations, and other times at the Soviet Union and its satellites. As Russia had been the object of demi-Orientalization since the eighteenth century, numerous intellectuals from the Third World saw it in a sympathetic light—an entity subjected to sometimes similar forms of discursive marginalization.[27]

If the First World looked down on cultural production from the Second and the Third Worlds, it is only natural that the Soviet Union tried to set up an alternative aesthetic system, which I discuss in more detail in chapter 2. The USSR aimed to attract intellectuals from the Third World who were disenchanted with the capitalist mode of cultural production and with the literary styles recognized by the Western publishing market. The Kremlin attempted to sway intellectuals from the former colonies, while writers' and filmmakers' unions in the USSR gave study scholarships to talented youth. Thus, some of the most important African filmmakers—such as Sembène and Abderrahmane Sissako—were trained in Moscow.[28]

Yet the aesthetic values preached in the "Fourth Rome," as Katerina Clark dubbed the earlier Moscow of the 1930s, with their emphasis on socialist realism and *partynost* (party spirit), were deliberately in conflict with those preached in Euro-American culture.[29] Aesthetic values evolved in different directions, and even whole sections of scholarship unfolded in parallel universes during the Cold War. Engaged leftist criticism did not see eye to eye with the depoliticized versions of poststructuralism that came to dominate the academic world in the West. The 1970s and 1980s consensus in the West that knowledge production should be apolitical, even when this requirement was contradicted by the more or less explicit ideological regimentation of academic knowledge, accounts for this methodological blind spot. These were not unprincipled or uneducated blind spots, but areas of penumbra generated by the extreme dichotomization of the political and cultural landscapes during the Cold War.

It is, of course, much easier to see large cultural patterns in retrospect. A few textual sites—the work of a handful of intellectuals like Aimé Césaire, Frantz Fanon, and C. L. R. James, to which I will return shortly—reveal the contours of the Cold War as a truly global conflict as early as the 1950s and 1960s.[30] However, by the 1980s and 1990s, their clearly formulated call to revolt against all forms of (neo)colonial domination had been dismissed in favor of poststructuralist approaches that focused on the complex intermeshing of power and knowledge production. In Neil Lazarus's words, the field of postcolonial studies that emerged in the 1980s was "predicated on a disavowal of liberationism, which it understands to have been rendered historically anachronistic" by the emergence of global capitalism and the collapse of the socialist regimes, yet at the same time opposed to Western mainstream antiliberationism and "the imperialist language of leading policy-makers."[31]

In scholarship written after the end of the Cold War, the work of the so-called anticolonial intellectuals—as opposed to their later counterparts, the postcolonial scholars—is often treated in a perfunctory manner, perceived as important pioneering work in the study of imperialism yet nonetheless burdened by unsubtle ideological commitments. Take, for instance, this assessment of anticolonialism in Bill Ashcroft, Gareth Griffiths, and Helen Tiffin's *Key Concepts in Post-Colonial Studies* (1998), a book that has shepherded numerous students and young scholars into the field:

> In the second half of the twentieth century, anti-colonialism was often articulated in terms of a radical, Marxist discourse of liberation, and in constructions that sought to reconcile the internationalist and anti-élitist demands of Marxism with the nationalist sentiments of the period (National Liberation Fronts), in the work and theory of early national liberationist thinkers such as C.L.R. James, Amílcar Cabral and Frantz Fanon.[32]

The implication that these intellectuals' work is ideologically regimented (they are "radical Marxists") and circumscribed to a specific national context ("early national liberationist thinkers") takes away from the important role they have played in the thorough and systematic analysis of forms of imperialism across the world. As chapter 3 shows in more detail, they could hardly be labeled "radical Marxists," unless by "radical" we understand a judicious adaptation of orthodox Marxism to local economic and political structures.

Despite such disparaging remarks, the works of Césaire, Fanon, and James reveal a keen awareness of the pitfalls of the new political configurations after World War II. One of the early essays that assesses the connections between colonial interests and the postwar Western capitalist culture is Césaire's "Discourse on Colonialism," published in its first form in 1950. The tremendous rhetorical energy that he arrays to critique the capitalist logic of profit and the disregard of human lives undergirding colonial rule (with the famous equation "colonization = thingification") leads to an equally important evaluation of the post–World War II political landscape. The essay concludes in Césaire's trademark aphoristic manner with a warning for those looking up to the United States of America as a champion of the oppressed: "American domination—the only domination from which one never recovers, I mean one never recovers unscarred."[33] Written a few years after the end of the war, the essay shows Césaire at a moment when he was beginning to discern the contours of a new global configuration of power, yet without having a full grasp of its pitfalls. His approving nod to the Soviet Union as a possible model for nations in the Caribbean and Africa is given at a time when he was still an active member of the French Communist Party.

However, by 1956, in his "Letter to Maurice Thorez," in which he renounces membership in the French Communist Party, Césaire shows a full grasp of the Cold War landscape and the imperial ambitions of both superpowers. Criticizing the French communists for their patronizing attitude toward leftists from the colonies, he also distances himself from the practices of the USSR, observing that Soviet fraternalism is a byword for new forms of paternalism and condescension toward people of color:

> Stalin is indeed the very one who reintroduced the notion of "advanced" and "backward" peoples into socialist thinking.
>
> And if he speaks of the duty of an advanced people (in this case, the Great Russians) to help peoples who are behind to catch up and overcome their delay, I do not know colonialist paternalism to proclaim any other intention.
>
> In the case of Stalin and those of his sect, it is perhaps not paternalism that is at stake. It is, however, definitely something that resembles it so closely as to be mistaken for it. Let us invent a word for it: "fraternalism." For we are indeed dealing with a brother, a big brother who, full of his own superiority and sure of his experience, takes you by the hand (alas, sometimes roughly) in order to lead you along the path to where he knows Reason and Progress can be found.[34]

Césaire's nimble argumentative strategy captures several problems with the USSR that, he points out, are not limited to the Stalinist abuses revealed and condemned by Nikita Khrushchev in his 1956 "Secret Speech."[35] The structure of the Soviet Union led to the creation of internal forms of colonialism that replicated the domination Russians had exercised over nations forcefully incorporated into the old empire. Equally significant is his critique of the Soviet Union's self-appointed paternalist role, the assumed leadership position that conceals forms of imperialism similar to those exercised by the West. By pointing out that the Soviet Union invoked the same Enlightenment principles ("Reason" and "Progress") that supported the Western colonial mentality, Césaire preceded by half a century the recent research outlining the forms of imperialism within the Soviet Union and inside the Eastern Bloc.[36]

If the neocolonial ambitions of the United States are well documented, new research on the USSR has pointed out that the help this superpower extended to countries emerging out of colonial rule was not disinterested. It was meant to augment or strengthen the Soviet sphere of influence. Starting in the 1920s, the Soviet Union, and later its Eastern European satellites, expressed interest in the fate of oppressed people of color and offered support for anticolonial revolutions, especially when led by communist forces.[37] Couched in internationalist terms, this much-avowed communist solidarity with oppressed peoples ("the brotherhood of nations") often camouflaged racial typecasting as well as neo-Orientalist discourses that formulated yet another "civilizing mission." The Eastern Bloc countries cast themselves in the role of selfless guides for young African nations in need of tutelage and protection.[38]

While Césaire remained a committed Marxist and activist to the end of his life, he nonetheless outlined the connections between the French left and colonialism and blew the whistle on the uglier aspects of the support the USSR gave colonized nations. This difficult balancing act of staying true to Marxism yet criticizing its institutional forms is quite rare at a time when many leftists in the West and in the Southern Hemisphere continued to summarily dismiss any censure of the Soviet Union's imperial ambitions as mere ventriloquism of capitalist interests. Indeed, criticism of either major actor in the Cold War was understood as a form of ideological subservience to the other side. This forced polarization blunted more nuanced arguments and rarely allowed for unregimented positions. In the early 1980s, Nadine Gordimer decried the "Manichean poisons" produced by the Cold War.[39] In Gordimer's South Africa, where, on the one hand, the government was quick to accuse leftist activists of subservience to Kremlin interests and, on the other hand, the African National Congress and its ally, the South African Communist Party, kept a united ideological front by sidelining dissenters, it was even more difficult to express discerning criticism of either side.

The subtly or overtly partisan nature of public discourse on both sides of the Iron Curtain oftentimes prevented scholars from seeing larger patterns of domination and similarities between the two blocs. As Césaire pointed out, the Cold War was not a competition between a neocolonial power (the United States) and a rival with a benign internationalist agenda (the Soviet Union). Rather, it was the cultural and political configuration generated by the rivalry between two imperial powers, with sometimes similar and other times different modes of operation. It is only this context of competing imperialisms that can truly make legible the cultural choices of intellectuals from the Third World in all their complexity. This struggle between superpowers, together with postcolonial intellectuals' attempts to dismantle or eschew the dichotomization of the world, is the indispensable background against which we are to reread African (and generally postcolonial) literature. It left its watermark on the production, circulation, and reception of postcolonial writing. By rereading African literature in this way—a process that is the object of this book—the continent and, by extrapolation, other regions of the Third World appear as not only battlefields and hot spots of a planetary conflict but also, more important, witnesses and contributors to the formation and development of a global Cold War culture.

Susan Buck-Morss has argued persuasively that, despite seemingly radical differences separating capitalist and communist polities during the Cold War, both sets of states wove mass-utopia narratives of progress and abundance rooted in a similar modernizing ethos.[40] The space race, the competition between the Soviet Union and the United States to launch the first satellites and put the first person on the moon, displayed both sides' confidence that human-made technology could outstrip the limitations of nature. As David Caute reminds us, while this contest at least on the surface seemed to focus on cultural competition, it "was possible only because both sides were agreed on cultural values to an extent that may seem astonishing, given the huge divide between a 'totalitarian' system and a pluralistic democracy."[41] Beyond a shared yet differently manifested belief in modernization, both the USSR and the USA acted as imperial powers, in a visible contradiction between their stated aims and their actual approaches. While both superpowers ostensibly supported decolonization struggles, "the methods they used in imposing their version of modernity on Third World countries were similar to those of the European empires that had gone before them."[42] The resistance to old and new forms of imperialism began at the Bandung Conference of 1955. Weaponizing the condescending term *Third World*, these African and Asian states asserted their need to level the playing field by creating a coalition of forces able to counterbalance the superpowers—a reminder that the process of decolonization took place against the background of the Cold War.[43]

Yet the forms of imperialism exercised by the USA and the USSR were not necessarily congruent, even if both sides supported coups and countercoups, propped up puppet regimes, and established economic treaties with their allies to expand their spheres of influence.[44] The discourses that cloaked each side's economic and political interests arose from different histories and would therefore take different forms. The United States claimed to support former colonies by playing up its own postrevolutionary development and promising to impart the democratic values and institutions it had achieved. Its commitment to support postcolonial states was also intended to address and dispel the dismal civil rights situation of the African American population during the 1950s and the early 1960s.[45] The USSR had incorporated Asian territories that had been part of the old Russian Empire, dominated the economies of its east-central European satellites, and strong-armed numerous communist parties around the world into toeing the ideological line. By playing up its internationalist credentials, it also attempted to assuage concerns about the forms of coercion and lack of freedom imposed on both its internal and external satellites.

This project therefore requires a redefinition of postcolonial studies. The narrow, traditional understanding reduces it to a field concerned with forms of Western domination as they evolved in tandem with the capitalist system. In some formulations from the 1980s and the 1990s—those primarily placing emphasis on forms of cultural imperialism—even the second part of the definition is optional.[46] I argue that postcolonial studies should instead address diachronically overlapping and synchronically interweaving forms of (neo)colonial domination.[47] Setting this more capacious scope for the field allows us to see, for instance, east-central Europe as the target of successive waves of imperialism (Ottoman, Russian, Habsburg, Soviet, American), and Vietnam as the playing field of French, American, Russian, and Chinese domination. The African continent, after achieving nominal independence from its colonial overlords, became the target of American and Soviet imperialism, while after the fall of the Berlin Wall, Western neoliberal capitalism and the interests of emerging economic powers such as China and Russia have continued the history of forms of imperialism on the continent.

## Knowledge Paradigms, Postcolonial Studies, and African Literary Criticism

Where does Africa stand in postcolonial studies? This question may seem redundant as postcolonial studies readily present themselves as the natural repository for research on African culture. However, the relation between the two research areas is more complicated. The field of postcolonial studies was founded with the publication of Edward Said's *Orientalism* in 1978—or so overviews of the discipline often let us know. This is the narrative we oftentimes teach our students in theory courses and specialized lectures on postcolonial literature. Yet the most cursory glance at the cultural criticism produced in the newly decolonized nations or countries awaiting independence from World War II to the 1970s shows us that the notions discussed by Said had been acerbically debated beforehand. Indeed, Neil Lazarus has observed that issues central to postcolonial studies, such as Said's injunction to "unthink Eurocentrism," were formulated a couple of decades earlier by African scholars and writers.[48] Similarly, we can point to the work of Aimé Césaire, who had already made visible the discursive incorporation of African peoples into European administrative, economic, political, and historical narratives, a process that he named "thingification."[49] Youssef El-Sebai, the Egyptian editor in chief of the journal *Lotus:*

*Afro-Asian Writings*, had likewise already outlined the high stakes of culture in the war against new forms of imperialism. Es'kia Mphahlele had formulated the task of decolonizing the scholarly perspective on African literature in the early 1960s, in the series of conferences he organized in 1962 (Kampala) and 1963 (Dakar and Freetown). The latter two conferences, dedicated to introducing African literature in the university curriculum, represented a concerted effort to undo the Eurocentric biases of higher education in Africa. Even the famous "Nairobi revolution," as Apollo Obonyo Amoko has named the call for the "abolition of the English Department," spearheaded by Ngũgĩ wa Thiong'o, Taban lo Liyong, and Henry Owuor-Anyumba's memorandum of October 1968, is oftentimes relegated to an intermediate position, between the efforts of anticolonial precursors and the plenitude of postcolonial analysis produced in the aftermath of the publication of *Orientalism*.[50]

How did this process of obscuring important research in African studies come to happen? What would it take to reset the narrative of postcolonial studies, and implicitly that of African literary scholarship? In an article from 1981, Wole Soyinka urged scholars to engage in a sociological analysis of literary critics, which would clarify the intellectual genealogies of the latter's scholarly concerns. "To my knowledge, very little has been attempted in studies of the critic as a socially-situated producer, and therefore as a creature of social conditioning, a conditioning which in fact offers no certitudes about the nature of his commitment to the subject which engages him, his motivations, or, indeed, about the very nature of his social existence."[51] His essay reminds us that during the Cold War the field of literary studies was besieged from both the right and the left. The right replicated the condescending fallacies of colonial discourse. The left imagined itself in the most radical terms and, according to Soyinka, altered the substance of the literary work for the sake of driving an argument home.[52] While starting from critics' statements about his work that he had found offensive and inaccurate, Soyinka's argument surpasses the level of personal discontent to show how either a pro-Western or a Marxist approach—both of which were inextricably tied to the context of the Cold War—can modify the dominant scholarly narratives in the field. His essay is a call to take a step back to contextualize and historicize the scholarly narratives about African literature and African writers.

If Said urged us to examine the forms of cultural imperialism and the knowledge production networks that manufactured the Orient as a discursive construct, we equally have to revisit the process of knowledge production during Cold War imperialism. Drawing on Said's approaches to cultural imperialism, Andrew N. Rubin labeled Western cultural domination during the Cold War "a way of knowing, a style of thought through which power worked to create divisions, distinctions, and discriminations."[53] This does not apply only to American neocolonialism; it is even more important to see the interpenetrating forms of Cold War imperialism as producers of knowledge paradigms. Historicizing the position of literary critics and essayists engaged in defining the field of African literature, as Soyinka urged us, will explain why Western forms of imperialism had more visibility during the Cold War for some African intellectuals, while others closed their eyes to the forms of control emanating from the West in order to repel the long arm of Soviet domination. To make visible the role of African cultural production within the larger field of postcolonial writing, we have to acknowledge the succession and interpenetration of forms of cultural and political imperialisms beyond the visible forms of domination exercised by the West. As long as postcolonial studies remains a field narrowly concerned with studying the long-term effects of Western colonialism, as long as we neglect to discuss the interlocking and overlapping forms of imperialism during the Cold War, African cultural production will remain only partly visible to scholarship.

What applies to culture is even more valid for the relation between material and cultural aspects. This book proposes to revisit African texts through a Cold War lens to see how they directly or obliquely mark the presence of overlapping imperialisms. This focus, which structures the second part of the book, can reveal the roots and the material traces of the marginalization of African cultures. Take, for instance, the startling example Ngũgĩ wa Thiong'o uses in *Decolonising the Mind* (1986) to explain the alienation induced by the imposition of a colonial language: "This [feeling of alienation] may in part explain why technology always appears to us as slightly external, *their* product and not *ours*. The word *missile* used to hold an alien far-away sound, until I recently learnt its equivalent in Gĩkũyũ, *ngurukuhĩ*, and it made me apprehend it differently."[54] The first missiles were used by Germany during World War II, yet the technology is associated with the Cold War and imposed itself on the consciousness of the world with the 1962 Cuban Missile Crisis, the event that threatened to turn the conflict into a nuclear conflagration. Thus, Ngũgĩ's comment draws attention to more than just the intertwined material and cultural imposition of Western (neo)colonialism; it illuminates the specific forms of imperialism arising from the Cold War competition between superpowers, which consigned Africans to a technological and linguistic penumbra. The Gĩkũyũ word Ngũgĩ selects as the equivalent of the term *missile* attempts to reintroduce a pastoralist culture in a world driven by the ethos of technological modernity: a ngurukuhĩ is a short, pointed stick that is thrown at a wayward cow to bring the animal back to the herd.⁵⁵ This archaic pastoralist term, antiquated in the context of contemporary Kenyan experience, represents the writer's attempt to salvage, preserve, and legitimize the forms of knowledge originally displaced by British colonialism and later by Cold War imperialisms. The wood cutting, planted in the earth to sprout a new plant (the Gĩkũyũ word's secondary meaning), is to take root and germinate a cultural experience different from the totalizing narratives put forth by the Cold War superpowers.

More important, what Ngũgĩ experienced as the alienating effects of the word *missile*, which in his Marxist interpretation reflects "the language of real life"—the relations of production—elsewhere in the West, may have actually been shaped by the gap between the American term *missile* and the corresponding Russian word *raketa* (rocket), or similarly the distance yet overlap between the words *astronaut* and *cosmonaut*.⁵⁶ To put it differently, there might have been different words to refer to the same technology on either side of the Iron Curtain, yet technology from each side was involved in expanding the superpowers' spheres of influence. Ngũgĩ is a fierce critic of neocolonialism, which, at that time, he understood to be a product of Western capitalism. In this book I argue instead that forms of neocolonialism in Africa were the result of the interplay and competition between Western and Eastern Bloc forms of imperialism, as the development of missile technology actually indicates. It is only the Cold War lens that does away with the relative marginalization of Africa in postcolonial studies and presents a more comprehensive account of twentieth-century forms of imperialism.

By revisiting the history of African literature and postcolonial studies through a Cold War lens we come to realize that scholars like Césaire correctly diagnosed the political and cultural situation. The multidirectional forms of imperialism—with the USA and the USSR as the main imperial powers—shaped cultural production during the second half of the twentieth century. It is a diagnostic that for the majority of us becomes visible only now, when both the blind spots created by the Cold War and the triumphalist discourse of the West in the wake of the fall of the Berlin Wall and the collapse of the socialist regimes no longer obstruct the view. To borrow and adapt an idea put forth by Jean and John Comaroff in *Theory from the South: Or, How Euro-America Is Evolving toward Africa*, looking at postcolonial theory from the vantage point of African cultural production during the Cold War reveals the contours of a competition of superpower imperialisms that had characterized the field and yet had been obstructed by the Euro-American methodologies on which the field rests.

## African Writers in the Crossfire of Cold War Imperialisms

Accustomed from films and spy fiction to an urbane yet lethal secret agent who is usually a far cry from the bookish type, it might surprise readers to realize that the literary and scholarly world—in the West, the Soviet Bloc, and the Third World—has known its fair share of intrigue and espionage during the Cold War. A 1958 North Atlantic Treaty Organization (NATO) confidential report on the Afro-Asian Writers' Conference in Tashkent—the cultural event that inaugurated the AAWA—highlights the surprisingly high degree of interest Western and Eastern Bloc states showed in writers from parts of the world that did not appear to be in the direct line of fire during the Cold War. Why would an intergovernmental military organization be concerned with the discussions Asian and African writers held in the capital of the Uzbek Soviet Socialist Republic? Compiling reports from the Ceylonese (Sri Lankan), Pakistani, and Indian delegations, as well as the account of a British Embassy official who encountered nine members of the Japanese delegation, the report focuses on the level of Soviet expenditure for the conference, English and French translations of international and local literature made available for the event, and the likelihood that the organizers managed to impress or even ideologically sway the participants. Written on behalf of the United Kingdom's delegation, the report displays a condescending attitude and repeats colonial clichés:

> From the point of view of serious literature the Writers' Conference had been practically worthless. Its only achievements had been to bring about some stimulating and interesting meetings between Asians and Africans, and to enable the Communist element to put out propaganda on the usual lines. . . . In this propaganda the emphasis had been mainly on the need to write on current themes (i.e. primarily anti-colonialism). This had had more effect on the Africans, who for the most part have no literary traditions, than on the Asians who have. Indeed, it was the Africans who, throughout the proceedings, played up more to the Soviet point of view, and spoke more violently.[57]

Two important points emerge from this document. First, the beginning of the Cold War and the concurrent period of decolonization did not do away with colonial discourse; it simply morphed into the new forms of imperialism wielded by the superpowers and their allies—the United States and Western Europe, on the one hand, and the Soviet Union with, and later against, China, on the other. Second, the ranking of Asian conference participants above their African counterparts based on the former's previous access to "literary traditions," which the latter putatively lacked, is not a mere rehearsal of the historically resilient and harmful representation of Africa as a continent devoid of historical consciousness, artistic accomplishments, and literary works. It demonstrates the importance accorded to cultural production in general, and literature in particular (at least literature in the forms recognized and validated by the two superpowers and their close allies), as a Cold War ideological instrument. As I discuss in more detail in chapter 1, culture became the proxy battlefield where the conflict unfolded. This faith in the power of literature explains why the USA and the USSR spent what, from this dismal moment of defunded humanities, appear like astounding figures for supporting the arts and cultural production at home and abroad.[58] Literary figures commanded authority. The election of two writers—Agostinho Neto and Léopold Sédar Senghor—as the first presidents of independent Angola and Senegal, respectively, reinforces the prestige of literary figures during those times of turmoil.

An interest in African literature was similarly expressed from the other side of the Iron Curtain. A few months after the landmark 1962 conference of African writers at Makerere College in Kampala, Uganda, *Voprosy Literatury*—one of the most influential scholarly publications on literary studies and philology in the Soviet Union—published a review of the event. As no Soviet representative had attended the conference, the reviewer relied on an account written by the event organizer, the South African writer Ezekiel (later Es'kia) Mphahlele. Much energy is dedicated to presenting African literature as a battlefield between progressive forces and regressive approaches—the former in keeping with other leftist literary developments, the latter directed by nefarious Western interests:

> Under the cover of "negritude" propaganda, some circles in the West try to prove the importance of retaining patriarchal order (tribalism), which impedes the political, social, and cultural progress of the countries of the "Black Continent." They push African literature toward idealization of the tribal past, and African writers toward the road of endless and harmful arguments getting in the way of their main task: the creation of a literature helping the peoples of Africa in the struggle against colonialism, a literature that would be the spokesman of the hopes and aspirations of the new African society. The Kampala conference showed that contemporary African literature successfully overcomes the "infantile disorders" of growth, sweeping away everything that gets in the way of her development.[59]

Mphahlele was a strong opponent of the Négritude movement, especially in the form promoted by the Senegalese president and poet Léopold Sédar

Senghor, and his criticism of its worldview likely had informed the Russian reviewer's response.[60] Yet beyond this understandable rejection of a romanticized view of the African past, there lies the weaponization of cultural theories to serve in the ideological battle between superpowers.

The congratulatory tone of the article is, moreover, undermined by occasional paternalistic formulations, as the author refers to African literary production as a literature overcoming its "'infantile disorders' of growth."[61] The syntagma placed within quotation marks references Vladimir Lenin's 1920 work *"Left-Wing" Communism: An Infantile Disorder*, and therefore suggests inevitable problems that can be surpassed with proper discipline and commitment. Nevertheless, Lenin's phrase, transplanted to an evaluation of African literature, reflects an undercurrent of superciliousness. The mirrored condescension in the NATO report and the Soviet review are chilling reminders that forms of (cultural) imperialism structured the Cold War geopolitical configurations.

During this prolonged conflict, much of the animosity and tensions between the superpowers was transmuted into and expressed through seemingly benevolent cultural diplomacy programs. Greg Barnhisel argues that "American cultural diplomacy had been founded on the premise that private, nongovernmental groups were the ideal cultural ambassadors and that the government's role should be to foster their involvement as much as possible."[62] Without appearing to be directly inimical to the other side, cultural diplomacy could act as a conduit of programs aiming to augment the superpowers' spheres of influence. For instance, the information programs developed under the umbrella of the United States Information Agency were "tasked with the job of telling America's story to the world."[63] Conversely, after the death of Stalin, the Soviet Union invested a lot of energy in cultural diplomacy, both with the West and the United States and also with the so-called Third World. The 1957 establishment of the Union of Soviet Societies of Friendship and Cultural Relations with Foreign Countries, and of the State Committee for Cultural Ties, as well as the firm hand that the Central Committee of the Communist Party kept on them, demonstrates the vision, shared by the superpowers, that culture granted access to each other's populations and could sway "hearts and minds" abroad.[64] Through exhibitions, cultural festivals, and educational cooperation, "cultural influence also became one of the most important instruments in the post-Stalin opening to the Third World, where the Soviet Union began to actively solicit the support of nationalist—but noncommunist—regimes."[65]

Most of the Cold War battles were fought at penpoint, yet gunpoints were directed at Third World countries as well. As David Caute points out, the Cold War was unlike any other confrontation between imperial powers, as the USA and the USSR did not dispatch armadas and troops in open combat; instead, they sent "their best ballerinas, violinists, poets, actors, playwrights, painters, composers, comedians and chess players into battle."[66] His assessment is only partly true: the war was cold only for the superpowers and their allies in the Northern Hemisphere, owing to the mutual-annihilation threat posed by a nuclear conflagration. Countries from the Third World, however, served as battlegrounds for hot conflicts, proxy wars, coups, and countercoups. The United States and the Soviet Union deflected their animosity through cultural efforts: they organized cultural events, promoted artists, offered scholarships, sent cultural ambassadors, and helped with the publication of ideologically aligned works in countries where they aimed to increase their visibility and solidify their grip. Indeed, the battle aimed to win both the hearts and minds of their own citizens and those of people across the world.[67] Quoting a 1949 statement by American philosopher Sidney Hook, the Central Intelligence Agency (CIA) website acknowledges that a cultural offensive oftentimes replaced military action during the Cold War: "Give me a hundred million dollars and a thousand dedicated people, and I will guarantee to generate such a wave of democratic unrest among the masses—yes, even among the soldiers—of Stalin's own empire, that all his problems for a long period of time to come will be internal. I can find the people."[68]

As chapter 1 shows in more detail, the superpowers targeted African intellectuals through publication programs and financial and logistical support for journals, literary events, and conferences. Some of the most important publications in the history of African literature received the financial backing of the two superpowers. For instance, journals and magazines that made significant contributions to the flourishing of the field of literary studies on the continent, *Black Orpheus* and *Transition*, on the one hand, and *Lotus: Afro-Asian Writings*, on the other, were supported by the United States and the Soviet Union, respectively. These investments in African culture were part of a larger global pattern. Recent research on UNESCO has revealed the ideological weaponization of culture and conceptions of literacy.[69]

During the first two decades of the Cold War, at the center of the United States' activities abroad was the Congress for Cultural Freedom (CCF). Established in 1950 as an anticommunist, antitotalitarian cultural organization, and headquartered in Paris to avoid suspicion of direct American involvement, it attracted both conservative and leftist intellectuals. In fact, leftist intellectuals were the target audience, in an attempt to rally them around Western values and distance them from political affiliation with the Soviet Union and the Eastern Bloc.[70] Frances Stonor Saunders has authored the most extensive and innovative research on the CCF to date. *The Cultural Cold War: The CIA and the World of Arts and Letters* underscores the extent of the CCF operations; it "had offices in thirty-five countries, employed dozens of personnel, published over twenty prestige magazines, held art exhibitions, owned a news and feature service, organized high-profile international conferences and rewarded musicians and artists with prizes and public performances."[71]

The CCF supported an impressive roster of journals, with the flagship *Encounter* (based in London) acting as a venue where some of the most important ideas of postwar culture were debated, validated, and reinforced. Other journals included *Der Monat* (Germany), *Preuves* (France), *Cuadernos del Congreso por la Libertad de la Cultura* (published in France for distribution in Latin America), *Tempo Presente* (Italy), *Forum* (Austria), *Cadernos Brasileiros* (Brazil), *Quadrant* (Australia), *Quest* (India), *Hiwar* (Lebanon), and, on the African continent, *Transition* and *Black Orpheus*.[72] The money was channeled through the Farfield Foundation, to give an air of political disinterestedness. According to Andrew Rubin, the CCF operation was at the center not only of the ideological conflict between East and West but also of a paradigm of imperial transfer of authority from Europe to the United States during the period of decolonization: "All these energies and resources, it was revealed, were enlisted to legitimize and culturally sustain the transfer of imperial power from Europe to the United States in the aftermath of the Second World War and refashion and reinvent the idea of world literature."[73] His assessment reminds us that Cold War–era imperialisms were overlapping and multidirectional, making actual resistance to co-optation a difficult-to-almost-impossible balancing act. While a lot of Soviet support unfolded more openly, therefore making it easier to identify and bypass institutions that served their interests, the covert CCF operation was nearly impossible to detect. Therefore, the 1966–1967 successive revelations of the vast network of cultural venues financed by the CIA devastated most of the intellectuals affiliated with the CCF.[74] The sense of betrayal they expressed is revealing with respect to the embedded presuppositions about the role of culture and literature in society. After the lessons of authoritarianism and totalitarianism (Nazi Germany and the USSR) were processed in the wake of World War II, the West positioned culture as an independent realm, not beholden to politics, a view ironically breached with this extensive intelligence operation. While the CCF reformed as the International Association for Cultural Freedom and continued its operations until 1979 with much-reduced funding, it is anyone's guess what the declassifying of archives in the next couple of decades might reveal as American government conduits for shaping cultural production around the world.[75]

Rubin's statement that the CCF participated in the refashioning of the idea of "world literature" is an important point that would warrant much more extensive treatment than afforded by the limited space in this introduction. This concept, which has become fashionable in the new millennium, especially with the publication of David Damrosch's *What Is World Literature* (2003) and Pascale Casanova's *The World Republic of Letters* (first published in French in 1999), has been vigorously challenged, especially from the left. The book *Combined and Uneven Development: Towards a New Theory of World-Literature* (2015), by the Warwick Research Collective (WReC), is the most sustained engagement of this type. As the hyphen in "world-literature" announces, this group of intellectuals from the University of Warwick challenges the premise of the earlier definitions and instead presents the relation between literary forms and genres and their geographical distribution as directly impacted by the capitalist world-system. In chapter 2 I return to this debate and, taking the WReC as interlocutors, propose a more comprehensive understanding, through the prism of the Cold War. The aesthetic system generated by the capitalist world-system was countered from the other side of the Iron Curtain, as the Soviet Union's investment in different modes of writing and a differently conceived social function of the writer attests. Indeed, as Maria Khotimsky argued, the Soviet Union had developed its own idea of world literature by the end of World War I. As Maxim Gorky founded Vsemirnaia Literatura (World Literature) Press, a long tradition of Soviet investment in culture and its political importance was concomitantly established.[76]

The institution on the eastern side of the Iron Curtain that forms the focus of much of part I of this volume is the Afro-Asian Writers Association (AAWA). Paradoxically, considering its later development, the AAWA's origins lie in the anti-imperial energies unleashed by the 1955 Bandung Conference of Asian and African nations. The groundwork was laid the following year in Delhi, where Mulk Raj Anand and other progressive Indian writers organized the first Asian writers' conference. There they formulated the desirability of a cross-continental alliance of writers from Asia and Africa. In 1958 the AAWA debuted with its first conference in Tashkent, the capital of Uzbekistan, one of the republics comprising the Soviet Union.

The newly constituted AAWA became one of the hot spots around which Cold War tensions manifested. True to the cloak-and-dagger atmosphere of the period, it entailed both physical and character assassinations. The AAWA was initially headquartered in Sri Lanka, and although the NATO confidential report mentioned earlier surmised that "in practice the thing would have to be run by the Soviet Embassy in Colombo," in 1965 pro-Soviet writers determined that the AAWA's Permanent Bureau would be moved to Cairo and placed under the leadership of Egyptian writer and future minister of culture Youssef El-Sebai, who was elected secretary-general.[77] Through El-Sebai the Permanent Bureau also acted as the cultural wing of the Afro-Asian People's Solidarity Organization (AAPSO). The change of location highlights the tensions brewing beneath the surface of what half a decade earlier might have appeared as a united anti-imperial and nonaligned front in the Third World. China had attended the Bandung Conference, despite numerous participants' apprehension that its leaders would act as mouthpieces for Soviet-style communism; yet the Sino-Soviet split soon placed the two states at odds. This fracture was reflected within the AAWA in the different ideological alignments of writers: pro-USSR versus pro-China intellectuals pulled the organization in different directions and, by 1966, split it.[78] The headquarters of the former were set up in Cairo; those of the latter in Beijing. More perplexing, the two factions continued to coexist in parallel, laying claim to the same name and history, with each side demanding to be recognized as the rightful inheritor.[79]

In 1968 the Cairo-based AAWA—which forms the object of this study—published the first issue of its journal *Lotus: Afro-Asian Writings*.[80] The same year, the pro-Chinese faction published a booklet entitled *The Struggle between the Two Lines in the Afro-Asian Writers' Movement*. The extravagant language of praise for Mao Zedong, with quotations printed in bold font, is matched only by the acrimonious tone directed at the Soviet Union: "Now it has become crystal clear that without acute uncompromising struggle against the Soviet revisionists, accomplices of U.S. imperialism, no success could be scored against U.S.-led imperialism, old and new colonialism and other reactionary forces."[81] While the Chinese approach is deeply problematic—for instance, the publication boasts that they have "purified" the ranks of the AAWA "by getting rid of Soviet renegades"—this parallel history points out that intellectuals from the Third World laid claim to an anti-imperialist vocabulary that criticized both American and Soviet forms of domination.[82]

The AAWA continued to be submerged in a Cold War espionage atmosphere for the next two decades. In 1978 an extremist Palestinian group gunned down El-Sebai while he was taking part in an AAPSO conference in Nicosia, Cyprus. In the ensuing attempt to find the murderers, who had taken thirty hostages in order to secure their own departure from Cyprus, an Egyptian military commando sent without the host country's permission clashed with Cypriot forces and almost created a diplomatic incident. El-Sebai had been killed for having accompanied Egypt's leader Anwar Sadat to Israel, for talks that the splinter Palestinian group had seen as a betrayal of its cause. It was a devastating turn, as El-Sebai had consistently used the space of *Lotus* as well as the AAWA and AAPSO events as platforms for supporting the Palestinian cause. This Cold War history, with its unexpected twists and turns, is scattered across continents and different languages and cultures, and is therefore impossible for a single researcher to piece together.[83]

Yet the story of *Lotus* and the AAWA does not stop in Cairo. It continues in Beirut, where the Permanent Bureau moved in the late 1970s, with the Pakistani poet Faiz Ahmed Faiz in charge, and later in Tunis, where it was headquartered in the early 1980s. Much of the history of the association, its administrative notes, and even some of the issues of the journal were lost or destroyed during the civil war in Lebanon. Of the *Lotus* issues published simultaneously in English, French, and Arabic, most of the surviving material from the 1980s is in Arabic. Yet, concomitantly, the activity of other members of the Permanent Bureau, such as the South African writer and secretary-general of AAWA from 1979 to 1985, Alex La Guma, wove connections between Havana, where he was headquartered, and the rest of the world. The Cold War was the background against which much of these intellectuals' literary careers unfolded and, more importantly, was the shaping force of their political and literary stance. This conspicuously absent angle in the evaluation of their work speaks to the blind spots created by the ideological fault lines of the latter half of the twentieth century in the development of the field of African postcolonial literature.

## Mapping the Cold War in African Literary History

To study the movement of ideas, the formation of literary networks, and notions of literary value on both sides of the Iron Curtain and within nonaligned spaces, I draw on both archival and textual evidence. Most of the documents and writings I consulted are in English; however, a number of journal articles, novels, and conference papers originally appeared in French, Portuguese, or Afrikaans. For the sake of accessibility and homogeneity, I used published translations in English, unless otherwise indicated. In geographical terms, most of the works draw on authors from or events that took place in West Africa (especially Ghana, Senegal, and Nigeria), East Africa (Kenya and Uganda, in particular), and southern Africa (Angola and South Africa). The emerging literary capitals Kampala, Dakar, Luanda, Accra, Johannesburg, Nairobi, and so on existed sometimes in an uneasy alliance with and at other times in open rebellion against literary metropolises such as London, Paris, Moscow, and New York. To map the networks and fault lines uniting and separating these locations, *At Penpoint: African Literatures, Postcolonial Studies, and the Cold War* takes a two-pronged methodological approach. The first part of the book comprises a historiographical assessment of the development of African literary studies, with a focus on the tenets of debates and literary venues. The latter half constitutes a thematic approach to representations of the Cold War in works from the continent.

Part I, "African Literary History and the Cold War," revisits some of the most important literary debates and the venues where they took place at the time when African literature was emerging as a scholarly field. I explore the direct impact of the Cold War on the production, circulation, and reception of African literature, with a focus on the late 1950s to the late 1980s. Chapter 1, "Pens and Guns: Literary Autonomy, Artistic Commitment, and Secret Sponsorships," proceeds from debates regarding the function of the writer in society during the second half of the twentieth century, asking, in Lewis Nkosi's words, whether writers should "separate the problem of gun-running from the problem of wielding the pen."[84] Are writers autonomous intellectuals, dissident figures who maintain their distance from the powers that be, concerned only with their craft? Or are they committed citizens who, by wielding pens and guns with equal adroitness, participate directly in decolonization struggles and the development of new societies? Cultural diplomacy programs financed by the superpowers, and writers' attempts to bypass such influences, shaped the divergent positions on the role of the writer in society. Looking at how the USA and the USSR attempted to sway African writers to their side, I discuss both the subtle and the direct forms of pressure the superpowers exercised. I draw my evidence by attending to essays, journalism, and archival material pertaining to the CCF with its sponsored literary venues in Africa (*Black Orpheus* and *Transition*); to the originally independent and gradually Soviet-influenced AAWA and its journal *Lotus: Afro-Asian Writings*; and to the Pan-Africanist and avowedly nonaligned journal *Présence Africaine*. The chapter demonstrates the impact of the Cold War: these publication and discussion venues promoted specific writers, author functions, and modes of writing, thus contributing to the formation of literary canons. It also draws attention to the history of committed art in the Third World.

Like chapter 1, which started from a debate on the role of the writer in society and thus is relevant to literary scholarship at large, chapter 2 reprises and redirects a debate that has galvanized scholars over the past two decades. "Aesthetic World-Systems: Mythologies of Modernism and Realism" takes up and problematizes an apparent dichotomy emerging between the supporters of modernism, largely identified with Euro-American aesthetic principles, and the backers of socialist realism, oftentimes perceived as an anachronistic artistic mode promoted within the Eastern Bloc. Instead of setting them up as yet another Cold War Manichean relation, I focus on the mythologies of realism and modernism as they were sedimented into literary consciousness owing to the aesthetic world-systems set up by the superpowers during the Cold War. The argument builds from essays by Ayi Kwei Armah, Es'kia Mphahlele, Micere Mugo, Lewis Nkosi, and Ngũgĩ wa Thiong'o and from proceedings and archival material pertaining to conferences in Cairo (1961), Kampala (1962), Dakar (1963), Freetown (1963), and Alma-Ata (1973). This abundance of materials reveals that theories of (world) literature were being formulated on the African continent at a time when the forces of aesthetic decolonization were intersecting with those produced by the global Cold War. The chapter ends with a quick survey of aesthetic shifts in Ngũgĩ's works, indicating that the cultural Cold War turned the antinomy between modernism and realism into two aesthetic world-systems that still affect the way we perceive literature today, by making invisible or illegible entire corpuses of texts.

Part II, "Reading through a Cold War Lens," proposes that we reread important works of African literature to identify the watermark left by this conflict. This type of reading expands established approaches to African literary history by suggesting new ways of articulating texts, of setting them in dialogue, while also allowing for a better understanding of the Cold War as a global conflict.

Chapter 3, "Creating Futures, Producing Theory: Strike, Revolution, and the Morning After," is concerned with literary renderings of imagined futures and the genealogy of ideas of revolution. The decolonization struggles of the 1950s–1960s, extending to the end of the Cold War in the case of southern Africa, drew on varied modes of action that energized the masses, from the strike represented in Ousmane Sembène's *God's Bits of Wood* (1960) to the armed struggle in Mongane Wally Serote's *To Every Birth Its Blood* (1981). The writers I look at think of revolution in leftist terms, yet their conception of transformative futures goes beyond the classics of Marxism-Leninism to engage with theorists of revolution in Africa—Frantz Fanon, Amílcar Cabral, and Steve Biko. The chapter starts from these writers' representations of the temporality of revolution and ends with interpretations of its aftermath. I read Ayi Kwei Armah's canonical novel *The Beautyful Ones Are Not Yet Born* (1968) as depicting not only the stagnation of neocolonialism (as most critics have done) but also the dead ends of African socialism. As with African perspectives on the function of literature and representational modes, the theories of revolution that emerge from the three authors discussed here contribute to enriching postcolonial studies.

Chapter 4, "The Hot Cold War: Rethinking the Global Conflict through Southern Africa," turns to another important theme that gives the lie to the very concept of cold war. It focuses on the changes in the literary representation of one of the hot spots of this global conflict: the war in Angola.[85] I look at a comprehensive regional panel of texts, from accounts written at the time of the conflict to retrospective narratives that commemorate this protracted proxy conflict. However, their visibility has varied, owing to the different overarching categories under which these works have been placed: South African memoirs and fiction of the Border War, lusophone literature of decolonization, African war fiction, and postmodern or magical realist writings. What do the shifts from literature based on the experience of conscripts, in Anthony Akerman's *Somewhere on the Border* (1986) and Mark Behr's *The Smell of Apples* (1993); to the realist or modernist novels of the decolonization period in southern Africa, such as Pepetela's *Mayombe* (1980), Nadine Gordimer's *July's People* (1981), and Sousa Jamba's *Patriots* (1990); to the contemporary magical realist fiction of Ondjaki's *Granma Nineteen and the Soviet's Secret* (2008) and Niq Mhlongo's *Way Back Home* (2013), tell us about the limits and strengths of specific genres in representing this conflict? I consider the trajectory of this body of works in formal terms, by contextualizing them in relation to global literary shifts in genre and by historicizing them in relation to the Cold War and its aftermath.

Southern Africa is a productive nexus of languages, literary genealogies, and cultural conflicts, yet only a continental and *longue durée* approach can give us a comprehensive perspective. In my preceding monograph, *South African Literature beyond the Cold War* (2010), I examined the previously overlooked impact of Eastern Europe in the postapartheid South African cultural imaginary. Yet, as I completed it, I discovered that the connections went deeper in time than the similarities between the 1990s transitions in the two regions, to their Cold War roots. The scope also has to be wider: both continental and global, tracing African intellectuals' axes of engagement with the United States and the Soviet Union as well as within Pan-African and Non-Aligned Movement networks.

What I hope I have unearthed in this book are both little-explored archives and new methodologies for reading texts in order to underscore the rich ways in which the Third World has contributed to the creation of global cultures *and* to theorizing them. Whether focusing on novels, essays, or conference ephemera, I show how we can reread African culture of the second half of the twentieth century through a Cold War lens. The stakes of such an exercise go well beyond completing the body of scholarship on writers' oeuvres with a perspective heretofore absent from this corpus. Like a chemical treatment or heat applied to invisible ink, the Cold War perspective acts as a developing substance that illuminates the political and ideological forces at work in postcolonial literatures, the aesthetic choices facing African writers, the specific forms taken by their critical reception, and even the blind spots in postcolonial scholarship. It reveals African intellectuals' contributions to various branches of cultural theory. I return to this point in the conclusion, which addresses again the impact of the Cold War on the disciplinary narratives in postcolonial studies and the developing field of world literature.

Part I

**African Literary History
and the Cold War**

# 1

## Pens and Guns

Literary Autonomy, Artistic Commitment, and Secret Sponsorships

In 1967, while taking part in the African-Scandinavian Writers' Conference in Stockholm, Alex La Guma exclaimed, "I, as a South African writer, am prepared to run guns and hold up radio stations, because in South Africa that is what we are faced with, whether we are writers or whether we are common laborers."[1] As expected, such a strong creed elicited equally robust responses from the other conference participants, who were a distinguished group of emerging and already established intellectuals that included Wole Soyinka, Ngũgĩ wa Thiong'o, and the revolutionary Algerian poet Kateb Yacine, as well as a celebrated group of South African writers that comprised Ezekiel (later Es'kia) Mphahlele, Lewis Nkosi, and Dennis Brutus. Counterintuitively, La Guma's remark and its evocation of violence likely appeared less jarring to his interlocutors than it would today: this was an era of decolonization and revolutions in Africa, when Frantz Fanon's call to arms in *The Wretched of the Earth* resounded across the continent. The coparticipants' reactions indicate that La Guma startled them by upending a piece of (Western) intellectual orthodoxy when stating that writers' duties include direct participation in social struggles. His stance, echoed by other writers yet contested by an equally large number of participants, asks us reappraise a debate on the role of the writer that was carried out during the Cold War.

I would like to revisit this moment because it offers insights into the formation and development of the field of African literature and its associated literary criticism. Some of the most important debates carried out from the end of World War II to the fall of the socialist regimes in 1989, such as those focusing on the role of the writer in society, have been forgotten, or their importance appears diminished today. This effect is not a consequence of their insignificance. Rather, the end of the Cold War, and the acerbic cultural battles it had sustained, as well as the global triumph of neoliberal capitalism, made some of these debates fade into oblivion. As a result, our current understanding of contemporary African literature and African literary criticism has been shaped by selective cultural memory and forgetfulness. To get past the blind spots created during and after the Cold War, we need to revisit and reactivate some of these debates, as they reveal a different distribution of cultural interests at the time when the study of African literature as an academic field was being born.

In order to paint a comprehensive view of these processes, I will position cultural debates among African intellectuals regarding the role of the writer in society within the Cold War–era discursive fields. This will allow me to discuss both the direct ways in which the superpowers influenced cultural production (funding, selective publication) and the interweaving structural forms of influence (cultural exchanges between like-minded intellectuals, publication networks, and conference circuits). As they subscribed to sometimes opposing views regarding the role of literary creation in society, African writers participated in and attested to transformations of Cold War–period global aesthetic discourses on realism, modernism, and postmodernism, to which I will turn in chapter 2. Finding themselves unwittingly embroiled in forms of cultural patronage, numerous African writers staunchly attempted to keep their distance from the aesthetic canons of the East and the West, which they saw as forms of cultural colonization. Instead, they drew on local traditions, Third World cultural alliances, and forms of Pan-African solidarity. Yet their evasive tactics further underline the impact of a Cold War–era polarized cultural field. In engaging with or distancing themselves from aesthetic categories backed by the West or the Eastern Bloc, writers became participants in the processes of cultural production shaped by the Cold War.

How do we assess the impact of Cold War political and cultural configurations, without either creating a crude image of literary puppets animated by the superpowers' interests or overemphasizing the agency of intellectuals at the cost of trivializing the effect of structural forms of influence? A comparative survey of three of the most important scholarly works dealing with specific aspects of the Cold War and African literary production shows us a gradation of emphases. In *Archives of Authority: Empire, Culture, and the Cold War*, Andrew N. Rubin looks at the role the United States, through the Congress for Cultural Freedom (CCF) and similarly oriented Western organizations, played in establishing "new regimes of consecration—a literary and cultural order through which certain authors became specifically identifiable as world authors in a new kind of international literary system."[2] By emphasizing the systemic aspects of this form of domination, Rubin forecloses much of the aesthetic freedom African writers had hoped to achieve when they shook off colonial bonds. To this astute yet grim view of literary production during the Cold War we can counterpose Peter Kalliney's more optimistic belief in the ability of writers to beat the system. Meticulously reading the Transcription Centre Records, Kalliney argues that for African writers "with a strong commitment to decolonization," Western aesthetic vocabularies, especially "modernist proclamations of intellectual and creative independence, held a profound appeal."[3] It follows that African writers were able to subvert the intentions of the American state and the CCF by appropriating Western aesthetics for their own purposes. Finally, looking at cultural production through the prism of socialist solidarity networks, Rossen Djagalov, in his book *From Internationalism to Postcolonialism: Literature and Cinema between the Second and the Third World*, focuses on the role of the Afro-Asian Writers Association (AAWA) in establishing a "contact zone" between the Second and the Third Worlds that eschews Western literary influences.[4] Acknowledging the complicated interweaving of idealism, bureaucratic oversight, and Soviet paternalism that brought the AAWA under the influence of the USSR, Djagalov focuses on the liberating and innovative processes the association spearheaded: it "aimed to establish direct South-to-South literary relations that would bypass the (neo)colonial metropoles of Paris, London, or New York."[5] Juxtaposing these three pronouncements, each substantiated by impressive research, shows that the study of Cold War literary production needs to orchestrate different perspectives in order to attend simultaneously to direct forms of imposition, structural forms of influence, and the sometimes small, and other times comprehensive, networks writers were able to create in order to disrupt established geopolitical configurations.

### From Dissident to Militant Writers

But first let us return to Stockholm and the meeting of African and Scandinavian writers.[6] In Lewis Nkosi's words, the debaters assessed whether writers should "separate the problem of gun-running from the problem of wielding the pen."[7] La Guma's bold statement came as a response to Wole Soyinka's keynote talk "The Writer in a Modern African State," in which Soyinka condemned African writers for becoming alienated from reality, mesmerized instead by a romanticized view of the past and glorified African humanism. This was a direct critique of the tenets of Négritude as proposed by the Senegalese poet and president Léopold Sédar Senghor. Soyinka criticized both the posturing of exiled writers who became inefficient United Nations fixtures and those who became embroiled in military coups in their own countries, by running guns and holding up radio stations. Ironically, two years earlier Soyinka himself had been imprisoned for using a radio station to criticize censorship and dictatorial tendencies in Nigeria; however, in Stockholm he was most likely addressing the increasing factionalism in Nigeria a few months before the Biafra War broke out.[8] According to Soyinka, what was compromised through this partisan political affiliation was the "integrity" of the writer and the writer's role as a "record of the mores and experience of his society and as the voice of vision in his own time."[9] These ideas are not new; they draw partly on the West African role of the griot as an oral historian and, more important for the argument here, on the European romantic tradition of the writer as prophet and the Euro-American modernist perception of the autonomous character of literature, which ought to maintain its "integrity" in relation to the ideologically tinted (or tainted) political field of action.[10]

La Guma's idea that writers, when confronted with oppression and denial of basic human rights, should not be squeamish about direct, violent intervention is less common today in literary criticism. This view of the revolutionary artist—wielding pen and gun with equal adroitness, and subsuming their craft as a writer to the duties of a conscientious citizen—held sway with many artists during the Cold War. I am emphasizing the Cold War setting of this debate because by historicizing the tenets of this dispute, we may elucidate the rise and decline of certain concerns in literary criticism during the latter half of the twentieth century.

La Guma posed the issue of the writer's function in society in terms close to how the Soviet Union as well as Marxist intellectuals in the West described the position of artists. Seen from this angle, the writer was a laborer among other skilled laborers, a working-class participant in the collective task of transforming and bettering society. Comparing his fellow participants to unskilled laborers and finding them lacking, La Guma asserted that "at conferences that I have attended of workers, either in the electrical industry or building industry or whatever, they have always known what they were and they have always discussed the problems from the point of view of knowing where they stood." He urged his fellow writers to determine first "what our functions are."[11] In other words, the writer could not stand aside and formulate social criticism from a detached, uninvolved position. Dennis Brutus would later take up this line of argument, aiming to "turn upside down . . . a series of widely accepted values": criticizing the class-blind opinion that writers engage in their creative process out of love for humanity, he explicitly drew on Mao Zedong to put down writers who distanced themselves from the people in the process of "making [themselves] special person[s]."[12] For Brutus and La Guma, writing was just another form of commitment to positive social transformation, a responsibility demanded of factory workers and intellectuals alike.

Soviet artists were not the only supporters of commitment in art. A second filiation for the idea of political engagement in literature comes from French existentialist philosopher and political activist Jean-Paul Sartre. "The 'committed' writer knows that words are action," he famously pronounced in his 1948 essay "What Is Literature?"[13] Deliberately distancing themselves from "art for art's sake," an aesthetic widely accepted in the West yet derided by Sartre and Soviet critics as a sign of bourgeois decadence, the African writers mentioned here signal their search for an alternative aesthetic system, one that they hoped would break the ideological restraints of capitalist societies. Some of them found it in socialist countries, especially the views promoted by Soviet artists, as well as within groups of sympathetic leftist intellectuals in the West and in Africa.

Arguing from a different perspective and discussing the pitfalls of establishing rules for what committed literature should look like, Es'kia Mphahlele argues that rigid formulas for engaged literature, like the one laid down by Sartre, risk transforming art into propaganda or having African literature be perceived as mere reportage. In *Voices in the Whirlwind and Other Essays*, Mphahlele works against formulas and a literature establishment that works by "decrees and orders," choosing his examples to show how a specific literary form or genre is necessary in one situation but might prove problematic in a different context: "Every writer is *committed* to something beyond his art, to a statement of value not purely aesthetic, to a 'criticism of life.'"[14]

In a 1974 article, the leftist critic Omafume F. Onoge surveyed the ways in which African writers addressed their social function "under the conceptual rubric of 'role,' 'responsibility' or 'commitment' of the writer to his society."[15] This persistent question raised at writers' conferences does not necessarily map directly to literary critics' approaches, which Onoge classifies under four rubrics: Western scholars who place a direct injunction against or a "subtle ban" on (anticolonial) political commitment (Lilyan Kesteloot, Dorothy Blair, and even Ulli Beier, Janheinz Jahn, and Gerald Moore); African supporters of "art for art's sake" who preach responsibility "strictly to the perfection of the form of [their] craft" (among whom he counts Lewis Nkosi and John Pepper Clark); critical realists (like Chinua Achebe and Wole Soyinka) who "advocate a literature that is *engaged* with the contemporary reality in a critical way"; and socialist realists (such as Ngũgĩ wa Thiong'o and Ousmane Sembène) who, "in addition to criticizing the surrounding reality," surpass critical realists in their "fundamental agreement with the aims of the working class and the emerging socialist world."[16] Onoge therefore brings Cold War ideological battles to bear on attitudes toward artistic craft and the function of the writer in society: according to his argument, the liberal critics and writers who wish literature to be autonomous serve the imperialist goals of the West by turning attention away from social suffering, while, at the other end of the spectrum, the socialist realists grasp the connections between capitalist and colonial exploitation and understand that cultural decolonization and the surpassing of social problems can happen only by "the *liquidation* of the capitalist state."[17]

Therefore, the Stockholm participants' divergent views were more than just a misunderstanding, an accidental comparison of the apples of "how to write" with the oranges of "how to be a writer." In fact, the supporters of the autonomy of the creative process did implicitly ascribe a function to the writer—that of a resister, a dissident voice, not co-opted by the powers that be and refusing to let itself be hired by the highest bidder.[18] The role assigned to such a dissident writer and some of the cultural institutions that promoted it will be detailed later in this chapter. The Stockholm dispute was a clear manifestation of Cold War ideological and artistic ruptures. However, the Cold War did not simply entail a binary configuration that forced writers to unequivocally associate themselves either with a model of literary autonomy completely evacuated of its political dimension or with a conception mandating the social role of artists that necessarily disdained the pursuit of craft and self-reflexive aesthetics. Even in Onoge's account, a complex gradation of positions emerges.

It is not my goal to point out the numerous ways in which many of the positions outlined thus far are idealistic or untenable. Nor is it my aim to decide which literary model or institution was the "right" one. Instead, my focus is on the development of literary discourses at war, animated by antagonistic political entities, which, in their clash, gave birth to the field of African literature and literary criticism. Finally, this chapter (and this book) is not concerned with choosing between First and Second World cultural models, between capitalist art and its socialist counterparts. In fact, most of the writers discussed hoped to extricate themselves from the many tutelary models imposed by successive waves of imperialism, whether those of old Western European colonial extraction or those of American neocolonialism or even Soviet imperialism.[19] Some of the most compelling positions on the function of the writer came out of the search for a third, unaffiliated or nonaligned, mode of cultural production, the dogged avoidance of choosing within a polarized world. Instead, in this chapter and the next one I revisit and reevaluate the literary debates and aesthetic choices available to African writers after World War II to determine how the current layout of the field came to be. To attend to the intermeshing forms of influence and resistance, I historicize these debates by placing them within their cultural and political contexts. Consequently, the historical processes that promoted certain African texts and authors to canonical status cast light on cultural developments around the globe.

## Autonomous Intellectuals and the State

The two opposing views expressed in Stockholm, one stressing the paramount importance of writers' "integrity" (as proposed by many Western intellectuals), and the other emphasizing social and political "commitment" (as argued by numerous Marxists on both sides of the Iron Curtain), bring us onto the battlefields of the Cold War. David Caute has emphasized the cultural dimensions of this confrontation, departing from traditional analyses that emphasized the political, military, and economic stakes. Instead of the "Armadas" deployed in past conflicts (an observation that unfortunately overlooks the heavy impact of proxy "hot conflicts" in the Third World), his analysis foregrounds cultural battles.[20] Cultural diplomacy, with its arsenal of international exhibitions and conferences, touring ensembles and "jazz ambassadors," scholarships for students and support for ideologically aligned publications, became one of the superpowers' main approaches.[21] Research carried out mostly on Cold War American and British cultural production, combined with an increasingly larger corpus of works on the Eastern Bloc, is showing the contours of a cultural battle that was global in scope. African writers were often unwittingly pulled into this contest, even when they tried to resist the cultural polarization of the globe.

Emerging archival evidence reveals the extent to which the two superpowers tried to sway African writers. Frances Stonor Saunders's *The Cultural Cold War: The CIA and the World of Arts and Letters* inaugurated a paradigm in the study of the forms of cultural influence deployed by the Central Intelligence Agency (CIA) through its umbrella organization, the CCF.[22] As described in the introduction, between 1950 and 1967, the CIA masterminded and financially supported a network of institutions, cultural venues, and literary forums clustered around the CCF. Maintaining offices in over thirty countries and publishing more than twenty magazines, the CCF built a constellation of institutions that dramatically shaped public taste and literary canons around the world.[23] The funds were channeled through a front organization, the Farfield Foundation, which provided an air of evenhanded and politically disinterested sponsorship. Without the knowledge of most of the participants involved, whether editors, writers, or scholars, important venues where African literature was promoted, published, and discussed had been bankrolled from the United States. These included the Transcription Centre in London (headed by Dennis Duerden); the Mbari Writers and Artists Club in Nigeria; the journal *Black Orpheus*, under the editorship of Ulli Beier; the Ugandan literary journal *Transition*, edited by Rajat Neogy; the Chemchemi Centre in Nairobi; and the Dakar and Freetown 1963 conferences on the teaching of African literature and, more important, the 1962 Makerere College conference, a pivotal point in debates about the field of African literature.[24] The CIA had used these cultural venues to attract intellectuals sympathetic to the political values of democracy, intellectual freedom, and—ironically—a principle of political detachment as a hallmark of literary value. Peter Kalliney has argued that the aesthetic vocabulary promoted by these institutions was modernism.[25]

At its headquarters in Paris, the CCF set up an African Program, originally headed by the African American intellectual Mercer Cook (1960–1961) and then, with significant impact, by the South African expatriate Es'kia Mphahlele (1961–1963).[26] It was with Mphahlele at its helm that the organization helped establish some of the most important venues where the contours of the field of African literature started to take shape. Literary forums in Africa had slightly predated this period. For instance, the Johannesburg-based magazine *Drum*, jam-packed with exciting journalism about music, literary events, and the attractions and terrors of black urban life, was read across the continent and beyond.[27] However, the temporally compact blossoming of literary hubs around the continent and the events sponsored by the CCF in the early 1960s initiated a sustained discussion intent on defining African literature, its languages of circulation, and its aesthetic values.

Adapting and enlarging the scope of Peter Benson's statement about the founding of the journal *Black Orpheus*, we can say that all the intellectuals and artists involved in the cultural debates patronized by the CCF from the late 1950s to the late 1960s defined the border between Euro-American and African literatures, implicitly setting up a field that was no longer "an exotic footnote" to metropolitan art: they "define[d] the nature of the goods" and "set the standards of valuation."[28] By setting the terms of the discussion—how African literature was defined, what formal aspects were considered important, what forms of literary criticism were to be imported or adapted to engage with the newly defined field—these primarily African (but also European and North American) intellectuals steered the course of the field for the decades to come. The participants themselves became canonical figures whose imprimatur later generations of writers and scholars sought to obtain.

As the director of the CCF's Africa Program, Mphahlele had access to funding to support local literary initiatives in Africa and to bring together artists from various parts of the continent and set them in dialogue with each other and with their counterparts from the West. It was an ideal position for Mphahlele's curatorial talent. He had already been directly involved in setting up one of these literary hubs while living in Nigeria. In 1957 the German art critic Ulli Beier set up the journal *Black Orpheus* in Nigeria, taking advantage of the cultural energy clustered around the University of Ibadan. The Mbari Artists and Writers Club blossomed out of this configuration, which brought together the important intellectual energies of Wole Soyinka, Demas Nwoko, John Pepper Clark, Mphahlele for a few years, and Abiola Irele later on.[29] After moving to Paris, Mphahlele offered money and logistical help for the Mbari Artists and Writers Club and supplied funding for *Black Orpheus*, which thus emerged as one of the most influential little magazines in Africa. The CCF also helped with sponsoring Mbari Publishers, which gave writers like Soyinka, Clark, Christopher Okigbo, and La Guma a venue for publishing their works before they found an audience with larger, commercial houses. From the helm of the Africa Program in Paris, Mphahlele administered a literary contest for black African writers organized by Mbari, which fellow South African writer La Guma won. It was also Mphahlele who propped up the brainchild of Rajat Neogy, the newly founded yet financially struggling Ugandan magazine *Transition*, which quickly became an important publication venue with a history that spanned Uganda, Ghana, and the United States, where it is still in print.[30]

Mphahlele's most important accomplishment was the organization—with CCF financial support—of the famous Makerere College Conference of African Writers of English Expression in 1962, setting up the foundation for literary-criticism debates in Africa. This event and the 1963 conferences he organized in Freetown (Sierra Leone) and Dakar (Senegal) spearheaded the debate on the importance of studying anglophone and francophone African literatures in the university, a rallying cry that was later successfully taken up by initiatives such as Ngũgĩ wa Thiong'o, Taban lo Liyong, and Henry Owuor-Anyumba's 1968 demand for the abolition of the English Department at the University of Nairobi and its replacement with a literature department that would foreground works written on the continent.[31] The Makerere conference brought together established writers like Chinua Achebe, Langston Hughes, and Mphahlele, as well as a diverse roster of emerging authors (among them James Ngugi (later Ngũgĩ wa Thiong'o), Soyinka, Nkosi, and Bloke Modisane), scholars, and the editors of several publications. The CCF photographs (like that in figure 1.1) as well as the archived papers capture the energetic exchanges, the playful spirit of some

Figure 1.1. 1962 Makerere conference session. The participants are identified on the back of the picture as Neville Rubin (editor), Mrs. [Elizabeth] Spio Garbrah (writer), and Wole Soyinka (writer). IACF Records, Special Collections Research Center, University of Chicago Library.

of the participants, and the genial atmosphere of this first meeting of African writers in such large numbers.

From Paris, the CCF also coordinated and sponsored the cultural activities organized by the Transcription Centre in London (1962–1977), an institution run by Dennis Duerden that brought together African artists—singers, performers, painters, writers—who were living in or passing through London.[32] The Transcription Centre ran the *Africa Abroad* radio program dedicated to African culture and politics, curated exhibitions, helped organize festivals (such as the Commonwealth Arts Festival of 1965), supported several theater and film projects, published the newsletter *Cultural Events in Africa*, and directed writers toward publications under the CCF umbrella.[33] As a result of the numerous conversations between artists hosted by the Transcription Centre, in 1972 Heinemann published a collection of interviews, *African Writers Talking*, edited by Duerden and Cosmo Pieterse.

When the CCF scandal broke and the extent of the CIA-sponsored network became apparent, journalists around the world turned toward the intellectuals at the helm of these publications and cultural venues to gauge—in interviews and analyses—the extent of their knowledge and involvement. It was an attempt to establish how political power can exert ideological pressure, whether in subtle or evident ways. Like today, the relationship between world-system(s) and cultural production fascinated scholars, even if in the 1960s, when the memory of Joseph McCarthy's communist witch hunt and the Stalinist purges was still fresh, the question resonated with the public in much more pressing ways. Rajat Neogy was interviewed in an article first carried in June 1967 by the Nairobi-based *Sunday Nation*, which Neogy then reprinted in his own publication.[34] Neogy was emphatic in establishing that he had no idea about the intelligence agency's involvement. Nor could it be said, he stated, that he was deliberately targeted and ensnared, as it was he who had reached out to Mphahlele and the CCF to ask for financial support when he ran out of the initial funds. In Neogy's analysis of this entanglement, his liberal values became both his most treasured intellectual asset and the Achilles's heel that made *Transition* a valuable target for the American government. "We pride our independence rather fiercely, even neurotically," Neogy stated, his word choice emphasizing the Cold War–era paranoid atmosphere that kept people always on their guard lest they be ideologically ensnared.[35] Although *Transition* was "perhaps the most Left-wing orientated" of the magazines supported by the CCF, this ideological tendency made it even more desirable for the CIA to bring into the fold.[36] Those in the know about the operation thought the magazine would act as a stabilizing political force in Uganda and elsewhere in East Africa.[37] Neogy surmised that the intelligence agency sensed a kindred spirit and shared values, even if driven by different political goals: "quite frankly, we do belong to the Western tradition of liberal inquiry."[38]

Given the CCF's decision to support *Transition*, it comes as no surprise that Neogy's views resonated with those of the founding figures of the CCF. In 1950, at the end of the Berlin congress, Arthur Koestler issued a manifesto proclaiming the importance of intellectual freedom, which writers should be able to exercise even when their opinions deviated from the views held by those in power.[39] Asserting that "liberalism is the toughest creed there is," Neogy believed that a good editor allows opposing views to coexist within the same publication, staging a truly democratic exchange of opinions. Aiming to go beyond the "aggressive assertiveness on the part of Marxist writers or [the] complacent close-mindedness of Western intellectuals," he trusted the value of "a rational dialogue between intellectuals of all persuasions."[40] Thus, Neogy was an important promoter in Africa of the model of the autonomous writer, not beholden to any ideology or state.

The poet and critic John Thompson, who served as the executive director of the Farfield Foundation—a CIA front organization—from 1956 to 1965, explained what he considered to have been the intentions of the intelligence agency in supporting *Transition* and similar publications by emphasizing the role of liberal intellectuals: "There was a small number of intellectuals and writers and our particular interest was in the literary people.... Our interest was in establishing an independent publishing program based on Africa and aiding African intellectuals to find their own feet on the ground."[41] Having written his discerning and comprehensive study on *Transition* and *Black Orpheus* in the 1980s, when the CCF documents were not yet available to the public, Peter Benson accepts the image of the CIA operation painted by Thompson: a project with little real oversight or rigorous planning, driven by a few intellectuals who believed that true art, universal in its values, builds democratic institutions through its emphasis on the freedom of speech and freedom of writing.[42] However, archival evidence suggests that much more oversight was involved, with the Farfield Foundation and the CCF demanding strict financial accountability.[43] Andrew N. Rubin points out the systemic aspects of this form of influencing cultural production: by braiding together the discourses of democracy and cultural freedom, the CCF "oversaw [what] had essentially become a global process, not simply of cultural reproduction but of cultural replication."[44] It is unclear whether those who designed the CCF program and other forms of state sponsorship accurately predicted their exact impact. Irrespective of the precise relation between aims and results, for the purposes of this book, the systemic aspects of the interaction between politics and cultural production are important. As Rubin correctly observes, "the activities of the CCF permitted [the writers'] work to travel in unlikely, unexpected, and influential ways."[45] *Transition* and *Black Orpheus* had a tremendous impact in endorsing, circulating, and canonizing authors and forms of writing, as I discuss in more detail further on.

There is no evidence of direct CIA oversight in the literary and cultural choices of *Transition*. Neogy would have resisted any direct interference or attempt at ideological guidance. However, his commitment to the values of liberalism aligns him with Western cultural and aesthetic values. While imprisoned by the Obote regime, he dreamed about the need for and urgency of a continuing "liberal conspiracy," a statement that inspired Peter Coleman's study of the relationship between liberalism, the CCF, and the new brand of American imperialism.[46] The CCF itself was birthed by a coalition of "liberals, social democrats, and anti-communist leftists," out of fear that Western intellectuals were succumbing to the dangerous totalitarian rhetoric spun by Moscow.[47] However, within the complex Cold War system of fault lines, citizens perceived liberal values differently depending on the context. While those on the right in the United States saw liberals as a "fifth column" intent on misrepresenting the threat posed by the Soviet Union and deceiving the population in order to steer the course of the country to the left, leftist critics had long seen liberalism as at least tacitly accepting, if not directly complicit in, (neo)colonial domination.[48]

If the CIA made sure that the cultural institutions it sponsored appeared independent of American interests, if most of the intellectuals affiliated with these forums were unaware of the secret sponsorship, if no direct pressure was exerted with respect to publication decisions, how did the American intelligence agency hope (and manage) to steer cultural life around the globe? Their tactics included the promotion of writers who supported Western values such as democracy, liberalism, and intellectual freedom; the circulation of works endorsing these values; invitations to various conferences that were extended to the same select group of intellectuals and the subsequent establishment of their authority and canonization; and the requirement to recommend and advertise other publications from within the network. In this way East African readers of *Transition* were aware of the West African *Black Orpheus*, and artists associated with the Transcription Centre in London would be familiar with the *Cultural Events in Africa* newsletter, and all would look up to the CCF flagship magazine *Encounter* as a paragon of intellectual rigor.[49]

When Mphahlele founded the Chemchemi Cultural Centre in Nairobi (1963-1965) with CCF support, his newsletter advertised other publications produced by the umbrella organization. For instance, in the first issue of the newsletter, published in March 1964, Mphahlele announced that eleven books published by Mbari Press (including Alex La Guma's *A Walk in the Night*, Christopher Okigbo's *Heavensgate*, and Dennis Brutus's *Sirens, Knuckles and Boots*) had been sent to Nairobi and would be available for purchase.[50] In the fifth issue of the newsletter (August 1964), the editor referred to *Transition* as "a most worthy magazine published in Kampala."[51] Moreover, the CCF often defrayed conference participation costs for authors it wanted to promote. For instance, shortly after Mphahlele had accepted the director position for the CCF's Africa Program, John Hunt had him invited to a conference on Africa, convened by the Cini Foundation in Venice: "I have written to the conference organizer, Mr. Vittore Branca, asking him to invite you," Hunt wrote in a decisive tone, strongly urging Mphahlele to abandon his earlier travel plans in order to attend this cultural event.[52] Thus, intellectuals like Mphahlele, Neogy, Duerden, and Beier inadvertently participated in the creation of a network of institutions and people who disseminated and solidified Western liberal ideology and its attending aesthetic principles for evaluating African writers and African literature.[53] The impact of their endeavors is still visible in the shape of the field today.

The conferences and literary forums organized by the CCF disseminated a distinctly Western liberal view of the role of the writer in society. Ironically—considering how these cultural networks were created—artists were seen as dissidents, people who had the courage to stand up to the regime and face prison sentences or even torture in detention centers. They were those who chose the distress of exile over the solace offered by kith and kin in their home countries. In Edward Said's formulation in the essay "Intellectual Exile," such a form of dissidence is more a state of mind than a material condition; it entails refusing to be part of the institutional machinery, choosing to always question the status quo and to avoid being co-opted.[54] While Said draws in this instance on Theodor Adorno's *Minima Moralia: Reflections on a Damaged Life* and is therefore informed by the immediate post–World War II context, the image of intellectual exile and moral dissidence that he paints is optimistic and rather simplified. It assumes a transparency of the political and cultural fields and entails a superhuman awareness of one's position within them—a difficult, if not impossible feat to achieve in the complex world of Cold War politics.

This inclination toward championing dissident figures in non-Western societies is evident when looking at the prestigious prizes bestowed on writers from other parts of the world. In 1986 the first African writer to win the Nobel Prize for literature was Wole Soyinka, twice imprisoned by the Nigerian government and celebrated for his detachment from political factionalism. Salman Rushdie, who opened up the path to international recognition for many postcolonial writers when he won the Booker Prize in 1981, was later both acclaimed and protected for his resistance to religious fundamentalism. The organization PEN International brought to international attention the plight of numerous writers persecuted by dictatorships and authoritarian regimes. In fact, the 1966 PEN congress organized in New York by its American branch, with financial backing from UNESCO, the Ford Foundation, and the Farfield Foundation, had as its central theme "The Writer as an Independent Spirit."[55] The CCF published censorship indexes and oftentimes focused on writers silenced by their governments. In 1965, when Yuli Daniel and Andrei Sinyavsky became the first Soviet writers to be brought to trial and imprisoned after the Stalin era, the CCF took a lively interest in their fate.[56] In his memoir *Afrika My Music*, Mphahlele triumphantly notes that the first literary competition organized by *Black Orpheus*, with CCF sponsorship, was a victory against the forces of censorship: "Alex La Guma, still under house arrest, ran off with the first prize for his powerful novella *A Walk in the Night*."[57] The formulation draws attention to the value Mphahlele and numerous other writers under the CCF umbrella placed on literary autonomy and resistance to ideological confinement as a freedom-creating mechanism.

This is a position sought and claimed by numerous Western writers and institutions from World War II to the 1990s. For instance, the charter of PEN International, which finds its origins in the struggle against totalitarianism, states that "in all circumstances, and particularly in time of war, works of art, the patrimony of humanity at large, should be left untouched by national or political passion."[58] This definition of literature is based on the assumption that art and artists must maintain an autonomous character, separate from the political domain. While quite understandable given the political perils during the second half of the twentieth century, it is nonetheless a normative understanding rooted in a modernist ethos, which separates literary production from civic engagement and other forms of social participation. Growing out of this definition of the function of art, dissidence was understood as a mode of resistance to the encroachment of the state and the political domain into the autonomous realm of creation.

As a result of this emphasis, during Mphahlele's tenure as the director of the CCF's Africa Program, his office sought to promote writers from the continent who shared a belief in the autonomous realm of creation and to perfect a support system that preserved this autonomy. After the 1962 Makerere conference, at the behest of the CCF, he engaged in a four-month tour of Africa to identify artistic communities in need of financial support. The letters he sent to local communities and the reports he filed with the congress show Mphahlele as extremely wary of creating top-down structures where his own views or those of the CCF would be imposed on African intellectuals. From the beginning he defined his role as that of "ascertaining local needs which Congress can assist in fulfilling, provided that the people themselves in any place invite our assistance."[59] Stating that "the arts will always defy polemics," the South African writer conceptualized a mode of sponsorship that pushed back from a top-down preferential model that would favor ideologically aligned artists and communities.[60] This belief that true art is bound to defy politics echoed the mandate of the CCF, as defined in a report by Edward Shils: "Congress does not seek to obtain subscriptions to an ideology. It does not seek to win intellectuals away from loyalty to their countries or to align them with or against particular parties or current of policy in their own country. It does aim, however, to heighten their attachment to universally valid standards of devotion to truth, to intellectual curiosity, and to the appreciation of creativity. It aims to cultivate an openness of spirit, a readiness to share experience and insight."[61] The disparity between the ideals expounded in this view and the reality of partisan sponsorship is a constitutive sign of the cultural Cold War.

Said and other postcolonial scholars have critiqued the belief that universal values in the arts exist independent of ideological systems and have exposed the Euro-American underpinnings of such universalism. "Counterfeit universals" are "designed to create consent and tacit approval."[62] This encompassing discourse was often couched in the terms of (Western) humanism, a discourse that in Said's analysis in his book *Humanism and Democratic Criticism* ties together other Cold War–era discourses, such as freedom and democratic values. Discussing the influence of the CCF, Said argued that "much of what was done in the name of freedom and democratic values, and fighting communist totalitarianism[,] contributed significantly to humanistic practice. It provided some of the overarching carapace and numerous programs and occasions for the promotion of humanism."[63] Said's analysis thus stresses the quiet, almost undetectable yet pervasive aspects of the system. Rubin's deft analysis of Said's later works, such as *Humanism and Democratic Criticism*, enables a view of the Cold War not merely as a political conflict but as a "way of knowing, a style of thought."[64]

It may seem at least ironic and at most highly contradictory that while Mphahlele and many of his colleagues had an impeccable record of intellectual and artistic dissidence in their countries, and defined their role as writers through their opposition to the state's encroachment on and domination of the field of artistic creation, their activity could be so easily subsumed to the aims of one of the superpowers. As we will see later on, this perplexity equally applies to left-leaning intellectuals and those who were sympathetic to the values of the Eastern Bloc. However, this is not the result of easy gullibility. The number of artists and scholars who experienced a sense of betrayal after the revelations about the CCF indicates the barely perceptible ways in which intellectuals were made part of the system, a process that oftentimes became visible only retrospectively. Their activity unfolded during the Cold War, when the superpowers vied for control of the field of artistic production.

If the CCF appears sinister to us retrospectively, it is important to understand that Mphahlele and many other intellectuals hired to run its various branches and publications most likely had no suspicion. After the extent of CIA involvement was revealed in 1967, Mphahlele participated in the meeting concerned with the reorganization of the congress (most likely owing to friendship and gratitude for the support John Hunt and Ivan Katz of the CCF had given him over the past years), and he insisted that there had been no form of coercion in the operation of the Africa Program. However, the consistent modernist aesthetic promoted in CCF's publications (to which I return in chapter

2), the cross-advertising for other CCF journals that editors were encouraged to do, and the referrals and recommendations of meritorious writers to other publication venues under the CCF umbrella promoted a group of writers with relatively cohesive aesthetic views, authors who have become emblematic of the African literary pantheon.

## Artistic Commitment and the Left beyond the Eastern Bloc

To further complicate matters, the Soviet Union extended its patronage over a network of institutions, congresses, and publication venues similar to that overseen by the United States. It promoted a different model of artistic engagement, according to which a writer was not to operate autonomously or pursue individual creative goals. The mandate of the artist was that of an active citizen, involved in the process of building a new society.[65] These ideas, grounded in the formulation of socialist realism at the Soviet Writers' Congress of 1934 and codified in successive documents of the Union of Soviet Writers, traveled to subordinate cultures in the Eastern Bloc or were rearticulated by sympathetic intellectuals from the Third World. Within the USSR, censorship controlled artistic output, and even visiting writers and filmmakers were placed under surveillance.[66] It is difficult to assess to what extent Soviet readers were genuinely interested in African literature or whether they paid lip service to an official rhetoric of the brotherhood of nations. Yet the Cold War, fought in part with a cultural arsenal that aimed to attract the newly decolonized nations, created publication venues and conversation spaces where African literature was discussed. As with the United States, the Soviet diffusion mechanisms for ideologically aligned art forms included conference invitations, publication forums, and exposure to new publics.

Foregrounding its tradition of internationalism, the Soviet Union was drawing attention to its commitment to learning about the cultural heritage of the African continent and to promoting the newest artistic developments. The literary works from Africa that Soviet publishers and critics endorsed were generally written in a realist style and dealt with class struggle or forms of colonial oppression. A 1966 article published in *Transition* provides a survey of the literary works by African writers that were translated into Russian and other languages of the USSR. These include Russian translations of books by Efua Sutherland (*Playtime in Africa*), Chinua Achebe (*Things Fall Apart*), Cyprian Ekwensi (*People of the City*), Alex La Guma (*A Walk in the Night*), Peter Abrahams (whose novel *The Path of Thunder* not only was translated and came out in twelve printings but was turned into a film and used for a ballet as well), and Mongo Beti (*The Accom-*

*plished Mission* and *The Poor Christ from Bomba*, which were translated not only into Russian but into Latvian, Estonian, and Lithuanian as well). Ngũgĩ's *Weep Not Child* and Mphahlele's *Down Second Avenue* were at the time in the process of being translated and published.[67] When La Guma visited the Soviet Union in the 1970s, he was deeply moved to find copies of his work translated into Russian even in a bookstore in Novosibirsk.[68] In the mid-1980s, an edition of his collected works was published in the country.

Without taking a cynical view that devalues the recognition offered to African writers in the Eastern Bloc, it is important to note that the publication system worked differently than in the West. Publication of ideologically aligned authors was controlled by the state, and the number of printed copies was not necessarily determined by the likelihood of selling numerous copies.[69] The impressive print runs that state-sponsored cultural production and distribution could boast greatly surpassed what African writers who signed publishing contracts with small local presses (like Mbari) or even with Western commercial presses (like Heinemann) could hope to achieve. For instance, Ramzes's report in *Transition* emphasizes the large public to which the Soviet and Eastern European cultural circuit would likely expose African authors: according to him, fifty thousand copies of the collection *Poets of Ghana* were printed in Moscow in 1963. The volume came on the heels of the Soviet public's acquaintance with writers from the first decolonized African country, such as Efua Sutherland and Cameron Duodu, at the 1958 inaugural conference of the AAWA in Tashkent. By 1964 Soviet statistics reported a staggering total of 7,652,000 copies of works by African writers hailing from twenty countries.[70] Thus, the USSR and its Eastern European satellites offered direct publication support to African writers and cultural organizations sympathetic to the cause of communism and, in a similar manner to the United States, worked to win over the hearts and minds of intellectuals from the Third World through subtle soft-power mechanisms, such as cultural diplomacy.

When in April 1967 a small U.S. publication, *Ramparts*, blew the whistle on the CCF and its various offspring, numerous writers wary of overt or covert Western influence clustered around the AAWA and its literary journal, *Lotus: Afro-Asian Writings*, which aimed to revive the spirit of the Bandung Conference of 1955, namely, Afro-Asian solidarity and nonalignment.[71] Although today mostly forgotten, the AAWA exercised an outsize influence on Third World cultural production. It was formed in 1958, following an Asian writers' initiative at the 1956 Delhi congress. The AAWA held its inaugural conference in Tashkent, the capital of the Uzbek Soviet Socialist Republic, an event that brought together delegates from thirty-seven Asian and African countries.[72]

This cultural organization had an abiding influence on numerous African intellectuals with leftist sympathies. It bestowed honors (the Lotus Prize for literature) on African writers such as Alex La Guma (South Africa), Agostinho Neto (Angola), Ousmane Sembène (Senegal), Marcelino dos Santos (Mozambique), Ngũgĩ wa Thiong'o (Kenya), Kateb Yacine (Algeria), Youssef El-Sebai (Egypt), Chinua Achebe (Nigeria), Meja Mwangi (Kenya), Antonio Jacinto (Angola), Atukwei Okai (Ghana), Assefa Gebremariam (Ethiopia), and Jose Craveirinha (Mozambique).[73] However, although it played an important role in the cultural politics of the Cold War era, it has recently fallen into oblivion. Two relatively recent articles by Hala Halim and Duncan Yoon, as well as Rossen Djagalov's book *From Internationalism to Postcolonialism*, are among the very few scholarly works that have engaged in depth with the association.[74] This neglect is likely rooted in the loss of most of the AAWA's documents during the years when the journal *Lotus* was based in Beirut, which partly overlapped with the civil war in Lebanon; the overall disregard for left-leaning cultural material associated with the Eastern Bloc in the immediate aftermath of the Cold War; and, finally, the difficulty in navigating the many languages in which material exists: *Lotus* was published in English, French, and Arabic, while some of the association's conference-related materials are also in Russian, Portuguese, and Hindi.[75] The publication of the English and French versions became erratic by the mid-1980s.

*Lotus* brought together a wide array of short stories and poetry, editorials and scholarly essays, book reviews, and articles on art. It was lavishly illustrated with images of sculpture, musical instruments, and ancient artifacts and oftentimes accompanied by conference minutes and reports of the AAWA's Permanent Bureau. Halim has argued that *Lotus*, with its richness and diversity of material, could play an important role in defining a new model of non-Eurocentric comparatism.[76] But with numerous cloak-and-dagger episodes that reflected global tensions at the time, the story of *Lotus* is also a Cold War story, with ideological fault lines and fissures as well as forms of solidarity.

Engaged in the cultural battles of the Cold War, the AAWA criticized the activities of the CCF in the first issue of *Lotus* in 1968.[77] In a resolution adopted at the Third Afro-Asian Writers' Conference, March 25–30, 1967, in Beirut, the AAWA warned artists to remain alert to "the danger of imperialist cultural infiltration" and named the CCF as an institution financed by the U.S. intelligence service.[78] On the verso of this exhortation to intellectual vigilance, the editors published a caricature by Alexander Saroukhan, an Armenian-Egyptian cartoonist of international acclaim (see figure 1.2). The image evokes a lupine representation of Uncle Sam who rattles cultural trinkets in front of an Asian

Figure 1.2. Alexander Saroukhan, *No More Eye-Bands: The Afro-Asians: Thank You! Now We Can See What Is Behind!*, *Afro-Asian Writings* 1, no. 1 (March 1968): 141.

and an African person, while his other hand conceals heavy chains behind his back. Yet the stand-ins for the newly independent peoples have removed their colonial blindfolds and are able to see through the disguise.[79]

However, the association was crying wolf while one of the beasts was unfortunately already in their midst. As mentioned before, the first conference of the AAWA took place in 1958 in Tashkent, the capital of the Uzbek Soviet Socialist Republic. Under the guise of promoting central Asian writers from its numerous component republics, the Soviet Union took on a central role in planning the meetings of the association, hosting several conferences, and providing funding as well as material for *Lotus*. Despite the diversity of the member countries, out of the eight conferences the AAWA organized—in 1958 in Tashkent, in 1962 in Cairo, in 1967 in Beirut, in 1970 in Delhi, in 1973 in Alma-Ata, in 1979 in Luanda, in 1983 in Tashkent, and in 1988 in Tunis—three were located in the USSR. Thus, the Soviet Union tacitly influenced the aesthetics and politics of the association, using it as one of its own cultural weapons against the United States.

Turning urban centers like Tashkent, Samarkand, Alma-Ata, Bukhara, Tbilisi, and Baku into "showcase cities" that advertised Soviet achievements in central Asia, the USSR also downplayed a history of Russian colonization in the area.[80] The aim was to provide ideological reinforcement for left-leaning international participants as well as to display, for the benefit of its own population, the reach of Marxist thought across the world. Photographs in the Soviet archives, such as the Sputnik collection of images from the 1958 Tashkent and 1973 Alma-Ata conferences, emphasize the racial diversity of the participants. The 1973 picture of the relaxed trio of winners—Sembène, Thu Bon, and Ngũgĩ—becomes an advertisement for the USSR's commitment to decolonization struggles around the globe and cultural inclusiveness at home (see figure 1.3). In Christine Evans's apt formulation, quoted by Djagalov, the Uzbek and Kazakh Soviet Socialist Republics "synthesized the dual, if contradictory, role the Soviet state sought to play, [namely,] a superpower offering a successful model of development and also the greatest Third-World country of all time."[81] The tension between these two Soviet masks inadvertently displayed the fissures between the USSR's official internationalist discourse, which pledged fierce support to anticolonial struggles, and its own imperialist agenda, aimed at expanding the Soviet state's global sphere of influence.

Indicative of the aesthetic journeys into the Eastern Bloc, the West, or the Third World that African writers undertook during the Cold War, Alex La Guma's argument quoted at the start of this chapter took up a question that animated the literary field in the Soviet Union in the 1920s and 1930s. In Boris

Figure 1.3. Winners of the Lotus Prize—from the left, Ousmane Sembène (Senegal), Thu Bon (Vietnam), and Ngũgĩ wa Thiong'o (Kenya)—at the Fifth Conference of the Afro-Asian Writers Association, 1973, Alma-Ata, Kazakhstan, USSR. Sputnik Images, International Information Agency Rossiya Segodnya.

Eikhenbaum's formulation, Soviet artists shifted the emphasis from the methodology of writing to the social role of the artist, from "how to write" to, instead, "how to be a writer."[82] This added emphasis on the social role of artists, occurring contemporaneously with the emergence of socialist realism as a guiding aesthetic principle, became part of the state-endorsed vision of intellectual work. Literature and art became involved and "committed," to appeal to a term used by leftist intellectuals at the time.

Other leftist writers contributing to the journal *Lotus* echoed La Guma's view of the role of the artist. In the editorial for the special issue of *Lotus* celebrating the ten-year anniversary of the AAWA, the editor in chief, Youssef El-Sebai, emphasized artists' "dual capacities as writers and loyal citizens" who, "armed with their pens," are "safeguarding their countries' independence, sovereignty and national character."[83] Drawing on an arsenal of war tropes frequently deployed in Eastern Bloc cultural discourse, El-Sebai seems to simultaneously disentangle the artists' task of producing their works from their civic function and infuse the writer function with ideological content. Their literary works are made valid by their "authentic" quality—a rather nebulous feature

52  Chapter One

that depended on the ability to draw on "ancient traditions," while updating literary concerns and form according to the "Modern Age with its scientific and spiritual trends."[84] In his formulation (in this essay and other editorials), the political function always short-circuits the vaguely defined formal aspects, drawing them back to the public function performed by the intellectual. Referring to the participants' discussions during the International Writers' Symposium, El-Sebai observed that whether the questions addressed at these meetings in Tashkent "are directly related to political or social issues of the hour, or are purely directed to literary matters, the speeches and discussions of the writers proved that all are closely linked and tend to one cause: the service of our people, their interests and the realization of their aspirations."[85]

This position echoes through the more than two decades of *Lotus*'s publication history, whether reinforced in El-Sebai's editorials; reprised by his successor, Faiz Ahmed Faiz; or foregrounded in the scholarly analyses of contributors. In the first issue of the journal, El-Sebai distinguished between the socioeconomic conditions in Afro-Asian countries and those in their Western counterparts, which were industrial societies that enjoyed both material prosperity and long traditions of "democratic rights and liberties."[86] This difference in the type of material base societies had translated into distinctive requirements for cultural production. If achieving freedom was an important objective in countries still experiencing forms of (neo)colonial subjugation, then writers from these cultures had important tasks to perform in the process of imagining and transitioning to new societies:

> Thus the Afro-Asian writer is not only committed to these causes—they are inevitably reflected in his consciousness and consequently in his work—but, over and above this he is called upon, as an enlightened human being to go even further beyond "commitment." Due to his abilities he should take a position as a leader among his people. He should move from the stage of commitment to the revolutionary phase, in all its aspects. This does not mean only armed struggle or the demand for change; it lies in participating in the process of transformation at both the individual and society levels.[87]

The problematic masculine terms in which El-Sebai paints the writer's function are commensurate with the gendered forms in which Cold War cultural production was defined across the globe. What strikes the reader in his exhortation is the leadership function he assigns to the writer, a vanguard role that subsumes even self-actualization to a process of betterment that extends from the individual to the totality of society. Dynamic, never simply descriptive, and ultimately performative, a writer's output "transform[s] silence into a driving force."[88] As David Caute has pointed out in *The Dancer Defects: The Struggle for Cultural Supremacy during the Cold War*, despite proclamations of revolutionary intent, Cold War Soviet art tastes tended to be quite conservative. Echoes of a romantic understanding of the function of writing (prophet, truth teller, motive force) appear both in Soviet art statements and in those of the *Lotus* writers.[89]

However, what we might reductively read as merely unthinking adoption or sinister imposition of Soviet speak was sometimes derailed, as with the address of Kamal Djumblatt, chairman of the Third Afro-Asian Writers' Conference, which took place in Beirut in March 1967. In his speech the materialist discourse of commitment shifts into a sometimes mystic, other times formalist understanding: "there is another type of commitment—commitment to form, to the sensory and intellectual image—commitment to the written word which makes itself understood."[90] This proclamation, which must have disquieted the leftist members in the audience, demonstrates that cultural production within what could be described as the superpowers' spheres of influence was not uniform. Yet clear patterns of emphasis show the structural aspects of cultural influence.

Opposing art for art's sake—in many ways a straw man that had long ceased to be a core tenet of Western art and which was difficult to homogenize under one rubric—was one of the important functions ascribed to the revolutionary writer in the pages of *Lotus*. In an analysis titled "The Role of Poetry in the Mozambican Revolution," Luis Bernardo Honwana proclaims the importance of "art for life's sake."[91] He throws out of balance El-Sebai's earlier-mentioned formula of the "dual capacities [of artists] as writers and loyal citizens" by prioritizing their militant function over intellectual exercise. Similarly, in 1985 the Marxist Indian writer Bhisham Sahni criticized the "damaging" notion of artistic autonomy promoted by Western intellectuals, for whom "freedom implies freedom from any kind of social commitment . . . from any set of convictions and beliefs. . . . We know that this is not freedom, this is total loss of freedom. Real freedom comes from . . . merging oneself into the life of one's fellow-beings."[92] Thus, through the intensification of Cold War ideological battles, autonomy and commitment become polar opposites that could be deployed to automatically assign writers to one camp or the other.

This history of influence and interference from both superpowers demonstrates that the USA and the USSR considered African literature, like other literary production from around the world, a desirable discursive field worth conquering. Thus, La Guma's startling declaration cuts to the quick of a debate on the function of the writer in the latter half of the twentieth century. In simplified form, this debate between the politically committed writer, on the one hand, and the detached, aesthetically autonomous writer dedicated only to his craft had ramifications not only within the field of African literary studies but also within branches of scholarship of general interest, such as the interest in the figure of the public intellectual.

## Aspiring to Nonalignment

While the superpowers were deeply invested in maneuvering intellectuals away from the opposing ideological camp, they also trod carefully owing to the increasing suspicions of intellectuals around the globe. This was a time when nations from the Third World fought geopolitical and cultural polarization by calling congresses and establishing nonaligned institutions. As Dennis Duerden reported in 1961, after his tour of Africa and before setting up the Transcription Centre in London, his interlocutors were suspicious of the aims of the organization, and although he had lived and taught in Nigeria for years, he had to answer questions regarding financial sponsorship: "Where does the money come from? It must be a subtle instrument of American politics." Even half a decade before journalists shone light on the scale of the CCF's operations, Duerden's interlocutor observed that "he would prefer it to come out in the open and admit what its politics are," underscoring numerous intellectuals' anxiety about being unwittingly involved in murky, undisclosed political aims.[93] In some ways the expectation that the USSR was bound to both tacitly manipulate and openly promote ideologically aligned intellectuals made the writers suddenly confronted with the CIA's involvement in such a large number of cultural institutions experience a heightened sense of betrayal and disenchantment.

In the 1950s and 1960s, at both the individual and the state level, attempts to found extra-bloc alliances combined with the ambition to make the political will of decolonizing or newly independent states count. In the shadow of dying colonialisms lay threatening forms of neocolonialism that had to be countered. The 1955 conference of Asian and African states that took place in the Indonesian city of Bandung marked the first concerted action taken by Third World nations to assert themselves in international politics, reject a subservient role, and, drawing on their sheer numbers when faced with sidelining, counter the old and new powers' financial, political, and institutional might. Although until relatively recently scholars have almost forgotten about Bandung, the conference was witnessed with excitement by people of color, who saw their political star beginning to rise: practically "the [whole] human race" was represented by the twenty-nine participant states, Ellen Wright, Richard Wright's wife, observed.[94] Yet, with China a participant, there was also anxiety about a possible communist takeover of the agenda. As Richard Wright described the atmosphere in the days preceding the conference in his travelogue *The Color Curtain: A Report on the Bandung Conference*, recently independent countries feared complex plots to lure them to one ideological side or the other, while new and old powers were anxious lest they lose their influence over much of the globe: "Such was the atmosphere, brooding, bitter, apprehensive, which greeted the projected conference. Everybody read into it his own fears; the conference loomed like a long-buried ghost rising from a muddy grave."[95] Even the title of the first section of Wright's book, "Bandung: Beyond Left and Right," announces not only the seeds of the Non-Aligned Movement but also the fear of ideological contamination, while the title of the volume itself cautiously redirects the attention from the Cold War to the manifold forms of race-based oppression and discrimination.[96]

Although the long-term political benefits arising from the conference were relatively few, as they gradually gave way to factionalism under the pressure of an increasingly polarized globe, the conference impressed the point that people of color represented a force to be reckoned with and bolstered the progressively vigorous anticolonial discourse. Simultaneously, the conference planted the seeds from which the Non-Aligned Movement sprang, inaugurated in Belgrade in 1961. The movement aimed to counteract the ideological and military polarization of the globe and saw the Third World as a counterbalancing force.

Political and cultural movements that assembled the energies of black people, such as Négritude and Pan-Africanism, both of which yielded rich literary outputs, had predated the Bandung Conference. It was in Paris, the avowed cultural capital of the world, that the Négritude movement had articulated its objectives in the 1930s and that the journal *Présence Africaine* was established in the aftermath of World War II. First printed in 1947, the journal served as a hub for black intellectuals in the diaspora. It disseminated the works of established and emerging thinkers like Aimé Césaire, Frantz Fanon, Léopold Sédar Senghor, Richard Wright, and Jacques Stephen Alexis, as well as the texts of supportive white French intellectuals like Jean-Paul Sartre and André Gide. Although most of its essays and literary pieces were written in French, side by side with these it also published works in English, while translations from one language into the other fulfilled an important function in its integration of a linguistically diverse global black diaspora.[97]

From 1947 to the present, *Présence Africaine* has been one of the most important venues for the discussion of African literary matters. Eschewing politics and framing its aim in cultural terms, the journal established an open approach to publication. The introductory lines of Alioune Diop's "Niam n'goura ou les raisons d'être de *Présence Africaine*" in the 1947 inaugural issue of the journal clearly state this nonaligned goal: "This magazine is not subservient to any philosophical or political ideology."[98] In the sixth issue of the journal, Diop reiterated the comprehensive scope of the publication that he had spearheaded: "All articles will be published, provided they are adequately written, are concerned with Africa, and are faithful to our anti-racialist and anti-colonialist purpose and to the solidarity of colonized peoples."[99] This second declaration of broad-minded inclusiveness is notably couched in less politicized terms. As Cedric Tolliver has convincingly argued, while Diop's definition of the role of culture in the global struggle against colonialism places politics in a secondary position among the journal's objectives, the intellectuals grouped around *Présence Africaine* understood that their anticolonial rhetoric was likely subject to state scrutiny and surveillance and that their publishing program was susceptible to falling prey to Cold War political machinations.[100] Thus, in the same foreword, Diop hints at a superimposition of old and new types of imperialism: "But the crushing weight of colonialism is now to be doubled. Europe, overshadowed by two giants," is likely to intensify its colonial exploitation in order to recover a modicum of the former authority lost to the postwar superpowers, the USA and the USSR, he warned.[101]

Even when writers were interacting in a seemingly friendly manner with other black intellectuals, suspicion of secret or not-so-secret ideological alignments ran high. For instance, in a confidential report on the 1963 Dakar conference on the teaching of African literature in universities, an event organized by the CCF, Mphahlele expressed his frustrations with the host country's leader, President Senghor, and the interference of *Présence Africaine*. He outlines a very complicated entanglement of contrasting intellectual approaches (e.g., the "unity of African culture" supported by the négritudinists at *Présence Africaine* versus the attention to national context supported by the CCF) and personal and ideological enmity or suspicion ("*Présence Africaine* does not miss any chance to run me down as an 'imperialist stooge,'" Mphahlele complained).[102] While the 1967 revelations about the funding behind the CCF appear to justify the suspicions of Diop and his collaborators toward Mphahlele, it is also important to note that distinguishing between political-based judgments and intellectual divergence—in this case over the teaching of the works of living

African writers in African universities—is difficult. This incident highlights both the justifiably skeptical approach of many intellectuals from the Third World and the near impossibility of keeping such cultural projects ideologically nonaligned.

Take, for instance, one of the leading events dedicated to the discussion of African cultural production—the First World Congress of Black Writers and Artists.[103] Organized in 1956 at the Sorbonne in Paris by a team of intellectuals associated with *Présence Africaine*, the congress reprised the ideals of Bandung in explicitly cultural terms. Out of the more than thirty intellectuals who gave papers, several participants invoked the conference in Indonesia as a touchstone for a new political and cultural direction of the world, spearheaded by the formerly colonized. For Senghor it was an opportunity to develop his ideas of Négritude and a putative "black spirit" by connecting the work of contemporary African intellectuals with the political project at Bandung and, further back in time, the foundations of an unadulterated African culture: "This means that if the Negro [w]riters and artists of to-day want to finish off the work in the Bandoeng spirit they must go to school in Negro Africa."[104] In the speech that opened the congress, Diop underlined that, irrespective of their religious or ideological affiliation, black intellectuals were dissatisfied with Occidental culture, a frustration that the Paris congress intended to channel into a cultural program.[105] Yet attempts at simultaneously avoiding openly politicized discussions while also complicating the relationship between politics and cultural production—Diop, for example, argued that historical narratives masquerading as universal and irrefutable representations of the world were in fact biased Western narratives—backfired several times throughout the conference.[106] For instance, Césaire's argument that all black people, whether from African or Caribbean countries or even from the United States, continue to wrestle with some form of colonialism that affects their forms of cultural production, was received with alarm by the American delegation. The diplomat and scholar Mercer Cook, who was later to become the first director of the Africa Program within the CCF, protested that, in light of Césaire's speech, the event in Paris appeared to be a political trap set by communist sympathizers. Tolliver vividly presents the overshadowing Cold War tensions by pointing out the partisan language in which James Baldwin couched his report from the congress, as well as the behind-the-scenes informing that took place.[107] However, just a month later it became obvious that Césaire had harbored no Soviet-dictated designs: in his famous "Letter to Maurice Thorez," he withdrew from the French Communist Party, outlining the forms of Soviet imperialism vis-à-vis nonwhite communists in other countries.

The overt and covert animosity between Diop and Senghor, on the one hand, and Mphahlele and the CCF, on the other, as well as the suspicion that the Soviet personnel within the AAWA harbored toward Diop, emphasizes the far-reaching impact of the Iron Curtain. Mphahlele had clashed repeatedly with Diop and Senghor over their continued preference for Négritude; Mphahlele's reports to his CCF higher-ups, Hunt and Katz, were often peppered with tirades against the former and their cultural agenda. When Mphahlele went to Nairobi to set up the Chemchemi Cultural Centre, the CCF saw itself in a territorial competition with Diop and *Présence Africaine*: "I have succeeded in interesting the [Kenyan] Minister of Education in our project. Présence Africaine has been and Diop has talked to almost every Cabinet Minister, I am told, and in each case there was vague interest but no idea what he really wanted to do. This [Chemchemi], from the patronage of two other Ministers—one that does not threaten to go out of hand—seems to be the thing Kenyans, indeed East Africans, have been waiting for. So the Minister has agreed to open the centre on November 16."[108] Mphahlele was equally careful to steer the activities of Chemchemi away from any possible overlaps with cultural venues under the patronage of the British Colonial Office.[109] Diop, on the other hand, pondered whether he should attend the AAWA inaugural conference in Tashkent in 1958. The CCF dissuaded him from participating, expressing concern about an event that happened under Soviet tutorship.[110] Moreover, the suspicion cut both ways: Soviet cultural bureaucracies had already decided that Diop was an intellectual best avoided.[111]

Given the danger of a world governed by superpower interests, the Bandung Conference inspired Third World solidarities, which in turn intersected with other political projects: Pan-Africanism, tricontinentalism, and late twentieth-century internationalisms. The layered interpenetrations between these projects are only today being excavated, as is the case with the development of Indian Ocean, South Atlantic, and Global South studies.[112] These solidarities that harnessed the energy of anti-imperial sentiments oftentimes (but not necessarily) presented themselves in nonaligned terms, an ideological neutrality that was mostly aspirational, in the same way in which the dream of building an alliance of "the wretched of the earth," to use Fanon's famous phrase, was an uphill battle. The opening line of Vijay Prashad's *The Darker Nations: A People's History of the Third World* insightfully establishes the laborious aspects of creating an ideal world: "The Third World was not a place. It was a project."[113]

The idea of tricontinentalism emerged with the first conference of the Organization of the Solidarity of the Peoples of Africa, Asia, and Latin America in Havana in 1966.[114] As the name of the organization indicates, it emphasized

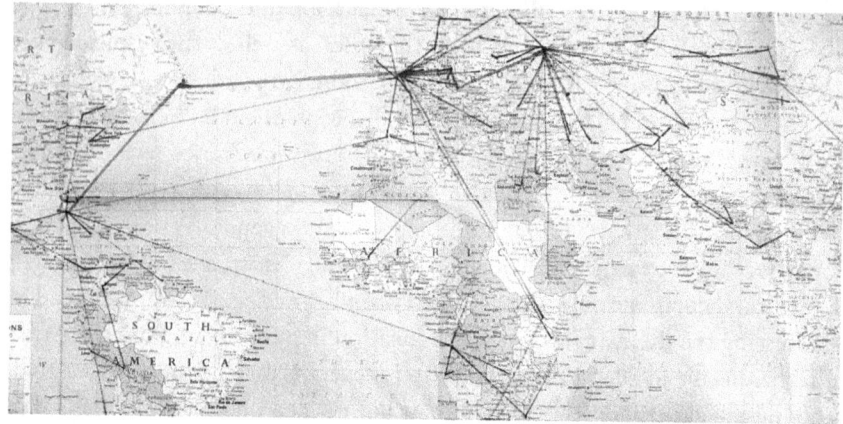

Figure 1.4. Alex La Guma's personal world map, with hand-marked flights. UWC-Robben Island Museum Mayibuye Archives. Photo courtesy of Christopher J. Lee.

the role of the Third World while eschewing the problematic hierarchical tones the latter term evoked and foregrounding instead forms of anti-imperialist solidarity. However, the movement could hardly be described as nonaligned: originating in Havana, where its flagship journal, *Tricontinental*, was published, it extolled the role of the Cuban revolution and its leader, Fidel Castro, and trained its criticism primarily on forms of American imperialism.[115] Nonetheless, the journal printed important cultural manifestos with Third World appeal, such as Fernando Solanas and Octavio Getino's "Toward a Third Cinema" (1969), and introduced literary figures from the three continents to a leftist public. For instance, after the death of Alex La Guma in 1985, the journal reprinted an earlier article by Samuel Omo Asein evaluating the global impact of the novelist's work.[116] La Guma had not only made vivid the horrors of apartheid, the article affirmed, but also established cultural solidarities between South Africans and readers around the world.

Indeed, La Guma's own work teems with the connections between oppressed people the world over. Like the map of the globe he kept with his personal papers and on which he drew connecting lines between the parts of the world he visited (see figure 1.4), his creative and political activity took him from London to Moscow to Tashkent and from Havana to Luanda to Lusaka.[117] In both imaginative and concrete political terms, his works penned in Cuba establish the cultural parameters of tricontinentalism. As Christopher J. Lee pointed out, this tricontinental pattern of his cultural interactions, which does not fit into the usual analytical paradigms, has led scholars of his earlier literary works to overlook much of his later corpus.[118] An antiapartheid activist and writer who was imprisoned and then held under house arrest in South Africa for speaking out against racism, La Guma established an international profile when the manuscript of his novella *A Walk in the Night* (1962) was successfully smuggled out of South Africa and published by Mbari Press. His short stories had already been featured prominently in *Black Orpheus*. While the early years of his career seem tied to institutions under the CCF umbrella, two of his following novels were published by the German Democratic Republic press Seven Seas, while his travelogue, *A Soviet Journey*, came out with the Moscow-based Progress Publishers. However, this seemingly equidistant pattern of publication venues does not signal a form of nonalignment. A member of the South African Communist Party, La Guma not only was deeply committed to a Marxist-Leninist view of historical processes but also followed the Moscow line.[119] Appointed representative of the African National Congress to Latin America and headquartered in Cuba until his premature death in 1985, he spent the last decade of his life forging alliances with left-leaning cultural institutions and governments, as illustrated by his short stories "Come Back to Tashkent" and "Thang's Bicycle," published in *Lotus*.[120]

Ngũgĩ wa Thiong'o's essays also illustrate an impetus to excavate and renew Third World alliances. For instance, in the preface to *Decolonising the Mind*, he enumerates his sources of inspiration and potential audiences among the unprivileged of the three southern continents—the workers and peasants of "South Africa, Namibia, Kenya, Zaire, Ivory Coast, El Salvador, Chile, Philippines, South Korea, Indonesia, Grenada, Fanon's 'Wretched of the Earth.'"[121] He expressed hope in alternative solidarities that would dismantle what he perceived as a renewed and more vicious form of imperialism—the neocolonial forms of domination in Africa and the rest of the Third World. The same thematic of remembered, unearthed, and rediscovered cultural and political solidarities around the Indian Ocean basin figures in a speech he delivered in 1973 in Alma-Ata, Kazakhstan, upon receiving the Lotus Prize conferred by the AAWA: "The Indian Ocean anyway has never been a barrier and for centuries East Africa peacefully traded with China, India and Arabia before the arrival of the Portuguese who turned this creative trade into a traffic of destroyed cities, cultures and human beings."[122] Beyond the geographical proximity that enables Afro-Asian solidarities, Ngũgĩ also proposes a solidarity of the suffering masses, "a United People's Republic of Africa joining hands with a United People's Republic of Asia in the service of the true Republic of man" based on a shared history of colonialism and oppression as well as the underrepresented creative energies of those populations.[123] Before Amitav Ghosh in *In an Antique Land* (1992) traced the contours of a flourishing cosmopolitan culture that linked northern Africa to the coasts of India at a time when Europe was steeped in the Middle Ages, before the emergence of Indian Ocean studies as a field of inquiry, Ngũgĩ had harnessed the spirit of tricontinentalism to evoke an alternative, erased history of African participation in commerce, arts, craftsmanship, and creation. His investment in the ethos of tricontinentalism is nonetheless tempered with the awareness that once such discourses of solidarity are institutionalized, private, sectarian, or national interests oftentimes hijack them.

While the arc of a sustained Afro-Asian and tricontinental thematic in Ngũgĩ's writing in the 1970s and 1980s is easily identifiable, what begs further scrutiny is how such a tricontinental alliance is imagined. As Antoinette Burton has pointed out, with the memory of Bandung having faded almost completely half a century later, "Bandung is typically conflated with 'Afro-Asian solidarity.'"[124] Literary research on the Cold War era needs to not only identify the traces of tricontinental solidarity but also understand how these convergences and disjunctions of interests evolved—the unsettled and contextual nature of such alliances.[125]

Similarly to La Guma or the participants in the Havana conference, Ngũgĩ did not hold an equidistant position to the superpowers that would match the stance advocated by the Non-Aligned Movement. In a paper delivered at the International Emergency Conference on Korea, held in Tokyo in August 1976, Ngũgĩ drew attention to the waning of the Bandung spirit and of the Non-Aligned Movement in the wake of intensified struggle between the West and the East for control over the Third World. He expressed the view that the Non-Aligned Movement, at least in the form embraced by the Kenyan government, served only to dissimulate the national leaders' subservience to the interests of the West. The essay was written at a time when Ngũgĩ intensified his protests against the neocolonial leadership of Kenya, as reflected in the scathing criticism of the comprador elites he delivered in the play *I Will Marry When I Want* and the novel *Petals of Blood*—both works depicting a postindependence universe populated by "black zombies, black animated cartoons dancing the master's dance to the master's voice."[126]

> I would like to make it clear that I'm not speaking for any organization in Kenya or Korea and that for the purposes of this meeting I am non-aligned: but then we were told that this conference was for non-aligned persons and was paralleling the Non-Aligned Nations Conference in Colombo! I am here in my capacity as a writer who tries to speak about myself and who tries to get his inspiration from the struggles of our people for total libera-

tion from imperialism and any form of foreign domination. That means that as a writer I can never be non-aligned. How can a writer, if he is to be meaningful, assume a non-aligned position amid a million voices crying out in unison for the right to control the natural and human resources of their own land; the right to control the fruits of their sweat, the products of their labour?[127]

The changing meaning of the term *nonaligned*, from a principle of authorial independence that refuses subordination to institutional politics, to a desire to eschew the Manichean binarism of Cold War superpower struggles, to the superficially equidistant stance of the Kenyan state, which used nonalignment as a ruse to preserve elite privileges, reflects Ngũgĩ's awareness of the transformation of world structures. Furthermore, as Ngũgĩ admitted, there was a contradiction between his location and his ideological position: in the 1980s he was writing against American imperialism from within the United States. A staunch Marxist, he conceded that although many American values contradicted his leftist stance, he nonetheless admired principles such as the rule of law.[128]

What happens, though, when intellectuals who are in fact partisan capture the language of nonalignment? "It is evident to me now that my duty is to state what I support without taking sides," writes Stephen Spender, the editor of the journal *Encounter*.[129] In his evaluation of the impact of CIA funding on the actual works and worldviews of intellectuals affiliated with the CCF, Peter Kalliney rightly points out that numerous contributors presented their approach as an uncompromising refusal of both East and West and cites Louis Fischer's sententious rejection of both sides: "Some are so obsessed with the crimes of the capitalist world that they remain blind to the crimes and bankruptcy of Bolshevism. Not a few use the defects of the West to divert attention from the horrors of Moscow. My own prescription is: Double Rejection. A free spirit, unfettered by economic bonds or intellectual bias, can turn his back on the evils of both worlds."[130] As we retrospectively recognize that the CCF-affiliated intellectuals were unwittingly co-opted for the American project, it becomes more important to understand how such statements of nonalignment operate within the polarized Cold War cultural climate.

It might appear tempting to automatically assign value to nonaligned, in-between approaches, at a time when superpowers pared down cultural production to an inflexible ideological backbone—those with us and those against us. Instead, we need to acknowledge a whole gradient of ideologically aligned and nonaligned approaches. Furthermore, the position of individual intellectuals and of cultural institutions and publication venues shifted from year to year and sometimes issue to issue depending on circumstances. Intellectuals' acts of distancing themselves from ideological commitment differed drastically in form and degree, from Césaire's continued engagement with a leftist agenda while prioritizing the political goals of people of color; to Kwame Nkrumah's declaration of principle that "we face neither East, nor West; we face Forward," contradicted by a Ghanaian economy deeply enmeshed with the Eastern Bloc's; to Mphahlele's denial of ideological affiliation under the mantra of an approach he later defined as African humanism.[131] Nonalignment then appears as a programmatic or declarative value rather than a reality.

This book does not seek to assign labels in a polarized or even triangular value system, and the terms *pro-Western*, *prosocialist*, and *nonaligned* are but positional relations within shifting configurations. Instead, I am interested in analyzing the complex ways in which the political and cultural fields influenced each other during the Cold War. The literary institutions and publication venues discussed here had an impact on the selection of texts for anthologies, the promotion of certain writers for literary prizes and their subsequent canonization, the adoption of texts for school curricula, and the promotion of certain forms of literary criticism. The current shape of the academic field of African literary studies is a clear product of the interpenetration between direct and structural modes of influence exerted during the Cold War.

# 2

# Aesthetic World-Systems

## Mythologies of Modernism and Realism

When I taught a graduate seminar on the global Cold War in 2014, I was delighted to see students keen to learn not only about specific themes and topics but also about the conflict's ramifications in terms of privileged literary genres, forms, and modes of writing. What took me by surprise, though, was the heated debate that broke out when we read Ngũgĩ wa Thiong'o's novel *Devil on the Cross* (1980). The novel, with its combination of allegorical structure, secondary orality, social(ist) realism, and explicit didactic strategies, does not resemble most of the texts graduate students encounter in their seminars.[1] While the majority of the class was hooked by Ngũgĩ's innovative novelistic techniques, one student simply refused to see it as a worthy literary text because, as he put it, the novel tells readers unambiguously what political position they are to take. He rejected the combination of didacticism and realist techniques, implying that representational straightforwardness and lack of interpretive ambiguity were artistic failures. Other students immediately came to the writer's defense. It was the most animated—and most illuminating—discussion I had ever had in a classroom. It made me see clearly the long-lasting legacy of literary models—or, rather, aesthetic systems, as I argue later in this chapter—cemented by the Cold War.

In slightly more sophisticated form, numerous critics have echoed such resistance to realist aesthetics and explicit didacticism, especially when coupled with leftist politics, denigrating politically committed writers or attempting to save them from themselves. For instance, of all the formal and ideological components of Ngũgĩ's works, his realist aesthetics and leftist politics have generated numerous paradoxical responses—sometimes praised, at other times treated as an embarrassment.² In an early 1980s article, Bernth Lindfors observes that "Ngũgĩ may have his heart in the right place, but the critical consensus seems to be that he does not always have his art where it should be," suggesting that artistic merit is tarnished through political engagement.³ Even when scholars assessed the innovative aspects of Ngũgĩ's Marxist aesthetics positively, his support of leftist politics was seen as partisan engagement that diminished the universal appeal of his work. Therefore, scholars sometimes apologized for the writer's political engagement, pleading for a purely literary evaluation of his work. Koku Amuzu entreated the reader: "While I do not deny the strong political nature of the novel or undervalue its social importance, I insist that regardless of the limitations from which it might suffer, *Petals of Blood* is foremost a literary work, an artistic creation, and if we look *closely enough*, we will discover its beauty."⁴ Political engagement, according to such a narrow interpretation, muddles formal aspects and makes it difficult to grasp the work's literariness.

What perspective can give us the key to such contradictory statements? These critical evaluations are not the consequence of scholars' ill-intentioned or limited engagement with the author's works. Quite the opposite: Lindfors, Amuzu, and many others have been fervent promoters of Ngũgĩ's literary oeuvre. Yet these pronouncements reduce realism to lack of technique or see explicit political content as an unnecessary burden that diminishes literary value. More dangerously, the statements also hint at a Euro-American aesthetic evaluation scheme that indirectly privileges modernist fiction over its realist counterparts.

Writing in a realist style and discarding modernist or postmodern techniques is never only an aesthetic choice. In the chapter dedicated to African fiction in his landmark study *Decolonising the Mind*, Ngũgĩ connects his aesthetic choices to his rejection of cultural colonialism, when he suggests that the African peasantry and working class should "appropriate the novel."⁵ The various forms in which African writers have taken control of poetry, drama, and the novel, whether by drawing on oral and written local traditions or hybridizing the former with modes of writing developed elsewhere, were shaped equally by the cultural politics of decolonization and by Cold War rifts and cultural alliances.

In this chapter I look at how modernism and realism were reshaped through the interactions between the superpowers, on the one hand, and the aims of writers seeking to decolonize literary canons and knowledge paradigms, on the other. These two modes of writing came to carry more meaning than the specific aesthetic strategies to which they initially referred, overdetermined by the cultural and ideological roles assigned to them during the Cold War. Therefore, I am not interested in assigning labels, calling specific texts for realism or modernism. Instead, I am addressing the mythologies of modernism and realism as they have become sedimented in literary criticism. I look at how African writers, like their counterparts around the world, perceived these modes of writing and how their preferences shaped the African literary canon presented in anthologies, literary histories, lists of prizes and awards, and the classroom. In short, I am interested in how the Cold War superpowers claimed these modes of writing as part of their aesthetic systems. There is a strong element of compulsion in these Cold War paradigms: beyond simple aesthetic choice—if such a simple choice was ever possible—they conveyed hierarchies that prioritized modernism over realism in the West, and the other way round in the Eastern Bloc. While a large part of the chapter will focus on the development of opposing aesthetic systems and the consequent hardening of positions in the last two decades of the Cold War, the last part of the chapter will return to Ngũgĩ's oeuvre as an example of these forces at work and of writers' capacity to surpass them.

In the first two decades following the end of World War II, the function of modernism and realism was mostly contextual. What counted was how authors drew on these modes of writing to achieve specific cultural aims. The late 1960s marked a turning point in the cultural narrative about realism and modernism. It was propelled by the revelation of extensive CIA intervention in cultural production across the globe and the subsequent increased Soviet efforts to match and outstrip the United States' influence, as described in chapter 1. In his book *Cold War Modernists: Art, Literature, and American Cultural Diplomacy*, Greg Barnhisel traces the transformation of modernism from a rebellious current, "a cause that intended to remake the world," into a style accepted and valorized by the American bourgeoisie.[6] The secret to this astonishing transformation, he argues, was the support offered by the American government after World War II, as it sought to counter the influence of the Soviet Union in the global arena of the Cold War. The state's shift from conservative suspicion of modernism and avant-garde art to embracing modernism as an expression of the American independent spirit was not a smooth one, but by the late 1940s, the "idea that Abstract Expressionism could become a vehicle for the [American] imperial burden began to take hold."[7] With the creation of the Congress for Cultural Freedom (CCF) in 1950 and its expansion beyond the boundaries of Europe and into the Third World to attract intellectuals to American values, the doyens of aesthetics in the Western world created an artificial dichotomy between modernism and realism.

A reductive assumption operated among both supporters of modernism and champions of realism. The devotees of modernism pushed against an imaginary reductive mimetic realism that could only present life in reportage style. Complexity, ambiguity, and irony became the mantra of those who wanted to claim a more nuanced understanding of the world. For its proponents, modernism came to represent the imaginative powers of individuals unencumbered by subservience to the state or other institutions, while realism, especially in its socialist realist iteration, came to denote a reckless abjuration of intellectual autonomy, politically and artistically subservient to the state and delinquent in the intellectuals' task to question and innovate. Conversely, the backers of realism argued that modernism, with its focus on form and craft, represented an abdication of moral and political responsibility and a narcissistic, self-involved channeling of creative energy. A zero-sum assumption seemed to operate on both sides.

There is, of course, a *longue durée* dialectic of realism and modernism as dominant modes of writing.[8] In the late nineteenth century, some artists rejected realism as an expression of bourgeois capitalist reification, and art for art's sake triumphed as a retreat from culture tainted by mercantilism. Various waves of avant-gardist experimentation in the early twentieth century imposed themselves, yet there was pushback from Soviet socialist realism, just as the influence of high modernism was spreading in the West. Writers and readers continued to celebrate late modernism in the period after World War II just as postmodernism, purportedly its antagonist yet sharing with modernism a penchant for retreat from politics, was making its entry on the world stage. Lauren M. E. Goodlad calls 1961 the annus mirabilis for realism's reappearance in literary criticism, although some of the attention it garnered was negative, with poststructuralist critics identifying realist novels as "instruments of Western ideology."[9] There is no teleological succession of literary modes: all throughout this time, modernism and realism coexisted, even if one of them appeared to be the dominant mode through the construction of a "selective tradition."[10] In fact, Susan Andrade has astutely argued that "realism, like modernism, can be and often is produced in the act of reading."[11]

The 1960s are also the decade when these mythologies of realism and modernism solidified against the background of the Cold War. Their respective supporters invested them with revolutionary character. For some, modernism was still wrapped up in the aura of its intellectually challenging, formally innovative experimentation of the early twentieth century: in social terms it was equivalent to the artist's refusal to submit to the dictates of bourgeois society. Seen as resisting official narratives, modernism and postmodernism have been particularly embraced in social contexts where the state took control of modes of representation, such as socialist dictatorships. Conversely, other intellectuals, like Georg Lukács and numerous (although not all) Marxist critics, championed realism as the mode of writing most receptive to social transformation: a style that surpassed the surface descriptions of naturalism and was capable of recording the dialectical processes through which a social class clashes with and eventually surpasses another.[12] Other defenders of realism as the true revolutionary form praised its ability to rupture the smoke-screen narratives of capitalism, speaking truth to colonialism and restituting erased histories to the oppressed. The pressures exerted by the system even on the most rebellious art forms meant, as Fredric Jameson has shown, that these art forms could still be co-opted into the mainstream.[13] Therefore, some readers absorbed the Marxist critiques of modernism and its ostensibly antagonistic sequel, postmodernism, as modes of writing connected with specific stages in capitalist society that lost their rebellious impulse and came to reflect the values of the bourgeoisie, the very class whose tastes they initially set off to upset.[14] Finally, the forms of socialist realism sanctified in the Soviet Union and adopted by the Eastern Bloc have long been decried in the West as a totalitarian mode of writing, the cultural reflection of a dictatorship that codified the ways in which artists were allowed to reflect on the world.[15]

While the preceding assessments tend to arrange realism and modernism as the poles of an aesthetic dichotomy, this chapter is not concerned with arbitrating between the African supporters of modernism and realism but with historicizing the creation of mythologies about them. To begin with, as Jameson has argued, realism is involved in a multitude of antinomies—"realism vs. romance, realism vs. epic, realism vs. melodrama, realism vs. idealism, realism vs. naturalism, (bourgeois or critical) realism vs. socialist realism, realism vs. the oriental tale, and of course, most frequently rehearsed of all, realism vs. modernism."[16] Furthermore, varieties of realism have been both condemned for their complacent acceptance of the bourgeois lifestyle *and* praised for their revolutionary political motivations and pedagogical salience.[17] The same holds true for varieties of modernism. Thus, attempting to adjudicate between a putatively progressive realist literature and a reactionary or complacent modernist style would be unproductive. In fact, some writers embraced one mode of writing in the earlier stages of their career, then articulated a different artistic creed later on, only to evince new stylistic features in more recent works, as I show in the last section of the chapter.

However, as described in chapter 1, the American and Soviet governments invested in specific modes of cultural production; as a result, modernism and realism became much more than simple stylistic choices. I am using the term *investment* deliberately to recall the connection Jameson and other leftist scholars established between culture and finance capital.[18] In the same way in which Jameson defined postmodernism as the cultural logic of a specific form of late capitalism, we can retrospectively extend this form of analysis to the conflict between modernism and realism. During the second half of the Cold War, not only did these two modes of writing articulate the symptoms of a specific form of economic and social organization and the effects of uneven development across the globe, but, owing to the infusion of funds by the USA and the USSR into cultural organizations that privileged, respectively, modernist and realist cultural production, they became superordinate categories, abstracted from their original function. Hence, I am interested in the mythologies of realism and modernism as they were taken up, defended, or rejected by various African writers and critics. In the process of debating these mythologies, writers and critics established the shape of African literature as an academic field and contributed to global debates on aesthetics.

In a chapter summing up the main debates in African literary criticism, Marxist critic Georg M. Gugelberger observed:

> African literature for quite some time now has struggled between modes of writing which are essentially modernist, Eliotic, and/or Poundian, longing for permanence and everlastingness (the increasing difficulty of Soyinka's style, particularly of his *Idanre*, 1967, and his modernist "miniature" epic *Ogun Abibiman*, 1978, are a case in point) and an aesthetic of resistance and commitment inherent in the writings of Okot p'Bitek, Ngũgĩ wa Thiong'o, Sembène Ousmane, Alex La Guma and others, writers who are less formalistically achieved but politically more engaged, even if they are less modernist. African writers themselves are fully aware of this bifurcation as can be witnessed in Okot p'Bitek's *Song of Lawino* and *Song of Ocol*, works which, according to one of the founders of African radical aesthetics, Grant Kamenju, are "the neo-colonial aesthetics of capitalism and subjugation" versus "the aesthetics of black pride, black affirmation, resistance and ultimate liberation."[19]

While realism is directly named elsewhere in the essay, Gugelberger's statement is one of the most striking examples of the polarization of African literature along Cold War ideological lines. It is surprising, though, that although Gugelberger champions the types of realism promoted by Ngũgĩ, La Guma, and Sembène, he still falls prey to the problematic assumption that political engagement equals attenuation of form.[20] Later on, I discuss the trajectory of and change of directions in Ngũgĩ's oeuvre under the impact of Cold War aesthetic debates. His commitment to finding the best literary form to express the conditions of neocolonialism in Kenya shows that political engagement and attention to form can and do coexist in productive ways.

Before ideological fissures turned literary options into veritable aesthetic camps, in the late 1950s and the 1960s there was a degree of overlap between African writers who published in the CCF venues and those patronized by the Afro-Asian Writers Association (AAWA). For instance, the South African writer Lewis Nkosi's work appeared both in *Transition* and in *Lotus*; Ngũgĩ attended the Makerere conference but then moved away from CCF venues and toward the AAWA. In the 1950s and 1960s, just as the two superpowers were ramping up their cultural patronage programs, the arts were paradoxically still perceived as a site of freedom that allowed writers to oppose brute politics. By the end of the 1960s, modernism and realism were no longer simple aesthetic modes African writers could deploy in their writings. They had become cogs in the superpowers' ideological machineries, and writers who sided with one or the other implicitly expressed sympathy for the aesthetic systems promoted within the West or the Eastern Bloc. In the 1970s and 1980s, the divisions deepened.[21]

In the last two decades of the Cold War, aesthetic statements had become acerbic. Part and parcel of knowledge paradigms that outlasted the fall of the Berlin Wall, those views on literature continued into the new global disposition. In 2003 Nkosi presented a poem at the Berlin International Literature Festival. Addressing the differences between poetry and prose in a problematically gendered allegory, his lines are an indirect testimony to how entrenched some Cold War–era aesthetic beliefs remain:

> Poetry is not like Prose
> conventional
> a thing of grime and slime
> full of blubber
> red-eyed, dishevelled
> a real skivy
> hitched to some one-eyed monster
> named Realism.[22]

This elitist paean to poetry is startling, first of all, because Nkosi, a practitioner of prose, was not an adept of writing in verse. More strikingly, he implies that the value of poetry lies in its tight and crafted form—the opposite of "dishevelled" prose "full of blubber." The marriage of prose to realism, a union that he subverted in his novel *Mating Birds* (1986), evokes a similar though unnamed pairing of verse and modernism. Just as, a few years earlier, Nkosi had reproached his fellow South African writers for a penchant for "technically brittle" reportage-like realism, to the detriment of artistic inventiveness, he still held the persistent suspicion that realism is a brutish and brutalizing mode of rendering reality.[23]

At the other end of the spectrum, in the early 1980s Gugelberger argued that "modernism . . . has a profound connection with the transition of the epoch of imperialism. Modernism is closely connected with reactionary politics. The perception of modernism in Africa is closely linked to neo-colonialism. One cannot be against imperialism and write in the tradition of T. S. Eliot and Ezra Pound."[24] Like Jameson, Gugelberger is interested in the connection between economic system and cultural production. Two major criticisms are leveled at this mode of writing: Eurocentric bias, along with cultural imperialism, and interiorization at the expense of participation in the community. Thus, by the late 1960s modernism and realism became shorthand for two larger aesthetic world-systems.

### Cold War Polarization and Aesthetic World-Systems

I am using the term *system* deliberately, as it harks back to the important contributions of Immanuel Wallerstein, the Africanist scholar who elaborated a theory of capitalism as a world-system.[25] Since the sixteenth century, he argued, the world has been dominated by an expanding capitalist economy that operates as a unified whole. The world-system does not have to encompass the entire globe, yet it subtends a sufficiently large number of states or political units.[26] This explanation is highly useful in the cultural realm, as the system impacts the exchange and circulation of knowledge. Expanding on Paulin Hountondji's ideas, Nicholas Brown describes the circuits of culture within such a world-system: African cultures (and Third World cultures by extension) "provide raw material[s] (local knowledges, African novels, musical idioms) that are shipped to the research centers of the First world to be converted into finished products (anthropology and pharmaceuticals, literary criticism, Paul Simon albums) that are sometimes reimported to the periphery."[27] As the products of authors who participated directly or indirectly in their countries' anticolonial movements or witnessed the independence moment, most of the literary works and theoretical interventions discussed in this book aim to oppose such easy incorporation within the capitalist world-system, fighting to destabilize it.

The Warwick Research Collective (WReC), in their coauthored book *Combined and Uneven Development: Towards a New Theory of World-Literature* (2015), have analyzed in depth the relations between world-system and literary production. Drawing on the work of Wallerstein and Leon Trotsky, and on the writings of Franco Moretti and Jameson in the literary-theory field, the WReC offers a compelling explanation for the simultaneous presence of different literary forms across the globe at a given moment.[28] According to them, capitalism, as a totalizing world-system, is responsible for the specific literary forms we encounter in world-literature, a hyphenated compound that emphasizes the systemic aspects of the phenomena: "A single but radically uneven world-system; a singular modernity, combined and uneven; and a literature that variously registers this combined unevenness in both its form and its content to reveal itself as, properly speaking, world-literature—these propositions sum up the kernel of our argument."[29] The unevenness of the modern world-system is most evident in the "peripheral" and "(semi-)peripheral" symbolic forms; therefore, the WReC's focus is on works from these parts of the world that "share not only common themes, plots and subjects, but also a range of formal features that we propose to call 'irrealist.'"[30] The WReC's approach is nuanced and compelling, taking into account the interaction between the cultural forces of the world-system, with its consecrated forms and genres, and writers' deliberate engagement with literary and nonliterary local forms.[31] Yet, while the operating logic of the underlying economic, political, and cultural model explains the status quo in the world today, as well as the historical processes engendered by the expansion of capitalism from the sixteenth to the mid-twentieth century, it does not account persuasively for the position of the socialist states during the Cold War. "The protocol commits us to arguing for a *single* world-literary system, rather than for world-literary *systems*," the WReC scholars state.[32] Yet what if it is more accurate to go against such a protocol to describe literary production during the Cold War?

In 1980 the reputed sociologist Peter Worsley countered Wallerstein's monistic model with a bipolar one that took into account the Cold War fault lines. To the capitalist world-system he opposed the "communist" one, acknowledging that there is unevenness even among the supposedly equalitarian and fraternal socialist states: "the communist 'world,' in this model, is decomposed, and its component countries also treated variously as core, peripheral, or semi-peripheral."[33] The model promoted by Wallerstein and his followers either completely overlooked socialist states, as if they did not exist, or made them fit an explanatory frame that was unnecessarily rigid.[34] For instance, Wallerstein argued that the Eastern Bloc did not comprise socialist states. As long as production was for profit and not for use, these countries were merely instances of what he termed "collective capitalist firm[s]."[35] States like the Soviet Union, which moved from semiperiphery to core, pursued their own interests; therefore, "their deteriorating relations" with "the revolutionary forces, particularly in the semiperipheral regions [can] be seen as the simple consequence of the promotion of the USSR from semiperiphery to core."[36] Wallerstein and his followers saw countries labeled as socialist as performing a spectrum of functions within the system, from that of further strengthening the capitalist order to a slightly destabilizing role to an antisystemic force, advancing its transformation to a socialist world-system.[37]

The so-called socialist states were far from attaining the types of equitable societies they purported to be. Inequality among the Eastern Bloc states and forms of imperialism exerted by the Soviet Union both within and outside its component republics created the image of a group of countries that was as stratified as the capitalist ones. Yet, whether the socialist states had succeeded in building an actual socialist world-system is beside the point for my argument here. To understand cultural production during the Cold War, it is enough to emphasize, with Zeev Gorin, that these societies perform an antisystemic function.[38] Wallerstein's and the WReC's approaches can take us a long way toward explaining the variety of literary forms and approaches in Africa after World War II, yet they still fall short of a full explanation owing to their emphasis on a single world-system.

Following a bipolar model, with a capitalist and a socialist world-system, for each of which the United States and the USSR served as center and catalyst, also allows us to understand elements of combined and uneven development within each system. For instance, this clarifies why Aimé Césaire criticized both the United States and the Soviet Union as imperialist centers. In the introduction I defined the Cold War as a configuration with two major imperial powers, the United States and the Soviet Union, operating on oftentimes similar principles, despite the apparent contradiction between their ideologies and modes of production; this similarity guaranteed their commensurability and the ability to work against each other.[39] Also, it elucidates why the AAWA split in two, with the China-based incarnation operating in parallel to the Soviet-backed one. China, during Mao's time, saw itself as a Third World country within a global distribution of economic power in which both the United States and the USSR were First World hubs.[40]

While I subscribe to the WReC's idea that "combined unevenness" is recorded in all literary forms, we may bypass the need for an umbrella "modernism." Under this rubric they extend modernism back in time to include "primitivism, early surrealism, Kafka's supernatural naturalism, even critical realism," thereby explaining the all-encompassing structuring effect of the capitalist world-system through the Jamesonian triad of modernization/modernity/modernism.[41] Their analytical strategy allows them to undo the spurious modernism-realism dichotomy, yet it masks the effects of the Cold War in the cultural realm, especially during the 1970s and 1980s, when the polarization between the supporters of the two modes of writing was further sharpened.[42]

Given the terminology in circulation during the Cold War, we may ask whether the world comprised three rather than two world-systems. Although interest in theorizing the Third World understandably declined after 1989, today numerous scholars are intent on revisiting and exploring its revolutionary potential. However, as Vijay Prashad argued in *The Darker Nations: A People's History of the Third World*, the Third World as a world-system was merely aspirational, a political dream woven at Bandung in 1955 out of the desire to create a network of mutual help that would bolster independent and decolonizing countries and keep them out of the tutelage of old and new imperial powers. This network failed under the increasing polarization of the globe during the Cold War and the pressures of realpolitik. While the Third World system failed, it left its cultural traces in the manifestos and literary works that attempted to break away from the various forms of cultural imperialism.

More important, the Second World, built around the USSR, aimed to become a true world-system: it promoted its own mode of economic organization, as well as an affiliated cultural and literary system. For more than seventy years, the Soviet Union tried to prove that the socialist (and eventually communist) way of life was better than the values and forms of political organization offered by the West.[43] In their engagement with Eastern Europe and Russia, the WReC bypasses the literary forms promoted within the Second World. For instance, their examples from this part of the world are solely what we could term 1990s postmodern writers, allowing them to sidestep the socialist realist novels of the earlier periods. In fact, they do not account for forms of realism that cannot be explained as effects of combined and uneven development of the capitalist world-system. Thus, we can complicate the explanation proposed by the WReC by saying that writers from the peripheries and semiperipheries of the capitalist world worked to disentangle themselves from or at least to signal the limits imposed by capitalism (in its various colonial and imperial guises); at the same time, some of them engaged with a noncapitalist mode of cultural production, ostensibly patronized by countries from the Eastern Bloc, even if this process ultimately led to new forms of cultural imperialism, from which a later generation of intellectuals would attempt to distance themselves.

Urging scholars to engage in a detailed literary historiography of the cultural effects of the Cold War, Joe Cleary gives us an entry into a possible analytical approach that both preserves the gains of world-system theory and also accounts for the radical polarization of the world: in the early twentieth century, the economic world-system that supported the literary field that gave us realism "entered a protracted period of crisis," and "the United States and the Soviet Union would dominate the new world-system already arising in the wake of the Great War."[44] As with everything co-opted or hijacked by the Cold War powers, the modernism-realism debate not only polarized these modes of writing but also hierarchized them, with "one of them being identified (and celebrated) as more progressive than the other, as more subversive or inventive or daring or resourceful."[45]

The very act of assessing literature became a Cold War playfield, as Alex La Guma unwittingly illustrates in an article discussing Alexander Solzhenitsyn's celebrity as a dissident Soviet writer: "From the standpoint of Western reviewers all this must have contributed to the 'unprecedented consensus that Solzhenitsyn is a great writer in the grand Russian tradition of ethical urgency and openness of life.' . . . But his Soviet colleagues did not think so. According to them in his work 'life is reflected in a distorting mirror, and moreover with an obvious anti-Soviet slant' as Soviet writer Nikolai Gribachev put it."[46]

The schism between "Western reviewers" and "Soviet colleagues" who see the same work as worthy or worthless, depending on which political, economic, and cultural world-system they are located in, shows us the far-reaching shadow cast by the Iron Curtain. The very institutions for the promotion, distribution, and consumption of literature—from prize committees to academia to writers' forums—became polarized during the Cold War, and the participants were fully aware of these fault lines. As the Cold War advanced, it became more and more difficult for writers to pursue their work without feeling inadvertently lured or outright hijacked into the ideological and aesthetic systems overseen by the USA and the USSR. Those who wanted to stay away from the long arm of the superpowers' specific forms of cultural imperialism, especially Pan-Africanists such as Ayi Kwei Armah, faced the challenge of setting up their own publishing venues, as the Ghanaian writer did with the Per Ankh press.[47]

At the same time, it is impossible and highly problematic to attempt to justify all literary production in Africa by making it fit a Cold War matrix. While opposing aesthetic systems were set up on the two sides of the Iron Curtain, in practice things were more complicated. For instance, La Guma won both the first competition run by the journal *Black Orpheus*, a contest organized with the support of the CCF, and also the first Lotus Prize, conferred by the AAWA.[48] Nkosi published both in *Lotus* and in numerous venues associated with the CCF. If the CCF and the AAWA were merely the ideological mouthpieces of war-locked superpowers, they could hardly be conferring cultural capital on the same intellectuals. If the cultural battles were simply staged between the supporters of modernism and the disciples of realism, there would probably be no room for mutual comprehension.

There are different genealogies of modernism and realism in African literature that have nothing to do with the Cold War. For instance, Mukoma wa Ngugi reminds us that literary history needs to account for the early twentieth-century South African "Afro-Modernists" and to set their work side by side with the realist novels of the "Makerere writers."[49] That the story of modernism and realism during the Cold War is much more complicated than a simple binary is obvious from the further bifurcation of the opponents of each mode of writing. Those who opposed modernism ranged from Marxist critics who saw it as a form of bourgeois navel-gazing, a subset of art for art's sake (such as Omafume F. Onoge, Gugelberger, and Grant Kamenju), to Africanists who equated it with Eurocentric culture (such as Chinweizu, Onwuchekwa Jemie, and Ihechukwu Madubuike), to those who thought that modernism was becoming antiquated and more innovative approaches had to be attempted. Those who could be termed supporters of realism (Ngũgĩ) or of modernism (Es'kia Mphahlele) both opposed the ideas and forms of art that came out of the Négritude movement. Finally, in her analysis of Kiswahili poetry, Meg Arenberg shows that local aesthetic debates were more complicated than simple infighting between traditionalists and modernists.[50]

One of the most important debates in the history of African literary criticism—usually referred to as the *Transition* debate, involving Wole Soyinka on one side and Chinweizu, Jemie, and Madubuike on the other—allows us to see these distinctive fault lines.[51] Launching a scathing attack on Soyinka and other writers from the Nsukka group, the three Nigerian critics accused their compatriots of producing neocolonial literature that emulated Western aesthetic models; instead, they recommended a return to African roots. It was a blunt and rather problematic accusation that did not recognize Soyinka's own deep investment in specific forms of African culture. The three critics identified a further bifurcation in the level of Western aesthetic influence in poetry versus prose, with critics telling poets to follow Anglo-modernist models, while novelists were being presented with premodernist examples.[52] Chinweizu, Jemie, and Madubuike argued that Eurocentric critics "embraced the modernist revolution of Eliot and Pound, and we find them enthusiastically rallying African poets to the standard of anglomodernist poetry."[53] This led to "cooperative tutelage in deracination," as the African poets subservient to Anglo-modernism adopted prescribed thematic and formal elements from colonial cultures, "with a marked preference for private topics" and "an injunction to obscurity."⁵⁴ Snubbed by Soyinka as "Neo-Tarzanism," and presenting numerous gross overgeneralizations, Chinweizu, Jemie, and Madubuike's book *Toward the Decolonization of African Literature: African Fiction and Poetry and Their Critics* (1980) nonetheless signaled the entanglement of individual authors' literary imagination with that of European writers. Moreover, Armah, Chinweizu, and other Africanist critics warned that the critical apparatus may have been inept at decolonizing the imagination because the very language and concepts of literary criticism came from elsewhere—whether Euro-American literary theory or the forms of criticism endorsed in the Eastern Bloc.

To counter the ideologically backed duels of modernism versus realism, African writers sought to introduce African literary conventions. In an article published in the journal *Transition*, John Pepper Clark set side by side European conventions of poetry—from the "well measured feet, falling to recurrent echoing sounds," of the romantic and Victorian poets to the jagged form of modernist poetry, which addresses the eye as much as the ear—and the "poetry of another convention," the oral literature of Africa.⁵⁵ Clark refuses hierarchies and introduces orature as another literary tradition, with its own codes, genres, and techniques: "The range then in 'oral tradition' as with the 'literate tradition' includes rhetoric, drama, lyric and epic—a living repertory for performance by a living people."⁵⁶ Yet the hardening of the political lines in the 1970s and 1980s nonetheless led to an unfortunate bifurcation and the creation of mythologies of realism and modernism.

Referring to the chasm separating capitalist and communist ideology during the Cold War, Timothy Brennan has pointed out that crossing from one ideologically determined aesthetic field into the other can happen only through an act akin to a religious conversion.⁵⁷ While he may slightly overstate the difficulty, his argument nonetheless makes evident the challenges posed by teaching and analyzing the realist and modernist aesthetic as they were championed by the superpowers and their allies during the Cold War. Furthermore, the impact of aesthetic world-systems lasted well beyond the end of the Cold War, perpetuating a sort of deafness to the literary vocabulary of the other camp.

## African Modernism and the Perils of Aestheticism

In African literary works that can be claimed for modernism in the first two decades of the Cold War, the writing mode is rarely if ever named as such. Instead, we can identify a work's affiliation by formal elements and named sources of inspiration and conversation, which are usually the tutelary figures of high modernism in Europe and America, such as T. S. Eliot and Ezra Pound. By contrast, the label "modernism" appears in the statements and articles written by these works' detractors. Furthermore, the supporters of modernism (and postmodernism) make their affiliation known by their views on the aesthetic of alienation and unreliable narrators, ambiguity and lack of interpretive closure, irony and opacity, or even the use of the fantastic to render national trauma during civil war or dictatorship.

As numerous scholars have already pointed out, at the forefront of the support for modernism in Africa sat two journals—*Black Orpheus* and *Transition*—and a cluster of venues, conferences, and other literary events, all functioning under the umbrella of the CCF.[58]

The modernist aesthetic of *Black Orpheus* is visible from the magazine's covers over the first decade of its existence: drawing on African masks and other cultural objects, the images were stylized into abstract shapes that could easily have been produced by Picasso in his primitivist phase (see figure 2.1). The tone was set with the very first issue, for which Suzanne Wenger, Ulli Beier's first wife, designed the cover. She and Georgina Betts Beier, the editor's second wife, acted as graphic designers for a large number of issues, unifying its visual impact under the sign of the same "bold simplicity of line and directness of effect characteristic of contemporary European graphic art."[59] Peter Benson, in his meticulous reconstruction of the history of the publication, cements this view by commending Ulli Beier's work during the first decade of the journal's existence and comparing his preference for a modernist aesthetic in art and poetry to that of Virginia Woolf.[60]

As elsewhere with the first generation of African cultural journals and magazines, the modernist perspective is not named as such. Rather, the aesthetic criteria transpire in the choice of pieces selected for publication as well as in the critical apparatus that processes cultural production into essays and book reviews. The Westerners who wrote for the magazine, such as Oscar Dathorne, Paul Theroux, and Beier himself, "sometimes showed a preference for the disillusioned styles of European modernism or for literary protagonists whose characters expressed ethical ambiguity or social dysfunction."[61] In *Black Orpheus* issue 10, Julian Beinart published an extensive essay on a brilliant young Mozambican painter, Malangatana Valente Ngwenya (otherwise known as Malangatana), whose oeuvre embodied all the features of the new art the magazine sought. While Malangatana's work matured into an indisputably original style that incorporated elements of southern African mythology and fabulation, some of his earlier paintings included in Beinart's article, such as *The Woman*

Figure 2.1. Cover of *Black Orpheus* 19 (March 1966).

*Who Cries*, follow the models of European artists like Picasso, even down to the title of the composition.[62]

Like the visual sensibility cultivated by the journal, Janheinz Jahn's essay on Aimé Césaire, published in the first issue of *Black Orpheus*, is indebted to Euro-American modernist assessment protocols, while at the same time displaying an awareness of such patterns of influence. To explain the creative forces at work in Césaire's oeuvre, Jahn establishes a dialectic between Martinique, represented as a raw volcanic force, and the educational years in Paris that made the writer partly lose himself even as he gained new knowledge. The critic deploys a modernist language of abstraction, evoking processes of paring down and transmutation to reflect on the gestation of Césaire's poems: "From the abstraction of ancient African conceptions . . . derives the power which is needed for the salvation of the occidental and colonial world of death."[63] Attributing to Césaire the same type of primitive energy that Picasso and fellow modernist painters ascribed to African art, Jahn praises the poet's creation as life-giving, the opposite of the deadening European culture and therefore a spring of rejuvenation for Western culture as well.

The reception protocols that allowed a writer like Césaire to be recognized by Western critics are also profoundly modernist. As Jahn himself accounts, for Césaire's career to be truly launched in Europe, André Breton had to misrecognize the writer from Martinique as a surrealist. However, Jahn is aware of the narcissistic tendencies that made European artists receptive to the work of poets, painters, and sculptors from the colonies: even in its most radical guise as avant-garde art, imperial culture expects to see itself mirrored and duplicated elsewhere. Take, for instance, the story of Breton's encounter with Césaire, which is based on misrecognition and the subsequent subsuming of Césaire's aesthetic under the surrealist banner: "Césaire's revaluations and reinterpretations of French words in the light of his African philosophy seemed to resemble (outwardly) Breton's own poetic techniques, and so Breton received him into the group of his disciples with much ado and began to proclaim his new discovery."[64] Jahn is therefore aware that Euro-American aesthetic vocabularies and evaluation schemas highjack material from the (former) colonies; nonetheless, he holds the hope that "surrealism—to many of us known as the uncomfortable game of an isolated intellect—develops here into a revolutionary expression."[65] The literary criticism deployed to evaluate African literature in the 1950s and 1960s was insufficiently equipped to deal with the subtle form of cultural colonialism at work, yet it was more complex than a simple tool of Euro-American imperialism.

Figure 2.2. Cover for the double issue marking *Transition* magazine's temporary renaming as *Ch'indaba*. *Transition* 50/*Ch'indaba* 1 (October 1975/March 1976).

Cultural borrowings from British and American high modernist artists are structurally embedded in the journal *Transition* as well (see figure 2.2). The covers of the magazine's issues, even when no longer edited by Rajat Neogy, preserved a pared-down abstract modernist look.[66] In the first issue, a brief editorial, most likely authored by Neogy, although no name is given, reflects on the goal of the journal. "Culture in Transition" begins from T. S. Eliot's inclusive and eclectic definition of culture—from Derby Day to "boiled cabbage cut into sections" to Gothic churches—and asks, "What is East African [culture]?"[67] The choice of a modernist writer as the arbiter of aesthetic and philosophical definitions and the aspiration to emulate the rebelliousness of a European avant-garde are some of the most notable ways in which Neogy perceives the watershed moment in East African culture.[68]

Neogy's own poems published in the first issue would be at home among the repertoire of Western modernist writers, with their common emphasis on internal turmoil, the crisis of the self, and the poetics of despair, as well as a rugged aesthetics reflected typographically in groups of indented lines:

> Curse: this vermin mind
> possessed with the I:
> Breeding ground of strangers
> Burning arrows in the sky[69]

If we are to take Neogy's prose poem "7T ONE == 7E TON" as a tone-setting piece for *Transition*, the experimental element dominates. In modernist fashion it invokes the breaking down of the meaning in contemporary experience: "myriad existences forgotten over a past tense and a vocabulary full of new cooked meanings meaning meaning but nothing else."[70] While we can see a general kinship in attitudes toward literature between the editor and British modernists, Neogy did not, however, impose a recipe on his contributors. As a result of the patronage the CCF afforded these publications as well as other cultural venues, such as a string of conferences in Kampala (1962) and Dakar and Freetown (1963), they all bear the hallmark of affinity with modernism and Western aesthetics, even if this inclination was far from the totalizing control Soviet institutions imposed at their literary events and publication venues.

The conferences organized by the CCF offer insight into the institutionalization of Euro-American modernism in some literary circles, at the very same time as other participants rejected this trend. There were plenty of initiatives that promoted African aesthetics, an African literature–centered curriculum, and the employment of readers from the continent or the West Indies to select publishable material for presses.[71] The very topic of the conferences in Dakar and Freetown was redressing the absence of African authors from literature syllabi in French- and English-language universities on the continent.

However, despite these laudable initiatives, Western academics at universities on the continent often deployed a patronizing approach to the oeuvre of African writers, appraising their work through a Eurocentric prism. Notwithstanding his tremendous work for the Mbari Club and *Black Orpheus*, and in contrast to the aims of the journal he edited, Ulli Beier's paper "Contemporary African Poetry in English," prepared for the Makerere conference, presents Euro-American modernism as the standard of good poetry. Comparing two talented Nigerian poets, he argued that "what Ezra Pound is to [Christopher] Okigbo, Eliot and Hopkins are to [John Pepper] Clark."[72] While already frequent in Beier's essay, comparisons with Eliot's and Pound's works proliferate in the *African Literature and the Universities* volume (1965) based on the Dakar and Freetown conferences. Gerald Moore, the editor of the volume, asserts that most of the poets producing their verse in English had not attempted to bring in qualities of African verse, choosing instead "masters" such as "Dylan Thomas (particularly noticeable in Gabriel Okara's early writing), the late poetry of W. B. Yeats, Eliot, Pound and Hopkins. . . . Only Soyinka seems to have been influenced by contemporary English poetry, by the poets who are writing now since the Second World War."[73] The language of subservience, temporal delay, and belatedness infuses his analysis. The expectation that talent in African poetry is measured by how contemporary one's English "masters" are illuminates the implicit assumption that literary models and standards are not set on the African continent.

Some participants, like Es'kia Mphahlele, pushed back against the insidious institutionalization of a critical vocabulary and, therefore, an aesthetic standard that promoted abstraction and a putative universal artistic model.[74] Others, like Eldred Jones, questioned the use of European models in Africa: "Pound is a very recondite poet. I think that one would use this word when one tries to describe him adequately—inaccessible to most people. Now, unless our audience is to be outside Africa, African poetry is not really ready to use a person like Pound as a model, with great profit."[75] Furthermore, Moore's edited volume gives a good sense of how forms of aesthetic influence operated in the 1950s and 1960s: divided between exegesis and discussion sections, with the former performed mostly by European academics and the latter allotted to a mix of African writers and the same academics, this CCF-funded book apportions much more space to those supporting a Euro-American modernist aesthetic.

The crystallization of mythologies of modernism (and realism) as a result of the Cold War political climate is also visible in the reception of Soyinka's work.

Gugelberger's edited collection *Marxism and African Literature* is symptomatic of Cold War anxieties about aesthetics, politics, and ideology. As the editor states in the introduction, "the reader of these essays might at first be startled by what appears to be an anti-Soyinka bias in some of the essays," yet "if the criticism of Soyinka is sometimes harsh, I hasten to add that not only Marxists are by now perturbed by Soyinka's position and some of his writings."[76] Yet, despite being presented by both Marxist and Africanist writers as a modernist author subservient to Euro-American aesthetic formulas, Soyinka attempted to stay aloof from Cold War ideological battles.[77] However, Gugelberger is quick to point out the stakes of this energetic debate: he sees African literature and African literary criticism as in danger of following "the pitfalls of Western art and literature which, for so long, have been based on the *aesthetic imperative* (from Kant's purposeful purposelessness via the Russian formalists to the dominant versions of New Criticism, French structuralism and beyond)."[78] These anxieties had to do with Cold War fault lines as described in chapter 1: whereas some critics emphasized the need for an autonomous creative field, others argued that the arts had to be involved in society.[79]

In this battle, postmodernism became subsumed to the aestheticist tendencies of modernism, despite the break with its predecessor announced by its very name. Nkosi observed that "the argument often made elsewhere against postmodernism [is] that it has the effect of 'disempowering' those struggling to dismantle imperialist discourses" and that "the case against postmodernism is invariably presented as a critique of an epistemological scepticism so extreme that it is seen as politically immobilizing."[80] In Chris Wanjala's formulation, Nkosi helped African intellectuals settle several important questions about the form and social function of their art, including their relationship to current and previous European aesthetic trends: "What value does the experimental line taken by twentieth-century Europe hold for Africa?"[81]

Marxist critics have long perceived modernism and its successor (though putative antagonist) postmodernism as apolitical artistic modes that could be captured by the state. Take, for instance, Michael Hardt and Antonio Negri's accusation, around the turn of the millennium, that postmodern and postcolonial cultural critique, with their emphasis on hybridity, diversity, and cosmopolitanism, have been outstripped and encircled by the neoliberal capitalist economy that has adopted their language for its own purposes.[82] Because *Black Orpheus* and *Transition* emerged at the height of the struggle for independence in Africa and yet turned out to be secretly financed by the CIA through the CCF, these publications problematize the relationship among American imperialism, modernist cultural forms, and decolonization. Is modernism necessarily a mode of writing that intentionally or inadvertently takes captive African cultural production and turns it into an instrument of imperial powers in the West? Most scholars have tried to answer this question in nuanced ways, without labeling participating African authors as flunkeys of Euro-American powers. For instance, Neil Lazarus, drawing on Simon Gikandi's assessment, poses the problem of the connection between modernism, presumably a liberating and rebellious mode of writing, and Western modernity, which is deeply interconnected with the colonial project: "'The men and women who came to produce modern African literature' felt the need to challenge the institutionalized forms of 'modernism,' which reached them, in still colonial or just decolonizing African contexts, as part and parcel of the colonial enterprise—as 'modernism' under the sway of a Eurocentric ideology of 'the modern,' and overdetermined in this respect by its minoritarianism (amounting de facto if not necessarily de jure to elitism), its appearance in European languages exclusively and its militantly partisan selectivity."[83] Pushing back against the simplistic and inflammatory assessment of Chinweizu, Jemie, and Madubuike, Lazarus concludes that African practitioners attempted to make it "their modernism," registering "their commitment to social self-determination."[84]

Similarly, in his important article on the role of the institutions of the CCF in promoting African literature, Peter Kalliney argues that "African writers of the early 1960s reinterpreted the legacy of interwar modernism to fit the needs of new cultural institutions founded in the context of decolonization and the Cold War. . . . At least five versions of artistic freedom were put into circulation through the institutions [of the CCF] examined in this essay: emancipation from colonialism; independence from the postcolonial nation-state; avoidance of politics in order to foster collaboration among multiple constituencies; freedom from politics altogether as a professional disposition; and ideological neutrality in the Cold War."[85] If for Kalliney, on the one hand, modernism enabled authorial autonomy and speaking truth to power, Rubin, on the other hand, has argued that this form of literature within the Third World was the product of Anglo-American imperial aesthetics.[86]

The essays published in *Black Orpheus* and *Transition* generally support the more sanguine view proposed by Gikandi and Kalliney. Introducing the readership to various African aesthetic concepts constitutes the bedrock of the magazines. The editorial in the first issue of *Black Orpheus* presents the aims of the magazine, stressing the importance of growing an audience and a literary-criticism community for contemporary African writers. Other aims are the preservation and display of the rich traditions of oral literature, as well as facilitating an alternative education that puts an end to acculturation.[87] For instance, an article on "Ijálá," the "speech-like song" dedicated to Ogún that Yoruba hunters and blacksmiths perform, appears in the first issue of *Black Orpheus*. Questions regarding translation practices and cultural contextualization come to the foreground: "Yoruba poetry has neither rhyme nor regular metre. The 'line' of Ijálá poetry is the sense group and its length varies. It was therefore considered that English blank verse might be the best medium of translation."[88] Finding commensurate elements within traditional Yoruba and modernist Western prosody indicates the editors' commitment to placing the various literary traditions in conversation as equals. In this respect, the aims of a magazine like *Black Orpheus* do not differ vastly from those of *Lotus: Afro-Asian Writings*. Where the two types of magazine diverge, and therefore reveal the competing views the superpowers attempted to insinuate in the publications, is the function of aesthetics, the role of the writer in society, and, despite some overlap in the writers they promoted, the relatively distinct rosters of artists. As the Cold War advanced, the aesthetic systems and associated modes of writing became more distinct.

In the introduction to their important special issue "Peripheral Realisms," Jed Esty and Colleen Lye synthesize Joe Cleary's position that "the Cold War skewed the aesthetic valuation of twentieth-century non-Euro-American literature: it masked their diversity by partitioning a liberal modernism from a socialist realism and thus inclining post-colonial critics based in metropolitan institutions toward modernist criteria."[89] They sum up the position of writers in rather sanguine tones: "Yet political nonalignment for the Third World writer in fact entailed an agnostic stance, with both modernist and realist forms usable for anticolonial expression."[90] However, the story is more complex and in need of a historicized approach. While this argument—supported by Gikandi and Kalliney as well—that (abstract) modernism was seized on by African writers as just one mode among the many available for literary expression holds true for the period from the end of World War II to the late 1960s, a hardening of ideological lines and aesthetic choices is visible from the 1970s onward. As Cleary has explained the initial dynamic, "once the Soviet Union took 'ownership' of realism . . . it was inevitable that its great Cold War antagonist would eventually, as a kind of reflex, espouse modernism."[91] The sharpening of positions coincides with the aftermath of the revelation that the CIA had set up the CCF to serve its purposes and the consequent soul-searching and redefinition of intellectual positions.

## Socialist Realism in Africa and the Dangers of Rigid Institutionalization

As with *modernism*, critics have sometimes used *realism* as a vague umbrella term without differentiating between its many varieties, from critical realism to naturalism, and from social realism to socialist realism and neorealism. This undifferentiated realism has been alternatively praised as a progressive style or criticized for its presumed subservience to bourgeois ideology.[92] For instance, in an essay entitled "Background to African Literature," printed in the first issue of *Lotus* (then published under the name *Afro-Asian Writings*), Mazisi Kunene speaks admiringly of the range of African literary forms (he enumerates the heroic poem, mythical and adventure stories, drama, and short lyrical pieces as possible genres) while also arguing for a specific mode of writing: "All this means that there is in African society a marked absence of any dogma. In literary terms this means that history and practical everyday actions determine the content of literature. Hence, as others have observed, there is no room for sentimentality; realism being the primary method of conceptualizing life situations."[93] In his statement Kunene sets up realism as the antinomy of romanticism rather than modernism, emphasizing realism's demystifying qualities. As Stefan Helgesson has observed, after World War II a large number of anglophone and lusophone writers—he mentions Fernando Monteiro de Castro Soromenho, Nadine Gordimer, Es'kia Mphahlele, Bloke Modisane, and Luís Bernardo Honwana—have used realism to subvert "misconceptions or outright lies" and as the most appropriate literary mode to resist "the ideological fabrications of [Portuguese] Salazarist and [South African] National Party propaganda or the self-serving myths of white communities."[94] Other authors, like Nkosi, pushed back against the assumption that African writers necessarily prefer a realist style because he saw in it a condescending implication of unimaginative mimetic rendering and an inferred accusation of disinterest in artistic craft.

Within the African context, forms of realism that might have been discarded as tired and surpassed in the West could be given new life when infused with a decolonizing agenda. The Cameroonian writer Mbella Sonne Dipoko identified a new form of realism in the literature of decolonized nations, where the anthropological focus of writers who originally explained their cultures for the West was replaced by sociological concerns: understanding the roots of social ills. He gives as an example the work of Ousmane Sembène, whose short novel *Le Mandat* (1966) he sees as a masterpiece of the new "dynamic realism" emerging in French African writing.[95] This underscoring assumption is also visible in the early issues of the journal *Lotus*, where realism as a descriptive label is used sparingly, mostly as a defining term for the works of participating writers. In the second issue of the journal, a report presented by the South African delegation to the 1967 conference of the AAWA in Beirut, Lebanon, names Alex La Guma "the undisputed great political realist short story writer."[96] By appending the adjective *political*, the report's authors highlight an important aspect of how realism was used and received by the readership: it fulfilled a direct function in societies still struggling against colonialism by critiquing inequality and racism. Yet La Guma's work, especially his early novella *A Walk in the Night*, has also been read as a perfect example of naturalism deployed to criticize apartheid.[97]

The genealogy of the forms of realism embraced by African writers is therefore diverse, even if some European and American authors' names come up repeatedly as interlocutors for the practitioners of realism on the continent. Reviewing for *Lotus* the collection *Modern African Stories* (1964), edited by Ellis Ayitey Komey and Es'kia Mphahlele, M. Shafeek Faind argues that the authors included in the volume "take their cues from American Negro literature and from realists like Dickens and some of the Russians."[98] In keeping with the aims of the journal, the reviewer identifies interlocutors among black American writers. By choosing conversation pieces ranging from nineteenth-century Russian works to contemporary African American novelists, the reviewer short-circuits the condescending assumption that African prose is an epigonal form influenced by Western European writers. However, Faind undercuts his attempts to underline the originality of African realist fiction by deploying a vocabulary of unidirectional influence and derivativeness, with writers from the continent taking their cue from elsewhere. Numerous African writers have staunchly opposed this center-periphery mode of conceptualizing culture from the continent, and maybe no other author's career better illustrates this departure than Ngũgĩ's, to whose work I return in the last section of the chapter.

These earlier, pre-1968 assessments of African realism are quite moderate in tone and do not display any of the hard-line arguments that we see during the last two decades of the Cold War. After the revelation of the extent of American programs designed to subsume cultural production in target countries to U.S. interests, numerous African writers rejected the modernist literature promoted by these programs. La Guma lashed out against writing that prided itself on its craft, works he (and Soviet critics) incorrectly dubbed "art for art's sake." Drawing on the work of Maxim Gorky, the classic of socialist realism, La Guma argued, "The purpose of all art, consciously or unconsciously, is to rouse certain feelings in men, to develop in them a certain attitude towards certain phenomena of life. The adherents of the so-called free 'art for art's sake' also profess this to be their purpose, although their attitude towards social tendencies is negative and even hostile."⁹⁹ The stark contradiction between the vehemence of La Guma's condemnation of such art forms and the vagueness of his statements—as illustrated by the repetition of the modifier *certain*—illustrates the increased stakes in the Cold War cultural battles. In 1986 in Tashkent, Sembène also declared his opposition to "art for art's sake," a category to which modernism and postmodernism were usually subsumed: "Such art fails to grow out of a living soil and cannot, therefore, be fruitful."¹⁰⁰

The covers of *Lotus* as well as the enclosed lavish color photographs frequently took a more utilitarian approach to art in order to better serve a decolonizing purpose (see figure 2.3). These are preponderantly photographs of traditional artifacts rendered in a mimetic style, with the goal of documenting and advertising the rich cultural traditions of formerly colonized people.¹⁰¹ By contrast, the schematic drawings that separate entries in the journal veer toward the abstract.

Leftist intellectuals sometimes created reductive dichotomies. In an otherwise nuanced 1985 essay on the relation between "culture and imperialism," the Kenyan playwright Micere Mugo set side by side two types of culture: "Utilitarian, pro-people culture can be liberating and fulfilling. Show/parade, anti-people culture on the other hand, can be decadent, suffocating, oppressive and enslaving towards the oppressed."¹⁰² This reductive perspective, which establishes absolute correspondences between decorative, form-oriented cultural production and social oppression, and between modernism and the modernity of imperialist cultures, is the obverse of the view held by supporters of modernism that hyperpoliticized forms of art, whether leftist or nativist, were no art at all.

In theory, the journal *Lotus* opened its pages democratically to all forms of art, without a prescriptive agenda. Its jacket underscored this commitment: "This Quarterly endeavours as far as utmost effort and possibilities permit to present models from Afro-Asian Literature, that are representative of various literary tendencies, currents, schools and experiments in various ages, whether classic, modern or contemporary, in the fields of creative and critical writings as well as in the fields of plastic arts and folklore."¹⁰³ However, under the influence of the journal's sponsors, a clear ideology of art developed in its pages from the 1970s onward.

Within the AAWA the dichotomy between realism and modernism became more charged once representatives of the Union of Soviet Writers began to assert their point of view in publications and at conferences, many of which they sponsored and organized. Take, for instance, this statement delivered by Mirza Ibrahimov at the Tashkent International Symposium on Literature and

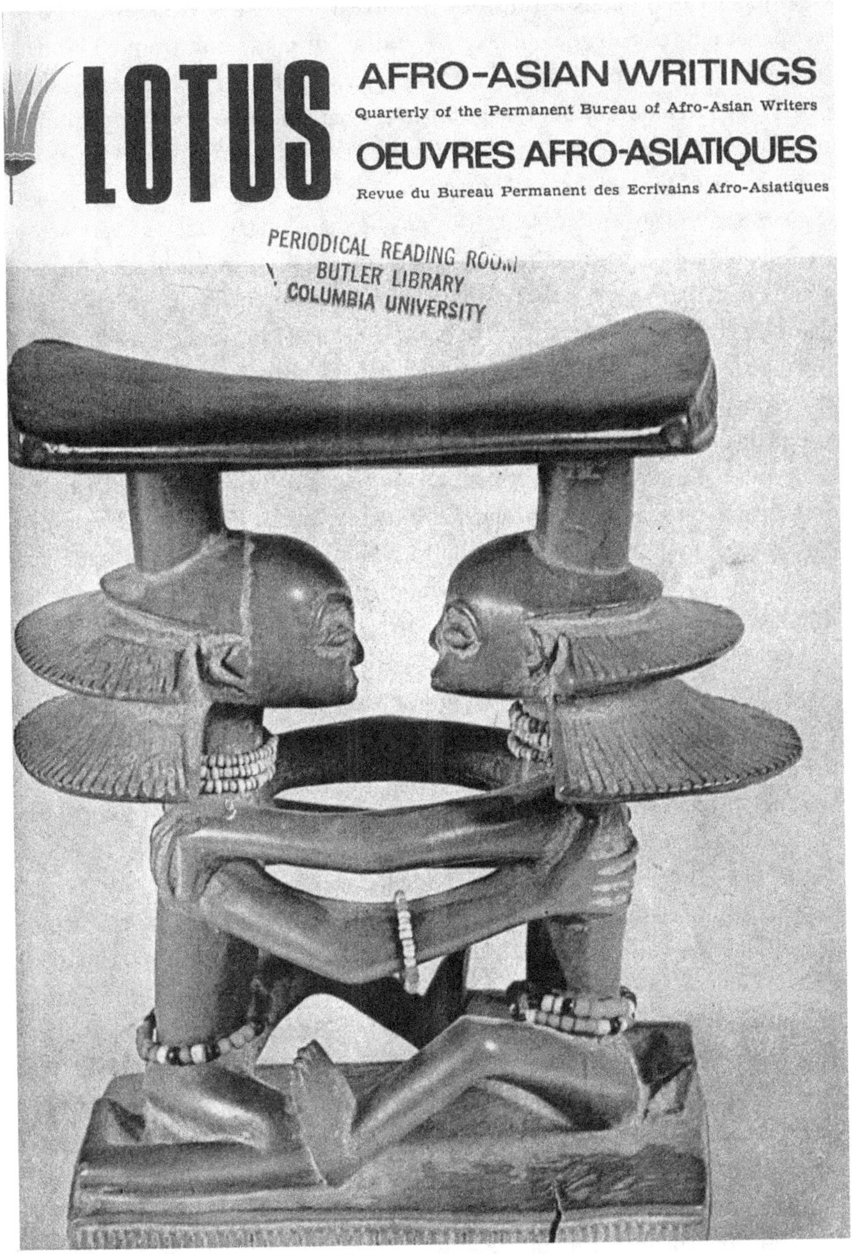

Figure 2.3. Cover of *Lotus: Afro-Asian Writings* 10 (October 1971), English edition.

the Modern Art, published in the fourth issue of *Lotus*: "We know only too well what ugly phenomena in creative endeavour may result from all kinds of 'innovational,' modernestic [sic] trends expressing internal emptiness and the decay of contemporary bourgeois culture; what tragedies develop from ultra-revolutionary but essentially crude vulgarizing attitudes that shackle the creative forces of writers, artists, composers. . . . Contemporary bourgeois modernism and vulgarisation cloaked in ultra-revolutionary attitudes are at one in their hatred of genuine innovation and the best examples of great artistic creativity. They detract creative thought from reality, from the real needs and requirements of the people."[104] While realism as a writing mode is not named as such in this excerpt, an emphasis on *real* and *reality* appears to crudely imply a correspondence between the social and economic structures in transformation and realism as the art form most capable of expressing them.

After the First Congress of the Union of Soviet Writers in 1934, formalism and "art for art's sake" were proscribed as empty, elitist Western aesthetics, divorced from politics.[105] Instead, socialist realism became the new artistic doctrine in the USSR—a loosely defined art form that by the 1950s had lost even the initial artistic coherence it had in the 1930s, when authors like Maxim Gorky and Mikhail Sholokhov lent their prestige and cultural authority to this project. Supporters of socialist realism represented it as a formulation of the artists' commitment to the transformation of society by raising the consciousness of their fellow citizens.

Socialist realism has long been regarded in the West as the expression of the intellectually inert cultural forms born in a totalitarian state. Even Katerina Clark's much-respected 1981 monograph *The Soviet Novel: History as Ritual* opens with an acknowledgment of the social and academic awkwardness of writing a book about Soviet socialist realist novels. "Soviet Socialist Realism is virtually a taboo topic in Western Slavic scholarship. It is not entirely taboo, for it can be discussed, but only in tones of outrage, bemusement, derision, or elegy."[106] If during the last decade of the Cold War Western literary critics would not consider socialist realism a topic worthy of inquiry, African or Asian writers who claimed to enjoy and emulate the works of their Soviet fellows were perceived with added skepticism and derision. Western critics oftentimes regarded them as politically naive or derelict in their duty to preserve the autonomy of literary creation from the intrusion of the state.

After World War II, the USSR's interest in expanding its sphere of influence over decolonizing nations ensured socialist realism's increased visibility abroad. As a promoter of internationalism, the Soviet Union projected itself as the champion and defender of the peoples of the Third World. It therefore sought to cement this leadership position by encouraging writers from newly decolonized nations to adopt what the Union of Soviet Writers had decreed to be revolutionary artistic strategies. Take, for instance, the International Symposium of Writers on "Literature and the Modern Art," convened in Tashkent in September 1968, a literary event that was extensively covered in the January 1970 issue of the *Lotus*. The inaugural speech delivered by Sarvar Azimov, chairman of the Soviet Liaison Committee with Afro-Asian Writers, goes beyond the usual vague call for "authentic forms" seen in several issues of *Lotus*. Establishing a difference between "progressive literature," which channels the creative energies of artists toward the shared goals of their nation, and "reactionary literature," which wastes them in unproductive forms, Azimov argued that "the definitive factor, which is something of a watershed between them, is the attitude to the problem of peace and socialism, to the liberation struggle of the peoples of Asia, Africa and Latin America. Reactionary literature has a pronounced tendency to depart into the world of the unreal, the subconscious, into the sphere of formal experiment. Hence its hypertrophied attention to diverse fashionable and superfashionable trends, which are indicative of the literature and art of the capitalist world."[107]

Progressive art is defined negatively, in counterdistinction to "reactionary literature." Social function supplants form in this definition. One of its most important features, though, is its tricontinental scope. The emphasis on former colonies and then-current targets of Western imperialism had been highlighted as early as the first Afro-Asian Writers' Conference, held in Tashkent in 1958. Soviet speakers emphasized the Bandung ideals upon which the association was forged.[108]

Yet did socialist realism make its way into the AAWA? In principle, the conditions for the spread of this mode of writing were in place, as the Soviet Union exercised a high degree of control over its operation, although the AAWA was created as an heir to the nonaligned principles of Bandung and although the association repeatedly pledged to fight imperialism, which was unilaterally understood as American and Western European imperialism. While there was some support for socialist realism in the journal *Lotus*, it is important to understand African and Asian writers' approving comments about this style as having more to do with a rebellious rejection of Western aesthetic principles than with a full-throated endorsement.

While African writers featured in *Lotus* embraced a leftist position with respect to the writer's role in society, and while the names of Soviet writers who have become bywords for socialist realism—Gorky and Sholokhov—are oftentimes mentioned, very few take up the banner of socialist realism.[109] When writers recorded their genuine support for it, oftentimes tautological statements ensued, such as La Guma's pronouncement, "Each real artist searches for the truth, seeks to depict the truth. . . . The main demand of socialist realism is to portray life truthfully, in its progressive development."[110] As we will see in the next section, Ngũgĩ's engagement with socialist realist aesthetics has less to do with a faithful emulation of the features encountered in early twentieth-century Soviet classics than with the creation of aesthetic solidarities that inscribed him within a progressive, Afro-Asian, or even tricontinental community of writers.

### Ngũgĩ wa Thiong'o's Decolonization of Writing Modes

Ngũgĩ wa Thiong'o's career has been an active search for the most appropriate style of writing to "decolonis[e] the mind" and "mov[e] the centre" away from the Euro-American canons. His literary practice has been part of the democratizing efforts of his oeuvre as well as the rejection of aesthetic and ideological shackles created by (neo)colonialism. This search has entailed an engagement with and surpassing of established modes of writing. While his earlier works, such as *A Grain of Wheat* (1967, revised 1986), display modernist features that have formed the object of numerous studies, he laid claim to a vigorous form of social realism in his midcareer works (*Petals of Blood, Devil on the Cross, Matigari*), a mode of writing cross-fertilized by oral traditions that allowed him to expose neocolonial exploitation, only to then exhibit a pattern-breaking combination of realism, fable, and fantastic elements in his most recent novel, *Wizard of the Crow*. I treat here only the transition from modernism to realism, foregrounding the changes between *A Grain of Wheat* and *Petals of Blood*, in order to illustrate the profound impact of Cold War aesthetic world-systems, as well as his solution for transcending them into a truly decolonized mode of writing. Like the chemical treatment or heat applied to invisible ink, the Cold War perspective acts as the developing substance that illuminates the ideological forces at work in postcolonial literature, the aesthetic choices facing African writers, and even the blind spots in postcolonial studies treating the works of these authors.

Simon Gikandi has argued that during the late 1970s—the moment when the shift between aesthetic world-systems becomes evident in Ngũgĩ's work—the author subscribed to "competing notions of culture" that ranged from a mostly surpassed liberal notion of culture, to a critical embracement of African nationalism, to a Marxist perspective on the role of literature in reflecting and effecting social change; hence, his aesthetics have given rise to contradictory assessments.[111] This assessment is probably even more accurate if we expand the span of time, from the late 1960s, after the publication of *A Grain of Wheat*, when Ngũgĩ began exploring the ideology of form, to the late 1970s and *Petals of Blood*.

The models of literature absorbed in the English colonial educational system influenced the earliest period of Ngũgĩ's career. While one signature chapter in *Decolonising the Mind* criticizes the 1962 Kampala conference for perpetuating the supremacy of the English language in Africa, the review he penned immediately after the event shows a less discerning eye. A college student at Makerere, Ngũgĩ had been invited to attend the watershed conference on the strength of several published short stories. Published in *Transition*, his review expressed enthusiasm at meeting established and rising writers from across the continent, while channeling Western European aesthetic principles. Chinua Achebe's first two novels "seem[ed] to herald the birth of a new society in which writers, freed from the burden of political protests and jibes at a disintegrating colonialism, can cast an unsentimental eye at human relationship in all its delicate and sometimes harsh intricacies."[112] Presenting African literary production as going through a ritual graduation from political contamination to abstracted forms, young Ngũgĩ's response highlights the hold of Western literary criteria on emerging anticolonial writers in the early 1960s. Political relevance was discarded, and the focus stayed on putatively universal features of human relations, in sharp contradiction with the cultural decolonization principles he later made famous. Equally striking is his emphasis on individuality rather than community: "A creative writer is concerned with the expression of the music and strife of his own soul."[113] The norms and aesthetic matrices imbued in a Eurocentric academic environment translated into modernist assumptions about individual interiority and psychological turmoil as hallmarks of good literature.

In a similar contextualizing move, Gikandi reflects on the pressure Western literary forms exerted in the Kenyan writer's earlier short stories "The Return" and "Goodbye Africa," where even the politics of decolonization are relegated to the background. Instead, the focus is on "master[ing] narrative forms built around the rhetoric of failure which, he had been taught at Makerere College, was the mark of good literature as defined by modernism."[114] At Makerere, Ngũgĩ was taught that writers should avoid "clouding" their works with political topics. After independence, young Ngũgĩ avers, writers in these new African societies can "sit down and observe," finally able to be concerned "with the music and strife of [their] soul."[115] In short, the view handed down to African students from the lecterns of colonial classrooms was that literature should aim toward autonomy, psychological individuality, and complex form.

The clearest reflection of the role of modernism in Ngũgĩ's early literary career—as well as relatively abrupt shift away from this mode of writing—is his celebrated novel *A Grain of Wheat*. Originally published in 1967 and reissued in a revised edition in 1986, the novel is torn between modernist and realist aesthetics. The first two chapters signal this bifurcation. In modernist fashion, the former zooms in on the anguish resulting from the guilty conscience of Mugo, a character who betrayed Kihika, the preeminent Mau Mau fighter. The latter chapter zooms out to present the historical panorama of community struggles under colonialism leading up to the Kenya Land and Freedom Army's insurrection; it largely employs realist techniques specific to historical novels. As Gikandi has pointed out, Ngũgĩ had absorbed the Euro-American modernist literary mandate, with its "themes of failure, disenchantment, and betrayal," a plot rent by ambiguity, and a writer sitting at a contemplative ironic distance.[116] That Ngũgĩ was under the spell of modernist masters is evident from the novel's critical reception: a large number of articles and book chapters describe in laudatory or critical terms the similarities and differences between *A Grain of Wheat* and Joseph Conrad's oeuvre, especially the novel *Under Western Eyes*.[117]

More relevant for this historical overview of transformations engendered by decolonization and the Cold War in Ngũgĩ's literary creed are the changes he introduced in the 1986 edition. Evan Mwangi has meticulously documented these changes: they range from removing some acts of violence that reproduced racist Western stereotypes of African men (the rape of Dr. Lynd is replaced by the killing of her dog) to clarifying and strengthening the political urgency embodied by some characters (Kihika and Lt. Koina no longer harbor doubts about the forms taken by the anticolonial struggle and are firm in their oppositional stance). With a few deft touches, African characters who play a part in the Mau Mau resistance are cleared of blame and justified in their wrath by previous suffering, while the British and their loyal henchmen are stripped of individual complexity to emphasize their violence as part of the larger colonial mechanism.[118] The revisions removed part of the novel's ambiguity and the characters' complexity—hallmarks of a modernist text—in favor of a clearer political message. Over two decades Ngũgĩ's aesthetic choices had changed under the twin forces of decolonization and the Cold War.

While each of Ngũgĩ's novels highlights important changes in his creative vision, *Petals of Blood* most clearly indicates a shift influenced by the Cold War aesthetic world-systems. The novel is a narrative tour de force that redresses the silences and imbalances of colonial versions of Kenyan history. It gives prominence to the Mau Mau resistance to British colonialism while also detailing the postindependence disenchantment with a new black elite. It builds an intricate murder plot and portrays four convincing main characters—the teacher Munira, the barmaid Wanja, the shopkeeper Abdulla, and the trade unionist Karega. Brought by circumstance to the isolated village of Ilmorog, they dedicate themselves to reviving its spirit, organize a long march to the capital when the drought decimates the farmers' cattle and already scant crops, and succeed in drawing the politicians' and entrepreneurs' attention to the region. The long-term results of economic development are, however, a far cry from what the protagonists envisioned: their initial gains are taken over by rich industrialists, the numbers of the unemployed and the *lumpenproletariat* are on the rise, and those who abused the protagonists in the past are at the top of the neocolonial hierarchy. At least five or six overarching meaning-making narrative structures are superimposed, as characters struggle to make sense of the past twelve years of their lives and the place of the postindependence period in Kenyan history. What has happened to the revolutionary spirit after uhuru? Why are the Kenyan peasantry and the emerging working class still struggling for basic means of subsistence if a black government is in power? What is to be learned from past struggles in order to achieve a different political and economic outcome in the future? These are some of the questions posed by the novel. All of these narrative arcs are concerned with the meaning of history, with linking events into causal patterns and ascribing interpretations to them.

An author's choice of a specific narrative structure and genre is informed by the historical and political context to which the writer responds: electing to use realist, magical realist, modernist, or postmodern techniques is a contextual decision partly informed by the historicity and locality of the respective genre and literary work. Ngũgĩ's decision to write *Petals of Blood* as a sweeping historical novel in the socialist realist vein, a novel that nonetheless presents characteristics of a whodunit, is the result of his informed dialogue with and contestation of contemporary literary genres against the background of the Cold War.[119] *Petals of Blood* conforms to some of the requirements of the detective genre, as literary critics have pointed out.[120] At least at a first level of interpretation, the novel is a crime mystery driven by the discovery of the corpses of the three directors of the Theng'eta Breweries. This plot element offers the pretext for Munira's detailed revisiting of the past twelve years of his life: "How does one tell of murder in a New Town? Murder of the spirit? Where does one begin? How to recreate the past so that one can show the operation of God's law?"[121] In this chain of rhetorical questions, the emphasis shifts from homicide as the object of a criminal investigation to murder as the object of psychological and sociological scrutiny. Munira's question illuminates a self-reflexive aspect of the literary work, as Ngũgĩ explores the formal literary options available to him in the mid- to late 1970s while witnessing the palpable deterioration of the Kenyan social fabric, the betrayal of the core ideals of the Mau Mau struggle, and the exhaustion of social patience.[122]

In his study *Detective Fiction and the African Scene,* Linus Asong reiterates Clifford Robson's earlier observation that "the ostensible framework of the book [is given by] the 'whodunit' element of the three deaths."[123] Ngũgĩ had become familiar with the thriller genre as a student at the Alliance High School, where he had immersed himself in classics of European literature like Charles Dickens and Leo Tolstoy and also enjoyed the formally less demanding pleasures of thrillers.[124] To this intimate acquaintance with the rules of the genre we can also trace back his use of the detective novel structure in *Petals of Blood,* where, however, the former imitative mode is transformed into a new aesthetic and political position. Observing the masterful *in medias res* opening of the novel and the drama and suspense created with the successive arrests of Munira, Abdulla, and Karega, as well as the long paragraph dedicated to the alleged professionalism of Inspector Godfrey (the police officer investigating the case), Asong considers the novel to be a successful incorporation of the elements of the whodunit genre. "Fortunately for Ngũgĩ," Asong proclaims, "the detective novel devices which he employed to hold the reader's attention to the end" save the author from being accused of having written a polemic, an overtly ideological narrative, rather than a work of fiction.[125] Recognizing that the detective genre is employed by Ngũgĩ to address the social issues characteristic of a nascent capitalist society, including the criminalization of the poor, Asong implies that the emphasis in *Petals of Blood* is placed on answering the question "whydunit?" rather than "whodunit?"

Instead of assuming that Ngũgĩ's decision to draw on detective fiction strategies was the saving grace that lifted the novel out of literary marginalization, I ask what Ngũgĩ intended to do with this formal element and how his decision to work with and ultimately discard the whodunit genre is rooted in aesthetic choices that are influenced by the Cold War. As Ngũgĩ acknowledged in a 1996 interview, "there is nothing wrong in the writer experimenting with different forms. I myself use in *Petals of Blood* [a] very popular thriller structure, a mix of thriller and detective structure . . . or the investigative detective structure and I use that for different reasons."[126]

If Ngũgĩ shows interest in the narrative opportunities afforded by the traditional detective novel that, popular with the masses and familiar as a mode of structuring the plot, would have garnered him a wider audience, he does not offer his readers any praiseworthy Sherlock Holmes or Hercule Poirot figure in Inspector Godfrey, the detective who investigates the crimes. On the contrary, we can say that Ngũgĩ intentionally employs this plot device in order to reveal its flaws: though formally a correct identification of the arson author, the detective's interpretation fails to grasp the larger historical significance of what has happened. Munira was indeed the author of the arson, as Inspector Godfrey intuits. Yet Wanja had already killed Kimeria, the man who had impregnated and abandoned her many years before, and Abdulla was contemplating the same revenge against the man who had been the means of his brother's death. The arson was the response of nascent forces resisting the transformation of Ilmorog, and by extension of Kenya, into a community divided by capitalist relations of production and neocolonial interests.

"One can use popular forms and subvert [the] ideology those popular forms have been serving in the past," the author observed.[127] Ngũgĩ suggests that an interpretation arising from a popular Western literary genre—a genre emanating from capitalist societies—would confuse or, worse, willfully obfuscate the roots of social unrest and violence in contemporary Kenya. As Gikandi points out, Ngũgĩ's aesthetics "was premised on a very specific [Marxist] understanding of the relation between society and the subject and form of literature."[128] The genres developed in what the author saw as capitalist-imperialist societies would not have been appropriate to represent the continued exploitation and marginalization of the Kenyan peasantry and working class. Therefore, with this reference to detective fiction, Ngũgĩ criticizes what he perceives as a failed epistemological mode arising from nineteenth-century Western literature that found renewed popularity during the Cold War. Countering the bourgeois worldview embodied by the detective genre, he introduced elements of the socialist realist genre.[129]

Critics have paid attention to the role British, and generally Western, literature has played in shaping Ngũgĩ's earlier view of literary craftsmanship, as well as his later integration of Gĩkũyũ oral narratives, leading up to his decision to renounce English as a literary language.[130] Yet, despite the interest in Ngũgĩ's literary Marxism, scholars have failed to establish a relationship between Ngũgĩ's leftist vision and his 1975 writing vacation in Yalta at the invitation of the Union of Soviet Writers, or between his admiration for Russian literature and the general Cold War context. In fact, in the same way in which Western literature has played a formative role in Ngũgĩ's development as a writer, we can equally speak of the role of the Eastern Bloc (and especially the Soviet Union) in Ngũgĩ's cultural imaginary.[131] In an article entitled "The Reds and the Blacks: The Historical Novel in the Soviet Union and in Postcolonial Africa," M. Keith Booker and Dubravka Juraga highlight the similarities between the historical novel in Africa and in the USSR. In both situations we deal with postrevolutionary texts that are "inherently political" and therefore need to be evaluated according to different aesthetic principles from those promoted in the West; the authors argue that such literature aims to seize historical interpretation from the hands of the bourgeoisie and recast the meaning of the past in order to open up new possibilities of political action.[132] Therefore, the emphasis on socialist realism is sometimes the result of African writers' deliberate departure from Western literary models and intentional dialogue with narrative strategies practiced in the Eastern Bloc, which they see as more compatible with the people's struggle. What then are the forms and the implications of Ngũgĩ's admiration for the Russian historical novel? How does he transform the socialist realist form to suit his aims?

Ngũgĩ's interviews underscore the influence of Russian writers, from the masters who shaped the global development of prose in the nineteenth century (Leo Tolstoy, Ivan Turgenev, Fyodor Dostoevsky) to the Soviet novelists who emphasized the tribulations and historical victories of the peasantry and the working class (Maxim Gorky, Mikhail Sholokhov).[133] His dialectical vision of history accounts for his understanding of the relationship between the economic structure of society, the forces of production, and the generation of cultural forms specific to each economic system. Based on this correlation, he identifies a kinship between the social transformation ushered in by the Russian Revolution and the liberation of the Kenyan people from British colonialism:

> What I liked with his [Sholokhov's] novel *And Quiet Flows the Don* was his mastery in depicting human beings being pulled, being torn, if you like, in the context of the Russian Revolution. This reveals his deep understanding of what you may call the dialectics of life. Really, I must have been under the spell of his *And Quiet Flows the Don* when I came to look at Kenyan history. I read his works at the same time I was writing *A Grain of Wheat* and later, before I wrote *Petals of Blood*. So I think his world outlook, his artistic rendering of the struggles of people, had a definite effect on me.[134]

Tracing the forces of progress (the working class and the peasantry) and the forms of consciousness engendered by the transition from one social order to another, the writer connects two apparently disparate events—the Bolshevik Revolution and the Mau Mau Uprising.[135] They led to a similar radical transformation of people's social consciousness, opening up the vision of freedom and equality, and simultaneously engendered the cultural instruments of liberation. However, although Ngũgĩ perceives the Mau Mau Uprising as an unfinished transformation, interrupted by the installation of an insidious neocolonial regime, he does not question whether the Soviet narrative of triumphant equality and participation in the new political structures gives a complete story of the state of affairs in the USSR.

Novels such as *Petals of Blood* borrow from earlier Soviet narrative models, like the early twentieth-century socialist realist genre, imagining the victorious march forward of progressive social forces. Post-perestroika research on the USSR has shown that such a vision, while invoked in official documents, was a projection oftentimes directly at odds with the reality experienced by the Soviet people in the late 1970s. For the purposes of this argument, it is irrelevant whether the writer was able to acquire an accurate understanding of the economic, political, and cultural situation in the USSR, either during his 1975 sojourn in Yalta or during his trip to the Soviet Union to attend the 1973 AAWA conference in Alma-Ata, Kazakhstan, where he was distinguished with the Lotus Prize. Shepherded by translators and closely monitored, foreign guests were oftentimes prevented from interacting with a disgruntled populace. What merits attention instead is the Kenyan writer's choice of literary forms that he borrowed from Soviet writers, along with other cultural influences, as well as the cultural routes traveled by these literary techniques during the Cold War.[136]

Ngũgĩ borrowed some aesthetic preoccupations and the attending revolutionary vision from the first generation of socialist realist writers, like Gorky and Sholokhov, yet he also tailored these features to speak to aspects of Kenyan society after independence. For instance, most Soviet socialist realist novels of this period foreground the consciousness of a "positive hero" whose life is patterned to represent "the forward movement of history."[137] However, despite Ngũgĩ's embrace of the genre, his polyphonic novel is fragmented by the diverging views of the four main characters and fraught with contradictions. The text ends with the imprisoned Karega's hopeful anticipation of "tomorrow," a word that announces both a renewed workers' strike to be held the following day and a future horizon of fulfillment for the downtrodden of Kenya.[138] Thus, the novel appears to endorse Karega's leftist worldview, which largely coincides with the author's political views stated in essays and interviews. However, in embracing the conflicting perspectives of all four protagonists, the author distances the reader's sympathies from Karega, who, led by revolutionary ardor and a mechanistic understanding of class conflict as the driving engine of history, ignores Wanja's sentiments and inadvertently hurts her. Instead of showing understanding for her suffering, Karega lectures her on history. Furthermore, Abdulla rejects Karega's workerist view of historical change and class conflict; instead, he emphasizes the role small traders and the unemployed might play in shaping the future of Kenya. As it is Abdulla who fathers Wanja's child and acts as the symbolic progenitor of a new generation, his perspective carries interpretive weight, counterbalancing Karega's leftist view at the close of the novel.

Critics have read *Petals of Blood* as an example of detective fiction, on the one hand, and socialist realism, on the other, yet a Cold War lens allows for an interpretation that accounts for the author's choice and deployment of both genres. Ngũgĩ used the detective novel structures only to discredit that genre's epistemology: Inspector Godfrey, representing individualist capitalism, cannot comprehend the clash between neocolonialism and progressive forces in Kenya. Similarly, the author borrows from the Russian historical novel and socialist realist techniques yet adjusts them to specific Kenyan concerns: Karega's Marxist view is complemented by that of Abdulla, an ex–Mau Mau fighter turned destitute small trader. Like numerous other African texts, Ngũgĩ's novel does not merely repeat Western or Eastern Bloc formal literary concerns but develops new genres adapted to the local cultural heritage that afford a better understanding of both the Kenyan and global dimensions of the Cold War. Neither the epistemology of the detective novel nor that of the socialist realist text completely fits his aims—the former is discarded as inadequate, the latter adapted to fit the Kenyan context. Ngũgĩ invites a cultural and political triangulation that includes the West, the Global South, and the East.

Ngũgĩ's subsequent novels—*Devil on the Cross* (first published in 1980 in Gĩkũyũ and in 1982 in English translation), *Matigari* (in 1986 in the original Gĩkũyũ and 1987 in English translation), and *Wizard of the Crow* (in 2004 in Gĩkũyũ and 2006 in English)—attest to his continuous distancing from formulas from elsewhere, whether Western or Eastern Bloc models, and the exploration of local aesthetic strategies in order to expand the capacity of the novel and turn it into an African genre. This is particularly evident in the role accorded *secondary orality*, to borrow Abiola Irele's term, channeling strategies encountered in oral narratives and epic poems to serve the purposes of a written genre, whether in a hyperbolic thieves' competition in *Devil on the Cross*, the fairy-tale female protagonist meets kung fu heroine in the same novel, or the subjects' competition to please the despotic ruler in *Wizard of the Crow*.[139] These novels also inaugurate a new (or rather an older) way of reception and consumption of novels, through public reading in bars and family homes, a communal form of sharing literature that Ngũgĩ particularly enjoyed recounting: "The process I'm describing is really, the appropriation of the novel into the oral tradition. *Caitaani mutharaba-Ini* (*Devil on the Cross*) was received into the age old tradition of storytelling around the fireside; and the tradition of group reception of art that enhances the aesthetic pleasure and provokes interpretation, comments and discussions."[140] In the same way in which Ousmane Sembène realized that novels—

given the requirements of literacy, leisure time, and higher income—could not reach the audience he intended, causing him to shift his efforts to film, Ngũgĩ has worked tirelessly since the early 1980s to democratize the novel form and make it accessible to the working class and peasantry.[141]

Referring to *Matigari*, Odun F. Balogun observed that in the same way in which the concept of realism has evolved in literary practice from its eighteenth-century roots, from formal realism to psychological realism, and from socialist realism to marvelous realism, Ngũgĩ further transformed this mode of writing "to create a new realism by returning to the previously neglected oral narrative aesthetic."[142] The Cold War cultural battles between the modernist and realist modes of writing have found in Ngũgĩ's post-1980 work their full resolution: the writer has indigenized and appropriated the novel, working against and breaking the hold of the aesthetic world-systems.

It is impossible to understand the impact of the Cold War without considering the career arc of productive writers like Ngũgĩ, because a snapshot at a specific moment is insufficient. It is only by historicizing the debates between the supporters of realism and modernism that we can understand the impact of the Cold War. The split between the two modes of writing has material effects, as the supporters of each side have contributed to disavowing the value of the other mode of writing. When aesthetics has the backing of empires, it inevitably has repercussions in the visibility or invisibility of specific writers. The two modes of writing have become entangled in writers' wars of position. They are equally entrenched in the critical apparatus. This, in turn, bequeathed us a nostalgia and desire to identify both "peripheral realisms" and "cosmopolitan modernisms," further solidifying the ideological split.[143]

The tenacity of aesthetic categories passed down in school curricula in the West and the Eastern Bloc translates into a certain tone-deaf response to the tenets of a different aesthetic. Such an approach forecloses the possibility of talking about a view of art that focuses on its social function. Conversely, a reductively Soviet approach shut down the ability to engage with formal innovation. Entire areas of African literary criticism produced during the Cold War were mutually invisible to each other. Historicizing the development of African literary criticism and of the most important discussion tenets would allow us to speak of literary styles and functions across the Iron Curtain and to see the emergence of African literature as a field that is part of a global interaction of aesthetic systems.

# Part II

# Reading through a Cold War Lens

# 3

# Creating Futures, Producing Theory

Strike, Revolution, and the Morning After

In a 2012 speech commemorating the death of the activist Ruth First, Albie Sachs bemoaned the "death of revolution" and the disappearance of the "tunnel vision" that had characterized the last decade of the antiapartheid struggle.[1] He mourned not only First but a sense of political purpose and clarity, which dissipated at the end of the 1980s, a moment that corresponds significantly with the end of the Cold War. The opinion expressed by the ex-freedom fighter and Constitutional Court judge also resonates across several recent literary texts: they articulate a nostalgia for the Cold War era as a temporal dimension structured by clearer moral and ideological principles than the disorienting present. In Zoë Wicomb's *David's Story* (2000), for example, the eponymous protagonist—an Umkhonto we Sizwe (MK) cell leader—contrasts the transparency of the rules of engagement, the moral and political code during the struggle, to the confusion brought about by the early 1990s: "Those were the days, David sighs, when things were clear and we knew what had to be fought, what had to come down."[2] In Mandla Langa's *The Memory of Stones* (2000), the narrative counterintuitively renders the recollected antiapartheid struggle as more present and alive than the decade succeeding the first democratic elections: a perception that translates into a narrative reversal. The narrator's use of the present tense enlivens past moments; his use of the past tense to recount recent events, by contrast, suggests the relative emotional remoteness of the present.[3] The energy of the antiapartheid struggle and the freedom fighters' commitment to bring about a new form of social organization elevated those years and set them apart in a temporal category of their own: revolutionary time. It is with this temporal dimension of revolution and violent social transformation in Africa that this chapter is concerned.

Revolution—as research topic—illuminates an important Cold War perspective on African literatures. The global conflict, with its bifurcated ideological landscape, shaped the types of postindependence futures available for decolonizing states. It molded actual and fictional representations of revolution and its aftermath. On the one hand, the erstwhile imperial powers exerted pressure on their former subjects, attempting to keep them within Western spheres of influence, promising that Euro-American modes of social and economic organization would offer new states the best chances to succeed. The preservation of European institutions guaranteed the West's continued ability to interfere and benefit from nominally independent states.[4] On the other hand, the Eastern Bloc promised alternative models of social and economic organization to be developed through revolution. The new non-European poster children of socialism—Cuba, China, the central Asian republics of the USSR, nations whose past of poverty and subjugation looked distinctly similar to that of other decolonizing states—held up the mirage of accelerated modernization and social justice. Besides, as Jeffrey James Byrne observed, aside from the statehood models offered by the Western world and the Eastern Bloc, newly independent nations could also contemplate regional unions or forms of social organization tailored to local traditions, as proposed by the supporters of African socialism.[5] Therefore, in the late 1950s and early 1960s, the end result of the decolonization process was not a foregone conclusion, and neither were the methods through which statehood could be attained. Negotiated transition, violent war of decolonization, revolutionary process entailing a change of the entire economic system—these were several avenues pursued by African countries.

Decolonization through revolution evoked different affective responses based on one's ideological vantage point and subject position. On the one hand, in Cary Fraser's words, for all participants—superpowers, former imperial centers, and (former) colonies—decolonization was more than just a political process: in the aftermath of World War II, "it was also a symbol of moral regeneration."[6] Even the British Empire disingenuously represented decolonization as a peaceful emancipatory process, according to which former colonies "graduated" into self-determination and sovereignty, thus disguising imperial violence as a benevolent process of political pedagogy. The stress on peaceful transformation removed the specter of revolution and violent overthrow of colonial regimes. The new superpowers, the USA and the USSR, used the mantle of anti-imperialism—all the while practicing new forms of imperialism—to draw countries within their spheres of influence. On the other hand, where colonial violence had been relentless, revolution appeared as the only available option. Frantz Fanon memorably argued that anticolonial violence is the natural response to the sustained violence inflicted by the colonizer; the deeply divided world created by oppressors encoded within it the only possible response from those crushed under its weight if they hoped to turn from objects into human beings.[7] However, he pointed out, the binary thinking that forced Third World nations to choose from "colonialism versus anticolonialism, indeed capitalism versus socialism," was to be discarded in order to zoom in on "the issue which blocks the horizon... the need for a redistribution of wealth."[8] In the same way in which, he argued, "Marxist analysis should always be slightly stretched" in the colonies, adapted to the specificities of African societies, socialism was not to be achieved by a recipe handed down from elsewhere, whether from the Eastern Bloc or leftist theorists in the West.[9]

This centering on the African conception and experience of revolution is given visual expression in the photographs captured by Jo Ractliffe of a triptych mural she discovered on a building in Viriambundo, Angola (see figure 3.1). Rendering the face of Agostinho Neto, the first president of Angola, flanked on one side by Cuban revolutionary Fidel Castro and on the other by the Soviet leader Leonid Brezhnev, the mural is one of numerous images Ractliffe documented in Angola that both acknowledge socialist internationalist sources of inspiration and supplement them with local material. The mural recognizes the imaginary of revolution-era Cuba and the Soviet Union fired up within the People's Movement for the Liberation of Angola (MPLA) as well as signposts the material support offered by the two countries and their specific leaders during Angola's protracted civil war. Yet, centered on Neto's face, the mural is incontrovertibly grounded in the African experience and the vision for Angola the MPLA held, a topic to which I return in more detail in chapter 4.

*Revolution*, a word striking terror in those associated with the interests of Western colonizers and conjuring the hopefulness of a new beginning for the colonized, structured the violence and disorder that Fanon evoked in his analysis. It is a concept that promised a specific process out of several possible paths to be taken by those involved in the struggle. Whether bringing forth the specter of the unprecedented Haitian Revolution, the first time the slaves managed to successfully overthrow their masters and set up their own state, or that of the radical changes introduced by the Bolshevik Revolution or, even more appropriately, the Cuban Revolution and the Chinese Great Leap Forward, decolonization through revolution conceptually encoded specific historical processes. "Decolonization, we know, is an historical process: In other words, it can only be understood, it can only find its significance and become self coherent inso-

Figure 3.1. Jo Ractliffe, *Mural Depicting Fidel Castro, Agostinho Neto and Leonid Brezhnev, circa 1975, Viriambundo 2009*. © Jo Ractliffe. Courtesy of Stevenson, Cape Town and Johannesburg.

far as we can discern the history-making movement which gives it form and substance."[10]

Fanon pleaded for an understanding of the historical forces leading to a specific process of decolonization. Likewise, the works I discuss in this chapter encode the ideas of revolution and attendant affective temporal structures specific to three moments: hopefulness in French West Africa in the late 1950s, when radical social change seemed almost at hand; the assiduously calculated trajectory of revolution in South Africa in the late 1970s; and the disappointment of failed African socialism—a putative social and economic revolution—in Ghana in the late 1960s. Instead of relying on generalizing chronologies of African or postcolonial literature, in this chapter I focus on smaller-scale perceptions of temporality that necessarily account for a writer's response to global blocs and fault lines while also attesting to the artist's embeddedness in local microstructures like class and generational position.

How is revolution perceived as it unfolds, and how does literature enable us to grasp this temporality? Does the topic lend itself to specific literary forms—a category of texts that could be labeled "novels of revolution"? If so, to what extent do local and global events combine to shape the form and themes of such texts? African novels depicting revolutionary situations record rapidly shifting perceptions of temporality, as those engaged in the struggle renew their commitment to the future, make sense of the present, and reckon with the past. I am interested in the ways in which literary texts like Ousmane Sembène's *Les bouts des bois de Dieu* (*God's Bits of Wood*, 1960) and Mongane Wally Serote's

*To Every Birth Its Blood* (1981) record this experience of temporality—the characters' perceptions of the present moment and the intuition of the advent of a larger structure that is becoming historical. I am equally intrigued by the change of tempo during what we could call the morning after independence, the loss of hopefulness that accompanies the shattered chances of revolutionary change, reflected with poignancy in Ayi Kwei Armah's *The Beautyful Ones Are Not Yet Born* (1968).[11] To do that, I introduce the concept of affective temporal structures.

Literary narratives are privileged sites where cultural critics can identify emergent ideas. Fascinated with the processual aspect of concept formation—the minute changes in dominant and submerged ideas that are legible only diachronically—Raymond Williams described these barely perceptible conceptual nuclei as "structures of feeling." He started from the observation that individuals do not experience the world in terms of fully articulated formulations of currents or ideologies but instead are caught in the ever-shifting and incompletely articulated experience of the present. Unlike other Marxist theorists concerned with a macroscopic view of society, Williams finessed the relation between art and society by attending to microscopic changes: "The idea of a structure of feeling can be specifically related to the evidence of forms and conventions—semantic figures—which, in art and literature, are often among the very first indications that such a new structure is forming."[12]

Instead of taking up Williams's term, I borrow some conceptual tools from the current affective turn in the humanities and the social sciences.[13] Recent developments in the theory of affects have highlighted their relevance for thinking not only about individuals but also about social bodies, by illuminating causal interrelations at work.[14] For instance, Lauren Berlant is interested in how aesthetically mediated affective responses exemplify a shared historical sense.[15] My argument develops from this social dimension of affect, yet it preserves the small-scale scope of analysis, attending to groups of people united in their perception of temporality by their geographical, sociopolitical, or cultural situatedness.

Affective temporal structures are ways of perceiving the present moment and establishing relations (whether of continuity or rupture) between the present, on the one hand, and the past and the future, on the other. Affective temporal structures are social, allowing individuals to see themselves in the community, to be affected by and to affect others. While informed by people's geopolitical location, as well as access to financial and cultural capital, they circumvent the need to make generalizations about the sense of historicity shared by a social class, nation, gender group, or generation. As affects are not yet articulated, they offer a way of addressing the transient moment and also ways of thinking about the world that are not yet conceptually fixed.[16] They allow us to conceive of emergent (or waning) ways of apprehending temporality without having to subsume artists to established ideological positions, accepting that even when politically involved, artists do not reflect the textbook version of ideas espoused by larger political or cultural entities.

Affective temporal structures generate narratives that we overlay on the concatenation of events; they make us see history as directional, or cyclical, or hopelessly fragmented. These structures refer to the desires, aspirations, or disillusionment that we invest in projections of the future.[17] To simplify: we may imagine a positive unfolding of the future, a good conclusion to our collective or personal life narratives, or we may see the future frustrating our aspirations to meaningfulness, to truthfulness to ourselves and to our ideals, or as a collapse of avenues of progress into a nightmarish repetitive cycle.

For instance, David Scott identifies a watershed shift in perceptions of temporality within his own generation of Caribbean intellectuals: this change was marked by the success of the Grenada Revolution in 1979 and then its defeat in 1983. It was not only the perception of the possible political futures for this small Caribbean nation that changed. While the revolution itself had been "a vindication and culmination of a certain organization of temporal expectation and political longing," its defeat led to a "palpable sense of dissolution of the political temporality of former futures."[18] In other words, the sense of defeat that accompanied the U.S. intervention in Grenada marked the way in which at least an entire generation of Caribbean leftist intellectuals came to see the future as depleted of any emancipatory hopefulness. Scott emphasizes the generational import of this event, in the same way in which intellectuals in Africa who witnessed the beginning of decolonization with Ghana's independence in 1957, or those who turned and returned compulsively to the pages of Fanon's *The Wretched of the Earth* in search of a blueprint to produce revolutionary futures, had a shared sense of what the temporal arc of past-present-future might produce. Reading the same texts and sharing similar sociopolitical circumstances is bound to engender similar, although not necessarily identical, affective temporal structures. As both archive and germinating fund for such perceptions of temporality, fiction presents us with a range of affective temporal structures that reflect the imaginative possibilities of this time frame.

### Developing a West African Strike Imaginary

Ousmane Sembène's most celebrated novel, *God's Bits of Wood* (1960), revives the memory of an important event in the history of anticolonial resistance in French West Africa.[19] The railroad workers' strike of 1947–1948 allows the writer to explore the labor union and worker communities in three cities—Bamako, Thiès, and Dakar—illuminating the systemic character of capitalist oppression under colonialism. Demanding a pay increase, family allowances, and a pension plan, the striking workers contend with indecision within their midst, fearmongering from the older generation, and the brutal intervention of the colonial administration. While *God's Bits of Wood* has deservedly acquired a hallowed place among the classics of postcolonial literature, in the following pages I read it as a prefiguration of ideas of anticolonial revolution. In other words, I argue that Sembène envisaged the railroad workers' strike as the germinating seed of larger social action that would simultaneously overturn the colonial regime and the capitalist system. The novel offers insight about available ideas of revolution in the late 1950s in French West Africa and the ideological pressure that the established Cold War camps exercised on the social and political avenues for change available to anticolonial intellectuals.

The finely tuned yet shifting balance between individual characters and crowd scenes allows Sembène to simultaneously advance a practice of novelistic form and a theory of revolution. While presenting us with memorable characters among the strikers and their families—especially the little girl Ad'jibid'ji, who lends her name to the first chapter; Tiémoko and Maïmouna in Bamako; Ramatoulaye and Daouda-Beaugosse in Dakar; and Penda in Thiès—the novel deploys an illuminating plot device. The most active strike leader, Bakayoko, is physically absent for most of the novel yet indirectly present in the aspirations and stories fellow characters weave around him. This device allows Sembène to engage with classic Marxist-Leninist literature on labor organization and the role of party leadership in revolutionary contexts, highlighting the extent to which such leadership is necessary to achieve success. If the first part of the novel places the spotlight on memorable characters, the communal energy of the strike translates into collective scenes and group chapter titles: "The March of the Women," "The Camp," and "The Meeting" showcase the power of organized protest. Likewise, the decisive role that female characters play inscribes Sembène among the supporters of African feminism. The strike becomes consequential only when the women of Thiès march to Dakar to protest the inhuman conditions they have to contend with, as colonial authorities weaponized a drought into an instrument of punishment and submission. Demonstrating women's importance in the strike—indeed, we may aver with F. Case that female characters are the true revolutionary engine of the novel, and Penda, not Bakayoko, the text's actual protagonist—Sembène also tweaks and adjusts abstract theories about revolution.[20]

The focus on revolutionary action highlights the importance of affective temporal structures—those within which Sembène himself was embedded as well as those he attributed to his characters. Published around the time of Senegal's independence in 1960, the novel looks back to another crucial moment in the history of French West Africa's resistance to colonialism, as the Dakar-Niger railway workers commenced strike actions in 1947. As the railway connected several regions of French West Africa and two future independent countries, Senegal and Mali, the strike became a focal point of both anticolonial and oppressive imperialist policies. The temporal distance between the narrative time and the political context at the time of publication allowed Sembène to portray both the gradual development of the characters' revolutionary consciousness and the retrospective hallowing of the strike, turning it into a seed for the later clamor for decolonization.[21] This distance permitted Sembène to retrospectively fit the strike into a teleological arc from anticolonial resistance to independence, infusing the workers' action with the messianic promise of a comprehensive movement that would sweep the French colonies.

While numerous critics have highlighted the revolutionary character of Sembène's works, addressing his commitment to representing the conditions of the working class and the political and economic impotence of a comprador bourgeoisie beholden to Western imperial powers, there has been relatively little scholarly interest in tracing the genealogy of the ideas of revolution in his works.[22] Samba Gadjigo's impressive biographical work, *Ousmane Sembène: The Making of a Militant Artist*, is one of the few monographs invested in identifying Sembène's interlocutors and acknowledging the formative books that shaped his worldview. Gadjigo pinpoints the shift from the awakening anticolonial sentiment Sembène experienced in Dakar in the immediate aftermath of World War II to his ever-deepening political consciousness in Marseille (1946–1960), where he joined the powerful General Confederation of Labor (CGT), the French Communist Party, and the Movement against Racism and for Friendship between Peoples.[23] The conditions of the black dockers amid whom he worked in Marseille clarified for him the interpenetration of two forms of exploitation: "In addition to my work as a CGT union leader, I was also the secretary-general of the Black workers in France. This enabled me to gain insight into both aspects, race- and class-based, of the situation."²⁴ Yet, while at the time Sembène considered that a separate labor movement for workers of color would be counterproductive, as all fellow dockers, irrespective of their skin color, were oppressed by the same system, and while by 1960 he continued to see the interconnection of racial and class-based oppression, in *God's Bits of Wood* he stressed the hierarchies established within the colony between white and black workers, with the former benefiting from better compensation and labor conditions as well as opportunities for promotion to skilled-labor positions.

Marxist readings, to which Sembène was introduced in Marseille, shaped his worldview and works from early on. In an interview he confirmed, "In *God's Bits of Wood*, I wanted to show that African unity cannot be envisioned outside of a Marxist purview."²⁵ As a representation of a strike that Sembène saw as prefiguring a generalized revolution against old and new forms of imperialism, the novel can be treated as an ideal debate site between two long-held socialist perspectives: the proponents of vanguardism and the supporters of spontaneity. The debate's long history can be traced back to the beginning of the twentieth century, when Vladimir Lenin and Rosa Luxemburg penned authoritative works supporting the two distinctive approaches. On the one hand, Luxemburg's *The Mass Strike* (1906) was a plea for the cooperation of organized and unorganized workers, arguing that "mass strikes and political mass struggles cannot . . . be carried through in Germany by the organised workers alone, nor can they be appraised by regular 'direction' from the central committee of a party."²⁶ On the other hand, in the impactful pamphlet *What Is to Be Done?* (1902), Lenin rejected the haphazard effects of spontaneous action. His argument for the necessity of organizing the workers, otherwise an easy prey to counterrevolutionary bourgeois ideology, and his support for the party's role as the vanguard of the social struggle became pillars of the Marxist-Leninist approach that Sembène imbibed during his time in Marseille. This view highlighted the importance of socialist ideology and the role of the party in conscientizing the workers, who might naturally gravitate toward socialism yet, under the spell of bourgeois ideology, could sabotage their own struggle.

In the novel the positive elements of both vanguardism and spontaneity are underscored in the counterpointing of strike organizing, with union officers in the main cities pondering the best approach, and the women starting at lightning speed their own supporting protest and march to Dakar. The relation between workers and strike leaders, who form a vanguard of the movement in *God's Bits of Wood*, highlights the importance of coordinated action, education of participants, and awareness of strategies to resist colonial sabotage techniques. Sembène unpacks the role of the union and activist leaders in Bakayoko's allegory of his job as a train engine driver:

> I wish I could make you understand something, too. When I am in the cabin of my engine, I take on a sense of absolute identity with everything that is in the train, no matter whether it is passengers or just freight. I experience everything that happens along its whole length. In the stations I observe the people, but once the engine is on its way, I forget everything else. My role then is nothing except to guide that machine to the spot where it is supposed to go. I don't even know any longer whether it is my heart that is beating to the rhythm of the engine, or the engine to the rhythm of my heart. And for me, that is the way it has to be with this strike—we must all take on a sense of identity with it.[27]

The sense of commitment and steadfast determination is one of the qualities the author underscores as a crucial feature of union leaders—the contextual equivalent of the party leadership in Lenin's text. Yet even more important seems to be the comprehensive view: readers understand Bakayoko's ability to "experience everything that happens along [the train's] whole length" to be the spatial equivalent of a temporal bird's-eye view, the aptitude to see the teleological arc of history. Yet embedded in the novel there is also an awareness of how a social group in which the interests of workers are vested, such as union leaders of other industries in Dakar, may turn into enemies of their own class. With Gaye, the trade unionist who does the bidding of a comprador class and their colonial masters, Sembène evokes not only Karl Marx's disparagement of a self-sabotaging middle class but also, closer to home, Fanon's pronouncement that wage laborers in African cities were the equivalent of the continental bourgeoisie.[28]

The relationship between individuality and collectivity is well mapped out in the novel, placing the text in conversation not only with the European classics of Marxism-Leninism but also, whether deliberately or implicitly, with Sembène's fellow revolutionary intellectuals—Fanon, Aimé Césaire, Amílcar Cabral, Ngũgĩ wa Thiong'o, and others.[29] While Sembène encountered some like-minded writers and activists during his time in France and came across the others' works in journals such as *Présence Africaine*, most of the ideas about revolution and social transformations in Africa illuminate shared affective temporal structures, a topic to which I return later in this chapter.[30] The titles of the chapters, divided into sections pertaining to the three main cities along the railway (Bamako, Thiès, and Dakar), at first vacillate between collectivities and individual characters, but after the women's march departs Thiès for

Dakar, the headings refer to collectivities or locations where communal action is undertaken. Within these collectivities, workers and women who become grassroots organizers continue to stand out as mobilizing figures. From N'Deye Touti, gently mocked by other women in her family for her Eurocentric aspirations, to the well-read Bakayoko, who indigenizes knowledge from Western cultures, to the admirable elders Fa Keïta and Ramatoulaye, who are aware of West African history and modes of resistance, Sembène presents a cast of characters that could serve as interlocutors to Fanon's portraits of African intellectuals. As with Fanon, the process of (re)discovery of the richness of local culture, ethics, and militant traditions is essential for Sembène's characters.[31] And like Fanon, Sembène nuances European theories of revolution, enriching them with the layered perspective from West Africa.

As Barbara Harlow pointed out, for most leaders of resistance movements, like Cabral, the anticolonial struggle was primarily supposed to bring about political and economic liberation; it was also supposed to transform modes of interaction and social structures into more democratic and inclusive ones.[32] It is the recognition that both local and European social structures were mired in sexism that sets apart some revolutionary intellectuals like Sembène or Fanon. The revolutionary from Martinique expressed hope that the strenuous conditions of the anticolonial struggle would dispel lingering Algerian patriarchal mentalities, changing gender roles: "Involved in the struggle, the husband or the father learns to look upon the relations between sexes in a new light. The militant man discovers the militant woman, and jointly they create new dimensions for Algerian society."[33] While the hoped-for transformation was hardly as comprehensive as Fanon had hoped, his groundbreaking essay "Algeria Unveiled" opened new scholarly perspectives by joining gender, nationalism, and the revolutionary process in a comprehensive analysis. Such work stands out even more in a cultural landscape where gender, as an analytical category, was largely illegible.[34] As Susan Andrade points out, in the 1960s even the scholarly environment was "inhospitable to feminism," which was perceived as a European import.[35]

A staunch belief in the transformative function of women's roles in the anticolonial struggle shines through in Sembène's novel, showing how the Senegalese intellectual both engaged with and outstripped many of his contemporaries' ideas of revolution.[36] As the female characters are not engaged in wage-earning labor, they are initially perceived as less than their male counterparts. When drought and poverty make cooking and housekeeping impossible, the women's decision to abandon entrenched daily patterns and find food by any means alters their image in their husbands' and fathers' eyes: "And the men began to understand that if the times were bringing forth a new breed of men, they were also bringing forth a new breed of women."[37] In language strikingly similar to that of Fanon, Sembène praises the transformative role of the strike and, by extension, the anticolonial struggle. As the women's march reaches Dakar, the male characters finally realize that they have to help women with obtaining water and food, a task previously perceived as demeaning. The transformation of their mentality is couched in leftist terms, as the overcoming of feudal attitudes, making room for new social relations and forms of consciousness: "Alioune had succeeded in persuading a considerable number of the men that their old feudal customs had no place in a situation like that," and instead men had to forage for water, wood for cooking fires, and food.[38] This co-construction of the new community is rendered in narrative terms reminiscent of both Marxist-Leninist literature and traditional Wolof tales, such as the legend of Goumba N'Diaye, the woman who measured her strength against that of men. It is on this note of unity between men and women that the novel ends, with the legend repurposed to render the social struggle against colonialism, a struggle that should be determined yet "without hatred."[39]

Sembène has a masterful sense of the affective temporal structures preceding the breakthrough of irreversible action. Throughout the novel descriptions of nature often function as an index of the collective character's mood, anticipating tensions, rebelliousness, and nearly exploding anger or prefiguring change.[40] The text opens with the image of the setting sun "striking brutally through the cloud curtain," "lash[ing]" at the governor's residence, with the verbs evoking violence and creating an impression that "all caught fire" in Bamako.[41] The temporality of the strike is punctuated by deliberation and decision-making, as well as plenty of moments charged with the tension of waiting for action to shape up or to diffuse. "And then the waiting began," the narrator observes, taking stock of the "long wait, broken into minutes, into seconds. The words that had been spoken were spoken again, and all the words that had been heard were pondered and studied again. Little by little, anxiety came, and a fear that settled heavily in their stomachs."[42] Comparisons with the failed strike of 1938, previous attempts at organizing, and their attendant problems plague the workers' memories. As long as decisive action is postponed, the workers, their families, and the entire community are trapped in the cycle of suffering and a life rhythm dictated by colonial authorities. Temporal markers that signal people's subservience to the capitalist system heighten this sense of entrapment in repetitive patterns: "When the siren screamed again, a shudder went through the crowd. . . . For as long as they could remember, that sound had meant obedience. As children they had seen their fathers, and even their grandfathers, begin to run when they heard it call."⁴³ The interference of labor hours in their private lives signals their regimentation in colonial structures.

When action does take place, it galvanizes everything: the characters' actions, their speech, and even the syntax and organization of the text. Take, for instance, the contrast between the long paragraphs marking the indeterminate mood in Thiès before the strike is declared and the one-sentence paragraph that marks the beginning of the confrontation: "That was when the soldiers charged."⁴⁴ The affective temporal structures are future-oriented and optimistic. Omafume F. Onoge observes that socialist realist literature, a rubric under which he registers Sembène's works, is optimistic because it believes in the ability of the masses to bring about revolution and transform the country's economic and political structures.⁴⁵ Indeed, the tomorrows are predicated on the idea of a generalized revolution that comprehends all oppressed people. The elder Fa Keïta observes, "Ibrahim Bakayoko said to me, not long ago: 'When we have succeeded in stirring up the people of this country, and making them one, we will go on and do the same thing between ourselves and the people on the other side of the ocean.' How all this will come about I do not know, but we can see it happening already, before our eyes."⁴⁶ This optimistic Pan-African vision has more to do with the moment when the novel was written and published (at the end of the 1950s) than with the hesitating beginnings of the anticolonial struggle in the late 1940s. The generous emphasis on a revolutionary movement that will transform for the better the lives of all oppressed peoples is another characteristic of the affective temporal structures within which *God's Bits of Wood* was born, a moment early in the Cold War when the political options for "the wretched of the earth" were not limited by the hardening of ideological fault lines.

In *God's Bits of Wood*, N'Deye Touti's depiction of Bakayoko as a man who conceives of connections between workers' movements around the world showcases both the extent and the limitations of this network in the years immediately following the end of World War II: "He always brought the discussion around to the problems of the workers. But he talked about all sorts of things—unemployment, the educational system, the war in Indochina; he talked about France and Spain, and even about countries as far away as America and Russia."⁴⁷ The global imaginary that connects peoples who suffer or struggle against oppression was rather sparse in 1947. The focus stayed on colonial ties with France and political developments in Europe, especially the civil war in Spain, which captured the imagination of leftists elsewhere. The resistance against French colonialism in Indochina had just started to place decolonization projects on the map. Indicative of the early stage of the Cold War the novel represents, the United States (America) and the Soviet Union (Russia) are mapped at the distant horizons of the revolutionary imagination, faraway locales that were only beginning to figure as political heavyweights.

In the late 1940s, when the West African rail workers' strike took place, the Soviet Union was not yet very visible in the anticolonial African and diasporic imaginary. Although several decades had passed from the Revolution of 1917, the positive image initially projected by the USSR for people of color around the world had been tarnished by Joseph Stalin's excesses, displays of paternalism, or even outright racism. The Trinidadian George Padmore, who lived in the USSR in the early 1930s, where he headed the Negro Bureau of the Communist International of Trade Unions and founded and edited the journal *Negro Worker*, was put off by Soviet vacillation in their support for anticolonial revolutions.[48] Although several West African intellectuals had traveled to the USSR before, it was only after 1956—when the Soviet Union took a stance against the Franco-British operation of the Suez Canal and their ill-fated intervention in Egypt—that Senegalese activists, trade unionists, and intellectuals began to see it as a potential source of support for the anticolonial movement.[49] Likewise, Soviet support for young African intellectuals and the project of forming cadres from the continent debuted only in 1958–1959, and its first concrete implementation was the scholarships offered for 179 African students to study at the newly inaugurated Peoples' Friendship University in 1960.[50]

Sembène is one of the artists with a clear, albeit little-explored, connection to the USSR. Most of this history of collaboration or artistic solidarity postdates the publication of *God's Bits of Wood*, yet in 1958 he attended the first conference of the Afro-Asian Writers Association in Tashkent. Later, Sembène was trained in filmmaking at the Gorky Studios in Moscow, under the direction of Mark Donskoy.[51] Sembène and Donskoy shared numerous interests, including a love for the novels of Maxim Gorky and a commitment to produce art that addressed significant social problems. "I profoundly believe that each [film] must treat an important issue, must resolve it in some fashion or at least suggest a solution. That's how Eisenstein and Dovzhenko made their pictures, pictures I studied in the Soviet Union," he declared.[52] This shared vision of art made Sembène a frequent guest of film festivals and writers' conferences in the USSR; his novels were translated into Russian, part of an approved canon of African writers available for the Soviet readership.[53]

Given this history of artistic kinship, it may surprise readers to see Sembène's reticent response to interviewers' requests to speak about his experiences as a student in filmmaking in the USSR: "I don't talk about my Russian experiences in America, just as I didn't talk of my American experiences in Russia. Every country has its methods and every system of education tries to perpetuate what it represents. Their teaching is socialist and communist just as teaching in America is linked to the establishment. You can take it or leave it. And since I was ignorant, I was forced to take what was given to me, and afterwards I used it as I thought I should."[54] On the one hand, the evenhanded reticence registered in the interview speaks indirectly about the divided Cold War landscape, as the Senegalese artist was aware that Western audiences would misinterpret any praise for the Soviet Union (or the other way round) as ideological subservience. It alerts us to forms of discourse that were seen as not quite permissible even for politically committed writers and filmmakers.[55] On the other hand, it shows that Sembène maintains a circumspect distance between his own development of the material assimilated at the Gorky Studios in Moscow and what he "was forced to take" by the education system in the USSR. In the same way in which he drew on classics of Marxism-Leninism and was inspired by the affective temporal structures characteristic of the late 1950s to draw up his own literary and political theory, resulting in a celebrated novel of revolution, Sembène skillfully navigated the divided Cold War landscape.

Raymond Williams spoke of the experience of a mode of perception that seems private yet later becomes codified into "institutions and formations."[56] Sembène's views on the revolutionary energy of a strike, which could galvanize the entire population into a rejection not only of capitalist structures but of the colonial ones as well, enmeshed as they were with each other, were not those that prevailed in Senegal. Sembène was later withering in his critique of Léopold Sédar Senghor and the neocolonial structures over which the latter presided. In the following decades, African writers added to a rich canon of novels of revolution, each of them nuancing the genre according to specific historical conditions and affective temporal structures.

## From Africanist to Marxist-Leninist Revolutionary Models

Mongane Wally Serote's 1981 novel *To Every Birth Its Blood* crystallizes a shift in perceptions of temporality, as it attempts to make sense of then-contemporary events in South Africa and the rest of the world. Begun at a moment when South African society was on the verge of going up in flames during the 1976 Soweto Uprising, the novel attests to a change in perceptions of temporality that Serote likely underwent at that time.[57] In dialogue with—yet not beholden to—mainstream ideas about social change, this novel reflects on the liberation struggle in southern Africa in the late 1970s and imagines its future trajectory into the 1980s. It prefigures the arduous road ahead in the struggle against apartheid. Serote's focus on process identifies his fiction as a privileged site for observing the emergence of new conceptual paradigms that envision social transformation.

With its emphasis on revolution, the novel charts a genealogy of the ideas of liberation in southern Africa—a lineage that intersects with various Cold War–era conceptions of social transformation. It ends with the blood-suffused image of a birthing mother to whom revolutionary Jully serves as midwife. It is a metaphor for the arduous process of decolonization that, despite its painful beginnings, announces the hopefulness of a new life. Serote's understanding of the temporality of revolution, viewed against the background of the Cold War, enables us to reassess the impact of this conflict on the cultural landscape in southern Africa. At first glance, the novel might display only superficial connections with the Cold War; however, its affective temporal structures, which I will discuss in more detail, connect it to this global conflict.

*To Every Birth Its Blood* has stimulated an energetic debate regarding its unusual form, more so, perhaps, than other literary texts from the same period. The novel has a bipartite structure that was deemed either disjointed, and therefore stylistically lacking, or singularly apposite to depict the mass struggle in the wake of the 1976 Soweto Uprising.[58] The first part of the novel presents daily oppression under apartheid through the lens of journalist Tsi Molope's first-person narrative of personal dilemmas; the latter half abandons the focus on the protagonist and democratically distributes the third-person narrative perspective among a multitude of focalizers. Onalena, John, Dikeledi, Tuki, Oupa, Themba, and eventually Tsi, who continues to narrate in the first person, convey the accelerating energies of revolution. Moving beyond rage and a feeling of helplessness after the 1976 Soweto Uprising was crushed, the characters discuss the violent character of the apartheid state, witness political trials, and hear about torture in detention; they are recruited into the antiapartheid movement and engage in sabotage actions, or they are driven to exile in neighboring countries from where they mount the final attack against the racist state. Initially at various stages of political consciousness and engagement with the struggle, this constellation of characters gradually comes to embrace a sense of imminent change and revolution.[59]

Although narrated in the past tense, Serote's novel conveys an acute sense of immediacy. Its combination of formal elements (clipped dialogue, increasingly shorter narrative vignettes, and the frequency of the present-tense adverb *now*, belying the past-tense narration) and thematic aspects (the characters' increasingly clearer political consciousness, the heightened tempo of strikes against the apartheid regime that the Movement mounts) gives the impression of unfolding events that might take unpredictable directions. At the same time, the antiapartheid struggle is presented as having continuity with the anticolonial battles of the past, in an ever-unfolding present of resistance: "The Movement is old. It is as old as the grave of the first San or Khoikhoi who was killed by a bullet that came from a ship which had anchored at Cape Town to establish a stop station. The Movement is as young as the idea of throwing stones, of hurling one's life at the armed men who believe in God and shoot with guns."[60]

The shift between overall past-tense narration and a present tense that paradoxically reflects a sense of historicity is only one of the startling ways in which Serote handles perceptions of temporality. Written during and in the aftermath of the Soweto Uprising, the novel moved with the events and ended up trying to anticipate the course of the struggle in the 1980s.[61] As Michael Green has pointed out, along with Nadine Gordimer's *July's People* (1981) and Christopher Hope's *Kruger's Alp* (1984), the novel is an example of the "future histories" penned in the 1980s. They are "works that seek to comment upon the past and present by projecting the implications of the past and the present forward in time."[62] Serote's novel charts the present moment as it accrues significance while the protagonists consider possible future outcomes.

There is an abrupt change in the affective temporal structures displayed by *To Every Birth Its Blood*, a shift that coincides with the transition from the first to the second part of the novel. More minute changes are also discernible in the second part. As Tsi Molope struggles to figure out the meaning of his life and his limited ability to connect to other people, hampered by apartheid-era racism, a spiraling, inward-looking, and pessimistic temporal structure is set in place. It is displaced in the second part, where the affective temporal structure becomes teleological and future-oriented, making the text a novel of revolution, committed to the world that is to be born. The ending of the novel takes place in an imaginary future in the 1980s, when a second student uprising propels the country into revolution. The Border War has spread from Angola to Botswana, where South African exiles and the local population alike are bombed by South African Defence Force planes and attacked by commando troops; yet Tsi, the narrator from part 1, is confident that this southern African expression of the Cold War will end with the victory of the antiapartheid movement. This shift in affective temporal structures from a pessimistic to an optimistic outlook appears to contradict established views about the periodization of contemporary African history. While macrolevel approaches cannot explain this transformation, a focus on understanding the present as process, as revealed through the concept of affective temporal structures, can give us an insight into these differences.

Large-scale attempts at periodization fail to explain the upsurge in optimistic perceptions of temporality that took place in South Africa in the 1980s. Cultural critics have made pronouncements about changes in the perception of temporality during the latter half of the twentieth century, changes driven by global events such as the tide of decolonization of the 1950s and early 1960s, or the hardening of Cold War ideological lines behind a rhetoric of militarization and the nuclear arms race, or the rise of an increasingly triumphalist neoliberal capitalist discourse in the 1980s. In the landmark article "Periodizing the American Century: Modernism, Postmodernism, and Postcolonialism in the Cold War Context," Ann Douglas divides the Cold War into two periods—an optimistic stage that lasted until the beginning of the 1960s and the collapse of optimism from the mid-1960s onward, when innocence and authenticity were no longer possible after neocolonial politics and interventionism had ruined the hopefulness of newly independent nations.[63] If we follow Douglas's argument, we expect that the affective temporal structures of the second half of the Cold War would correspond to the skepticism and pessimism that characterize numerous African novels from the late 1960s onward, such as Ayi Kwei Armah's *The Beautyful Ones Are Not Yet Born* (1968) and Ousmane Sembène's *Xala* (1973), or South African texts like Christopher Hope's *Kruger's Alp* (1984) and J. M. Coetzee's *Waiting for the Barbarians* (1980).

However, as mentioned earlier, David Scott places the tidal change at the beginning of the 1980s, when the revolution in Grenada was defeated and intellectuals on the left had to reassess their perception of past, present, and future: the years ahead no longer holding the possibility of socialist victory, the postcolonial dreams smashed under new forms of imperialism. While both Douglas and Scott agree that at some point during the second half of the twentieth century the effervescence of the post–World War II independence movements and people's former belief in the possibility of attaining social justice died out, they do not necessarily agree when this turn took place. If we add to the mix—as I did at the beginning of this chapter—the South African intellectuals' nostalgia for the 1980s as a period of hopefulness, political clarity, and purposefulness, the picture becomes even more confusing.

The decolonization struggles in southern Africa were still in full swing during the second half of the Cold War, as Angola and Mozambique gained their independence in 1975 yet continued to battle internal and external enemies; Zimbabwe shrugged off white rule in 1980, Namibia in 1990, and South Africa only in 1994. Thus, a number of southern African novels bring an important contribution to the postcolonial literary archive by displaying cautiously optimistic affective temporal structures, such as those underlying Serote's novel

*To Every Birth Its Blood*. This optimistic affective temporal structure, which we see in other works of fiction (for instance, the promise of change at the end of Alex La Guma's *In the Fog of the Season's End* and *Time of the Butcherbird* or Nadine Gordimer's *A Sport of Nature*), is primarily due to the fact that South Africa, unlike other former colonies, had not experienced either the elation of independence or the disappointment of the "morning after" that we see in numerous postcolonial novels, such as Armah's *The Beautyful Ones Are Not Yet Born*. Therefore, numerous 1970s and 1980s South African texts penned by writers associated with the antiapartheid struggle upheld the optimistic affective temporal structures that had characterized 1950s and 1960s decolonization literature elsewhere on the continent.[64]

The concept of affective temporal structures allows us to record the minute changes in the perception of the present as experienced by characters, reflecting shifts in levels of political consciousness and commitment, and to relate them to literary strategies. This focus on emerging structures illustrates Serote's own changing position, as he gradually abandoned the Black Consciousness (BC) perspective and embraced a view of revolution in consonance with that of the African National Congress (ANC)–South African Communist Party (SACP) alliance. The novel fictionalizes some of Serote's formative experiences. For instance, Tuki and Dikeledi are part of a township theater group that stages plays reflective of the lived experience in Alexandra. Similarly, Serote and artist Thami Mnyele cofounded the Mihloti Black Theatre in Alexandra in 1971.[65] Together the artists read and discussed works by Frantz Fanon, Amílcar Cabral, Agostinho Neto, Malcolm X, and Marcus Garvey.[66] Later Serote expressed his belief in the value of togetherness and community action, an idea that finds an echo in the shift from individualistic self-absorption in the first part of the novel to the multiple yet conjoined action of characters in the second part of the novel: "Changes take place when people are informed, when people are conscious, when people identify common goals and common objectives, and in certain circumstances are prepared to make sacrifices for that."[67] This belief in collective action is informed by and has ramifications for the affective temporal structures displayed; it also highlights the genealogy of political concepts that informed Serote's vision of revolution.

Serote has been described as a revolutionary writer who, during the apartheid era, was ready to use both words and weapons to overturn the regime.[68] But what does revolution mean in his literary works? Who is to participate, and how does it unfold? Does political action suffice, or is blood to be shed? How long is revolution supposed to last? His novel offers a snapshot of the mélange of emergent, crystallized, and vanishing political ideas, with their attendant affective temporal structures, during the late 1970s and early 1980s. I explore the genealogy of Serote's idea of social transformation in South Africa to tease out the cultural texts and programs reflected in his writing and, simultaneously, his contribution to shaping the conceptual components and aesthetics of revolution in South Africa. The intellectual history of the idea of revolution as reflected in South African fiction not only displays its conceptual makeup but also highlights the cultural forces and the global political landscapes that have modified or supplanted this idea. To revisit the concept of revolution is to find new ways of thinking about the period and of historicizing the scholarship that engaged with or circumvented it.

Consistent with Serote's idea of literature as a form of social commitment—he encouraged readers to think of authors as "cultural workers"—writing about revolution also entailed writing the revolution into being in South Africa.[69] In a roundtable with Ngũgĩ wa Thiong'o in 1988, Serote was asked whether his political involvement in the liberation struggle or his interest in writing came first. His response followed a line oftentimes expressed by ANC-SACP activists in the 1980s, which gave culture an instrumental role, turning it into a "weapon of the struggle": "Participation in the struggle became an inspiration. Because one wanted to express the condition of one's people, one also had to further understand what it is that made us become an oppressed and exploited people, what it was that was going to liberate us."[70] This view of the function of the writer is the distillation of his political journey, from an adept of BC philosophy to an ANC cadre, as he became a "poet of revolution."[71] This progression, which unfolds against the background of the Cold War, is also inscribed in the novel's focus on the present and the text's shifting affective temporal structures. The novel is able to record these minute changes otherwise difficult to chart in history studies because, as Raymond Williams pointed out, the "practical consciousness" recorded in literature and the arts "is almost always different from official consciousness."[72]

Writing about the meaning of revolution and social transformation in Africa in the late 1970s and early 1980s happened in a variety of venues, from strategy and policy-making documents issued by the political entities involved in liberation struggles to essays and analyses penned by those close to decision-making structures, and from journalism and academic writing to fiction. When Tuki, one of the main characters in Serote's *To Every Birth Its Blood*, proclaims, "South Africa is going to be a socialist country, this is going to come about through the will, knowledge and determination of the people," his statement obliquely speaks to a history of conceptual road maps for surpassing apartheid that had variously clashed or coexisted.⁷³ As mentioned earlier, during the first wave of decolonization in the late 1950s, it was not clear what specific forms of social organization would emerge in Africa and whether they would be established by means of revolution or negotiated transition.⁷⁴ As the euphoria of new beginnings started to dissipate and the reality of neocolonialism and a sharply polarized Cold War climate set in, fewer real options remained for southern African countries seeking independence in the 1970s and the 1980s. Until the Pretoria government became interested in negotiating with the ANC in the late 1980s, thereby creating a glimmer of hope for a peaceful transition to a democratic form of organization, the ANC-SACP alliance had envisioned revolution and armed struggle as the only available roads for social transformation in South Africa.⁷⁵ This process of conceiving trajectories for social transformation came to a head with the Soweto Uprising of 1976.

Serote is one of the few South African novelists who rendered "the Power days," the moment of the antiapartheid struggle spearheaded by the BC movement that culminated in the Soweto Uprising.⁷⁶ His novel records the shift in public consciousness from a focus on BC philosophy to a growing awareness of "the Movement" (Serote's fictional representation of the ANC-SACP alliance) as the leader of the struggle. The militancy and the immediacy of the response (black pride, the resumption of African names, street battles, and the refusal to surrender the townships to state control) change into a longer-term perspective (initiation into the Movement, study groups to conscientize freedom fighters, underground operations, and the continuation of the struggle in exile). As an ANC member who came to political consciousness under the influence of BC yet who received military training in Botswana, Angola, and the USSR as an Umkhonto we Sizwe (MK) member, Serote is exceptionally positioned to understand the elements of ideological continuity and disjuncture within the antiapartheid struggle during the late 1970s and the early 1980s.⁷⁷

The revolutionary method and the time frame within which apartheid could be abolished had preoccupied the ANC leadership from the early 1960s, when Nelson Mandela rejected the efficacy of nonviolent protest and spearheaded the formation of the armed branch of the party, MK. In the aftermath of the 1963–1964 Rivonia trial, the ANC-SACP alliance was seriously debilitated in its power to strike back against the apartheid state, as a result of the imprisonment or escape into exile of the MK high command. The model of revolution or political change that had worked in other African colonies was impracticable in South Africa, where the white minority was entrenched in its controlling position over the political, economic, and legal apparatuses. After the ANC and the

SACP regrouped in exile, in the wake of the 1969 Morogoro conference, they set in place a new strategy for conducting the armed struggle. However, the resilience of the Portuguese empire and the obstructing presence of white minority rule in Rhodesia and South-West Africa prevented guerrillas from infiltrating and launching operations within South Africa.[78] The early 1970s were marked by the clash between the leaders' long-term approach and the rank-and-file members' impatience, as the latter desired to be sent home immediately after receiving military training abroad in order to start a revolutionary war.[79] It was only after 1975, when Angola and Mozambique became independent, and 1980, when Zimbabwe did, that the idea of revolutionary warfare could actually be concretized.

This politically favorable situation was ideologically strengthened by the impact of BC, in turn boosted by dialogue with the Fanonist school of thought as well as the Black Power and civil rights movements in the United States. Serote's oeuvre reflects the growth of his revolutionary consciousness under the influence of Steve Biko and the BC movement, especially in his first two volumes of poetry, *Yakhal'inkomo* (1972) and *Tsetlo* (1974).[80] Fanon's idea of violence as a cathartic reappropriation of the activist's abused self and as a means of recapturing the pride of being black entered the South African discursive field with the BC movement.

Fanon had influenced Serote's thinking as a young writer, as evidenced by his invocation of the Martinican activist and philosopher as part of a line of secular, revolutionary saints:

I've been a looked after
black seed; by black saints and prophets
by Sobukwe Mandela Sisulu
Fanon Malcolm X George Jackson.[81]

In *To Every Birth Its Blood*, Dikeledi draws on the famous Fanonian argument to summarize the idea that freedom can only be brought about through struggle: "She felt sad because she knew, she understood so well that South Africa had shut out all other choices. . . . She understood that there was no such thing as freedom being asked for, that freedom must be fetched, must be won, must be fought for."[82] Fanon had pointed out that the psychological damage inflicted by colonialism—the fear and self-hatred experienced by the colonized—could only be undone through cathartic violence, participation in revolution, and a "change [of] the order of the world."[83] The idea of revolutionary transformation through insurrection and armed struggle, through a necessary period of violence that would make space for a new world, is epitomized in the title of

Serote's novel. *To Every Birth Its Blood* establishes a correlation between the birth of the postapartheid society and revolutionary violence.

However, Serote's relationship with revolutionary violence has been far from straightforward. While he saw the resort to arms as a normal expression of the anger felt by his generation, which marked a new form of "consciousness and responsibility" that enabled their rise as political interlocutors to be reckoned with, "the gun was never an end in itself for me, although the struggle to use it responsibly was never easy. It was part of a bigger quest for a goal that reached beyond killing."[84] *To Every Birth Its Blood* reflects this uneasy relation with violence: characters are recruited to be part of the Movement (John and Dikeledi are inducted by Oupa), and the members plant bombs to destroy governmental targets (Onalena detonates a bomb in a parking lot outside a state institution); they kill black collaborators (Mandla executes a policeman who had terrorized Alexandra during the Power days), retaliate against state violence by attacking its representatives (Tuki, Mandla, John, and Onalena participate in a dangerous mission to kill officers responsible for numerous township deaths), and finally extend the armed struggle into the countryside by "dealing with" farmers. Described euphemistically or in a matter-of-fact style, the escalating violence imagined by Serote in the novel as a necessary component of the revolutionary struggle in the 1980s was at odds with the changing ANC-SACP policies, which varied between acknowledging their limited resources and hopes of starting an urban-based "people's war."[85] "My writing enabled me to understand what I was doing and why I was doing it," Serote observed, as he had to reconcile a superseded Fanonist emphasis on the psychological benefits of violence, the humanist abhorrence of bloodshed inherited from his grandmother, and changing ANC-SACP strategies in the late 1970s and early 1980s.[86]

However, as the characters progress through various stages of political involvement, the novel makes clear that Fanonism and BC are insufficient intellectual and tactical weapons, and the truly revolutionary program is the one proposed by the Movement: "While he [Dikeledi's father] encouraged her, he also made it clear, somehow, that he regarded what was going on as something which still had to be cooked, looked into. Whenever they talked, he was careful. He questioned her. Made it known when he thought something was wrong, or when he disagreed. 'I want you to understand that colour here must not be the issue. Once we get to understand that, then we can talk on, but I am afraid that you have put too much emphasis on the colour question,' Ramono used to say to her."[87]

Serote implies that a race-based alliance as advocated by Pan-Africanism and BC is not tenable. As further proof, Yaone—the artist in exile in the United

States—professes that African Americans are not able to fully grasp the situation in South Africa. As Americans and citizens of a neocolonial power, they are indirectly complicit in apartheid.[88]

In a move that places the novel squarely within the international Cold War context and draws attention to the role of the superpowers in creating or enabling crisis situations in the rest of the world, Yaone voices his concern with American complicity: "They call it Soweto here. Sometimes, when I am sitting around and talking about the Soweto issue, with both the black and the white Yankees, I feel like saying okay now, you bloody shits, did you know that as I am sitting here and talking, I think that you are directly responsible for the deaths in this, *your* Soweto?"[89] This view of the responsibility of old and new imperial powers for creating and maintaining iniquitous regimes is in keeping with both the ideas put forth by Kwame Nkrumah in his pathbreaking analysis of neocolonialism and the astute social and political analysis produced by members of the ANC-SACP coalition such as Ruth First.[90]

The novel traces the process of acquiring social and political literacy, starting from John's observation of seemingly disparate realities that he intuits to be nonetheless interlinked by means of opaque economic mechanisms and moving to his realization that change must be brought on by the people through a necessarily violent overthrow of the regime: "The people of this country are locked in a tight embrace which is going to destroy them. The white people. The black people. The gold. The diamonds. The guns. The bombs. South Africa, such a beautiful country. The bright sun, the warm days and nights, the rainy days, the mountains, trees, rivers, such a unique country. John felt *illiterate*, naïve and stupid, thinking all these things. What had all these to do with a reality which was death?"[91]

The questions John tries to answer connect apparently disparate entities. Rendered in short sentences consisting mostly of noun phrases, the seeming disjuncture between these proximate yet conflicting elements highlights the contradiction between the bountiful landscape of South Africa and the poverty and violence to which the majority of its inhabitants are subjected. A few pages later, Oupa points out that the police defend the property of the big owners, indicating that the deployment of state violence served financial and industrial interests.[92] As a writer and ANC member, Serote takes part in the ANC-SACP coalition's efforts in the 1970s to present apartheid as a systematic and far-reaching denial of human rights. These extended over the political, economic, legal, social, and cultural realms and had beneficiaries across the globe. As Ruth First, one of the strongest intellectual voices against apartheid, pointed out in the coauthored *The South African Connection: Western Investment in Apartheid*

(1972), the vested interest in preserving the political status quo was made evident by a study of international business interests and investments in material and human resources in South Africa. To preserve control over gold, diamonds, and fertile land, the white minority in power deployed violence and technologies of subjugation, such as guns and bombs. Without spelling it out, John's musings imply that death not only was dispensed by the apartheid state but was also inextricably connected to international powers that tacitly accepted the situation or permitted South Africa to acquire or manufacture military equipment.[93] Posed as a puzzle that cannot be articulated in complete sentences yet, this enumeration of disparate yet invisibly interconnected elements enables John, intradiegetically, and the readers, extradiegetically, to begin to become politically literate. Apartheid is therefore presented as having far-reaching ramifications and as being entangled in the Cold War global setup.

In keeping with ANC-SACP strategy, the novel suggests that this entanglement of interests could be counteracted only through a well-planned revolutionary solution. The "Strategy and Tactics" document adopted at the 1969 Morogoro conference in Tanzania proposed a long-term plan for seizing power in South Africa.[94] In the aftermath of the Soweto Uprising, with numerous young people secretly leaving the country to join the MK training camps, the militarization of the movement increased, and, consequently, the idea of revolution carried more weight.

Revolution is envisioned differently by various characters: the younger generation, like Oupa, are impatient for action; those who came of age during the BC movement and the Soweto Uprising wonder whether the people will have sufficient strength to fight apartheid successfully; at the same time, Michael Ramono, Dikeledi's father, a spokesperson for the older generation in the ANC, advocates long-term strategy and careful planning for decisive action: "This is a long, long struggle; it has long been here, we used to talk about the same things which you are talking about."[95] One of the leitmotifs of the second half of the novel is the statement "they have heard that before," which reflects a repeating stalemate with apartheid forces that this time, despite initial doubts, propels the characters into action. For instance, both John and Dikeledi had participated in protests during the Power days and had lost loved ones or were marked by violence; they had been mobilized by revolutionary thoughts, yet later they lapsed into an uneasy adjustment to the tense life in the townships. However, when the still-teenage Oupa displays his faith in the Movement and its transformative powers, they agree to be recruited. Their views of temporality, vacillating between hopefulness, despondency, and confidence again, trace some of the affective temporal structures crystallized in this novel.

As the antiapartheid struggle was a protracted process spanning four decades, therefore taking much longer than decolonization struggles in other parts of the African continent, the characters have to negotiate between an ominous sense of repetition and a distant horizon of hopefulness, on the one hand, and the realization that a different strategy and the clear leadership of the Movement will lead to liberation, on the other. "When the Power days were over, there was silence," John observes, while also keeping an ear attuned to what new local and international events indicated.[96] Serote is interested in rendering the formation of revolutionary energies as well as the characters' increased confidence in the success of the struggle. *To Every Birth Its Blood* makes room for the processual dimension—the formation of mass consciousness, people's new or renewed commitment to the future as they become convinced of the necessity to join the struggle and follow the program laid out by the Movement.

Both the ANC's 1969 "Strategy and Tactics" document and the SACP's 1962 program *The Road to South African Freedom: The Programme of the South African Communist Party* envisioned the struggle as a two-stage transformation—a national revolution that would eliminate racial discrimination, followed by a socialist revolution that would transform the economy of the country by empowering the working class and abolishing private property.[97] Oupa's statement that the Movement stands for "the destruction of oppression and exploitation" alludes, through its precise choice of nouns, to the two stages of revolution endorsed by the ANC-SACP coalition.[98] At the same time, read retrospectively, the novel serves as a reminder that the options and models available during the late Cold War era necessarily informed the ANC-SACP strategy. At the beginning of the 1980s, neither the antiapartheid movement nor writers could envision the collapse of the Eastern Bloc, the invalidation of socialism, or the possibility of peaceful transition to a democratic society as it actually came to happen.[99] Therefore, the imagined futures were shaped by Cold War geopolitical landscapes.

Nonetheless, as Serote's novel is not the ideological mouthpiece of the ANC-SACP alliance, the characters debate the meaning and substance of revolutionary action and the time necessary to carry it out. For instance, Oupa reads Lenin's *What Is to Be Done?*, a political pamphlet that criticizes the reliance on the spontaneous revolt of the masses and emphasizes the party's leadership role. Despite his engagement with this pamphlet, Oupa favors spontaneity, arguing that "this is the moment to hit," contrary to what "The Center of Directives" advises.[100] Characters debate and contest the possibility of relying on models. While Oupa foreshortens the affective temporal structures by focusing on immediate action, his elder peers take a longer-term approach:

[Oupa:] "The boers are fighting us, as simple as that. We have to pitch up a battle, fight back, that is all. All this that is happening now, happened to many other people. It happened in Guinea Bissau, Algeria, Angola, Mozambique, Vietnam, Cuba, you know: the people there pitted their strength against the mighty, the strong.... We too have to fight and win our country back."

Both John and Dikeledi looked anxiously at Oupa but said nothing. They were alarmed by the enthusiasm that suddenly lit up his face as he said this. They wondered whether he knew what he was saying. They had heard this so many times.[101]

Beyond their concern for a generation that seems too young to be thrown into battle, John and Dikeledi are also alert to the simplifying comparisons that propose Mozambique or Algeria (with their extremely violent conflicts drawn out by Western interventionism), not to mention Angola or Vietnam (true Cold War battlefields), as examples to be followed by the antiapartheid movement. Also, as part of a slightly older generation that came to political consciousness with the BC movement, Dikeledi and John are initially uncertain whether the end of the antiapartheid struggle could be foreseen. The corresponding affective temporal structures are similarly without a clear future horizon. "Now, there was a sense of loss, a sense of defeat; there were no more fists and shouts of Power. It seemed quiet," Dikeledi observes, meditating on the difference between the years when the BC movement was spearheading the struggle and the early 1980s.[102] Having been faced with the violent response of the state, Dikeledi and John lack the strategy and the vision that the Movement brings. Elsewhere Serote discussed his sense that BC had exhausted its energy by 1974, when he left South Africa to pursue a master of fine arts in the United States.[103] It was the encounter with a determined group of ANC activists in Botswana in the late 1970s that persuaded him that the party's vision for the future, with its attention to political, military, ideological, and cultural aspects of the struggle, was worth following.[104]

Serote suggests that with its echelons bridging generations—from the older Michael Ramono, to the middle-aged Mandla, to young comrades like Oupa—the Movement provides the strategy, the teleological outlook, and the belief in victory. The affective temporal structure emerging at the end of the novel looks confidently toward the future. "Push, push, push" are the final words of the novel, referring both to Jully's injunction to the mother-to-be and the collective effort of pushing through the final arduous stretch of the battle against the state.[105]

Two revolutions are taking place in Serote's novel: while it is evident that the novel envisions the struggle and radical social transformation in South Africa, the text also participates in a writing revolution that discards a high modernist style of writing (seemingly embraced in the first half of the novel) for a more apposite prose style, a literature that participates in the struggle. As Michael Titlestad has persuasively explained, the novel "sounds a cautionary note in its exploration of the limits of modernist improvisation in the face of violent oppression."[106] He argues that by relinquishing the narrative mode of organization based on jazz and improvisation, as well as the modernist rendering of individual breakdown, *To Every Birth Its Blood* makes a statement about the forms of literature appropriate for a society in crisis. A narrative that renders the growth of the political consciousness of a multitude of characters and their unity of purpose is preferable to the solipsism of one consciousness, even if the latter is presented in a formally innovative way. Serote implies that a revolutionary writer disdains the claims to the autonomy of fiction, which was a distinctive mark of modernist authors. Instead, he sees the writer as just another type of worker, a cultural worker, who contributes to the creation of a new society. This movement away from the belief in the autonomy of art to a collective effort of creation it is a journey undertaken by other African writers.[107] Not only thematically, but also by means of its form, the novel allows Serote to enter a dialogue with his contemporaries regarding the role of art in times of social turmoil and transformation. The emphasis on the social function of the writer and the thematic focus on revolution signal that the Cold War was the background against which these cultural battles unfolded.[108]

If in the later decades of the twentieth century, critics paid attention to Serote's politically committed fiction because it addressed important contemporary issues, today we can revisit novels like *To Every Birth Its Blood* because they offer insight into the unexpected resurgence of optimistic and forward-looking affective temporal structures in southern Africa in the late 1970s and 1980s. The very possibility of such perceptions of temporality seemed to have been negated by the late 1960s, when numerous countries that had won independence had experienced the disappointments of incomplete revolutions and inadequate social changes or had had their aspirations for a better future stymied by assassinations and coups plotted in Western capitals. In other words, the intersection of decolonization and Cold War politics had placed what Bhakti Shringarpure calls a "triple bind of time" on newly independent states, rupturing their trajectories.[109]

## The Morning after African Socialism

Nowhere is the central tenet of the second part of this book—that we should revisit canonical African literature through a Cold War lens in order to reveal previously indiscernible aspects—more poignantly visible than with Ayi Kwei Armah's 1968 novel of postcolonial disenchantment, *The Beautyful Ones Are Not Yet Born*. This final section of the chapter looks at representations of "the morning after" or, in Neil Lazarus's insightful formulation, "the mourning after" independence.[110] While literary critics have astutely analyzed the forms of neocolonial corruption that compromised the accomplishments of newly independent Ghana, they have overlooked the impact of African socialism, the ideology embraced by Kwame Nkrumah after decolonization. African socialism, fleetingly invoked by name several times in the novel, affords added depth to the analysis of the social crisis Armah depicts, while also functioning in an indexical way. It points to the Cold War background against which the drama of Nkrumah's last days in office and the economic hardships of Ghanaians unfolded, and it allows us to better understand the affective temporal structures characteristic of this novel and its historical moment.

It has become customary for literary critics to read *The Beautyful Ones Are Not Yet Born* as a literary illustration of Fanon's premonitory warning about the failures of the national bourgeoisie, its underdeveloped character, and the betrayal of the masses by leaders who pursue and protect the interests of their class. The most compelling reading of Armah's indebtedness to Fanon unfolds in Lazarus's *Resistance in Postcolonial African Fiction*. For Lazarus, the failure of Nkrumah's leadership happened because of his and his government's inability to think beyond the colonial capitalist state apparatus inherited from Britain: "To the extent that anticolonial nationalism directed its efforts solely at what Nkrumah called 'the political kingdom' of the colonial state, its labor was oriented toward the appropriation of a *capitalist* apparatus."[111] While here Lazarus is discussing more widely the failures of nationalist anticolonialism across the continent and its inability to deliver the revolutionary transformations the colonized had dreamed of, his analysis emphasizes the structures inherited from the British colonial state and their intersection with American neocolonialism as the corrupting elements in postindependence Ghana. Yet why should we read the corrupt Ghanaian society pictured in the novel as representative only of Western neocolonialism, when the novel could actually be an exemplary depiction of the overlap of American and Soviet imperialism during the Cold War and their damaging effects in postcolonial societies? Lazarus overlooks the other political and ideological molding factor that contributed to destabilizing

Ghana after independence: the Soviet Union and the Eastern Bloc, with which Nkrumah's government developed relations of economic cooperation.

I propose instead to revisit the novel bearing in mind the Cold War background and the different ways in which Nkrumah's rule has been interpreted. What is visible or invisible in the novel and in its attendant literary scholarship is telling about the blind spots created by the Cold War political and cultural landscape. Nkrumah has been variously seen as a doctrinaire follower of Marxism-Leninism, a cross between "Africa's Lenin" and "Ghana's czar," a dictator who stifled the mechanisms of democracy in his country, a well-intentioned leader who was bamboozled by Soviet propaganda, a proponent of African socialism who astutely adapted Marxism-Leninism to specific conditions in Africa, or a Pan-African leader who augmented the role and visibility of the continent on the world stage.[112] While Nkrumah is revered by some for his insightful theoretical pronouncements and for leading the first African state to independence, his legacy still elicits different responses according to the audience. This should not be surprising, considering the Cold War ideological fractures that pitted supporters of socialism against defenders of Western liberal democracy. A man who considered propaganda, perceived as political blasphemy in the West, as "a means of liberation, an instrument of clarification, information, education and mobilization," was bound to be seen by some as a courageous political leader and by others as a mere puppet of the Eastern Bloc.[113] The oppressive aspects of his regime intensified, especially as, following an assassination attempt, he made Ghana a one-party state in 1964 and proclaimed himself president for life.[114] Yet, as Charles Adom Boateng pointed out, the Ghanaian leader was "an elder statesman of the African continent," whose ideas (whether successful or failed) have provided a theoretical and practical framework within which to understand the problems confronting former colonies.[115]

"We face neither East, nor West: we face Forward" is a much-quoted Nkrumah dictum, epitomizing the dangerous political landscape of the late 1950s and early 1960s; it was a moment when the Cold War ideological trenches were deepening, and navigating between the superpowers' Scylla and Charybdis required the governments of newly independent nations to be vigilant.[116] Nkrumah, the preeminent theorist of neocolonialism, was rightfully wary of the long arm of the former British overlords and the rapacious intentions of the new Western superpower, the United States. Drawing on Lenin's theory of the stages of imperialism, he saw contemporary neocolonialism as the most dangerous form of imperialism: "The essence of neo-colonialism is that the State which is subject to it is, in theory, independent and has all the outward trappings of international sovereignty. In reality its economic system and thus its political system is directed from outside."[117] To counter the dangers Western neocolonialism posed, Nkrumah established economic and political relations with the Eastern Bloc, despite subscribing to a rhetoric of nonalignment.[118] In 1961 Nkrumah toured several Eastern Bloc countries, traveling from Moscow to Warsaw and Budapest, and from Tashkent to Belgrade, Prague, and Bucharest. A publication of the Ghanaian Ministry of Information and Broadcasting showcases these visits with their focus on ceremonial time, the exchange of "fraternal greetings" with the leaderships of the corresponding communist parties, and the collection of photographic evidence of warm receptions in these countries, including by a group of African students in Moscow.[119] The objectives of these visits highlight what Nkrumah was hoping to accomplish: to "strengthen further the cordial relations that exist between our two countries"; "reinforce our determination to crush imperialism, colonialism and neocolonialism in Africa"; and observe "projects [collective farms, irrigation systems] [that] are object lessons for us in Ghana."[120] In theory at least, Nkrumah attempted to temper and adapt both socialist and capitalist principles by explaining their coexistence through the framework of Non-Alignment.[121]

Nkrumah's view of the forms of socialism to be achieved in Africa differed radically from the perspective of the supporters of nationalist, humanist "African socialism" of the type endorsed by Léopold Sédar Senghor. In fact, in a paper delivered at the October 1966 Cairo seminar on national and social revolution in Africa, Nkrumah expressed his concern with the meaninglessness and irrelevance of the term *African socialism* to describe political programs embraced on the continent, taking Senghor to task for the "metaphysics of knowledge" that evacuates the term *socialism* of any meaning.[122] Embracing a materialist perspective, he argued that "socialism is not spontaneous. It does not arise of itself. It has abiding principles according to which the major means of production and distribution ought to be socialised if exploitation of the many by the few is to be prevented."[123] In fact, he drew parallels between the Marxism–social democracy split at the Second International, on the one hand, and the divergence between the scientific forms of socialism he envisioned as necessary for the continent and the problematic theorizations of "African socialism," on the other.[124]

I am not interested in prioritizing Nkrumah's perspective over the competing views held by his contemporaries, or in explaining away and dissimulating the negative aspects of his rule. The focus of this chapter is representations of revolution and intellectual genealogies of revolution in literary works. The emphasis, therefore, is on what aspects Armah chose to address or overlook in his grim representation of postindependence Ghana and on the author's take on Nkrumah's failed leadership. Why, given the differences between Senghor and

Nkrumah, does the latter's view not register with intellectuals like Armah? Why does Nkrumah come to be seen as either one more corrupt postindependence leader who betrayed the masses to neocolonial interests, as most literary critics of *The Beautyful Ones Are Not Yet Born* see him, or a proponent of African socialism who ventriloquized spurious ideas about traditional and contemporary African societies, as Armah did? The blind spots arise from the Cold War background: as a result, literary scholarship either completely erases socialism or treats it as a straw man not worthy of careful consideration.

The plot of the novel is sparse, and it is subsumed to the relentlessly grim mood of Ghana on the verge of the coup that ousted Nkrumah from power. The protagonist of the novel is an unnamed man who ponders the ethical dilemmas posed by a corrupt society that enmeshes reluctant and willing participants alike. Although he holds a white-collar job with the railway company and works endless hours, he is unable to bring home enough money to feed his family and satisfy his wife's and mother-in-law's dream of climbing the social ladder. As he turns down a bribe from a lumberman who wants to reserve a train wagon to transport his timber, he is propelled into an ethical crisis. His angered wife reproaches him that, in a corrupt system, his vaunted incorruptibility entails belittling those around him. The man's moral confusion leads him to visit Teacher, and their conversation about love, duty toward family, ethical principles, and the failure of the promises of independence constitutes a turning point in the novel. In contrast to the moral values the man prizes, materialism, commodity fetishism, and individualism are the driving forces in the new Ghana. The man's wife and mother-in-law would like to strike a deal with Joseph Koomson, a corrupt government minister, that would involve buying a fishing boat with money lent by the official. The deal fails just as Nkrumah and his government are toppled from power in a military coup. In a vindicating finale, Koomson has to escape through the man's latrine, becoming immersed in the excrement that his corrupt class had come to symbolize.

The novel's almost unyielding bleakness has earned Armah both accusations of indiscriminately transposing existentialist philosophy and European novelistic techniques to postindependence Ghana and praise for his unflinching scrutiny of the rapid unraveling of hope under Nkrumah's regime.[125] Literary critics have dwelled in detail on the cycle of all-pervasive corruption that affects Ghanaian society in Armah's novel and the chains of metaphors, similes, and extended analogies that structure the plot: physical objects (the banister at the Railway and Harbour Administration, bank notes, latrines) rot or emit foul smells; elites stuffed to bursting on expensive foods become metonyms for the ill health of the nation; and even abstractions like dreams of revolution are perverted.[126] The existentialist interlude between the man and Teacher highlights the dead end to any hope that Ghanaians could find ethical solutions to the pervasive corruption. Armah's dystopian assessment has attracted harsh censure from literary critics, including accusations that the author set himself above his contemporaries and pontificated from an untenable moral high ground, denunciations of his putative shortsightedness and inability to dig deeper into the postindependence situation, and charges of groundless philosophizing.[127] The novel "refers to no real Africa but to some abstract human condition," concludes Charles Nnolim.[128] Yet the bleakness of Armah's vision is interrupted at the end by the image of the "bird with a song that was strangely happy" and the flower on the misspelled bus sign that gives the novel its title.[129] As ambivalent as the final glimmer of hope is, considering that the last sentence of the text returns to the weariness and toil facing the protagonist, the ending is commensurate with the temporality announced in the title. Despite the grimness, the affective temporal structures are those of a deferred fulfillment of the promises of independence.

If Armah was indeed drawing on existentialist philosophy in his novel, he was equally in conversation—whether friendly or combative—with African theorists of revolution. Thus, he drew on Fanon's ideas about the narcissistic personality of the middle class and the fetishism of consumerism that overtook Ghana and other countries after independence. However, as Armah argued, Fanon's theory of revolution could become practice in Africa only at a later point, when the residues of previous forms of oppression, masquerading as independence, would have proven their irrelevance: "Fanon will be relevant when both the windy 'African Revolution' and its sequel, the reaction, are finished."[130] Using quotation marks to signal his derision for the empty claims of revolution contemporary African leaders made, Armah launched a withering critique of African socialism in an article published just a year before the release of *The Beautyful Ones Are Not Yet Born*. "African Socialism: Utopian or Scientific?" harshly criticized Senghor and Nkrumah: "African Socialism may be regarded as a gimmick, a set of magical prop slogans, or as an ideology in the Mannheimian sense. Its value as a sloganeering gimmick is obvious: there is the aggressive affirmation of Africanness, coupled with the defiant invocation of a revolutionary system opposed to the former master's."[131] In this article Armah sides instead with Marxist scientific socialism, an opinion that he later overturned in his 1984 essay "Masks and Marx: The Marxist Ethos vis-à-vis African Revolutionary Theory and Praxis."

What becomes obvious within this enlarged cultural context is Armah's profound interest in stasis, social transformation, and revolution. What kind of social movements are capable of breaking stagnation and corruption? When is a change of political regime truly revolutionary, and when does it fall into the same patterns that privilege the upper middle classes? These are some of the questions, carrying the hallmark of the Cold War years, that Armah's novel also attempts to answer. Yet, although Ghana was supposedly building a form of African socialism under Nkrumah's leadership, socialism does not get an extensive treatment in the novel. In fact, it simply features as one of the manifold forms of betrayal of the promises of independence on the continent. Koomson is a "Hero of Socialist Labor," which does not prevent him from finding illicit means of monetary gain.[132] His thinking and actions are at odds with the principles of socialism, which he actually perceives as stumbling blocks for his advancement. Koomson's wife, Estella, protests that "it's this foolish socialism that will spoil everybody's peace," while her husband expresses skepticism that socialism could actually be established in Ghana: "It is not possible here," he concludes, protesting that Nkrumah himself "does not believe in it."[133] As Armah had already indicated in "African Socialism," in Ghana socialism had been reduced to slogans that were used as weapons to prevent one's fellow citizens from accumulating wealth. Thus, Koomson bemoans that "when people see you doing something to get ahead, they become jealous and shout the slogans against you."[134]

While evidence of older forms of colonialism (the fetishism of English lifestyles, English houses, and English names) and new forms of imperialism (the lure of consumer goods of American provenance) is highly visible in the novel, the landscape of the city is sprinkled with new forms of social organization introduced by Nkrumah's pursuit of socialism. Koomson is a "Hero of Socialist Labor," the government has initiated a (failed) campaign to "KEEP YOUR COUNTRY CLEAN BY KEEPING YOUR CITY CLEAN," citizens are familiar with party slogans and some climb up the social ladder by reproducing them zealously, and those who run afoul of the new leadership have slogans shouted back at them or are branded saboteurs.[135] These modes of interpellating citizens are familiar to any readers who have lived in the Eastern Bloc or other socialist states. The Ghana represented by Armah in *The Beautyful Ones Are Not Yet Born* is in the Cold War crucible, caught between lingering and new ideologies that combine to further oppress the population.

In his book on contemporary Guinea, *A Socialist Peace? Explaining the Absence of War in an African Country*, Mike McGovern looks at the fraught yet long-lasting legacy of Sékou Touré's regime during the postsocialist period. He draws on Lauren Berlant's exploration of "cruel optimism" to account for the tenacious mental and social dispositions set in place during socialism as well as on researchers of Eastern Bloc cultures to understand the type of temporality instituted under a socialist regime. With the latter set of countries he identifies several forms of experiencing time under socialism, from the "accelerated time" that allowed governments to plan for catching up with development markers to the "revolutionary time" that entailed reaching a "messianic limit of accelerated time," and from the "anniversarial" and "festive time" that compelled or outright forced citizens to celebrate the achievements of the state to the "interrupted time" that decreed people had to participate in patriotic or artistic duties.[136] McGovern's astute intervention reminds us that it is problematic to think only in terms of affective temporal structures resulting from neocolonialism, underdevelopment, and continuous dependence on the West, neglecting the effect of socialist dispositions on perceptions of temporality.

The novel's affective temporal structures—characterized by despair and a loss of hopefulness—are the result of the overlapping legacies of neocolonial capitalism and the version of African socialism that Nkrumah's government established in Ghana. In a superb tour de force, Lazarus showcased the Fanonist aspects of Armah's novels, especially in *The Beautyful Ones Are Not Yet Born*, in the process delivering a keen reading of the tensions in Fanon's writings about revolution, especially the tensions between the "partyist" and "spontaneist" aspects in the latter's thinking. Lazarus presents the image of a young Armah who was disenchanted with what could be accomplished from the elitist heights of Harvard, where he had gone to study, and who was driven instead to consider practical ways in which he could contribute to transforming the continent.[137] Under the spell of Fanon's *The Wretched of the Earth* and driven by the twin forces of "Africanity" and revolutionism, Armah traveled across Africa, Asia, and Latin America, only to realize that "so-called revolutions were being recuperated and institutionalized, and new regimes were moving smartly to enthrone themselves in the very positions of power and privilege only lately vacated by departing colonial administrations."[138] As a result of this disappointment, Lazarus concludes poignantly, Armah's early novels, from *The Beautyful Ones Are Not Yet Born* (1968) to *Fragments* (1970) to *Why Are We So Blest?* (1972), are torn between the messianism the writer inherited from Fanon and the recognition of mechanisms that led to the failure of the emancipatory potential of postindependence states.

We see this bifurcation at the level of the text, as Teacher's cynical interpretation and the man's somber reflections allow us to delve into how social change and revolution are portrayed in the novel. According to Reinhart Koselleck, there is a productive tension within the meaning of the term *revolution*, as it evolved from a concept that described a cyclical movement to an idea that stood for radical rupture and new beginnings.[139] This tension is foregrounded in Armah's novel, where the Fanonian messianism undergirding the novel without becoming fully expressed is continuously syncopated by the suspicion that revolution as radical rupture and a qualitative jump forward is a political sham that disguises the return of the same class of beneficiaries to positions of domination: "We were ready here for big and beautiful things, but what we had was our own black men hugging new paunches scrambling to ask the white man to welcome them onto our backs. These men who were to lead us out of our despair, they came like men already grown fat and cynical with the eating of centuries of power they had never struggled for, old before they had even been born into power, and ready only for the grave."[140]

The lexical and grammatical choices in that excerpt—the vacillation between future in the past, past tense, and past perfect, as well as between the adverbs *already* and *never*—display the interpenetration of past and future, the inevitability of decay yet also the hope of some new beginning, however distant. In contrast, the popular wisdom of latrine graffiti "SOCIALISM CHOP MAKE I CHOP," with its uninflected verb forms, keeps citizens in the eternity of the present.[141] Lazarus correctly points out that, despite its bleakness, Armah's novel is not devoid of a certain hopefulness embedded in its messianic vision: "The social environment of 'the man' is profoundly unrevolutionary, but the specter of revolution figures in its margins nevertheless."[142] The protagonist is torn between the dream of a radical departure from the misery of past and present and the acknowledgment of the wisdom of an older, circular understanding of temporality and the cycle of suffering.

For Teacher, the dreamer turned cynic, revolution ushers in a circular pattern that moves from the hopefulness of new beginnings to reinstated forms of exploitation and suffering, not just in Ghana but across the world, short-circuiting the hopefulness and political options introduced by socialist countries and the Eastern Bloc: "When Teacher had talked of people standing up and deciding then and there to do what ages and millions had called impossible, had talked of the Chinese Mao and the Cuban Castro struggling in the face of all reasonable hope, even then Teacher's mind would look beyond the clear awakening and see after the dawn the bright morning and the noonday, the afternoon, dusk, and then another night of darkness and fatigue."[143]

The choice of representative midcentury revolutionary movements is telling: neither "the wretched of the earth" in Asia who embraced socialism as the solution to oppression nor those in Latin America, neither Mao nor Castro, had found a way to break the cycle and create truly revolutionary states. There is no mention of the Soviet Union or its Eastern European satellites, and this absence, by implication, damns their social models as even more corrupt. After all, these are the countries with which Ghana had established trade relations, where Nkrumah had traveled to link up with the leadership of communist parties, and which had failed to deliver on the fraternal bonds they were supposed to cherish.

The end of the novel briefly mentions the military coup that ousted Nkrumah from power. The man finds out from his fellow railway workers that there had been "no six o'clock news this morning. Only some strange announcement by a man with a strange name, then *soja* music."[144] Aside from mentions of the coup in passing a few times, a matter-of-factly treated military roadblock that does not alert the regular citizens, and a chapter dedicated to Koomson's escape from the new authorities through the man's latrine, the novel marks no modification of the pace of life. The change of regime, Armah implies, is no revolution, in the same way as the independence of Ghana from the British Empire, as radical as it seemed, was not a revolution. "The power shifts we have got into the habit of calling 'Independence' are not revolutions. Reform would be a more accurate term," Armah indicated in his article "African Socialism."[145] In Fanonian fashion, Armah has reduced the political and social structures erected under Nkrumah's rule to yet another example of disappointing leadership and betrayal of the masses by the leadership encountered in many other countries across the continent.

Affective temporal structures that highlight stagnation and deferred revolution are characteristic of most of Africa from the end of the 1960s onward, with some small exceptions like southern Africa, where the struggle for liberation infused perceptions of temporality with optimism until the end of the 1980s. The reality of the "mourning after" independence, to borrow again Lazarus's term, with the effects of (neo)colonialism expressed in poor leadership, economic crises, and military coups, changed perceptions of temporality for many writers across the continent, ushering in a period of cynicism and despondency. Moreover, as Shringarpure has poignantly argued, the assassinations of leaders like "Patrice Lumumba, Amílcar Cabral, and Thomas Sankara are not only tragic events that bring the individual trajectories of these young revolutionaries to an abrupt end but they cut across what can be called 'nation time,' the deeply layered, complicated chronopolitics that newly formed nation-states struggle with."[146] Under these conditions, revolution is represented as a political option continuously deferred by the interference of internal and especially external powers.

The prominence of revolution as a political modality of breaking the constraints of the present across the African continent and the Third World decreased in the 1980s. Concurrently, its specific affective temporal structures also waned toward the end of the Cold War, although they maintained their significance in places like South Africa, where the revolution was still seen as the only way to break oppression and political deadlock. Although today we are no longer immersed in these affective temporal structures, the increasing distance from the years of anticolonial resistance and the emergence of documents that were kept secret or were difficult to access at that time give us the possibility to revisit them in a new light now, set them in dialogue, and see how themes articulated in cultural texts find echoes in political documents and vice versa. As a result, a submerged Cold War landscape, sometimes tacitly grasped yet other times completely invisible, can now be traced in all its manifestations.

To conclude, writers' engagement with revolution helps us better conceive the historical conditions they represent in their work. However, the more important contribution they bring is an intervention in the terminology that allows us to conceptualize revolution. Koselleck has made some of the most important observations about the historical trajectory of the terminology of revolution. He has drawn attention to the (sometimes exaggerated) elasticity of the word, a word that can change a situation through its evocative power: "It almost seems that the word 'revolution' itself possesses such revolutionary power that it is constantly extending itself to include every last element on our globe."[147] Quoting Hannah Arendt, he points out that before the current understanding of the term *revolution*, one "possessed no word which could have characterized a transformation in which the subjects themselves became rulers."[148] Therefore, the focus on revolution in African literary works, which this chapter has traced, effects several transformations. First, it brings forth a new mode of social organization—oftentimes willing it into being, as with Sembène and Serote. Second, and equally important, by setting down the descriptive terms in which revolution is to be represented, it wrests the term from its Eurocentric grounding, challenging accepted filiations. In their stead, it creates new intellectual genealogies for conceiving revolution, in which the voice of African thinkers is given primacy.

# 4

# The Hot Cold War

Rethinking the
Global Conflict through
Southern Africa

The desolate landscape in Jo Ractliffe's photographs reveals two cement slabs surrounded by gum trees (figure 4.1). They could be anything—the beginning of a building project or two abandoned pieces of construction material. There are no other signposts in the pictures' foreground or background. Only the captions, identifying them as mass graves at Cassinga, jolt the viewer into realization. The inscription on each of the cement slabs, "Massacre at Cassinga, 4 May 1978" and "We Will Always Remember Them"—just a fraction of which emerges in the first picture and which is completely invisible in the second photograph—foregrounds the contradiction between the memorializing gesture and the erasure of this outrage from international memory.[1] The pictures are drawn from Ractliffe's photography book *As Terras do Fim do Mundo*, a work that wrestles with the impermanence of the memory of the war in Angola and the fading of the traumatic events that culminated in the biggest battles on African soil since the end of World War II.[2] Following Ractliffe's lead, this chapter focuses on South African and Angolan literary representations of the first part (1975–1991) of the conflict problematically labeled "the Angolan Civil War."[3] The literary texts that I discuss similarly reflect on the vagaries of public memory; they demonstrate that this protracted struggle was an integral part of the global Cold War and contradict the very idea of a "cold" conflict. A thematic constellation exposes a slippage from binary certainties to fuzzy and intermeshing ideological perspectives. Additionally, the transition from predominantly realist techniques of representation in the late 1970s and 1980s to magical realism and fragmented narrative structures from the 1990s onward shows that,

Figure 4.1. Jo Ractliffe, *Mass Grave at Cassinga I*, 2010. © Jo Ractliffe. Courtesy of Stevenson, Cape Town and Johannesburg.

despite accumulated knowledge about the conflict, the remembrance project poses more, rather than fewer, challenges.

I am proposing a new reading of literature on the war in Angola that brings together texts from two combatant countries (South Africa and Angola) and two oftentimes nonintersecting postcolonial literary traditions (anglophone and lusophone), thereby uniting works that are rarely read and discussed together. If it is unsurprising that Angolan writers have focused on the war that devastated their country, the obsessive return of their South African counterparts to this topic demonstrates the conflict's impact in the region's cultural imaginary. The texts range from literature based on the experience of white South African conscripts in Anthony Akerman's *Somewhere on the Border* (1986) and Mark Behr's *The Smell of Apples* (1993) to the retrospective novels rendering the experience of their black Umkhonto we Sizwe (MK) counterparts in Mongane Wally Serote's *Scatter the Ashes and Go* (2002), and from the realist or modernist novels of the decolonization period in southern Africa, such as Pepetela's *Mayombe* (1980), Sousa Jamba's *Patriots* (1990), and Nadine Gordimer's *July's People* (1981), to the contemporary magical realist prose of Ondjaki's *Granma Nine-*

*teen and the Soviet's Secret* (2008) and Niq Mhlongo's *Way Back Home* (2013). The visibility of these texts has varied owing to the different overarching categories under which these works have been placed: South African memoirs and fiction of the Border War, lusophone literature of decolonization, African war fiction, and postmodern or magical realist writings.[4] While disorienting plot devices and fantastic elements were already present in the earlier texts, their predominance in the post-1990 literary works, as well as the increased fragmentation of the narratives, reveals the persistent difficulties of telling the story of the war in Angola. To underscore these challenging aspects, I focus on several topoi: conflicting perspectives and the literal and ideological borders they evoke, the blurring of demarcation lines, betrayals, and the persistence of secrets and unsolved mysteries. The literature I discuss turns the story of the war in Angola from a local conflict in southern Africa to a crucial event that reshapes our understanding of the Cold War and the second half of the twentieth century. This approach challenges simplistic historical accounts that narrow down the Cold War to a conflict between the West and the East, the USA and the USSR. From the entangled southern African accounts, with ideological borders that are difficult to trace with clarity, there arises a complex narrative of a global conflict, in which Third World countries were important participants and stakeholders.

## Silences, Censorship, and Academic Compartmentalization

Before plunging into the discussions of the literary texts, let us return to Jo Ractliffe's photographs, as they adumbrate an important topos in the works discussed in this chapter. The unobtrusive presence of the graves, almost invisible against the background of the gum trees, contrasts dramatically with the aftermath images of the massacre. The international press focused, albeit briefly, on innocent casualties and the magnitude of the horror. During the South African Defence Force (SADF) air and land raid at Cassinga in 1978, a raid that crossed the border from South West Africa (later Namibia) into Angola, over six hundred people were killed. Most of them were Namibian refugees. As a result, the lives of hundreds of men, women, and children, along with a number of Cuban soldiers responding to the bombing at Cassinga, were obliterated in a South African operation that army commanders described as a successful antiterrorist operation.[5] While the United Nations High Commissioner for Refugees and the World Health Organization accused South Africa of killing civilians, the regime in Pretoria rationalized the attack as an operation against enemy military installations. The contradictory narratives over Cassinga underscore the radically polarized views about the nature of the conflict in Angola. For South

Africa and its supporters, Cassinga was a military camp of the People's Liberation Army of Namibia (PLAN), which was the armed wing of the South West Africa People's Organization, the political movement that led the struggle to decolonize Namibia; therefore, according to the SADF, it was a legitimate target in what South Africa claimed was a war against terrorist destabilization driven by the *rooi gevaar* (the red threat). On the other side of the front line, the South West Africa People's Organization, sympathetic regional entities (such as the Popular Movement for the Liberation of Angola [MPLA], in charge of the government of Angola), Eastern Bloc allies, and Western humanitarian organizations saw it for the outrage that it was.[6]

A photograph of the larger of two mass graves brought the massacre to international attention. Taken from the foot of the grave, the picture reveals the horror meeting the foreign journalists: "First we saw gaily coloured frocks, blue jeans, shirts and a few uniforms. Then there was the sight of the bodies inside them. Swollen, blood-stained, they were the bodies of young girls, young men, a few older adults, all apparently recent arrivals from Namibia," announces the best-known caption of the photograph.[7] The photographic evidence, drawing attention to the civilian victims, seemed to settle the debate, pointing accusingly to South African war crimes.

Responding to the picture's implicit injunction to speak up, South African writer Anthony Akerman dedicated his play *Somewhere on the Border* (written in 1982 and first performed in South Africa in 1986) to the memory of the Cassinga massacre.[8] While the village of Cassinga is never mentioned within the diegesis, the memory of the massacre is evoked at the end of the play when Paul Marais, a young Afrikaner conscript, has a nervous breakdown upon realizing that many of the targets of his company's attack were children. The dedication highlights the growing urgency to stand up against South Africa's participation in the war: "No one got out of [conscription in South Africa]. Most of us thought it was a waste of time. But in the back of your mind, you knew you could be used to maintain the status quo. Now the boys are sent to the border. Now the boys are sent to Cassinga."[9] While initially it was seen as a problematic hijacking of a young man's life by the state, army service, with its almost mandatory tour to the Namibia-Angola border, became an act of complicity with the apartheid regime and a crime against humanity. Akerman's play declares the stakes of literature and art: at a time when the South African government erased the traces of its crimes, thus making it almost impossible for historians or social scientists to properly evaluate the events, artists had to sound the alarm.

How do we get from the imperative to see and witness—as the photograph of the dead enjoins the viewer—to the desolation and forgetting documented by Ractliffe's pictures in 2009–2010? Today, over four decades after the massacre, with declassified military information, the production of detailed historical narratives, and, in recent years, a flood of memoirs and fiction on the topic, we know much more about those events. Yet the silence persists. "There is no sound. It takes a while for me to register this, to recognize what I am experiencing is silence"—these are the opening lines of Ractliffe's narrative about her journey to Angola to visually document the battlegrounds where SADF conscripts were sent.[10] The soundlessness that opens her book suggests a more problematic epistemological silence. In his groundbreaking book *Silencing the Past: Power and the Production of History*, Michel-Rolph Trouillot argues that "silences enter the process of historical production at four crucial moments: the moment of fact creation (the making of *sources*); the moment of fact assembly (the making of *archives*); the making of fact retrieval (the making of *narratives*); and the moment of retrospective significance (the making of *history* in the final instance)."[11] Journalists, historians, and political scientists have been debating the constitutive facts, sources, archives, narratives, and their significance, targeting the forms of silencing at various constitutive levels. In time, their emphasis has moved from fact retrieval and questioning of the relevant archives to a more nuanced understanding of representation and narrative visibility. Likewise, writers and artists who have addressed the participants' voicelessness or amnesia have seen their function differently throughout the decades according to the historical moment when they intervened. The thematic and formal aspects of their works signal their changing priorities. For some of the authors discussed in this chapter, naming events, spelling out forms of complicity, and combating their compatriots' apathy are the main priorities; for others, the task shifts from a personal undertaking (wrestling with the trauma of participation) to a national scope (combating collective amnesia); and for yet another group of writers, it is the recognition of an epistemological conundrum that must be foregrounded: the story has to be told with subtlety and nuance, while still acknowledging the impossibility of attending to all its complexity.

As shown in the introduction, (post)colonial polities seldom featured as full-fledged Cold War participants in scholarly accounts until recently. The hot conflicts involving Angola, the Horn of Africa, and even Vietnam or Cuba appeared as footnotes to a text in which the superpowers were cast as protagonists.[12] In these accounts, either the legacy of colonial subordination to Western powers is overlooked, and the respective country's ideological alignment with the capitalist or socialist bloc prioritized, or vice versa. The Angolan conflict was one of the hot spots of the Cold War where the government forces of the MPLA, Cuban troops sent to support the fledgling leftist administration, Soviet tactical support, PLAN, and MK soldiers from the Namibian and South African liberation movements came face to face with the soldiers of the National Union for the Total Independence of Angola (UNITA) and the SADF, backed by CIA political and financial support. A third liberation movement, the National Front for the Liberation of Angola (FNLA), received financial and tactical support from sources across the ideological spectrum—China, Romania, Israel, the United States, and Zaire—further complicating the intricate relations between the warring parties.[13]

It is only in the past decade that scholars working on southern Africa have truly started to address this omission by focusing on the cultural resonances of the war in Angola. The main scholarly texts that redirected attention toward this conflict are the interdisciplinary essay collections *Beyond the Border War: New Perspectives on Southern Africa's Late-Cold War Conflicts*, edited by Gary Baines and Peter Vale (2008), and *Cold War in Southern Africa: White Power, Black Liberation* (2009), a volume edited by Sue Onslow, along with more specialized contributions like Piero Gleijeses's *Conflicting Missions: Havana, Washington, and Africa, 1959–1976* (2002) and *Visions of Freedom: Havana, Washington, Pretoria and the Struggle for Southern Africa, 1976–1991* (2013), Vladimir Shubin's *The Hot "Cold War": The USSR in Southern Africa* (2008), and, more recently, Gary Baines's *South Africa's "Border War": Contested Narratives and Conflicting Memories* (2014). These works of scholarship signal a turn in public memory about two decades after the major powers' withdrawal from this conflict.

In the new millennium, political scientists and historians are turning their attention to the war in Angola as more than just a civil war (an unfortunate internal affair) or a regional conflict (as the South African descriptor "Border War" implies), therefore acknowledging it as a proxy war for the superpowers. However, less attention has been paid to the ways in which cultural production from the area has been shaped by the conflict and has influenced its representation in equal measure. When critics finally started attending to these texts, they usually focused on the national context within which they had been produced.[14] As anglophone and lusophone literatures from southern Africa are seldom treated together, largely owing to language barriers that are further complicated by the presence of texts in Afrikaans and local African languages, a highly compartmentalized scholarly landscape persists. While recognizing the limitations of working with texts in their English translation, this chapter gestures toward the need to think about this body of texts transnationally, both in terms of regional influences or mutual incomprehension and within a global Cold War context. The literary texts discussed here thereby appear as the source of a much more nuanced narrative about the conflict. The transnational circuits they evoke could be conceived differently: across the South Atlantic (to include cultural relations with Brazil or Cuba) and within the Global South; with Eastern Bloc countries (especially but not exclusively the Soviet Union); and, quite obviously, with former and neocolonial powers in the West. I return to these alternative cultural circuits (and theoretical frameworks) in the conclusion.

Angolan literature is one of the sites where we can identify with clarity the connections between the struggle for independence and its postindependence successor, the so-called civil war that was a miniaturized version of Cold War interests at full-blown violent capability. While the main political parties—the MPLA, UNITA, and FNLA—continued from the colonial period to after independence, their adversaries were no longer solely the Portuguese colonizers but included South Africa and the United States, or Cuba and the USSR, depending on the writers' ideological orientation. Angolan authors took up the anticolonial and then anti-imperial topic from the 1950s onward, in prison writing, novels, and collections of poems that addressed their compatriots' suffering under Portuguese colonial domination as well as the nefarious influence regional or (aspiring) global powers had in prolonging the bloodshed. The New Intellectuals of Angola, a group that coalesced in Luanda and published a short-lived yet impactful journal, *Mensagem* (Message), produced many writers sympathetic to the MPLA's cause. José Luandino Vieira's *Luuanda* (1964, *Luuanda: Short Stories of Angola* in the 1980 English translation) transformed the creolized Portuguese influenced by Kimbundu into a literary language.[15] Artur Pestana dos Santos, better known by his pen name Pepetela, became one of the most important writers of historical novels: *As aventuras de Ngunga* (1972, translated into English as *Ngunga's Adventures: A Story of Angola* in 1988), *Mayombe* (1980, translated into English in 1982), and *A gloriosa família* (The glorious family, 1997) are novels that position the contemporary tribulations of Angola within a *longue durée* perspective on forms of imperialism. Manuel Rui's work, especially his novel *Quem me dera ser onda* (Oh that I were a wave in the ocean!, 1982), began addressing the complex situation after independence, a sociopolitical reality that could not be reduced to a Manichean Cold War binary of good and bad protagonists. This "social satire, tinged with political parody, ... was audacious for those times of implicit, if not official, socialist realism."[16] In fact, it paved the way for more equivocal renderings of the Angolan war, as we will see in Sousa Jamba's novel *Patriots* (1990).

As with Ngũgĩ wa Thiong'o and Ousmane Sembène, Angolan intellectuals were concerned with understanding the role that the medium and language of artistic endeavor had in making their works accessible to a larger local and international public, connecting them with the peasantry and the working class, as well as with anti-imperialist struggles around the world. In the context of an already ideologically polarized Cold War world, the Portuguese language confined the circulation of many of these writers' works to Portugal and its (former) colonies. Therefore, both translation and participation in multilingual cultural venues were important strategies in raising the visibility of the Angolan struggle. The international profile of Agostinho Neto, then an imprisoned poet and later the first president of Angola, gained from the publication of a collection of poems entitled *Sacred Hope* (1974) in English translation.[17] Several of the literary venues discussed in part I of this book were also conduits for the translation and dissemination of Angolan literature, therefore making the Angolans' plight during the war better known on Pan-African, tricontinental, or internationalist circuits. For instance, Mário Pinto de Andrade served as the private secretary of Alioune Diop and later as the editor in chief for *Présence Africaine*.[18] The July 1972 issue of *Lotus: Afro-Asian Writings* featured a special section on Angola, with translated poems by Neto, Fernando Costa Andrade, and António Jacinto, as well as a chapter from Fernando de Castro Soromenho's novel *Camaxilo*.[19] The 1979 conference of the Afro-Asian Writers Association brought to Luanda sympathetic writers from around the world.

Yet the relatively small international readership supportive of the anti-imperial struggle was hardly the only audience Angola's writers wanted to address. The function of the writer in a society in the process of revolutionary transformation features prominently in the literary works discussed in this chapter. Both Neto and Jonas Savimbi—the former with more success, the latter with less—assumed the mantle of popular poets energizing their constituencies. For instance, Neto's poem "Havemos de Voltar" (We must return), written in prison, became a popular song with MPLA soldiers, as did several of his later creations.[20] In her pathbreaking study *The People's Right to the Novel: War in the Postcolony*, Eleni Coundouriotis points out that, unlike the postcolonial bildungsroman, which is oftentimes pitched to or easily assimilated by an international audience, the war novel in Africa is "introverted," focused on a "people's history" and addressing a collective "'we' who experienced the war and must come to recognize the correspondences across the many and varied stories of war."[21] This turn to national audiences is visible in both the Angolan and South African works examined here.

South Africa's participation in the Angolan war has generated a number of memoirs and fictional accounts most often dismissed as partisan state propaganda—and with good reason. They comprise military history books that eulogize the role of combatants, such as Jan Breytenbach's *Forged in Battle* (1986).

Films like *Boetie gaan border toe* (1984) and *Boetie op manoeuvers* (1985) romanticize the war by portraying the conduct of SADF soldiers as chivalrous. *Grensliteratuur*, or border literature, is a body of writing representing fictionalized accounts penned mostly by white Afrikaner conscripts. Critics still debate the literary value and ideological orientation of these texts: while some consider them to be the expression of bourgeois political interests, others have pointed out the intellectual complexity and antiapartheid message expressed by works like Alexander Strachan's *'n Wêreld sonder grense* (1983), Louis Kruger's *'n Basis oorkant die grens* (1984), or Gawie Kellerman's *Wie de hel het jou vertel?* (1988).[22] Indeed, not all literature written by former conscripts should be dismissed as propaganda. As we will see later on, Mark Behr's novel *The Smell of Apples* works to dismantle the effects of ideology and its long-lasting impact on conscripts, who were interpellated by the state as defenders of the white republic from the "godless" forces of communism.[23] The corpus of works that, in the 1980s, challenged South Africa's increasing militarization is predominantly written in Afrikaans; it comprises short stories like Koos Prinsloo's "Grensverhaal" (1987) and George Weideman's collection *Tuin van klip en vuur* (1983), as well as plays like Deon Opperman's *Môre is 'n lang dag* (1986).[24] A smaller number of works were published in English, among them Peter Wilhelm's *LM and Other Stories* (1975) and *At the End of a War* (1981) and Damon Galgut's *The Beautiful Screaming of Pigs* (1991). These texts often reflect the young men's moral dilemma of choosing among three unappealing options: compulsory military service, which by the 1980s amounted to a two-year conscription, with a minimum of six months in or near the Operational Zone on the border; an increasingly longer prison term for those refusing enrollment; or self-imposed exile.[25] Those unaware of the full ramifications of their decision, who reached the border without comprehending that military service demanded full ideological acquiescence and support of the status quo, were often permanently scarred by the waste of lives and senseless violence.

More recently, a growing body of memoirs as well as visual material assembled on the internet by veterans attests to the different ways in which ex-combatants are dealing with trauma, ambivalence, and, in some cases, nostalgia for the apartheid period. A compilation of soldiers' stories and anecdotes significantly entitled *An Unpopular War: From Afkak to Bosbefok; Voices of South African National Servicemen* (edited by J. H. Thomson, 2006), which joined ranks with Clive Holt's *At Thy Call We Did Not Falter* (2005) and Rick Andrew's *Buried in the Sky* (2001), signaled a turn in public memory toward the events of the Angolan war in the new millennium. These books revisit the battlefield not only to establish the events but also to criticize the war in a tone that few contemporary firsthand or fictional accounts had the courage to adopt.[26] In 2011 Anthony Akerman bemoaned the lack of memoirs and literature written by black South Africans; however, it is worth noting that the participation of MK soldiers in Angola features prominently in Mandla Langa's novel *The Memory of Stones* (2000), Mongane Wally Serote's *Scatter the Ashes and Go* (2002), and Niq Mhlongo's *Way Back Home* (2013), as well as in flashbacks in Serote's *Rumours* (2013).[27] The publication of these memoirs and fictional works coincides with the emergence of what promises to become a sustained scholarly interest in South Africa's participation in the Angolan war.

## Physical Borders and Mental Boundaries

Given that the South African government labeled the conflict in which they were involved "the Border War"—a euphemism that dissimulated its larger spatial and political implications—borders, both as real spaces and as mental constructs, represent the conflict's most obvious thematic expression in literary works. The Border War was a conflict with multiple dimensions, simultaneously a real event with a real location on the border between Namibia and Angola and a distant, imprecise setting, nonetheless made continuously present through its psychological and ideological proximity. Akerman's play *Somewhere on the Border* masterfully evokes the overlap of several conceptualizations of the border. While the territorial boundary and the infamous Caprivi Strip (used by the SADF for training and military experiments) were concrete topographies, they became culturally vague locations in the name of preserving military secrets. The conversation between two conscripts, Campbell and Marais, at the end of act 1, scene 3, blends into a radio broadcast for servicemen, which purports to keep them in touch with their families: a card with the family's prayers and good wishes is read for "Corporal Brian Adams, somewhere on the border."[28] Paradoxically, the lack of concrete information about the conscripts' real place of deployment, compounded with radio and TV broadcasts that glorified and romanticized the frontier as a space of fabulous military exploits, turned the border into a topography of permanent psychological proximity, in which every white member of the nation had a stake.[29]

For most conscripts, it was a dreaded location they hoped to avoid. Their commanding officers, like the brutalizing Kotze in Akerman's play, regard the Operational Zone as a circumstance that "sorts out the weeds from the men"—distinguishing those who have internalized the regime's militarized code of masculinity from the psychologically weak who go *bosbefok*.[30] The proximity of the border conflict, and implicitly of the Cold War, is reflected in its inscription on the body, a biological frontier demarcating the margins of the community. As with many nationalist discourses, the body politic is imagined as a feminized entity whose defense is entrusted to "real men" and whose preservation is intimately connected with the biological survival and reproduction of the ethnic and racial group. Kotze describes the threat posed by the enemy as a violation of the female members of the white community: "If that enemy get past you, he's going to rape your mother and your sister and burn your house," he states, suggesting that the reproductive power of the white nation would be seized by the enemy.[31] More important, biological procreation becomes synonymous with ideological reproduction, hence the imperative to stem communism by barring politically unsound marriages: "Do you want your sister to marry a Russian?" Kotze asks rhetorically, suggesting that such an alliance would represent the ultimate Cold War defeat of white South Africa.[32] The numerous sexual innuendos, jokes, and machismo tales shared by the conscripts in the play highlight that the stakes involve control over the reproductive capacity of the nation, signaling that the *swart* and rooi gevaar were seen as a combined assault on the ethnic, racial, and ideological borders of the community.[33]

Aside from grensliteratuur that makes the Border War its central concern, we find echoes of the conflict in unexpected novels. Nadine Gordimer's *July's People*, a novel that imagines a white family's ways of coping with a generalized antiapartheid revolution, does not address the Border War or the larger Cold War context directly. However, the author's experience of the militarization of the media in the late 1970s must have informed her rendering of the broadcasts in the novel: Maureen and Bam are fascinated by the alternation of martial sounds and complete silence emanating from their radio set. The descriptions of both MARNET, the Military Area Radio Network, "that had been developed originally to supplement vulnerable telephone communications on the border in the Namibian war, and lately extended to the whole country," and the civilian radio station that "had always concealed so much," even when it broadcast "stolidly bureaucratic-sounding reports quoting 'authoritative sources,'" render visible the role of the media in creating and elaborating a war-zone imaginary.[34] In fact, we could argue that Gordimer imagined the apocalyptic scenario in order to criticize the government's "total onslaught" premise.[35] The Border War was not only a flesh-and-blood confrontation; it became a mental landscape, with the frontier represented by government propaganda as a vulnerable topography of alien encroachment and cultural subversion. Mathilde Rogez has argued that we could read J. M. Coetzee's *Waiting for the Barbarians* in a similar vein: the torture and violence that take place on the frontier of an unnamed empire are the emanation of a nation that feels itself under siege.[36]

The object of this exercise is not simply to enumerate and recuperate a corpus of texts that might have fallen into oblivion or that have never been scrutinized from this angle. These literary texts also illuminate a complicated political landscape created by the border conflict. The convergence of various forces in Angola shows that the Cold War political imaginary is not organized into neat categories, an us-versus-them scenario, but includes numerous blurred allegiances and circumstantial alliances. While the conscripts in Akerman's play are encouraged to think of themselves as a tightly knit unit, there are internal tensions between the English-speaking Campbell's initial antiwar attitude and the Afrikaner soldiers' ideological support of the Border War, between the Jewish conscript Levitt's attempts to integrate and Mowbray's relentless anti-Semitism, between Marais's religious conviction that innocent children should be spared and Kotze's indiscriminate racism, and even between Campbell's initial pacifist, culture-loving attitude and the individualistic survival mode he adopts by the end of the play. Campbell sides with a black man at the beginning of the play but shirks all responsibility for the civilian massacre by the final act. A literary work like *Somewhere on the Border* reminds us that what purports to be a united ideological front (the generic supporters of Western values against the minions of communism, in this case) is crisscrossed by various interests, which in southern Africa are further multiplied by the historical fault lines and bridges that separate or unite identities.

### From the Iron Curtain to Collapsing Ideological Borders

If the term *Iron Curtain*—which was put in circulation by Winston Churchill in 1946—suggests impassable ideological barriers between the West and the Eastern Bloc, the war in Angola highlights fractures within communities that were supposed to be on the same side and affinities between groups portrayed as the absolute opposite of each other. "Communism [is] the highest form of capitalism," the head of the South African Security Branch, Major-General Hendrik van den Bergh, declared in 1966, in a nonchalant statement that short-circuited the staple binaries of Cold War discourse.[37] The officer's political illiteracy aside, his oxymoronic formulation may actually unwittingly reveal points of convergence in the discursive strategies churned out by supporters of communism and capitalism alike. Singular as it might seem, this curious little sentence speaks of a larger conundrum that placed South Africa in an uneasy ideological spot between the Scylla and Charybdis of the Cold War. With its uncomfortable position in relation to Western capitalism and Soviet communism, South Africa becomes a privileged site for exploring Cold War contradictions.

These contradictions become most explicit in the simplified ideological positions distilled for young Afrikaners, who were trained into proper citizens of the nation during the apartheid years. This ideological battle with the Soviet power did not entail a perfect alignment between South African and American foreign policy. Both historical documents and, more importantly for this argument, literary texts reflect the disdain the Pretoria rulers had for their American counterparts, whom they perceived as weakened and needlessly encumbered by multiculturalism and human rights concerns. A study of Cold War ideologies as reflected in South African and Angolan literature renders a much more complex picture than a bipolar confrontation between supporters of communism and capitalism. Several discourses rooted in Cold War politics existed simultaneously and interacted with each other in ways that are quite revealing at both the local and the global levels.

The dilemma that communism and capitalism posed for the old Pretoria government arose from the National Party's economic and cultural values. On the one hand, South Africa had the highest percentage of state-owned companies outside of the socialist bloc, making the country dangerously akin to socialist polities.[38] On the other hand, the Afrikaner abhorrence of leftist atheism and embrace of the cultural values of the West (the government saw itself as a last bastion defending Occidental values in Africa) led South Africa to reject the USSR and its allies as the ultimate enemies. The Marxist orientation of many freedom fighters provided sufficient grounds for the apartheid government to label the African National Congress (ANC) and the South African Communist Party (SACP) as puppet extensions of the Kremlin authorities. The conundrum was not solved but merely deferred by the options opened up in the 1990s. As the so-called Second World bid farewell to communist utopias with previously unsuspected alacrity, there was no credible socialist model left standing after 1989 for the leftist members of the post-1994 government. Under pressure to make the South African economy viable and to garner Western support, the ANC changed its leftist discourse to open up to the demands of an increasingly integrated global economy, and South African society as a whole deferred the debate on the Cold War's impact on its cultural imaginary. Concerned with the more pressing goal of decolonizing knowledge systems previously controlled by the apartheid regime, cultural and literary criticism left Cold War tensions and incongruences brewing below the surface.

Mark Behr's novel *The Smell of Apples* is one of the few 1990s fictional works that explicitly foreground the impact of Cold War rhetoric on South African children. Marnus Erasmus, its central character, moves from internalizing the values of Afrikanerdom to acting them out in the war against MPLA and Cuban forces in Angola. The narrative straddles two time frames: while most of the events take place in December 1973, as eleven-year-old Marnus prepares for the end of the school year and the Christmas vacation ahead of him, this story line is interspersed with 1988 episodes from Marnus's service in the army during South Africa's secret war in Angola. Much of the novel's narrative energy is directed at unmasking the nationalist and masculinist culture in which Afrikaner children were raised.

The child of the youngest general in the SADF and of an opera singer turned dedicated housewife, Marnus trusts the political knowledge he imbibes from his parents and never fails to reproduce it for the benefit of the readers: "Dad says things are looking bad up north. They've even started planting bombs in Southwest Africa. Things are worse than when Dad was in Rhodesia. The Communists muddle up people's brains so that in the end you can't trust anyone. The Communists indoctrinate everyone."[39] Indoctrinated himself with the values of Afrikanerdom, Marnus is less a self-determined agent than a performer of the role of obedient, respectful, and hard-working child assigned to him by his parents. "Quietpoliteandinthebackground," Marnus repeats to himself over and over again, thus internalizing the conduct rules set out by his parents and schoolteachers.

In proposing national narratives and devising role models for youngsters to enact, state ideology reveals its inner contradictions. To oppose communism during the Cold War meant to embrace Western capitalist culture. Yet the conservative Christian nationalist outlook of the Erasmus family (and of Afrikaner nationalists in general) rejects the West as debauched and immoral. American politics are regarded as muddled backwaters, with leaders lacking the vision they preach to their allies: "Dad says Nixon will be out of the White House before Christmas and it looks like the Americans are going to lose the war against the communists in Vietnam. Dad says it's typical of the Americans to try and prescribe to the Republic how we should run our country while their own president is such a rubbish. Dad says you don't tell someone else how to make his bed when your own house looks like a pigsty."[40]

Aside from the repeated assertion of paternal authority, as Marnus argues by means of quotation, what transpires from this fragment is South Africa's imperfect alignment with the American camp within the binaries established by the Cold War. General Erasmus treats "communist terrorists" like hunting trophies (he tortures, murders, and displays them for photo shoots) without any signs of uneasiness, yet his Christian morality shivers at the thought of entering a jazz bar—a site of American depravity. Afrikaner culture shared strategies and discursive patterns with the very ideologies it combated most fiercely.

Thus, many of its authoritative patterns are characteristic not only of patriarchal, militarist systems but also of the communist dictatorships they despised and feared so much.

On the Angolan side, two novels—Pepetela's *Mayombe* (1980) and Sousa Jamba's *Patriots* (1990)—take up the topic of problematic binaries, reductive categories, and confused ideological affiliation. Although Pepetela wrote *Mayombe* in the early 1970s, before Angola had freed itself from Portuguese colonial domination, and although it attends to the challenges of the liberation struggle, it is a novel of the Cold War. Its focus on leftist revolutionary approaches (How does a country transcend ethnic divisions? What is the role of the party as a vanguard of the revolution?) makes it relevant to the problems that beset the MPLA as it attempted to govern Angola while fighting against UNITA and its foreign supporters. Further proof of the book's relevance comes from the support it received from Angola's postindependence leader, Agostinho Neto, despite opposition to its publication from an influential group within the MPLA leadership.[41]

The challenging aspect that rankled MPLA officials arises from Pepetela's recognition of blurred lines of allegiance in a world that insisted on simplifying Manichean dichotomies. A liberation movement does not comprise only good people fighting against despicable enemies; being part of a guerrilla movement does not guarantee uniform ideology within the group. This theme is present from the first lines of the novel, as the fighter dubbed Theory, although wounded and in pain, wishes to prove himself a worthy member of the group. In doing so, he hopes to transcend "the Manichean Universe" and find "room for maybe," for people like him, of mixed white and black ancestry, who could not neatly fit into predetermined categories:[42] "Is it my fault if men insist on purity and reject compounds? Am I the one who must turn me into a yes or a no? Or must men accept the maybe? In the face of this essential problem, people are divided in my view into two categories: Manicheans and the rest. It is worth explaining that the rest are rare; the World generally is Manichean."[43]

Here the arbitrariness of racial categories stands in for other binaries as well. The alienating role of labels and categories is amplified throughout the novel to include ethnic, class, and gendered identities. Thus, the novel is a Cold War text in the sense that it wrestles with the limitations of labels and categories and the harmful inflexibility of political lines created by ironclad ideologies.

To respond to these challenges, Pepetela brings readers to the vast immensity of the forest of Mayombe, in the Cabinda enclave of Angola, where a guerrilla group affiliated with the MPLA is engaged in sabotage actions against the

Portuguese colonial authorities and is forging ties with the local community to raise their anticolonial consciousness. While official narratives that retrospectively address the anticolonial struggle in postindependence states almost always gloss over tensions within the new nation, Pepetela, drawing on his experience as an MPLA fighter, foregrounds the cracks in the national narrative, fissures that became magnified after the collapse of the Portuguese empire. There is deep suspicion between the Kimbundu, Ovimbundu, and Bakongo members of the group, despite the Commissar's attempts to raise their consciousness and transcend ethnic divisions. Furthermore, the peasant fighters are suspicious of their educated comrades who tend to occupy command positions. The narrative strategies reflect the difficulty of harmonizing numerous distinct perspectives on the struggle. Several guerrillas become point-of-view narrators, with the switch self-reflexively marked in the text: the declaration "I, the narrator, am Theory" is the first of numerous italicized passages in which Theory, Miracle, New World, Muatianvua, Andre, Stores Chief, Operations Chief, Struggle, and finally the Political Commissar take on the mantle of narrator. The rest of the novel embraces a third-person omniscient perspective, as if attempting to harmonize the different perspectives. It is worth noting that a reductive reading of the text, maybe emphasizing the love triangle that is prefigured and dismissed, would focus on Fearless, the guerrilla group's leader; Ondine, the only female character; and the young Political Commissar as protagonists. By denying the first two a role in the narrative relay and by allowing the Political Commissar only the narration of the epilogue, Pepetela emphasizes the need to incorporate as many voices as possible, even if, or especially when, their perspective is intolerant and problematic.

Indeed, the function of literature in a time of war and revolution is at the heart of Pepetela's novel, as the author implicitly reflects on his own choices as a white Angolan man of Portuguese descent, choices that are distilled through the perspective of one of the book's main characters. For Fearless, the group's Commander, literature and revolution bifurcate as two options in life: "As I was not the type to remain just making up stories, I had only two courses open in life: to write them or to live them. The Revolution gave me an opportunity to create them in action. If it had not been for the revolution, I should certainly have ended up a writer."[44]

Pepetela reconciled these choices with the writing of *Mayombe*, a novel that has been variously characterized as a narrative of "epic proportions"; "a broad examination of national culture, past and present, with an eye to the construction of a coherent, multifaceted Angolan self-awareness and mythology"; and a "polyglottic arrangement" of different narrative perspectives that questions the ideological motivations of the diverse characters, while also permitting "a narrative self-representation of [the Angolan] nation within a type of collective discourse."[45]

The role of culture in the formation of a new national consciousness is articulated in terms that resonate with black intellectuals involved in decolonization struggles, especially Frantz Fanon and Amílcar Cabral, while also echoing the Marxist-Leninist classics. Several chapters, especially those staging discussions between Fearless and the Commissar, read as fictionalized versions of poignant theoretical questions: the role of intellectuals within the party, charismatic leaders and their ability to change the world, the blurred lines between religious and revolutionary institutions, the potentially perilous function of utopian belief in a perfect postcolonial society, nation building and ethnic tensions, class and nationalism, discipline within the movement, dogmatism and centralism and their challenges to equal participation, and revolutionary commitment and disillusionment.[46] The novel ends with Fearless sacrificing himself for the success of the mission. As such, the Commissar must travel to take up the former's position with a different group of MPLA guerrillas. The stress falls on individual transformation while preserving group coherence: "From the depths of Bie, a thousand kilometers from Mayombe, after a month's marching, surrounded by new friends, where I came to take the place that he had not filled, I contemplate the past and the future. And I see how ludicrous is the existence of an individual. However, it is what marks the passage of time."[47]

As the Commissar contemplates the trajectory of individual versus national history, his words close the world of the novel but keep open the debate about the function of literature and individual writers in the formation of national culture. Pepetela implies that narratives need to be focalized by individuals whose lived experience of history is necessarily idiosyncratic and temporally bound by a life span, in nuanced terms that official history can never attain.

Yet, at the same time, how does one write with an eye to representing the entire group instead of focusing on personal tribulations? For Fanon, the revolution entails the development of inclusive cultural forms with a focus on the epic and drama, to the exclusion of lighthearted genres such as comedy and farce. The emphasis moves away from "the intellectual's tormented conscience," and by discarding its characteristics of "despair and revolt," drama becomes "the people's daily lot, . . . part of an action in the making or already in progress."[48] Fanon's take becomes amplified and detailed in Ngũgĩ wa Thiong'o's criticism of the literature of the petite bourgeoisie, with its "vacillating mentality, the evasive self-contemplation, the existential anguished human condition, or [its] man-torn-between-two-worlds-facedness."[49] Both Fanon and Cabral have drawn attention to the class-based character of national culture, insisting that, in order to be effective, literature must represent the mass of the people, a desideratum that Pepetela's work embodies.⁵⁰

Sousa Jamba's *Patriots* (1990) is the natural interlocutor to Pepetela's novel, even if it was published a decade after *Mayombe*, at a time when the hot Cold War conflict in Angola was cooling down owing to the withdrawal of the Cuban and South African troops. *Patriots*, written from a UNITA perspective, reveals a similarly ideologically scrambled society. It focuses on the journey of a young man, Hosi Mbueti, who travels from the relative safety of exile in Zambia to his country of birth, Angola, to fight alongside the UNITA troops. Serving as narrator for most of the novel, and sharing numerous biographical details with the writer, Hosi begins as a naive yet trustworthy narrator; however, using irony, Jamba distances Hosi from the reader when his intellectually threadbare meditations yet confident dreams of authorial fame are revealed. If the naive young man originally sees ironclad forms of affiliation—communities of patriotic citizens separated from traitors by an ideological chasm—he later comes to understand the complex nature of the war in Angola.

In the first part of the novel, the characters find reassurance in ethnic ties that are supposed to clarify political and ideological belonging: "'Yeah, I am an Ovimbundu,' Hosi said. 'There is no place for me in the MPLA.'"⁵¹ Similarly, the teacher Xavier Ramos is won over to the FNLA when a relative speaks warmly about the glorious past of the Bakongo. Meanwhile, the characters of mixed ancestry find the Marxist internationalist ideology of the MPLA, with its disdain of ethnonationalism and emphasis on class-based alliances, the most reassuring and accepting of them. However, these comforting ethnic and political allegiances dissipate in the second part of the novel, as confusion becomes widespread. Despite detesting the Soviet model, UNITA party structures include a commissar in charge of the ideological training of the recruits, who introduces himself as "Comrade Second Lieutenant Raimundo."⁵² Notwithstanding his preference for communist nomenclature, the commissar declares that marijuana "is for the MPLA soldiers, the Cubans, the Soviets and all the dogs furthering Soviet imperialism."⁵³ As a new recruit, Hosi is told to read a brochure entitled UNITA—*the Constitution and Statute of Internal Regulations*, which proclaims, similarly to the ANC-SACP alliance in South Africa, that the "national and democratic revolution must be followed by a socialist revolution."⁵⁴ The perplexing declaration makes Hosi consider his political beliefs in a new light:

> He felt very confused. He asked himself whether UNITA was socialist or capitalist. From what he had read, it struck him that it was socialist....

Hosi subscribed to UNITA because he was Ovimbundu, but he liked to think that part of the reason for his loyalty was ideological: the MPLA stood for communism, which was evil, while UNITA stood for democracy, which was good. Now, as he lay on the bed, he felt confused. He asked himself why the booklet went on about socialism. The MPLA talked about creating a new man—one who was revolutionary and versed in Marxism. UNITA too talked of creating a new man—one who was versed in socialism and in the Paramount Thought, for that was how the ideas of the Elder were described.[55]

Hosi is disoriented by the amalgamation of Marxist, socialist, communist, and capitalist ideology and religious beliefs in his country as well as by the slippage in everyday parlance between ideological outlooks and the political forms they take. Although the main two warring political entities, with the help of their international supporters, attempt to present their political stances as diametrically opposite, Hosi's lived experience dismantles this framework. He hopes to obtain clarity like his compatriots—by joining the struggle. Yet his idealist thoughts about the war are quickly dispelled when he realizes the ease with which combatants opportunistically switch sides. The similarity between the terror tactics employed by UNITA's and MPLA's secret police as well as peasants' disenchantment with revolutionary ideology in comparison to materialistic concerns (they care only about getting radios and tape recorders) serves to highlight how self-interest is the narrative's true driving force. Throughout the novel the characters prioritize individual concerns: obtaining promotions, protecting loved ones, finding glory in ascetic forms of ideological purity, and even writing are all revealed to be self-serving.

The full meaning of the novel's title transpires in the concluding section, a purloined piece of literature, namely, the diary of Hosi's friend Raul. If at the beginning of the text we might have suspected that the titular patriots were those, like Hosi, fighting on the side of UNITA, the denouement clarifies Jamba's ironic take: "Who is a true patriot? Of course, the number one patriots are the Elders, and all those who aspire to be true patriots should emulate them.... They love Angola so much. How I wish we could all love Angola as much as they do!"[56] The switch from the singular form "the Elder," which references Savimbi in UNITA political discourse, to the plural form "the Elders" indicates that other Angolan political leaders were similarly made the subjects of meaningless hagiography. Indirectly, Agostinho Neto is cast as the other protagonist in the melodrama of empty patriotic discourse that has torn Angola apart.

Both the MPLA and UNITA embraced the tradition of the *écrivain engagé* (engaged writer), although in Jamba's novel this literary mold is depicted as more akin to a personality cult. Both parties proclaimed their political leader the most accomplished poet, an insistence that reminds us that literature played an important role in the Cold War. Reducing art to ideological guidelines, various characters perceive poetry as both a measurement of patriotic character and an activity that can influence the future: "Debora thought for a while and then said: 'There are too many poets in Angola. That is why we have problems. We just need one leading poet, or one leading thinker, and the rest of us should follow. Then there will be peace. As it is now, you just have to switch on the radio to see the confusion. The people in Luanda are going on about this and the people in Jamba are going on about that.'"[57]

If, in Debora's interpretation, one of the most devastating Cold War conflicts could be brought to an end by setting a single literary model, then poetry is both weaponized as an ideological tool and simultaneously transformed into an instrument of censorship. Jamba seems to be skeptical of the *littérature engagée* model, which, in his novel, produces only self-involved drivel and an inflated ego in its practitioners.

Jamba's treatment of literature moves between modernist belief in the uncensored coexistence of a plurality of literary forms not beholden to any political authority and criticism of the self-interested dreams of characters with poetic aspirations. Hosi holds such ambitions himself: the hope that UNITA would send him to the United Kingdom to study, rather than political commitment, is what draws him from Zambia to Angola: "He wanted to pen novels that would not only win literary prizes but put African writers of repute, such as Achebe, Ngugi and Laye, to shame. His novels would lay bare the core of the African soul to the world, would be part of school syllabuses and would encourage students the world over to delve into his life in order to understand his work."[58]

Hosi's literary dreams switch quickly from inclusive representation of a putative "African soul" to narcissistic self-representation. It is "the intellectual's tormented conscience" and the "evasive self-contemplation," which Fanon and Ngũgĩ, respectively, had discarded as inappropriate topics of revolutionary literature, that are being satirized here as caricatures of modernist self-aggrandizing posturing.[59] While it is not fully clear from the text, Jamba could be satirizing the modernist model of literary autonomy, centered on the figure of the writer not beholden to any political authority. For instance, Hosi finds out that other UNITA soldiers are eager to tell him their stories because they see him as "a political virgin," "a *tabula rasa*—a blank sheet waiting to be filled in on the principles of the struggle."[60] In that case, neither the model of the committed writer nor that of the autonomous author—both of which are discussed in detail in chapter 1—prevails in Jamba's novel.

Pepetela, Jamba, and Behr are examples of writers who draw on realist and modernist strategies—while also vigorously questioning the function of literature at a time of war—to present a much more nuanced Cold War landscape.

## Secrets and Betrayal as Challenges to the Linear Plot

Another topos of Cold War culture that we can trace in southern African texts consists of secrets, which range from suppressed military intelligence to destructive personal and family secrets. The pervasive atmosphere of fear and suspicion, directed against internal and external enemies, amplifies secrecy as a thematic concern. Compared to numerous overlooked Cold War literary themes, scholars have paid abundant attention to the proliferation of secrets, intrigue, and espionage in American and British fiction.[61] The works of Graham Greene, Ken Follett, Dashiell Hammett, and John le Carré, as well as spy films such as the popular James Bond series, have endorsed the idea of a world climate of distrust best navigated by inquisitive minds that look beyond appearances.

In an article concerned with periodizing American literature in relation to the Cold War, Ann Douglas anchors cultural phenomena usually ascribed to postmodern sensibility in the Cold War mentality: the perceived uncertainty of knowledge, paradoxically augmented by the bombardment with information through the development of new media; the disenchantment with grand narratives, especially those offered by the state; the paranoia about external foes and even more insidious internal enemies, as illustrated by the Red Scare in the United States; and anxiety about the unreliability of one's own body when subjected to psychological or biochemical experimentation are all features of the climate of political mistrust induced by the Cold War.[62]

A similar atmosphere of secrecy characterized South African culture during the Border War. Apartheid media long denied or downplayed the country's participation in this conflict.[63] The presence of South African troops north of the Namibian border was contradicted or put down to "preemptive strikes" against PLAN and MK bases that allegedly threatened to bring communism and "total onslaught" into South Africa.[64] In fact, a quasi-blackout was in effect in the media, with only selective access to information granted to a few skilled propaganda spinners. It went from denial of the government's military intervention in 1975 to limited and well-orchestrated releases of news during the 1980s. Historians complain about the lack of verifiable information at the beginning of this conflict, as each of the warring parties refused to allow foreign correspondents on the battlefield, and each deployed propaganda machines that aimed to aggrandize its victories, project a higher popularity, and conceal unorthodox or covert help. This was due, in part, to the fact that an acknowledged collaboration with the racist apartheid regime would have tainted the image of both UNITA and the United States in 1975. Operation Savannah, as the South African offensive was known to the military leadership, was kept secret until leaked by journalists to the Western press in November 1975.[65] In the following years, the apartheid state, with the help of the South African Broadcast Corporation (SABC), presented events that fit neatly into the grander narrative of an apartheid state that did not behave aggressively toward its neighbors but merely defended its frontiers—a state that made overt attempts at African détente. In the 1980s South African television and radio programs started to incorporate references to the war in which the communist danger was magnified while the patriotism and devotion of the conscripts were abundantly praised.[66]

Reflecting this distrust of official media, the radio no longer functions as a source of reliable information in Behr's *The Smell of Apples*: "I remember Xangongo, New Year '84. We were two hundred kilometres inside Angola, listening to the Voice of America. Then Dad's voice came over the airwaves, and everyone looked at me. He was telling the world that there wasn't a single South African soldier inside Angola. The rest of the interview was lost, as everyone around the radio roared with laughter."[67] This passage highlights the magnitude of image construction in the South African media as well as the role of secrets—military and personal—in the structure of the novel. As Rita Barnard has argued, both the Erasmus family microcosm and the Afrikaner macrocosm rely on a code of secrecy that binds characters together.[68] Kerry Bystrom has elucidated the importance of secret alliances between governments that pretended to have no contact during the Cold War. The relationship between Marnus's father and the visiting Chilean general articulates "Augusto Pinochet's Chile as an uncanny double for apartheid South Africa," gesturing toward "Cold War anticommunist military and political networks—often routed through the United States but also existing bilaterally among Argentina, Brazil, Chile, Uruguay, Paraguay, and South Africa—that allowed for the circulation of both technologies and cultures of state-sponsored terror."[69]

The conflict in Angola cannot be narrated through a linear, continuous narrative arc, and writers turned to fragmented plot structures to address the disorienting secrets their protagonists (and readers) have to parse. This is what the failed bildungsroman structure of *The Smell of Apples* signifies: Marnus dies during the Cuban attack on the Calueque dam in May 1988, expecting to "escape from history" following his death. However, this release from history does not happen in the novel. The oppressive structures and binaries created by apartheid, various forms of imperialism, and the Cold War are reinforced: the narrative returns to the 1973 events and ends with Marnus's collusion with his father's ideals and his implicit surrender to a government that militarizes young boys while mentally and physically violating them. This ending comes on the heels of a bombardment with slogans and half-processed ideological sound bites to which Marnus and his companions have been subjected at home, at school, in church, in the army, and through the media.

Under this ideological bombardment from all sides, the stakes of identifying allies versus enemies (especially when the latter appeared as potential supporters) increased. For many leftists (and this holds especially true for South African Marxists), Western values were closely aligned with colonial exploitation and hence untrustworthy. As Gordimer observed, in the dualistic imaginary generated by the polarized Cold War political field, for most leftists in South Africa the Western world was synonymous with imperialism and therefore antagonistic to the antiapartheid struggle: "It is difficult to point out to black South Africans that the forms of Western capitalism are changing towards a broad social justice in the example of countries like Sweden, Denmark, Holland, and Austria, with their mixed welfare economies, when all black South Africans know of Western capitalism is political and economic terror. And this terror is not some relic of the colonial past; it is being financed now by Western democracies—concurrently with Western capitalist democracy's own evolution towards social justice."[70]

Leftist intellectuals associated with the SACP have often described apartheid as a form of internal colonialism based on the accumulation of the means of production and economic resources in the hands of a white minority, so that the capitalist exploitation of the black majority was supported by, and in its turn maintained, racial segregation.[71]

By contrast, the socialist system in the Eastern Bloc promised values that, at least in form, stood as the opposite of the capitalist exploitation and racial discrimination witnessed in South Africa. As a result, leftist writers like Alex La Guma and Mongane Wally Serote lauded the virtues of the socialist system and presented the Soviet Union and the Eastern Bloc as beacons of hope for anticolonial struggles. The USSR adopted the role of defender of the oppressed across the globe. State propaganda pointed out that the Soviet Union was built on anticolonial principles: it had putatively rescued central and eastern Asian nations from the yoke of tsarist imperialism and given them an equal place among the other republics. As La Guma explained, the model set by the USSR promised to fast-forward the creation of societies organized on socialist principles and to level the field by equaling or surpassing the economic development of Occidental powers: "One of the most important developments of the Great October Revolution for the colonial countries was the feasibility of liberated colonies advancing towards socialism without going through the stage of capitalism."[72] In La Guma's eyes, the merits of the Soviet system were both material (the seemingly fulfilled and surpassed five-year-plan targets) and philosophical (the model of development it offered for colonized nations). The material and ideological support that the Soviet Union and other countries from the Eastern Bloc delivered to decolonization struggles in the Southern Hemisphere gave credence to this view. Indeed, the ANC-SACP alliance received financial support, military aid in the form of weapons and training facilities, and educational assistance for cadres who wished to study.[73] However, recent research has questioned the disinterestedness of the Soviet Union's support, pointing to the political capital gained by the Kremlin leaders among Third World nations and the socialist power's intentions of expanding its global sphere of influence.[74] Furthermore, recent research on Eastern European cultures has developed the idea that the Soviet Union was an imperial power that exercised tight-fisted ideological, economic, and political control over both its component republics and the satellite states from the Eastern Bloc.[75] However, observations on the Soviet Union's imperialist role during the Cold War, a form of domination similar in many ways to that exercised by the United States, need to be formulated with particular care in the southern African political context to avoid duplicating the self-serving propaganda put forth by the Pretoria regime and UNITA, which relied on similar accusations of Soviet imperialism.

A well-orchestrated discourse that demonized the Eastern Bloc and its African supporters was meant to exonerate the South African government from its political and human rights abuses in the name of defense against a concerted attack on its borders and economic interests. The rooi gevaar and a putative "total onslaught" unleashed by the Soviet Union, which allegedly demanded a "total strategy," were the main ideological components of the paranoia whipped up by the government. News broadcasts and newspaper articles released in South Africa and abroad presented the USSR as a colonizing force that was sponsoring and fanning the flames of black nationalism in the front-line states: "Soviet colonizers" who made their way into Angola to support the fledgling MPLA government were said to represent the "biggest imperialist power the world ha[d] ever seen."[76] Through official channels and news outlets, the government attempted to persuade Western powers that South Africa was both a strategic territory that should be defended from communist encroachment and a valuable ally in the Cold War conflict. In April 1976, in an address to the American Security Council Foundation, Roelof Frederik "Pik" Botha, at that time South

Africa's ambassador to the United States, described Soviet involvement in Angola in hyperbolic terms intended to raise concern about the Eastern Bloc's interests in Africa and to link the political security of the republic to that of North America. The Russians, he warned, would "straddle Africa, divide it in two, get a thousand miles chunk of African country across, ocean to ocean. And then, at what point in time will the United States stop this? Will you stop it by the time they get to Canada?"[77] Botha's speech evokes the late nineteenth-century Anglo-French animosity and the Scramble for Africa as the two powers attempted to craft a large corridor of colonies across the African continent, from south to north in the case of the British Crown, and from west to east for France. Botha further insinuated that the Cold War conflict might move to Canada, on North American soil, and that the Americans and the Russians would clash in the same way in which the British and the French had fought for domination over Africa. Harnessing the memory of historical events that changed the dynamic between and status of Western powers, the authorities in Pretoria attempted to highlight white South African rulers' crucial role in the Cold War global configuration.

This disorienting ideological landscape, riddled with secrets and potentially treacherous allies, constitutes the background of Mongane Wally Serote's novel *Scatter the Ashes and Go* (2002). The first half of the novel takes place in the late 1980s and leads up to the moment of Nelson Mandela's release from prison in February 1990. Antiapartheid activists move from country to country; they live the peripatetic existence of MK cadres in exile who might meet and connect with each other in Zambia, reconnect on a sabotage mission deep within South Africa, and then miss seeing each other in Botswana, but who are bound to reassemble at one of the ANC's training camps in Angola. Oupa, the narrator, an MK cadre and commander, wonders where his love interest, Sizakele, might have met Jackie, a nurse he had known in Angola: "Sizakele said she had long ago met Junior in England, in Italy, in Portugal. Where have people met Jackie? Where have people met me? Where have people met Ralph? We are such wanderers!"[78] This spatial dispersion captures the wandering, meandering spirit of the novel and its narrative strategy. *Scatter the Ashes and Go* does not offer a traditional plot; that is replaced by Oupa's and his comrades' reflections on the goals of the antiapartheid struggle. They meditate on the facilitating synergies and the debilitating tensions arising between individual and organizational goals, on the role of personal and political friendship in the face of multifaceted forms of betrayal, and on the function of nationalism and its enabling or hindering role in ushering in a new South Africa.

The title of the novel announces a moment of impermanence, an injunction to movement and transformation, thereby sketching out a larger historical vista on southern Africa at the end of the 1980s than research concerned with national trends of literary development could hope to achieve. A telescoping narrative perspective—now zooming in on the thoughts of a character and then immediately zooming out with a comment that involves seemingly remote political actors—enjoins readers to relinquish traditional ways of thinking about South African literature, in particular, and African cultural trends, in general.

At the start of the novel, the narrator imagines his friend Vusi's state of mind shortly before the latter's death at the hands of a South African hit squad that penetrated into Zambia in the early 1990s. Despite Mandela's release from prison on February 11, 1990, and the unbanning of the ANC and the SACP, the period that immediately followed these watershed events was wrought with suspicion and tension. The antiapartheid movement engaged in negotiations with the Pretoria government while the former enemies were still conducting covert military operations. It is within this fraught context that Serote introduces the theme of insider betrayal—whether betrayal by one's own mind beset by illness and madness, treachery sown within the MK by Pretoria-trained agents, or disloyalty shown by international entities that had long acted as political supporters.[79] A hallmark of American Cold War fiction, the fear of betrayal, duplicity, and espionage seeped into the thematic content of literature of the period across the globe.[80] An *impimpi*, an informer, opens fire on the MK soldiers at night, inducing anxiety and distrust in the ANC camp in Angola:

> The comrade, no, the bandit... what are people who are treacherous called? Mpimpi?! Woke up at night, uncocked his rifle and started to shoot blindly at the sleeping comrades. Vusi remembers this very well, for, that night, very bad news had reached the camp. The news was that large demonstrations, demonstrations of thousands and thousands of Germans, in the GDR, were demanding that the communist leadership must stand down in that country. He, and other comrades, had listened to the news. Each word from the news came as a stunning blow. Blow for blow the words came stunning him, staggering him and blinding him.[81]

The juxtaposition of the two events—the government mole's murderous spree and the East German demonstrations that led to the fall of the Berlin Wall and the entire Eastern Bloc—highlights the close, fraternal relationship that ANC and SACP members imagined they had with the socialist countries and their populace. The novel dwells on stories of personal betrayal: Oupa killed the woman he loved, Naomi, because she had betrayed him by engaging in an affair with a policeman; Ndaba joins the MK training camps in Angola because his wife sold him to the security forces in an act of vengeance for his marital infidelity. In the MK camp administered by Oupa, Sarah, a government agent posing as a fellow cadre, elicits potentially dangerous information from her sexual partners. And as the narrative emphasis on the anticommunist protests in Eastern Europe suggests, betrayal by political allies is similarly taxing. Intimate ties connect people but also compromise their security. With its focus on epistemological confusion (Who is a friend, and who is a foe? What is a good political decision, and what is a destructive one?), *Scatter the Ashes and Go* is a novel of the aftermath of the antiapartheid struggle, unimaginable in the 1980s, when Serote and many of his comrades subscribed to a vision of culture as an instrument of the struggle.

In a paragraph that reflects on the shifting political landscape of the globe in the late 1980s, Oupa observes, "We had to change plans. It is not so long ago, twenty years gone by in a life, but in history it is nothing. It is not so long ago that seventy years of history told us, there was hope for the oppressed and now, slowly, that hope evaporates with one after the other of the Eastern block [sic] countries falling apart. Soon, the Soviet Union will be no more—prophets predict it in the West, the most reliable prophets, say so."[82]

By varying the length of the sentences, from a contracted format to elaborate subordinate clauses, Serote also shifts the scope of the meditation from the narrow contingencies of the antiapartheid struggle to the larger twentieth-century panorama of efforts to produce social justice. The change in tactics that the ANC-SACP coalition (and their armed branch, the MK) had to implement responded to the situation in Angola, where numerous MK soldiers were quartered, in late 1989 and early 1990. The order to move out of Angola was triggered by the change in political configurations not only in the host country but in the world as well. In the aftermath of the battle of Cuito Cuanavale, despite the heavy losses incurred by UNITA and their SADF allies, the superpowers brokered an agreement that included the withdrawal of Cuban forces and MK bases and soldiers in Angola; in exchange, their departure allowed South West Africa to be freed from the grasp of the Pretoria government and paved the way for the country's independence under the new name of Namibia.[83]

Connecting disparate historical scenes and political landscapes, this moment in the novel clarifies the requirement of understanding the events in southern Africa in the 1980s through a Cold War lens. The elliptical formulation enjoins the reader to reflect on which events twenty and seventy years earlier, respectively, had set up a vision of freedom now challenged by a shifting global political landscape. In what way did those earlier events clash or collide with contemporary developments, creating a disorienting situation?

Twenty years before 1989, the command structures of the ANC in exile had met at the watershed Morogoro conference in April 1969. It led to the adoption of a new document and guidelines regarding the unfolding of the antiapartheid struggle. The conference took place in Tanzania, a country that under the leadership of its first president, Julius Nyerere, was developing a form of African socialism. *Ujamaa*, as Nyerere called this concept, relied on the idea of the extended family and mutual support, at both the national and the Pan-African level.[84] The development of ANC camps in the country, with educational and training facilities, spoke to a Pan-African vision of unity in the face of oppression. Serote's oblique allusion to this document summons the vision of a united Africa that in the late 1960s and 1970s was building a common front against the various forms of neocolonialism and oppression. The "Strategy and Tactics" document adopted at the Morogoro conference guided the actions of the ANC in the following two decades, until the collapse of the Eastern Bloc and the concomitant withdrawal of its financial and tactical support forced antiapartheid activists to reconceptualize their strategy.[85]

Serote suggests that it was not only the practical plans—namely, what operations were still viable and which camps and hosting countries were still available—that had to change. Shaken by the winds of history at the end of the 1980s, the ANC-SACP coalition's historical vision of a two-stage revolution, which would involve a national struggle of liberation followed by a socialist transformation of society, was no longer tenable.[86] For seventy years the Soviet Union had served not simply as a political entity to which formerly colonized nations and their political representatives often turned for support, especially during the Cold War. More important, the USSR represented a beacon of hope, a society perceived (even if incorrectly) as an example of an equalitarian form of social organization. Not only were the material benefits (training camps, support for the armed wing of the ANC, scholarships for meritorious students, financial backing, and ideological training) withdrawn with the collapse of the USSR, but the very vision that an equalitarian society could be established collapsed.[87]

An ironic substitution takes place in the previous paragraph, as the messianic vision of socialist societies (the belief that all forms of inequality can be abolished) is replaced by the so-called prophetic formulations of Western pundits. Political scientists and commentators on both sides of the Iron Curtain were notoriously unable to foresee the fall of the Eastern Bloc. Foretelling the collapse of the USSR after the democratic transformations in its Eastern

European satellites is a mean act of prediction—meager in vision and cruel in its destruction of South African hopes. This exchange of prophetic vision for charlatan predictions, and of revolutionary dreams for despair, is reinforced by the tension between the metasignificance of the USSR (beacon of hope and supporter of liberation struggles) and the Soviet Union's decision to pull out of southern Africa, while also enforcing the withdrawal of its Cuban ally.[88]

The Eastern Bloc's dismantling of the communist system and the rejection of the utopia that these countries stood for dismayed numerous South Africans. The ANC and the SACP, the two parties at the vanguard of the antiapartheid movement, accepted it only belatedly and with much reluctance. The alacrity with which these former allies discarded socialism and embraced capitalism and a Western lifestyle was initially taken as a betrayal, the unexpected transformation of an ideological sibling into a rival. The news of the fall of the communist regimes came at the same time as orders for the MK troops to leave Angola. As the host country was disentangling its politics from the Cold War stronghold, the MPLA's leftist allies were also cut loose. The "hope for the oppressed" represented by the USSR's seven-decade existence evaporated, and leftist freedom fighters had to rebuild the view of how the future would unfold.[89] "Most of the people we had sent to the Soviet Union, to the GDR, and others of those countries, are coming back. They come back with news we know, but because the news is unfamiliar, perhaps unacceptable, and also, because it has serious consequences it shocks us and presents us with too many unknowns."[90] The end of the Cold War signified that what used to be politically safe travel routes—journeys to allied countries—were reversed, and ties were severed. The diasporic networks were swiftly reconfigured within a few months.

The epistemological shock experienced by Vusi and his MK comrades mirrors Serote's experience. The writer was in Moscow during the second half of 1989, being trained to seize power in South Africa by armed struggle; when the Soviet Union disintegrated, he confessed, his whole world collapsed.[91] The ontological condition Zygmunt Bauman called "living without [a political] alternative" left numerous people around the world rudderless.[92] At the narrative level, the dismantling of physical and ideological routes that leftist activists had been taking to the Eastern Bloc translates into a directionless plot. The friendships and enmities that had animated the Cold War years entailed sharply delineated literary and political plotlines. Struggle literature, the poetry and prose written by antiapartheid intellectuals during the 1970s and 1980s, was animated by a clear sense of political goals, partnerships, and enmities and driven by the faith in the ultimate triumph of the liberation struggle.

In *Scatter the Ashes and Go*, Serote revisits the tortuous transition from struggle to postapartheid democracy, a transition that overlapped with similarly radical transformations in the Eastern Bloc—the collapse of the communist regimes and the inauguration of democratic rule for the respective countries. This period, paradoxically characterized by a simultaneous "retreat from communism and anti-communism," challenged Marxist orthodoxies at the core of the struggle and the teleological vision of revolutionary triumph.[93] The dichotomies of the Cold War era were both divisive (pressuring intellectuals into choosing one camp over the other) and reassuring. There was clarity, even if superficial, of goals and alliances: apartheid was to be defeated, and those who supported the ANC-SACP alliance belonged in the same camp. With the hindsight of more than a decade since the end of the Cold War, *Scatter the Ashes and Go* shows how blurred the lines between belonging and separateness, commitment and betrayal, actually were. This confusion comes to be represented in fiction as a disruption of the teleological narratives that had dominated the struggle literature of the 1970s and 1980s. A plotline that followed internal and external tensions, hardships overcome, and revolution finally accomplished was now no longer a plausible scenario.[94] Meandering plots and a blurred experience of temporality replaced the earlier clarity. *Scatter the Ashes and Go* revisits this period of uncertainty, the interregnum that discarded what Albie Sachs called "the tunnel vision" characterizing the years of the struggle and, as South Africa advanced toward its first free elections, gradually replaced it with newly articulated narratives, such as that of the rainbow nation.[95]

### War Ghosts and the Specter of Internationalism

The near impossibility of narrating the trauma of the war in Angola in a straightforward manner and the war's continued impact on the present are defining elements of Niq Mhlongo's novel *Way Back Home* (2013).[96] The plot moves between contemporary events in South Africa and incidents that took place in Angola in the late 1980s. In the contemporary narrative, the life of prosperous businessman Kimathi Fezile Tito begins to spiral out of control under the pressure of nightmares, a shattered family life, and addiction to alcohol, sex, and status-defining consumer goods. The chapters focused on Kimathi's challenges are interspersed with sections treating events that took place toward the end of the Cold War in an ANC prison camp in Angola, where a group of Mbokodo officers (the MK secret police) torture and kill their fellow revolutionaries with impunity. Comrades Pilate and Idi beat and torture fellow cadre Bambata into a false testimony against Comrade Mkabayi, an outspoken and fearless female soldier. Mhlongo braids together two of the most violent secrets of the MK camps in exile: the rape, torture, and murder of Comrade Mkabayi is a reference to both numerous (unreported) cases of sexual assault in the camps and to the infamous Quatro camp in Angola, where cadres suspected of being informers were imprisoned, tortured, and murdered.[97] The readers begin to suspect that there is a connection between Kimathi and his fellow tenderpreneur Ludwe, on the one hand, and the MK soldiers who in Angola go by their noms de guerre Pilate, Idi, and Bambata, on the other, even if it is not clear how the characters from the two temporal spheres map onto each other.[98]

Mhlongo's novel demonstrates that it is the failure of public memory as well as the individual wish to forget that makes it difficult for South Africans to see how the war in Angola continues to influence contemporary social and political affairs.[99] The trauma induced by witnessing and participating in senseless violence across and within combatant lines, and the secrets that military commanders of yesteryear turned politicians of today want to leave behind, trouble the emphasis on memory, witnessing, and accountability that the Truth and Reconciliation Commission was supposed to produce. Kimathi's encounter with Senami, a beautiful young woman who turns out to be the ghost of a young MK comrade who died in exile in Angola, confirms the connection between the 1988 and 2007 narratives. The plot structure, with its flashbacks and seemingly separate subplots that are reconciled only at the end, when Kimathi is revealed to be the ruthless and treacherous Comrade Pilate and the ghost of Senami/Mkabayi finds rest and vengeance as the man who raped and murdered her hangs himself, points unequivocally to the near impossibility of a linear, chronological rendering of this tragic episode of recent southern African history. Moreover, fantastic elements suggest the limitations of mimetic modes of representation.[100]

While the temporally split narrative structure seems to suggest that past and present are separate spheres, in the same way in which life and death are ontologically different categories, the trope of the ghost gives flesh to a more complex, spiritual understanding of the reverberations of actions across time. Mhlongo replaces Western ways of perceiving temporality as a string of discrete, successive moments with local epistemologies that allow for interlinked past and present events as well as here-and-there dimensions. By uniting the two narratives through traveling spirits that are able to break temporal and place barriers, Mhlongo shows us that past, present, and future are imbricated. In this respect the absence of the definite article *the* in the novel's title marks a deliberate ambiguity: the text can be read as expressing both Senami's spirit's journey to find her way back home and equivocality as to what the true home of the revolutionary struggle and its rainbow-nation aftermath is: South Africa or Angola? This ambiguity is confirmed when Kimathi, upon accompanying Senami's parents to Angola to find their daughter's remains and give them a proper burial in South Africa, exclaims, "This trip feels like I'm on my way back home."[101] Furthermore, the fusion of a construction that could have temporal connotations, "way back" in the distant past, with "home," a spatial noun that indicates a recognizable point of reference, generates the *Unheimlichkeit* that accompanies Kimathi's encounter with Senami: she is both familiar and new, and her avenging spirit drives home the moment when he betrayed the ideals of the revolution.

The use of magical realist strategies, especially the presence of the ghost, introduces an indigenous South African spiritual dimension: Kimathi suffers from mental health problems for which he is on medication, a condition that could explain his interactions with Senami as merely the result of stress-induced hallucination. However, Mhlongo does not want us to read the narrative in this light. It is the disturbance produced by the rape and murder of Senami/Mkabayi, in a place that was supposed to forward the interests of oppressed South Africans, that generates an ontological disturbance and ruptures the barrier between the world of the living and the world of the dead. Similar to the short stories of Ben Okri that address the civil war and subsequent military dictatorships in Nigeria, the presence of ghosts and spirits among the living is an expression of an ailing society in spiritual crisis.[102]

The reverberation of spirit throughout time and history is also visible in the politics of naming. Senami chose Mkabayi as her nom de guerre, thus channeling both the strength and the ambivalence evoked by the eighteenth-century Princess Mkabayi kaJama of the Zulu people.[103] The biblical resonances of Comrade Pilate's name as well as the chilling reference to Uganda's dictator Idi Amin in Comrade Idi's name put us on guard against these characters. The main character's actual name evokes a web of internationalist solidarity—Kimathi Fezile Tito, born in the Morogoro ANC camp in Tanzania, is named after the Kenyan Mau Mau leader Dedan Kimathi and his Xhosa paternal grandfather Fezile, while the family name evokes the Yugoslav leader Josip Broz Tito. Yet the most ambivalent symbolism pertains to the fictional name of the MK prison camp where Comrades Pilate and Idi rape and murder Comrade Mkabayi: Amílcar Cabral camp, with its name inspired by the revolutionary icon from Guinea-Bissau, is a stand-in for the notorious Quatro prison camp. From Kimathi's pledge of allegiance to the South African revolution and his oath to be "committed to the struggle for justice . . . in the service of the people," a pledge that serves as the novel's epigraph, we move swiftly to the torture scene at Amílcar Cabral camp in chapter 1.[104] This abrupt switch from revolutionary ideals of justice in the name of the oppressed masses to the violent disregard of human rights within the MK military machine foreshadows Mhlongo's depiction of South Africa's plunge from a cherished model of peaceful postapartheid reconciliation to a greed-driven economy ruled by a new business elite in alliance with global capitalism.[105]

Achille Mbembe has argued that necropower is historically linked to the plantation system, colonialism, and various forms of imperialism. He observed that since the mid-1970s, in the era of globalization, the power of death operates through war machines and brutal technologies of annihilation that control whole categories of people: "a patchwork of overlapping and incomplete rights to rule emerges, inextricably superimposed and tangled, in which different de facto juridical instances are geographically interwoven and plural allegiances, asymmetrical suzerainties, and enclaves abound."[106] Expanding Mbembe's model, we may consider how the war in Angola exemplified this new form of necropower: the conflict was generated by the superimposition of larger and smaller war machines, hired by or belonging to the superpowers (the United States and USSR) or their smaller local and global allies (South Africa and Cuba) and channeled through the factionalism dividing Angola (MPLA, UNITA, FNLA), further amplified through the participation of MK and PLAN forces. To invoke Mbembe again, these war machines have both "the features of political organization[s] and mercantile compan[ies]."[107] According to Mhlongo, in this zone of death, the ideological platforms of the warring parts are discarded: the Marxist ideals that baptized the camp "Amílcar Cabral" have turned into a mere facade, and the war economy in the prison camp, based on deceit, grabs for power, and transactions in human lives, is the foundation on which the equally corrupt postapartheid tenderpreneur economy is built (as Comrade Pilate and Idi metamorphose into the business tycoons Kimathi and Ludwe)—an economy that is plugged into contemporary global capitalist circuits.

A disorienting ideological topography emerges in Mhlongo's novel: Kimathi claims to have received a masters in fine arts from the "Underground People's University of Siberia," while one of his partners obtained a degree from the same (nonexistent) university with a thesis on the Soviet dissident writer Aleksandr Solzhenitsyn's *Gulag Archipelago*, a putative feat that combines Soviet internationalist solidarity with resistance to the Soviet death camps. Similarly, the revolutionary chant "a luta continua" becomes in Senami's rendering "[a] looter continua, Mr Politician!," a slogan fit for the corrupt South African economy.[108] What Albie Sachs described as the "tunnel vision" offered by the struggle years, namely, a form of commitment to the social and political goal that easily distinguishes one's comrades from one's ideological adversaries, was lost after the end of apartheid. In its stead, a muddled ideological landscape, with faded leftist aspirations in a world dominated by capitalism, emerged.

A similarly confusing ideological landscape materializes in the Angolan writer Ondjaki's novel *AvóDezanove e o Segredo do Soviético* (2008), translated into English as *Granma Nineteen and the Soviet's Secret* (2014).[109] Ondjaki reflects on his compatriots' perceptions of the Cuban and Soviet soldiers and personnel who supported the MPLA during the war. *Granma Nineteen and the Soviet's Secret* challenges the rhetoric of tricontinentalist solidarity, asking whether there was a mismatch between Cuban, Angolan, and Soviet official declarations of brotherly love and mutual support, on the one hand, and the ways in which the population on the ground perceived the presence of soldiers and personnel from fraternal nations, on the other. From a Cold War interpretive perspective, two aspects stand out in this novel: first, both child and adult characters are deeply suspicious of the Soviet military and its motives, a relationship that is spatially represented as that between foreign invaders and a resisting local population; and, second, Angolan characters create hierarchies of trust and friendship, preferring the Cubans quartered in Angola to their Soviet counterparts.

At the heart of Ondjaki's novel is a mausoleum that commemorates Agostinho Neto, Angola's first president after its independence from Portugal and one of the most important writers from this country (see figure 4.2). The mausoleum is an actual landmark in Luanda; its literary counterpart is blown up at the beginning of Ondjaki's novel. The destruction of the mausoleum becomes an expression of ordinary people's resentment of the formalized ways in which internationalist support was expressed in policies during the Cold War. When Neto passed away in Moscow in 1979, the specialists entrusted with the upkeep of Vladimir Lenin's remains also embalmed the Angolan president's body, a service they performed for leaders of several other socialist countries. According to Neto's Russian biographer, the embalmed remains were supposed to become part of an imposing memorial complex in Luanda, with a rocket-shaped mausoleum at its center and "a political-administrative complex, which [would] house the Presidential Palace, the central Committee, the Council of Ministers, and the Ministry of Defense, the security organs and the courts. The entire complex [would] occupy 152 hectares in Luanda."[110] Conceived in the grandiose yet austere style of communist buildings, the complex was an expression of ideological kinship, the repetition of Soviet memorializing methods on Angolan soil. While the mausoleum was built and, with its striking vertical profile, continues to tower over the skyline of Luanda, the rest of the complex remained

Figure 4.2. Agostinho Neto Mausoleum, Luanda, Angola. Photograph by Frank van den Bergh. © Frank van den Bergh.

unfinished. Neto's embalmed body was eventually removed from the decaying mausoleum and interred.[111]

With its rocket-shaped profile, the mausoleum is a reminder of the Cold War in ways that go beyond its status as a gift from the Soviet Union. Reminiscent of the space race and the aspirations of peoples around the world to conquer outer space with the help of technology, the monument both embodies the hopefulness of a newly independent state and is indexical of the ways in which the Cold War stymied those aspirations. The antagonism between the superpowers was outwardly staged through a seemingly peaceful competition to demonstrate the best space technology, while proxy hot conflicts (like the one in Angola) absorbed the militaristic and destructive elements of the contest, destroying the very chances such young nations had to join the space race. This tension is at the heart of Kiluanji Kia Henda's 2008 exhibition *Icarus 13*, which imagines the first African space mission to explore the sun. Using photographs of Neto's mausoleum, the installation recalls the bold dreams of postcolonial African nations to surpass the feats of space missions like *Apollo 13*, while also underscoring the illusory character of those hopes by evoking the myth of Icarus and the danger of flying too close to the sun.

In a recent article, Kerry Bystrom productively reads Ondjaki's novel side by side with another art project that incorporates the Neto mausoleum, Jo Ractliffe's *Terreno Ocupado* (2008). The explosion of artistic interest in this monument in the years following the end of the conflict in Angola demonstrates, in Bystrom's terms, the public investment in "debates about the legacy of international socialism and contemporary urban politics in Luanda."[112] Like Mhlongo, these artists identify a perplexing continuity between the seemingly opposite discourse of solidarity between socialist states during the Cold War and the self-serving nationalism of the postwar elites. Under the pressure of new configurations of global imperialism, the MPLA had transformed from "workers' party to petrocapitalist oligarchy."[113]

In Ondjaki's imaginative development, the mausoleum becomes the focus of the local population's animosity, of all the tensions and misunderstandings that the official solidarity discourse overlooked or deliberately disguised. The construction of the grandiose complex in the Bishop's Beach neighborhood unfolds under the supervision of Soviet troops. Yet, to make room for the monumental project, the old neighborhood is slated for eviction and demolition. The story, narrated from the perspective of a boy living with his grandmothers and cousins in this neighborhood, takes off in an unexpected direction, as the narrator and his friend Pinduca (Pi) plan to "dexplode" the mausoleum to prevent the planned destruction of the neighborhood. The child perspective, with its mix of insightful observations and unfiltered ventriloquizing of adults' words, displaces the official narrative about the postindependence period in Angola and the MPLA's battle against UNITA and its imperialist supporters. The MPLA's focus on internationalist solidarity and appreciation for Soviet tactical and financial support and for Cuban military, medical, and scientific help is discarded or repurposed.[114] Instead, the novel foregrounds tensions between the local population and the Soviet military presence.

Ondjaki confronts the reader with the possibility that the much-avowed socialist solidarity might have been perceived as a form of colonization and that the supposed fraternal aid given by the Soviet Union and Cuba could have been seen as brutal intervention that destroyed Angolan ways of life. In the same way in which in the 1950s Aimé Césaire expressed revulsion for the racist and paternalist nuances in the policy of communist parties within the Soviet orbit, Ondjaki shines light on the Angolan population's discontent with the Soviet presence. There are numerous Soviet soldiers and workers in the Bishop's Beach community, tasked with erecting and guarding the mausoleum. The locals perceive their presence as an imposition.

The Soviet visitors are simultaneously seen as unwelcome invaders and colonizers, using their technological prowess to take over the community, and also as uncivilized savages, who are therefore subjected to an Orientalizing discourse.[115] Outraged by the takeover of the beautiful Bishop's Beach—a source of food, relaxation, and aesthetic pleasure for the community—one of the characters observes, "We never went to Russia or the Soviet Union to close or open or inaugurate or invade a Soviet beach."[116] If the Soviet presence is seen as an act of occupation, the locals express their animosity by deriding Soviet culture and the Russian language. The "Soviet language" is viewed as an aggressive foreign tongue, "half-spitted," "really weird and impossible to understand."[117] While Cubans, given the similarities between Portuguese and Spanish, find it much easier to interact with Angolans, the Soviet troops and workers are seen as a "disgrace to linguistic socialism."[118] Comrade Bilhardov, one of the workers in charge of the construction site, is saddled with the nicknames Goodafterov and B.o.-dorov, disparaged equally for his linguistic clumsiness and persistent body odor, a sign of uncouth manners and undiscerning sartorial choices.

Soviet and Cuban soldiers and workers are supposed to cooperate equally with the Angolan population to help build the new state; however, a hierarchy of internationalist sentiment is established, with Angolans preferring Cubans over their Soviet counterparts. In the novel this competition plays out as the courtship that Bilhardov and the Cuban doctor Rafael "KnockKnock" pay to Granma Agnette (the eponymous Granma Nineteen of the title). While linguistic kinship helps cement the Cuban-Angolan friendship, the children also express the hierarchy in racialized terms: "I don't know anything, but Cuba's got sun, beaches and pretty mulattas, I saw it all on television. Do you want to compare that with snow, frozen water that turns into ice and whitish women with minuscule boobs?" asks Pinduca.[119] The Cubans sent to Angola, many of whom were black, were generally considered "more sociable, easy-going and more racially tolerant than their Soviet and East German comrades."[120] However, as Anne Garland Mahler astutely observes, Cuban tricontinentalist discourse "often used a racial vocabulary to mark ideological position rather than physical appearance, attributing color as a signifier of subaltern resistance to phenotypically white people who shared its views, and in this way, it sought to destabilize racially essentialist claims to belonging."[121] Thus, in the universe of Ondjaki's novel, the Russians' whiteness makes them easier to reject as socialist brothers to Angolans and casts them in the position of unwelcome occupiers and colonizers.

Ondjaki seems very much concerned with not only exploring how internationalist discourse played out during the war in Angola, in the actual interactions between the local population and Cuban and Soviet personnel, but also with short-circuiting the negative assumptions Angolans made about Russians. As the mausoleum explodes in a dazzling display of color, and as the narrator and his friend Pinduca try to figure out how their feeble attempts to blow it up could have actually worked out, a letter from Bilhardov clarifies their questions: "Forgive if explozhun in Muzzleum make problem, but Dona Nhéte family get time and they must start verk again. Bilhardov cover dinamite with sea salt for booteful effect in Luanda sky. The kildren like? One day kildren can rite tell how was Bishop beach after fireverk."[122] Distraught that the expanding mausoleum complex entailed the bulldozing of the neighborhood and the displacement of people for whom he felt affection, Bilhardov sabotages the Soviet project for which he and his comrades had labored for years. Moreover, he adds an aesthetic element to the destruction, creating a spectacle of fireworks and color for the neighborhood children. Ondjaki therefore implies that interpersonal transnational relations succeed, while official internationalist cooperation projects are doomed. The local population is likely to see the latter as an imposition, rather than real assistance. Attending to the complexity of Soviet-Angolan relations in the novel, Bystrom observes that the novel "at once peels back a kind of solidarity-nostalgia about Soviet involvement in Angola, and recuperates a more modest but perhaps more useful vision of internationalist friendship."[123] Ondjaki offers a very nuanced interpretation of the discourse of Soviet interests in Africa, emphasizing individual people's goodwill while also criticizing the formalized ways in which politicians expressed them.

The explosion of the mausoleum, with the rocket-like structure taking off in a vortex of color, in an ironic fulfillment of its shape, is represented in Ondjaki's novel through a lyrical stream-of-consciousness description bordering on magical realism. While less explicitly fantastic than the ghost elements in Mhlongo's prose, Ondjaki's formal choices reflect a specific dilemma of representational history. Why do Ondjaki and Mhlongo turn to elements of magical realism to render in retrospect the Cold War conflict in Angola? Why do realism or modernism, which had served an earlier generation of writers well, appear as insufficient representational modes? How does this formal aspect relate to the theme of memory retrieval? Like postmodernism (discussed in more detail in chapter 2), the political credentials of magical realism have been questioned. Homi K. Bhabha, praising Salman Rushdie's prose, proclaimed that "'Magical Realism,' after the Latin American Boom, becomes the literary language of the emergent post-colonial world."[124] However, Aijaz Ahmad critiqued Bhabha and writers like Rushdie: Rushdie's use of irony and laughter acts as "linguistic quicksand," and it entails that "not only his text but he, himself, 'exists at a slight angle to reality.'"[125] A more nuanced understanding appears in Jean Franco's work. Writing about the Latin American boom and the turn to previously suppressed indigenous belief systems, Franco acknowledges that the lure of magical realism lies in "reenchant[ing] the world by drawing into literature popular beliefs and practices as a form of dissent from post-Enlightenment rationalism."[126] However, she differentiates between indigenous belief systems and their appropriation by intellectual elites to gain currency on the international literary circuit.

Addressing magical realism in West African literature, Brenda Cooper acknowledges the conundrum at the heart of this mode of writing: "Magical realist writers have an urge to demonstrate, capture and celebrate ways of being and of seeing that are uncontaminated by European domination. But at the same time, such authors are inevitably a hybrid mixture, of which European culture is a fundamental part."[127]

The critics' censure implies that magical realism is a literary gimmick that capitalizes on the cultural resources of the masses without actually giving back to the nation. The association of magical realism with postcolonial writers who achieved success in Western metropolitan centers further confirms these writers' absorption into a system of literary recognition that equates magical realism with the exotic.[128]

Given this mixed reception, it is not surprising that an author like Ngũgĩ wa Thiong'o distances himself from the terminology of magical realism, insisting instead that he is "more influenced by African oral traditions and folk tales."[129] Magalí Armillas-Tiseyra concurs, observing that the African novel is much too often packaged into a preexisting literary terminology used to describe non-Western literatures, rather than being read on its own terms.[130] Therefore, the magical realist paradigm might be constraining when dealing with a larger range of phenomena that do not have the same genealogy as their Latin American or South Asian counterparts. Ondjaki's and Mhlongo's novels display similar types of dysfunctional society and hallucinating levels of corruption as those rendered in magical realist terms in the Latin American boom novel. However, these southern African novelists writing in the new millennium might be more akin to Eastern European writers like Victor Pelevin and Mircea Cărtărescu. The latter express through fantastic elements the breakdown of grand narratives and the epistemological disorientation brought on by the collapse of socialist regimes in 1989. The discourses of the past haunting Mhlongo's and Ondjaki's novels corroborate the perilous transformation of

Marxist and internationalist discourses into insubstantial ghosts in the neoliberal order; at the same time, they also confirm the need for a reinvigorated analysis of neoliberal capitalism.

The war in Angola created forms of anomie that reached fantastic levels, destabilizing the boundary between life and death, as social oppression became the equivalent of death in life. It also generated a culture of disenchantment with the certainties and optimism of leftist discourse (such as that of the MPLA government or of the ANC-SACP coalition), suggesting that it bore no actual relation to reality. In both Mhlongo's and Ondjaki's novels, leftist discourse is associated with forms of abuse that are given a facade of anticolonial respectability, as well as with the creation of more insidious forms of imperialism that come dressed up as internationalist solidarity. With this representational rupture, the earnestness of realism appeared insufficient, replaced by new literary forms that bear similarities with magical realism elsewhere.

At the end of *Grandma Nineteen and the Soviet's Secret*, the narrator questions his grandmother:

> "Is that what tales from before were like a long time ago?"
> "Yes, son."
> "So before is a time, Granma?"
> "Before is a place."
> "A place really far away?"
> "A place really deep inside."[131]

The spatialization of time and the unsettled marker *before*—does it refer to stories in wartime, or does it point to modes of narration before colonial and imperial domination?—create a disorienting effect. And so it should. It is an apt conclusion for Ondjaki's novel, with its nuanced stories of internationalist solidarity made visible, as well as a summation of the narrative challenges posed by the war in Angola. How southern African writers access the conflict, and how they render the vagaries of public memory, has changed over time: the texts have moved from documentary or autobiographical form, with the witnessing function as the first imperative, to realist and late-modernist novels that explicitly engage in national culture projects, to the fragmented and haunted recent texts, an explicit nod to complicated national or group memory politics. In the conclusion I return to some of these themes as I discuss new theoretical avenues opened by the Cold War in Africa.

CONCLUSION

# From Postcolonial to World Literature Studies

The Continued Relevance of the Cold War

Some seventeen years ago a computer scientist friend asked me why literary scholars necessarily think that the more complex a work—the more there is to decode—the higher its quality.[1] At the time the question seemed a no-brainer: a complex work that could not be reduced to a single, authoritative meaning is an artwork that stands in opposition to dogma and propaganda. A stylistically sophisticated, formally complex work counters a simplistic understanding of the world; it likely evinces a nuanced rendering of a complex reality. It has taken me a while to come to place my earlier assumptions within their historical context: the automatic equation of formal complexity and abstraction with heightened artistic quality was a reflex of my education in the Eastern Bloc in the immediate aftermath of the Cold War. Postmodernism, which many of us in the Eastern Bloc in the late 1980s and 1990s saw as the ultimate resistance to state-dictated forms of cultural production, appeared as the height of literary sophistication. It allowed writers and readers to find the necessary ironic distance from the grand narratives the socialist state had forced on its citizenry. Western critics who praised the rebellious posture of postmodern literature cemented this view. A decade after the fall of the socialist regimes, while living in North America, I was to encounter a completely different view of postmodernism: Fredric Jameson's assessment that postmodernism is the cultural logic of a specific manifestation of capitalism.[2] Both views are pertinent to my discussion here: they reflect the knowledge paradigms that invisibly yet comprehensively shaped my view of the world.

The Cold War ended with the fall of the Berlin Wall, and so did its cultural impact. This is what we used to assume. Yet what if the knowledge paradigms specific to the global conflict linger on, shaping the intellectual instruments we use to explain literary phenomena today? What if the impact of the two world-systems persists beyond the demise of one of the superpowers, manifesting itself in the triumph of neoliberal capitalism and the preservation of the West's cultural and aesthetic structures?[3] What if the ways we understand literature today—the canons inscribed in anthologies, the prizes bestowed, the forms of criticism preferred—are at least in part shaped by the remnants of the Cold War? There are no precise answers; however, a connection between the victory of the West and the easy availability of journals published by Occidental institutions is no easy-to-dismiss suspicion. Many of the Congress for Cultural Freedom's publications are available in digital format; their counterparts from the Afro-Asian Writers Association are buried in a handful of libraries around the globe.[4] Writers who have produced a staggering corpus of works but demonstrate a commitment to leftist activism, like Ngũgĩ wa Thiong'o, have been bypassed for major prizes in favor of authors who have displayed artistic values cherished in the West. African literary stars celebrated in the 1970s and 1980s for their anticolonial work (Alex La Guma, Pepetela, and Nadine Gordimer) gradually slipped into oblivion after 1990, while postmodern writers and adepts of magical realism (J. M. Coetzee, Ben Okri, and Mia Couto) shot to prominence. The global preference for postmodern aesthetics from the late 1980s onward and the simultaneous retirement of the figure of the revolutionary artist are symptoms of the aftermath of the Cold War. There is no conspiracy per se to deny visibility to the former; instead, the aesthetic world-system associated with capitalism continues to affect selections for anthologies, prizes, and classroom syllabi.

To the victor, the spoils: the triumph of the United States over the USSR did not lead to the end of history, as Francis Fukuyama had foretold, but rather the West's victory created the illusion that debates about forms of social organization had been settled for good.[5] Like the colonial and postindependence experience, the Cold War has shaped disciplinary knowledge systems. Since the 1970s cultural theorists and philosophers such as Michel Foucault, Edward Said, and Fredric Jameson have discussed the relation between forms of political and economic organization and knowledge production, whether to illuminate the genealogy of modern power, the invention of the Orient in tandem with the expansion of the European empires, or the development of postmodern culture as the cultural logic of late capitalism. In this book I have attempted to address the knowledge paradigms established during the Cold War, which oftentimes have extended into the present, reinforced by neoliberal capitalism.

The boom in postcolonial studies in the 1990s and, subsequently, the rise of the world literature paradigm are two research areas that could benefit from historicization of their development in relation to the end of the Cold War. Since in the past three decades African literature has been slotted first under the postcolonial rubric and later under that of world literature, I briefly turn to them here, pointing out possible future research avenues.

Cold War–era literary criticism in the West was "a refusal of politics disguised as a high moral or political argument," Tobin Siebers observed.[6] Timothy Brennan likewise argued that the brand of theory that became fashionable in American academic circles in the late 1970s and 1980s—"revolutionary in posture . . . characterized as Marxist by the media"—in fact embraced the values of American liberalism.[7] Even postcolonial scholarship, ostensibly treating the relation between forms of (neo)colonial power and knowledge production, became strangely depoliticized, as Brennan and David Scott have pointed out.[8] Blind spots developed, and scholars designed circumventing strategies, which, for instance, allowed a critic to analyze Marxist aesthetics and criticize Western neocolonialism on the condition that it did not simultaneously entail adhering to what was seen as an Eastern Bloc ideological perspective. This scholarly approach in the West was matched in the Eastern Bloc by equally one-sided formulations: to deliberately speak of writers' leftist politics was to enhance their desirability in the eyes of publishers, to remove the threat of censorship, or, conversely, discreetly intimate an anticommunist stance.

In *Refashioning Futures: Criticism after Postcoloniality*, David Scott traced the development of postcolonial studies as a field as it grew from anticolonial theory, focused on liberationist politics of decolonization, to a postcolonial emphasis on decolonizing representation.[9] This latter moment, with its emphasis on forms of cultural imperialism and cultural modes of analysis and resistance, became identified with the field of postcolonial studies itself, erasing or marginalizing much of its predecessors' efforts to analyze the material forms of oppression. While Robert J. C. Young is slightly more sanguine, positing postcolonial theory as the "dialectic of Marxist and French poststructuralist thought," Scott sees the emergence of postcolonial studies as the result of the depoliticization of scholarship during the Cold War.[10] It is only by reengagement with the political, without succumbing to the "oppositional languages of emancipation" of the old left politics, that the study of imperialism can find a way forward, Scott argues.[11] Such a reengagement with activism and politics can find the forgotten roots of studies of imperialism in the twentieth century. It requires carefully historicizing the impact of the Cold War on the forms of cultural production that we have subsumed as the object of postcolonial studies.

By returning to the works of African intellectuals during the Cold War period, we can bring back to light a vigorous leftist tradition of critique of imperialism, erased by the focus on postcolonial cultural analysis in the academy. For instance, Micere Mugo's work exemplifies the types of questions leftist intellectuals ask in order to establish the foundations of their analyses. Mugo dismisses the premises on which the *Concise Oxford Dictionary* explains *culture* as "improvement (by mental or physical training); intellectual development; particular form; stage of intellectual development of civilization," and she challenges the static snapshot offered by such a definition, proposing instead a probing approach into the mechanics of cultural transformation, marginalization, and institutionalization.[12] Mugo argues that a Western-based approach "leaves us with an abstract statement that does not take us very far. For instance, who sets the standards used to define the level of 'intellectual development'? Under imperialism the reference point would be the West and the terms would be dictated by its ruling class intellectuals."[13] Mugo addresses both international structures of domination and intranational class hierarchies. She is against isolating aspects of culture (such as form) from the historical contexts within which they have been produced, arguing for a grounded, material analysis of cultural production.

The 1990s were the heyday of postcolonial studies in the West, and the field's methodologies and assumptions were directly shaped by the political context: the fall of the Berlin Wall and of the communist regimes in Eastern Europe.[14] Epistemologically, the decade was a time frame "without an alternative," to use Zygmunt Bauman's words—in not only ideological but also methodological terms.[15] The protocols of the Western academy stole the limelight, especially the forms of postcolonial analysis indebted to poststructuralism. In Brennan's words, "purportedly driven by the desire to combat Eurocentrism, the field emerged speaking a language that was Eurocentric reflexively and automatically, one in which Europe existed speaking the language of 'difference.'"[16] On the false assumption that the collapse of the communist regimes invalidated Marxist methodologies as well, leftist analytical approaches to the study of imperialism became unfashionable, incorrectly regarded as oversimplifying and as narrowly focused on economic aspects. Leftist scholars like Benita Parry and Arif Dirlik were relatively marginal voices. This was, after all, the era of "hybrid," "liminal," and "in-between" identities, "textual gaps," and "always already" constituted forms of resistance.[17] In *Cold War Assemblages: Decolonization to Digital*, Bhakti Shringarpure identifies "the deeply entangled, symbiotic relationship between American universities and American imperial interests" during and in the immediate aftermath of the Cold War, which translated into the reduction of postcolonial studies to tame, poststructuralist exegesis.[18]

About two decades after the heyday of postcolonial studies in the 1990s, the hypernuanced, carefully hedged, and cautious critique of imperialism it delivered appears depoliticized and suspect in its investment in texts.[19] This might be largely an issue of altered perception, as Edward Said's and Gayatri Chakravorty Spivak's scholarship has always been politically committed and engaged with material aspects of domination. It is mostly the forms in which their scholarship was consumed and reinterpreted that elided the materialist underpinnings of their work. In Shringarpure's formulation, "the long arm of the Cold War" is visible in the cooptation of the humanities "in the service of sanitizing radical discourses and making them palatable in an academic setting."[20] Only at the beginning of the new millennium, after society had seen the extent of neoliberal capitalist depredations when unopposed by even the deeply flawed socialist bloc, did Marxist criticism in postcolonial studies stage a comeback. *Marxism, Modernity, and Postcolonial Studies* (2002), a collection of essays edited by Crystal Bartolovich and Neil Lazarus, reminded readers that Marxism and postcolonial studies had shared a research object for many decades.[21] In fact, leftist intellectuals had been writing against imperialism at least since Vladimir Lenin's acerbic critique in *Imperialism: The Highest Stage of Capitalism* (1917).

Therefore, the task of rewriting the history of postcolonial studies through a Cold War lens entails rediscovering the radical forms of writing that were excluded from the history of the discipline and that had been dismissed for their leftist or Afrocentric emphases. African critics have contributed radically not only to the analysis of imperialism and forms of cultural colonialism—the names of Frantz Fanon, Amílcar Cabral, Ngũgĩ wa Thiong'o, and Walter Rodney immediately spring to mind—but also to the decolonization of leftist tools of analysis, which, during the Cold War, had been claimed by the Soviet Union as their domain. In his important essay "Masks and Marx: The Marxist Ethos vis-à-vis African Revolutionary Theory and Praxis," Ayi Kwei Armah observed that "Marxism, in its approach to non-European societies and values, is decidedly colonialist, Western, Eurocentric, and hegemonistic. Marxists do not present their philosophy as a European variant of communist theory—which would be the accurate, intelligent and honest thing to do. Marxists in Africa exhibit a desire to institutionalize European communist hypotheses as the only correct philosophy. Some of the most enthusiastic believers go so far as to pretend to think that Marxism is not just a philosophy but a science, the only correct science of liberation."[22]

While leftist intellectuals have argued that such a critique is blunt and lacking in nuance, Armah's admonition is particularly relevant now as materialist modes of analysis are again proving their usefulness in analyzing the exacerbated contemporary phenomena associated with capitalism.[23] He urges us to consider the ways in which the most radical intellectual tools—be they produced in academic circles in the West or the Eastern Bloc—could be appropriated by imperial powers, concomitantly eclipsing pioneering developments in African cultural philosophy and theory.

As the appeal of postcolonial studies as a vantage point on African literature has waned, to be replaced by world literature approaches, we need to pay the same scrutinizing attention to the history of this latter field and its institutionalized narratives. Could this purportedly inclusive approach also disguise forgotten alternative genealogies? The Cold War context explains why some views on world literature, while dominant in specific literary circles during the twentieth century, have disappeared today from among the prevailing narratives in this field. The revival of interest in the idea of world literature since the 1990s is a result of the end of the Cold War, the disappearance of the "three worlds" mode of conceptualizing cultural production, and the rise of a global purview for the study of literature, commensurate with the global reach of neoliberal capitalism.

It might appear unfair to tie the resurgence of scholarly interest in world literature to the triumph of neoliberal capitalism, especially since its scholars, from David Damrosch to Pascale Casanova, have striven to create inclusive models that attend to and integrate literary production from the former Third World; moreover, many of its theorists, from Franco Moretti to the Warwick Research Collective, operate with a Marxist methodological apparatus.[24] In fact, the relative consensus on the role of world literature has been to see it as resisting the encroachment of capitalism and as responding with a rich display of diversity to the homogenizing forces of globalization. Yet the Cold War, with its fault lines and its competing aesthetic world-systems, pitted against each other divergent ideas about the function of literature in general and the position to be occupied by African writers within these systems. Maria Khotimsky, Rossen Djagalov, and Galin Tihanov have most helpfully unpacked the parallel development of an idea of world literature within the Soviet Union, nowadays erased from institutional memory. It started with the establishment of Vsemirnaia Literatura (World Literature) Publishing House in Moscow in 1918 and continued with the development of what Djagalov called the "Soviet republic of letters."[25] Such research opens up the idea of competing theories and understandings of what world literature is, revealing a cultural history obscured by Cold War ideological partisanship.

In the first issue of the journal *Lotus: Afro-Asian Writings* (March 1968), the editor Youssef El-Sebai invokes in passing the term *world literature* by stating that "the writers of Asia and Africa have made a significant contribution to the treasury of world literature."[26] While here the concept seems to be understood merely as a collection of formative, impactful writings from around the globe, the term is reprised in South African writer Alex La Guma's 1970 speech upon receiving the Lotus Prize conferred by the Afro-Asian Writers Association. La Guma draws on a tradition of understanding world literature that has largely been erased from contemporary scholarship, namely, that of Maxim Gorky and the Eastern Bloc writing traditions. Hala Halim, in her foundational appraisal of the role the Afro-Asian Writers Association played during the second half of the twentieth century, names the journal *Lotus* as the site for the development of an alternative idea of world literature.[27]

An argument in favor of going back to the decades of the Cold War to rethink the history of world literature is also given by Andrew Rubin. Discussing the role of the CIA-financed Congress for Cultural Freedom, Rubin observes that the CCF's operation participated in "refashion[ing] and reinvent[ing] the idea of world literature."[28] His assessment indicates that ideas of literariness later deployed in the formation of a world literature canon were shaped in the crucible of the Cold War. If we follow Rubin's argument to its ultimate conclusion, we come to see that current models of analyzing world literature arose against the background of the dominating episteme at the end of the Cold War and the beginning of the era of global neoliberal capitalism.

Instead, more comprehensive and democratic models of world literature arise from the former colonies, what we call today the Global South. The Warwick Research Collective reminds us that although the capitalist world-system keeps cultural economies in its grip and although there is unevenness within the system, the flow of cultural information and literary models is not unidirectional. While the collective's emphasis is on the predatory aspects of the system, there are also destabilizing and antisystemic forces at work.[29] During the Cold War and in its aftermath, the circulation of ideas from the peripheries and semiperipheries to the center challenged settled theories of literature and culture. Based on these flows, Ngũgĩ has proposed a globalectical way of conceiving of world literature, according to which a journal founded in Uganda can shape the development of postcolonial literature:

> In terms of migration of ideas, a good example is the birth of *Transition* magazine. The journal, founded in the early sixties and edited by Rajat Neogy, whose birth, upbringing, and entire schooling was in Kampala, be-

came synonymous with the birth of the postcolonial African intellectual. It opened its pages to such luminaries, then in their youth, as Ali Mazrui, Wole Soyinka, and Peter Nazareth, and featured the 1962 conference of writers of English expression. When Neogy moved to America, his journal went with him, from Ghana to Harvard. It has been going strong ever since, fifty years now. A French-language parallel is the Paris-based *Présence Africaine*, founded by the Senegalese Alioune Diop even before *Transition*.[30]

Ngũgĩ's vision treats each point on the circumference of the globe as a center, allowing it to reveal the wealth of cultural material it produces and shares with other locales.[31] What we need to add to this important perspective is the Cold War history that shaped the production of *Transition* and *Présence Africaine*: the superpowers' attempts to sway the editors and leading intellectuals affiliated with these journals, the forms of financial and cultural support they received, and the complex reasons for which they have enjoyed such a robust presence within international cultural circuits—in short, the Cold War literary historiography I explored in chapter 1.

The history of world literature therefore needs to be rewritten with a more inclusive genealogy. Along with traditional references to Goethe and Marx, it incorporates moments that the triumph of the West at the end of the Cold War has erased, such as the discussions around the abolition of the English Department at the University of Nairobi in 1968, or the rise and impact of journals like *Transition* and *Lotus* with the support of, or in defiance of, the superpowers' imperialist interventions.[32] The works of African writers during the Cold War give us a different perspective on the intellectual genealogy of postcolonial and world literature studies.

# NOTES

## Acknowledgments

1 Wainaina, *One Day*, 105.

## Introduction: Genres of Cold War Theory

1 Ngũgĩ was a visiting associate professor at Northwestern University in Evanston, Illinois, in 1970–1971. During the 1970–1975 period, when he was a faculty member at the University of Nairobi, he must have visited his birthplace, Limuru, quite frequently. He spent a month in Yalta in 1975 at the invitation of the Union of Soviet Writers, at "Chekhov's Writers House on the Caucasian Mountain overlooking Yalta on the Black Sea." Ngũgĩ, "In Chekhov's House," 21.

2 Ngũgĩ emphasized the Cold War symbolism of the locations where the novel was completed: "It was, I suppose, my contribution to 'détente' since the novel was really started in Evanston, Illinois and completed at Yalta where Roosevelt and Churchill and Stalin met after the Second World War." *Ngũgĩ wa Thiong'o Speaks*, 57. "This was the sixties when the centre of the universe was moving from Europe or, to put it another way, when many countries particularly in Asia and Africa were demanding and asserting their right to define themselves and their relationship to the universe from their own centres in Africa and Asia." Ngũgĩ, *Moving the Centre*, 20. In a recently published essay, Ngũgĩ confirmed this global Cold War perspective: "I like to think of my novel, *Petals of Blood*, as the book that built a bridge across the East, West and Third World divide of the Cold War." Ngũgĩ, "In Chekhov's House," 21.

3 While leaders like Kwame Nkrumah (Ghana), Léopold Sédar Senghor (Senegal), and Agostinho Neto (Angola) sought cultural recognition for their countries, undemocratic regimes, such as the military dictatorships in Nigeria and Uganda, persecuted writers and artists and curtailed cultural programs.

4 The program of the Makarere conference lists the event name as the "Conference of English-Speaking African Writers," TC Records, folder 1.3. Festac '77 was the Second World Black and African Festival of Arts and Cultures, organized near Lagos, Nigeria, in January–February 1977, with major support from the Nigerian state, which wanted to display its cultural and political prowess. See Apter, *Oil, Blood and Money*; and Iwara and Mveng, *Black Civilization and Education*.

5 See Casanova, *World Republic of Letters*.

6 My book title pays homage to Ngũgĩ's collection of essays *Penpoints, Gunpoints*

and Dreams: Towards a Critical Theory of the Arts and the State in Africa* as well as to the revolutionary force of his oeuvre.

7   *Postcolonial/ism* is a notoriously slippery term, criticized from its first decade of existence. It confusingly encompasses both cultural production from the former colonies and a field of studies with a nebulous inception date. Robert Young observed that "writing about the postcolonial while claiming to stand outside it in fact typically characterizes postcolonial writing itself." Young, "Ideologies of the Postcolonial," 5. Different approaches to periodizing the postcolonial era further complicate the use of the term; see Scott, *Refashioning Futures*; and Comaroff and Comaroff, "Naturing the Nation."

8   Although today it sounds outdated, I prefer the term *Third World* (as opposed to the contemporary *Global South*) as it evokes the Cold War context. Vijay Prashad famously opens his book *The Darker Nations: A People's History of the Third World* with the sentences "The Third World was not a place. It was a project" (xv), to evoke the aspirations of formerly colonized countries after World War II. However, in the tug of war between the two superpowers, vying to expand their ideological, economic, and political dominance over the rest of the world, the Third World became also a place shaped by these power relations. For the emergence of the term *Global South* as a successor to *the Third World*, see Dirlik, "Global South"; and Prashad, *Poorer Nations*.

9   For instance, despite the existence of a vigorous Marxist approach in postcolonial studies (e.g., Aijaz Ahmad's *In Theory: Classes, Nations, Literatures* [1992] or Fredric Jameson's "Third-World Literature in the Era of Multinational Capitalism" [1986]), only in the 2002 collection of essays *Marxism, Modernity and Postcolonial Studies* do the editors, Crystal Bartolovich and Neil Lazarus, remind readers that Marxism and postcolonial studies "have something to say to each other" (1). However, despite sporadic references to the Cold War, the contributing authors do not treat the Cold War as a knowledge-producing paradigm that shaped and was shaped in turn by the emergence of postcolonial studies.

10  Armah, *Remembering the Dismembered Continent*, 145.

11  African literature obviously predates the birth of the discipline with the same name by centuries. Individual scholarship on African oral and written literature likewise predates the beginning of the Cold War. What interests me is the impact of the Cold War knowledge paradigms on the development of the academic field concerned with the study of African literature.

12  Young (dir.), *Dr. No* (1962).

13  Hamilton (dir.), *Diamonds Are Forever* (1971).

14  As recently as 2012, doubt (in the shape of a question mark) still accompanied the idea of going "Beyond the East-West Axis?," as the title of a panel at the multidisciplinary conference East-West Cultural Exchanges and the Cold War (University of Jyväskylä, Finland, June 2012) attests.

15  As an example of such omissions, see Winkler, *Cold War*; the only reference to Africa is in relation to the Suez Canal crisis (77).

16  The two collections of essays edited by Andrew Hammond—*Cold War Literature:*

*Writing the Global Conflict* (2006) and *Global Cold War Literature: Western, Eastern and Postcolonial Perspectives* (2012)—are an important exception to this bias. However, out of the fourteen essays in the former, only one addresses African literature. The same applies to the second volume. For a literary treatment of regional aspects of the Cold War in southern Africa, see Popescu, "Reading"; and Baines and Vale, *Beyond the Border War*.

17  Westad, *Global Cold War*, 4.
18  For a summary of early Cold War studies, see Hanhimäki and Westad, *Cold War*, ix–x. For pioneering approaches that bring together the decolonization struggle and the Cold War, see Pietz, "'Post-colonialism'"; and Brennan, "Cuts of Language."
19  See, for instance, the equivocal language in Said's discussion of states and institutions that promoted opposition to colonialism: "A far from negligible part was played by the Soviet Union and by the United Nations, not always in good faith, and in the case of the former not for altruistic reasons; nearly every successful Third World liberation movement after World War Two was helped by the Soviet Union's counter-balancing influence against the United States, Britain, France, Portugal, and Holland." Said, *Culture and Imperialism*, 242.
20  For recent exceptions to this tendency see Lee, *Making a World after Empire*; Prashad, *The Darker Nations*; and Young, *Postcolonialism*.
21  For some exceptions see Lee and La Guma, "Addressing an Afro-Asian Public"; Lee, "Introduction: Anti-Imperial Eyes"; Popescu, *South African Literature*; and Djagalov, *From Internationalism to Postcolonialism*.
22  Balogun, *Ngugi*; Gikandi, *Ngugi wa Thiong'o*; Gugelberger, "Marxism and African Literature"; and Kamenju, "*Petals of Blood*."
23  Heonik Kwon describes the Cold War as "a battle for the appropriation of meaning between two competing teleological systems of historical progress." Kwon, *Other Cold War*, 5. Jini Kim Watson and Gary Wilder exhort us to understand "the complexity of our postcolonial present as simultaneously configured by Cold War imaginaries and aftermaths." Watson and Wilder, "Introduction," 21.
24  David Chioni Moore "Is the Post- in Postcolonial the Post- in Post-Soviet?"; Popescu, "Lewis Nkosi in Warsaw"; Ram, *Imperial Sublime*; and Șandru, *Worlds Apart?* However, politically motivated statements about the imperial nature of the Soviet Union were all too common during the Cold War. For instance, the apartheid government oftentimes presented South Africa as a Western bastion against the encroachment of Soviet imperialism in southern Africa.
25  Brennan, "Cuts of Language," 39.
26  Pietz, "'Post-colonialism,'" 55, 58.
27  See Wolff, *Inventing Eastern Europe*; and Todorova, *Imagining the Balkans*.
28  The relations between the Soviet Union and African intellectuals had developed on the basis of an already existing tradition of black fellow travelers visiting the USSR in the first half of the twentieth century. See Baldwin, *Beyond the Color Line*; and C. Tolliver, *Of Vagabonds*.
29  In *Moscow, the Fourth Rome: Stalinism, Cosmopolitanism, and the Evolution of Soviet*

*Culture, 1931–1941*, Clark refers to Moscow as an emerging cultural center in the 1930s. However, her emphasis on Sergey Eisenstein's 1933 description of Moscow as a concept that represents "the concentration of the socialist future of the entire world" (1) easily translates into the cultural and political role assumed by the Soviet capital during the Cold War.

30 For Fanon and the Cold War, see Lazarus, *The Postcolonial Unconscious*; and Shringarpure, "The Afterlives of Frantz Fanon and the Reconstruction of Postcolonial Studies."

31 Lazarus, *The Postcolonial Unconscious*, 10.

32 Ashcroft, Griffiths, and Tiffin, *Key Concepts*, 15.

33 Césaire, *Discourse on Colonialism*, 337. Consulted in the original French, *Discours sur le colonialisme*, but citations are from the English translation.

34 Césaire, "Letter to Maurice Thorez," 149. Consulted in the original French, *Lettre à Maurice Thorez*, but citations are from the English translation.

35 Khrushchev, "Nikita Khrushchev's Secret Speech, 1956," 247–49. For a further discussion of the relation between Césaire's "Letter to Maurice Thorez" and contemporary events, see also Kemedjio, "When the Detour Leads Home," 195–96.

36 Césaire sounds a note of optimism for the development of a different form of socialism in China: "Without being very familiar with [Chinese communism], I have a very strong prejudice in its favor. And I expect it not to slip into the monstrous errors that have disfigured European communism." "Letter to Maurice Thorez," 150. For the Sino-Soviet split as the background of this reorientation, see the various documents pertaining to relations between China and the USSR in Hanhimäki and Westad, *Cold War*, 198–208.

37 For a history of Soviet interest in the Third World and decolonization struggles, see Westad, *Global Cold War*, 49–78.

38 Quist-Adade, "From Paternalism to Ethnocentrism," 81; and Matusevich, "Journeys of Hope." For the early Cold War, see Baldwin, *Beyond the Color Line*. Not all such aid was Machiavellian in intent; also, African revolutionaries and intellectuals were oftentimes aware of the downsides of this patronage yet accepted support from where it was available.

39 Gordimer, *The Essential Gesture*, 263.

40 Buck-Morss, *Dreamworld and Catastrophe*, xv, 31.

41 Caute, *The Dancer Defects*, 4. See also Westad, *Global Cold War*, 397.

42 Westad, *Global Cold War*, 397.

43 "The Third World project (the ideology and institutions) enabled the powerless to hold a dialogue with the powerful, and to try to hold them accountable." Prashad, *The Darker Nations*, xviii–xix.

44 Westad, *Global Cold War*, 159, 241–48. While taking into account the U.S. bias in Gaddis's study, see also Gaddis, *We Now Know*, 26–27, on the asymmetry of the two empires.

45 Baldwin, *Beyond the Color Line*, 136; and C. Tolliver, *Of Vagabonds*, 95–96. See also Zien, *Sovereign Acts*, for the entanglement of American imperial interests, the

46. For an early critique of the poststructuralist takeover in postcolonial studies, see Ahmad, *In Theory*.
47. For the continuity-in-transformation of forms of imperialism throughout the twentieth and twenty-first centuries, see Said, *Culture and Imperialism*, xvii; and Hammond, "Frontlines of Writing," 1.
48. Lazarus, "Modernism and African Literature," 228.
49. *Chosification* in the original *Discours sur le colonialisme*, 13.
50. Amoko, *Postcolonialism in the Wake of the Nairobi Revolution*.
51. Soyinka, "Critic and Society," 133.
52. "Marxism has created for our Leftocracy a system that declares itself complete, controlled and controlling: an immanent reflection of every facet of human history, conduct, and striving, an end known in advance and only delayed by the explicable motions of economic production and development." Soyinka, "Critic and Society," 142.
53. Rubin, *Archives of Authority*, 103.
54. Ngũgĩ, *Decolonising the Mind*, 16–17.
55. I am grateful to Chalo'a Waya for clarifying this linguistic aspect. According to T. G. Benson's 1964 *Kikuyu-English Dictionary*, the nouns *rũkurukuhĩ* and *ngurukuhĩ* mean a "short piece of stick used as missile" and a "cutting put into earth to take root, slip."
56. The quoted phrase is from Ngũgĩ, *Decolonising the Mind*, 13.
57. "Committee on Information and Cultural Relations: Afro-Asian Writers' Conference, Tashkent, October 1959 [sic]," NATO Confidential Document AC/52-D(58)59 (Declassified), 1. The document is dated November 18, 1958, yet the title incorrectly identifies the conference year as 1959. http://archives.nato.int/uploads/r/null/1/4/14871/AC_52-D_58_59_ENG.pdf
58. Barnhisel, *Cold War Modernists*, 74, 103.
59. S. Mitin, "African Writers Talk about Literature," *Voprosy Literatury*, March 1963, 157. I am grateful to Rossen Djagalov for the translation from Russian.
60. At the 1963 Dakar Conference on African Literature in French and the University Curriculum, which Mphahlele helped organize with funding from the Congress for Cultural Freedom, he had vigorously rebutted the ideas of Négritude: "Who is so stupid as to deny the historical fact of *négritude* as both a protest and a positive assertion of African cultural values? All this is valid. What I do not accept is the way in which too much of the poetry inspired by it romanticizes Africa—as a symbol of innocence, purity and artless primitiveness." "Remarks on Negritude," box 71, folder 8, 2, International Association for Cultural Freedom (IACF) Records, Special Collections Research Center, University of Chicago, Chicago (henceforth cited as IACF Records).
61. Mitin, "African Writers Talk about Literature," 157.
62. Barnhisel, *Cold War Modernists*, 69.
63. Barnhisel, *Cold War Modernists*, 75.

64 Gould-Davies, "Soviet Cultural Diplomacy," 205–6. The Union of Soviet Societies of Friendship and Cultural Relations with Foreign Countries was a restructured version of the All-Soviet Society for Cultural Relations with Foreign Countries. For the latter's role in cultural diplomacy, see Fox, *Showcasing the Great Experiment*, 40–46.

65 Gould-Davies, "Soviet Cultural Diplomacy," 203–4.

66 Caute, *The Dancer Defects*, 5.

67 "Winning hearts and minds" was a strategy used by the United States during the Vietnam War, but the concept precedes this conflict. "The year 1952 also saw the debut of a series called My Credo, in which high-profile American artists and writers—including, among others, Steinbeck, John Marquand, Claude Rains, Thomas Hart Benton, Robert Frost, and Marianne Moore—'open their hearts and minds to overseas listeners on the importance of spiritual freedom in their artistic creations.'" Barnhisel, *Cold War Modernists*, 228–29.

68 Hook quoted in "Origins of the Congress for Cultural Freedom, 1949–50." Central Intelligence Agency, posted April 14, 2007, https://www.cia.gov/library/center-for-the-study-of-intelligence/csi-publications/csi-studies/studies/95unclass/Warner.html.

69 See Brouillette, "UNESCO and the Book"; Brouillette, "US-Soviet Antagonism"; and Dorn and Ghodsee, "Cold War Politicization."

70 Coleman, *Liberal Conspiracy*, 9; and Saunders, *Cultural Cold War*, 1.

71 Saunders, *Cultural Cold War*, 1. The book was originally published in the United Kingdom in 1999 as *Who Paid the Piper?* For other important studies on the CCF, see Coleman, *Liberal Conspiracy*; Wilford, *Mighty Wurlitzer*; Scott-Smith, *Politics of Apolitical Culture*; and, in the African context, P. Benson, *Black Orpheus*; and Rubin, *Archives of Authority*.

72 For years of operation and locations, see Rubin, *Archives of Authority*, 11.

73 Rubin, *Archives of Authority*, 12.

74 Saunders, *Cultural Cold War*, 4, 320.

75 For the International Association for Cultural Freedom, see Saunders, *Cultural Cold War*, 346–48; and the IACF Records.

76 Khotimsky, "World Literature, Soviet Style," 120.

77 NATO Confidential Document AC/52-D(58)59, 2. For a detailed account of the infighting within the AAWA and the decision to move the Permanent Bureau from Colombo to Cairo, away from Chinese influence, see Djagalov, *From Internationalism to Postcolonialism*, ch. 2, "The Afro-Asian Writers Association and Its Literary Field," especially 75–96.

78 Yoon, "Our Forces Have Redoubled," 234.

79 For a more detailed account of the China-supported AAWA, see Yoon, "Our Forces Have Redoubled."

80 The journal, first published in English and French in 1968, was first titled *Afro-Asian Writings*, with *Lotus* added to its name from the sixth issue. The publication year is misprinted on the covers of the English and French editions as 1967,

an error that might have been generated by the occasional lag between the Arabic version and those in English and French.

81  Afro-Asian Writers' Bureau, *Struggle between the Two Lines*, 3.
82  Afro-Asian Writers' Bureau, *Struggle between the Two Lines*, 4.
83  In a series of blog posts ("Lotus Notes") based on interviews, travel to Cairo and Beirut, and diligent assembly of information, Nida Ghouse pieced together this almost unbelievable episode from the history of *Lotus*. Two working groups dedicated to researching the history of AAWA have also been established: a group (of which I am a member) spearheaded by a 2017 workshop at New York University, as well as a group based at the American University of Beirut. "The Lotus Project," Anis Makdisi Program in Literature, American University of Beirut, accessed August 2019, https://www.aub.edu.lb/fas/ampl/Pages/lotus.aspx.
84  Nkosi's comments appear in the discussion section following Soyinka's talk "The Writer in an African Modern State." In Wästberg, *Writer in Modern Africa*, 27.
85  The title of this chapter is indebted to the historians and political scientists who have studied the conflict in Angola as an expression of the global Cold War. More specifically it draws on the title of Vladimir Shubin's *The Hot "Cold War": The USSR in Southern Africa*.

## Chapter 1: Pens and Guns

1  La Guma's comments are part of the discussion section following Wole Soyinka's talk "The Writer in a Modern African State." In Wästberg, *Writer in Modern Africa*, 22.
2  Rubin, *Archives of Authority*, 9.
3  Kalliney, "Modernism," 334.
4  Djagalov, *From Internationalism to Postcolonialism*, 17–19 and ch. 4.
5  Djagalov, *From Internationalism to Postcolonialism*, 28.
6  Co-convened by the Scandinavian Institute of African Studies, the Swedish Institute for Cultural Relations with Foreign Countries, and the Council for Swedish Information Abroad, the conference included "twenty-four African writers and about as many writers and critics from Sweden, Denmark, Norway and Finland." Wästberg, *Writer in Modern Africa*, 7. African and Scandinavian writers were brought together by the desire to define the literature of the African continent as well as by a perceived experience of being "outsiders" (10) to the Western world.
7  Nkosi's comments appear in the discussion section following Soyinka's talk "The Writer in an African Modern State." In Wästberg, *Writer in Modern Africa*, 27.
8  The Biafra War, or Nigerian Civil War, unfolded between July 1967 and January 1970, when the Igbo-dominant region of Biafra attempted to secede from the Nigerian federation.
9  Soyinka, "The Writer in a Modern African State," 16, 21.

10 For the development of the concept of autonomy within Western modernist art, see Barnhisel, *Cold War Modernists*, 33–39. Also, Kalliney helpfully points to the turn-of-the-twentieth-century Dreyfus affair and Émile Zola's spirited intervention as one of the early defining moments for the "complicated relationship among autonomy, politics, and the practice of intellectuals" in the West. "Zola tried to finesse his entry into the sordid field of politics by claiming that he was motivated solely by nonpolitical criteria, that his attachment to objective standards of truth and fairness trumped any other concern." Kalliney, "Modernism," 335n1.

11 La Guma's comments appear in the discussion section following Soyinka's talk "The Writer in a Modern African State." In Wästberg, *Writer in Modern Africa*, 21.

12 Brutus, *Poetry and Protest*, 205.

13 Sartre, *What Is Literature?*, 37. Odile Cazenave and Patricia Célérier's *Contemporary Francophone African Writers and the Burden of Commitment* looks at contemporary forms of commitment in francophone African literature.

14 Mphahlele, *Voices in the Whirlwind*, 187 (emphasis mine).

15 Onoge, "Crisis of Consciousness," 21. The article was originally published in 1974 and republished in 1985 in Gugelberger, *Marxism and African Literature*.

16 Onoge, "Crisis of Consciousness," 31–32, 33, 35 (emphasis in original), 36.

17 Onoge, "Crisis of Consciousness," 38 (emphasis in original).

18 Drawing on an earlier argument put forth by Biodun Jeyifo, Ato Quayson observes that "there are always elaborate socio-cultural and political dynamics to the interpretation of the relationship between literature and politics." Quayson, *Postcolonialism*, 77.

19 For instance, Kalliney argues that African writers deployed the concept of "literary autonomy," conventionally associated with Western modernism, in "malleable, even contradictory" ways, to proclaim their "intellectual and creative independence." Kalliney, "Modernism," 334.

20 Caute, *Dancer Defects*, 5.

21 See Barnhisel, *Cold War Modernists*, especially 69–75, 101–2; Caute, *Dancer Defects*; Von Eschen, *Satchmo Blows Up*; and Gould-Davies, "Soviet Cultural Diplomacy."

22 For a detailed analysis of the activities of the CCF, see also Wilford, *Mighty Wurlitzer*; Coleman, *Liberal Conspiracy*; and Scott-Smith, *Politics of Apolitical Culture*; and for the CCF's impact in Africa, see P. Benson, *Black Orpheus*; Kalliney, "Modernism"; G. Moore, "The Transcription Centre"; and Rubin, *Archives of Authority*.

23 Saunders, *Cultural Cold War*, 1.

24 Archival sources on their operation include the International Association for Cultural Freedom (IACF) Records, Special Collections Research Center, University of Chicago (especially boxes 68, 70, 71, 364, 422, 440, 441, 442, 542); the Transcription Centre (TC) Records, Harry Ransom Center, the University of Texas at Austin (especially Series I, Subseries A, B, and D, and Series III); and

25. Kalliney, "Modernism," 337, 341–42. For the CIA's preference for modernist writers as editors of the CCF journals, see E. Holt, "Cold War," 229.
26. See "Historical News," 287; and Mphahlele, *Afrika My Music*, 30, 80.
27. For the flourishing of African-owned newspapers in British colonial West Africa, see Newell, "Articulating Empire." See also Lewis Nkosi's broadcast "African Little Magazines," TC Records, folder 8.5, item 47.8.
28. P. Benson, "'Border Operators,'" 432. For an account of aspects that Benson missed, see Adesokan, "Retelling a Forgettable Tale."
29. In his memoir Mphahlele, who was teaching at the University of Ibadan at that time, places himself within the inner circle that founded Mbari: "I was invited by Ulli Beier and the Nigerian writers to help form the Mbari Artists and Writers Club in Ibadan." Mphahlele, *Afrika My Music*, 33.
30. For a detailed history of *Black Orpheus* and *Transition*, see P. Benson, *Black Orpheus*. For an emphasis on the CCF involvement, see Kalliney, "Modernism"; and Coleman, *Liberal Conspiracy*. For Mphahlele's account of his role in steering these literary hubs, see *Afrika My Music*. It is important to observe that, unlike all the cultural venues that folded once CIA involvement in the CCF was revealed and its financial support was withdrawn, *Transition* was chosen by the reformed International Association for Cultural Freedom (IACF) as a journal to save and continue to publish. After the magazine's founder and original editor, Rajat Neogy, was charged with sedition and imprisoned by Milton Obote's regime, the IACF supported its continued publication in Ghana (with Soyinka as editor); then, after its demise in 1976, it was reactivated by Henry Louis Gates Jr. in the United States. For further information on Neogy see Paul Theroux, "Rajat Neogy Remembered," *Transition* 69 (1996): 4–7.
31. For what Apollo Obonyo Amoko terms the "Nairobi revolution," see Amoko, *Postcolonialism*, 4–13.
32. After the CCF scandal in 1967, the Transcription Centre received (reduced) funding from other foundations. For instance, between 1966 and 1970, radio programs were sponsored by Deutsche Welle. See Harry Ransom Center, the University of Texas at Austin, "The Transcription Centre: An Inventory of Its Records at the Harry Ransom Center," accessed March 1, 2018, https://norman.hrc.utexas.edu/fasearch/findingAid.cfm?kw=citation&x=0&y=0&eadid=00447&showrequest=1.
33. For the aims of the center, see the correspondence between Duerden and John Hunt, TC Records, container 21.6.
34. Originally published as "On the Carpet" in the June 11, 1967, issue of the *Sunday Nation*, it was republished as "Rajat Neogy on the CIA," interview by Tony Hall, in *Transition* 32 (August-September 1967): 44–47.
35. Neogy, "Rajat Neogy on the CIA," 45.
36. Neogy, "Ragat Neogy on the CIA," 45.
37. P. Benson, *Black Orpheus*, 161–63.

38  Neogy, "Ragat Neogy on the CIA," 46.
39  See the "Manifesto of the Congress for Cultural Freedom," reproduced in Coleman, *Liberal Conspiracy*, 247–52. Following the revelations about the extent of the CIA operation, Neogy characterized this contradiction between avowed aims and methods as a perversion of the very foundational principles of American democracy, a painful and baffling spectacle of "a snake eat[ing] its tail." Neogy, "Rajat Neogy on the CIA," 45.
40  Neogy, "Rajat Neogy on the CIA," 46. This ability to integrate opposing views and stage a true debate within the pages of *Transition* was apparent when several politically divisive events took place. For instance, shortly after the first president of Ghana and prominent Pan-Africanist Kwame Nkrumah was deposed in a military coup in February 1966, Ali Mazrui, a frequent contributor to *Transition*, penned an evaluation of the West African statesman and instigated a heated debate that carried across several issues of the journal.
41  Quoted in P. Benson, *Black Orpheus*, 161.
42  Thompson met Neogy in Kampala and approved of his journalistic zeal, so that when, in the wake of the Makerere conference, Neogy approached Mphahlele for funding from the CCF, the Farfield Foundation purse was readily available. Benson points out that neither Neogy nor Mphahlele mentioned their relation with or knowledge of Thompson, further removing themselves from the CIA operation. P. Benson, *Black Orpheus*, 161–63.
43  Unlike Thompson's suggestion (which Benson reproduces in *Black Orpheus*, 162) that, given the small amounts of money available for Africa, the top officers in the CIA never concerned themselves with checking the financial details, the CCF and Transcription Centre archives reveal a high level of oversight over and accountability for Mphahlele's and Neogy's expenses. See, for instance, Ivan Katz's memo to John Hunt regarding Chemchemi, IACF Records, box 71, folders 6 and 7; box 304, folder 4, gives an image of the money squabbles between Neogy and Hunt; and box 70, folder 3, contains documents regarding the daily running of Mbari Club.
44  Rubin, *Archives of Authority*, 17.
45  Rubin, *Archives of Authority*, 17.
46  Coleman, *Liberal Conspiracy*, vii.
47  Coleman, *Liberal Conspiracy*, 2.
48  Coleman, *Liberal Conspiracy*, 2. For instance, the South African leftists criticized the complicity of liberalism in a capitalist economy dependent on segregation.
49  In a rather ungenerous interpretation, Rubin implies that Wole Soyinka's success was largely obtained through the backing of CCF institutions: "Soyinka's drama, *Dear Parent and Ogre*, was first produced by the Mbari Writers Club (which was supported by the CCF), reviewed in *Transition* . . . and then promoted in *Encounter* magazine, which had introduced Soyinka to its readership by previously awarding a literary prize to *The Dance of the Forest*. Further aggregating Soyinka's reputation, it awarded an accolade to *Dear Parent and Ogre* on the occasion of Nigeria's independence. The self-reflexive, self-aggrandizing, and self-

serving activities of the CCF saturated and subsequently shaped the limits of a whole generation of postcolonial Anglophone writing in Africa." Rubin, *Archives of Authority*, 59.

50  IACF Records, box 68, folder 2. It is important to note that Mphahlele's lack of knowledge with respect to his actual sponsors' aims translated into crossed ideological fault lines: in the same issue of the Chemchemi newsletter, he also announces new publications put out by the German Democratic Republic's Seven Seas Press.

51  IACF Records, box 68, folder 2. See also the Chemchemi Cultural Centre materials, Kenya National Archives.

52  John Hunt was a CIA operative and Operations Officer for the Congress for Cultural Freedom. IACF Records, box 364, folder 1. Also, for the Cini Foundation see box 322, folder 7.

53  After the CCF scandal, Mphahlele replaced "the modernist language promoted by US cultural diplomacy programs" with a "renovated form of 'African humanism.'" Eatough, "Critic as Modernist," 139.

54  Said, *Representations of the Intellectual*, 52–53.

55  Doherty, "PEN International," 332–34.

56  For more detail on the Daniel-Sinyavsky trial, see Caute, *Politics and the Novel*, 219–27. Also IACF Records, box 277, folders 7–9.

57  Mphahlele, *Afrika My Music*, 33. The cowinner of the prize was Brutus's volume of poetry *Sirens, Knuckles and Boots*. A selection of the poems from Brutus's award-winning volume can be found in Brutus, *Poetry and Protest*.

58  PEN International, "PEN Charter," accessed March 5, 2018, http://www.pen-international.org/pen-charter/.

59  Mphahlele, letter to Tom Mboya, IACF Records, box 71, folder 1.

60  Mphahlele, "Chemchemi Cultural Centre: Highlights 1963–1964," IACF Records, box 68, folder 2.

61  Edward Shils, "Further Thoughts on the Congress in the 60s," IACF Records, box 71, folder 2.

62  Said, *Humanism and Democratic Criticism*, 31. See also Rubin's insightful engagement with Said's career against the background of the Cold War in *Archives of Authority*.

63  Said, *Humanism and Democratic Criticism*, 36.

64  Rubin, *Archives of Authority*, 103.

65  "Socialist Realism was, above all, a political–aesthetic doctrine based upon certain 'principles of the artistic method,' such as 'ideological commitment' (*ideinost'*), 'party-mindedness' (*partiinost'*), 'popular spirit' (*narodnost'*), 'historicism,' and 'typicality.'" Dobrenko, "Socialist Realism," 100.

66  Personal accounts of traveling through the USSR, such as La Guma's *A Soviet Journey*, reveal the well-orchestrated itineraries of foreign visitors and the omnipresence of translators as mediators of official Soviet policy. See also Matusevich, "Journeys of Hope," 73, for the experience of African students in the USSR.

67  Victor Ramzes, "African Literature in Russia," *Transition* 25 (1966): 41. This arti-

cle demonstrates Neogy's commitment to an open publication policy, irrespective of an article's political orientation.
68   La Guma, *Soviet Journey*, 209.
69   For a detailed history of the creation of the Soviet public, see Dobrenko, *Making of the State*.
70   Ramzes, "African Literature in Russia," 42. While the figures are indeed impressive, the publication market in the socialist countries was not for profit, and there are no definitive figures that indicate how many of these books were actually purchased. Also, according to Maxim Matusevich, the Soviet Union had violated the copyright and did not pay royalties for works by Nigerian writers like Ekwensi and Soyinka. Matusevich, *No Easy Row*, 167.
71   For the *Ramparts* article and the CIA counteroffensive, see Saunders, *Cultural Cold War*, 320–21.
72   W. E. B. Du Bois was one of the high-profile participants, and the archives housing his materials at the University of Massachusetts also contain valuable images from this event.
73   See Djagalov, *From Internationalism to Postcolonialism*, appendix, 227–28, for a list of all the winners of the Lotus Prize by year.
74   Halim, "Lotus"; Yoon, "Our Forces Have Redoubled"; and Djagalov, *From Internationalism to Postcolonialism*. There is fresh interest in the AAWA, as shown by the formation of two working groups dedicated to researching its cultural impact. One group, of which I am a founding member, together with Djagalov, Yoon, Halim, and Leah Feldman, had its inaugural workshop at New York University in May 2017. The other group is based at the American University in Beirut.
75   Nida Ghouse calls it a "little magazine," a term used to describe noncommercial magazines. This is at odds with the aims and publication history of this journal, which enjoyed state funding and editorial support from the Eastern Bloc. Ghouse, "Lotus Notes."
76   Halim, "Lotus," 563–65.
77   For the first few issues, the journal had the title *Afro-Asian Writings*. The decision to change it to *Lotus: Afro-Asian Writings* was made at the editorial board meeting in Moscow in June 1969, and it was announced in the seventh issue in January 1971. The publication date of the first issue is misprinted on the covers of the English and French editions as 1967 (instead of 1968). Throughout the years, some issues featured a volume number, while others did not.
78   Resolution "On the Counter-action to Imperialist and Neo-colonialist Infiltration in the Cultural Field," *Afro-Asian Writings* 1, no. 1 (March 1968): 142.
79   *Afro-Asian Writings* 1, no. 1 (March 1968): 141–42.
80   Djagalov, *From Internationalism to Postcolonialism*, 17.
81   Quoted in Djagalov, *From Internationalism to Postcolonialism*, 70.
82   Eikhenbaum, "Literary Environment," 58.
83   Youssef El-Sebai, "Editorial: Tashkent and the Afro-Asian Writers," *Afro-Asian Writings* 1, no. 4 (January 1970): 8.

84   El-Sebai, "Editorial," 8.
85   El-Sebai, "Editorial," 9.
86   Youssef El-Sebai, "The Role of Afro-Asian Literature and the National Liberation Movements," *Afro-Asian Writings* 1, no. 1 (March 1968): 8. This first editorial strikes a more balanced note than the starkly Manichean image of the world El-Sebai painted in subsequent issues.
87   El-Sebai, "Role of Afro-Asian Literature," 9. It is interesting to observe the bifurcation of the discourse of freedom during the Cold War, with its different idioms and referents in the West and the Eastern Bloc.
88   El-Sebai, "Role of Afro-Asian Literature," 5.
89   For "revolutionary romanticism" and its differences from nineteenth-century romanticism, see Clark, *Soviet Novel*, 33–34.
90   Kamal Djumblatt, "The Cause of Freedom as Reflected in Afro-Asian Literature," *Afro-Asian Writings* 1, no. 4 (January 1970): 42.
91   Luis Bernardo Honwana, "The Role of Poetry in the Mozambican Revolution," *Lotus: Afro-Asian Writings* no. 8 (April 1971): 155.
92   Bhisham Sahni, "The Struggle against Cultural and Ideological Imperialist Expansionism," *Lotus: Afro-Asian Writings* no. 56 (Summer 1985): 98.
93   Duerden, 1961 report, quoted in G. Moore, "Transcription Centre," 169.
94   Quoted in R. Wright, *Color Curtain*, 14. For recent studies on the cultural afterlives of Bandung, see especially Prashad, *The Darker Nations*; Lee, *Making a World after Empire*; and Burton, *Brown over Black*. The conference made visible the power that the united will of (formerly) colonized nations could wield and the consequent anxiety of the Western world: "But I hope that this Conference will give *more* than understanding only and good will only—I hope that it will falsify and give the lie to the saying of one diplomat from far abroad: 'We will turn this Asian-African Conference into an afternoon-tea meeting.'" "Sukarno Speaks at Bandung, 1955," in Hanhimäki and Westad, *Cold War*, 349.
95   R. Wright, *Color Curtain*, 93. Wright's travels to Indonesia were actually sponsored by the CCF, which allowed him to publish a series of institutionally unaffiliated articles that were later collected as *The Color Curtain*. As with other cultural enterprises it sponsored, the CCF (and the CIA) preferred to maneuver unobtrusively from the shadows. Roberts, *Artistic Ambassadors*, 147–48.
96   Richard Wright gave up his Communist Party membership in the early 1940s, contributed to the anticommunist volume *The God That Failed* (a collection of essays by disenchanted former communists, edited by Arthur Koestler et al.), and, while living in France, whether for reasons of protection or out of conviction, reported on communist activities to U.S. embassy officials in Paris. C. Tolliver, "Making Culture Capital," 215.
97   Edwards, "Uses of Diaspora," 47–48.
98   My translation. The original reads, "Cette revue ne se place sous l'obédience d'aucune idéologie philosophique ou politique." Alioune Diop, "Niam n'goura ou les raisons d'être de *Présence Africaine*," *Présence Africaine* 1, no. 1 (1947): 7.
99   Alioune Diop, foreword, *Présence Africaine* 1–2 (1955): 8.

100 C. Tolliver, "Making Culture Capital," 205, 208.
101 Diop, foreword, 9.
102 Es'kia Mphahlele, "Conferences on African Literature in French and English and the University Curriculum," TC Records, box 17, folder 15, pp. 2, 5.
103 In French, Le premier Congrès mondial des écrivains et artistes noirs.
104 L. S. Senghor, "The Spirit of Civilization or the Laws of African Negro Culture," *Présence Africaine* 8–10 (June–November 1956): 51.
105 Alioune Diop, "Discours d'ouverture," *Présence Africaine* 8–10 (1956): 15.
106 Diop, "Discours d'ouverture," 9, 11.
107 C. Tolliver, "Making Culture Capital," 215.
108 I. Katz, memo to J. Hunt, "Memo on Zeke's Progress in Africa since His Arrival," October 4, 1963, IACF Records, box 71, folder 6.
109 E. Mphahlele memo to J. Hunt, "Africa Memo 15," September 6, 1962, IACF Records, box 364, folder 2.
110 For more details see "American Society of African Culture, August 1, 1958–December 31, 1958," the Horace Mann Bond Papers, University of Massachusetts, Amherst, 49. I am grateful to Cedric Tolliver for bringing this letter exchange to my attention.
111 Djagalov, *From Internationalism to Postcolonialism*, 77.
112 For Indian Ocean studies, see Hofmeyr, "Black Atlantic Meets"; and Gupta, Hofmeyr, and Pearson, *Eyes across the Water*. For defining the South Atlantic as a cultural exchange zone, see the 2017 collection *The Global South Atlantic*, edited by Kerry Bystrom and Joseph Slaughter. The Global South is also defined positionally, "to refer both to a global and decentralized system of inequity that affects diverse peoples across a fluid geographical space and to a transnational resistance that is unified around ideological rather than trait-based affinities." Mahler, *From the Tricontinental*, 26. According to Alfred López, the Global South is "the mutual recognition among the world's subalterns of their shared condition at the margins of the brave new neoliberal world of globalization." López, "Introduction," 3.
113 Prashad, *Darker Nations*, xv.
114 R. Young, *Postcolonialism*, 4–5.
115 For an authoritative discussion of tricontinentalism and the *Tricontinental*, see Mahler, *From the Tricontinental*.
116 Asein, "Ideas de Alex La Guma." See also Gonzales, "Alex La Guma."
117 Roger Field's magisterial literary political biography of Alex La Guma, especially ch. 8 and ch. 9, presents a detailed account of the writer's travels. See also Lee, "Introduction."
118 Lee, *Making a World*, 283.
119 See Popescu, *South African Literature*, 26.
120 Alex La Guma, "Come Back to Tashkent," *Afro-Asian Writings* 1, no. 4 (January 1970): 208–10; Alex La Guma, "Thang's Bicycle," *Lotus: Afro-Asian Writings* 29, no. 3 (July–September 1976): 42–47.
121 Ngũgĩ, *Decolonising the Mind*, 3.

122  Ngũgĩ, "The Links That Bind Us," in *Writers in Politics*, 102.
123  Ngũgĩ, "The Links That Bind Us," in *Writers in Politics*, 106. Also, the unnamed narrator of Ngũgĩ's *Petals of Blood*, who traces the story of the Ilmorog plains back to immemorial times, asks, "Where went all the Kenyan people who used to trade with China, India, Arabia long before Vasco da Gama came to the scene and on the strength of gunpowder ushered in an era of blood and terror and instability?" (67).
124  Burton, "The Sodalities of Bandung," 352.
125  For a detailed analysis of the formation and unraveling of such contextual alliances in Dar es Salaam during the 1960s, see Ivaska, "Movement Youth."
126  Ngũgĩ, *Petals of Blood*, 163.
127  Ngũgĩ, "The South Korean People's Struggle," in *Writers in Politics*, 117. The 1976 International Emergency Conference on Korea was called in Japan in order to discuss and take a stance against political oppression under Park Chung Hee's military dictatorship in South Korea. Ngũgĩ, *Writers in Politics*, 107.
128  Quoted in Indangasi, "Ngugi's Ideal Reader," 193.
129  Spender, "Stephen Spender," 272. When the CIA involvement in the CCF became evident, Spender resigned and argued that he never knew about it.
130  Fischer, "Louis Fischer," 223. For a more in-depth discussion, see also Kalliney, "Modernism," 346.
131  Nkrumah, speech at the Positive Action Conference.

## Chapter 2: Aesthetic World-Systems

1  *Secondary orality* is a term introduced by Abiola Irele to describe written texts that emphasize the transfer of modes of oral expression into print. Irele, "Orality, Literacy," 79. For socialist realist features, see Gikandi, *Ngugi wa Thiong'o*, 135, 156, 225.
2  For features of Ngũgĩ's Marxist aesthetics, see Balogun, *Ngugi*.
3  Lindfors, "*Petals of Blood*," 51.
4  Amuzu, *Beyond Ideology*, 20 (emphasis mine).
5  Ngũgĩ, *Decolonising the Mind*, 68.
6  Nathan Glazer, quoted in Barnhisel, *Cold War Modernists*, 1–2.
7  Saunders, *Cultural Cold War*, 215. For a detailed account of this shift, see Saunders, *Cultural Cold War*, 212–15. For the role of the Museum of Modern Art in promoting abstract expressionism, see Barnhisel, *Cold War Modernists*, 5–6.
8  See R. Williams, *Politics of Modernism*; Jameson, *Antinomies of Realism*, especially pt. 1; and Goodlad, "Introduction."
9  Goodlad, "Introduction," 186.
10  See R. Williams, "When Was Modernism," in *Politics of Modernism*, 32.
11  Andrade, "Realism, Reception," 293.
12  See Lukács, especially "Narrate or Describe?" in *Writer and Critic*. However, the realism-modernism debate was not just a discussion between Marxists and non-Marxists; within the leftist camp, some of the most acerbic debates took place between Lukács and Theodor Adorno. See Adorno et al., *Aesthetics and Politics*.

13  Jameson, "Culture and Finance Capital," 256.
14  Jameson, "Culture and Finance Capital," 256.
15  See Katerina Clark's assessment of the perception of socialist realism in the West in *The Soviet Novel: History as Ritual*.
16  Jameson, *Antinomies of Realism*, 2.
17  Jameson, *Antinomies of Realism*, 1–11.
18  See Jameson, "Culture and Finance Capital." Addressing the increased abstraction that characterizes both finance capital and modernism, Jameson observed that "modernism faithfully—even 'realistically'—reproduced and represented the increasing abstraction and deterritorialization of Lenin's 'imperialist stage.' Today, what is called postmodernity articulates the symptomatology of yet another stage of abstraction, qualitatively and structurally distinct from the previous one, . . . the finance capital moment of globalized society, the abstractions brought with it by cybernetic technology" (252).
19  Gugelberger, "Marxist Literary Debates," 2.
20  A much more nuanced and insightful analysis of form in relation to ideology in Soyinka's and Ngũgĩ's plays is put forth by Biodun Jeyifo: "Ngũgĩ is everywhere insistent that as far as theatre is concerned, modernity in Africa lives or dies with workers and farmers especially. . . . For him, the unity and communalism of *Ujamaa* are solidly class-based. By contrast, Soyinka's faith, as quiet as it is kept, is in a radical-liberal bourgeoisie of gifted and conscientious individuals and groups." Jeyifo, "Ayan Contra *Ujamaa*," 13.
21  The hardening of conservatism in the United States and the United Kingdom, the triumph of CIA-backed dictatorships, and the continuous onslaught on culture and education as putative bastions of the left contributed to the polarization of the cultural field. Consequently, numerous cultural figures retreated into the apolitical world of poststructuralist theory. Brennan, *Wars of Position*, 42, 96–99; and Scott, *Refashioning Futures*, 196.
22  Nkosi, "What Makes Poetry Not Prose," quoted in Lombardozzi, "An Introduction to the Poetry of Lewis Nkosi," 137.
23  Nkosi, "Postmodernism and Black Writing," 83. For Nkosi's perspectives on African literature in the 1970s, see his collection of essays *Tasks and Masks*.
24  Gugelberger, "Marxist Literary Debates," 16.
25  A good collection of essays that reflects Wallerstein's interests is his 1979 *The Capitalist World-Economy*.
26  Peter Worsley explains some of the challenges scholars posed to Wallerstein's idea and the latter's response. See especially Worsley, "One World or Three?," 299–300.
27  Brown, *Utopian Generations*, 4.
28  The members of this praiseworthy collective initiative are Sharae Deckard, Nicholas Lawrence, Neil Lazarus, Graeme Macdonald, Upamanyu Pablo Mukherjee, Benita Parry, and Stephen Shapiro.
29  WReC, *Combined and Uneven Development*, 49.
30  WReC, *Combined and Uneven Development*, 55, 51. Their case studies include

"Tayeb Salih's *Season of Migration to the North* (Sudan, 1969), Victor Pelevin's *The Sacred Book of the Werewolf* (Russia, 2005), Peter Pist'anek's *Rivers of Babylon* (Slovakia, 1991), Pio Baroja's *The Quest* (Spain, 1922), Halldor Laxness's *The Atom Station* (Iceland, 1948), James Kelman's *The Busconductor Hines* (Scotland, 1984) and Ivan Vladislavic's *Portrait with Keys* (South Africa, 2006)" (51).

31 WReC, *Combined and Uneven Development*, 52.
32 WReC, *Combined and Uneven Development*, 8.
33 Worsley, "One World or Three?," 301, 302.
34 Worsley characterized Wallerstein's theory as "over-deterministic": "it is a picture of a world so determined by capitalism, and particularly by those who control the core capitalist states, that it leads logically to fatalism and resignation, for it becomes difficult to see how any part of such a tightly-knit system can possibly break away." Worsley, "One World or Three?," 305.
35 Wallerstein, *Capitalist World-Economy*, 68, 74–75; and Gorin, "Socialist Societies," 335–37.
36 Wallerstein, *Capitalist World-Economy*, 90.
37 Gorin, "Socialist Societies," 336.
38 This is demonstrated by the acerbic forms the Cold War battles took and the fact that each bloc of states interacted primarily among themselves rather than across blocs. Gorin, "Socialist Societies," 336–38.
39 In a brilliant conference paper on cultural arbitrage and the movement of art across the Iron Curtain, Kevin M. F. Platt underscored the fallacy of theorizing a single (capitalist) market and argued in favor of taking into account the relations between the socialist and the capitalist systems. Platt, "Global Exchange, Aesthetics, Arbitrage."
40 Worsley, "One World or Three?," 317.
41 WReC, *Combined and Uneven Development*, 22. This analytical move allows them to include "the work written by writers celebrated as 'modernist' alongside coeval and even antecedent work by writers from peripheral and semi-peripheral locations—Pérez Galdós, Machado de Assis, José Rizal, Hristo Botev, Knut Hamsun, Lu Xun, for instance—writers seldom considered in this context because critics have rarely thought through the full implications of the link between modernism, modernity and modernisation" (18).
42 "We need to do away once and for all with the still-dominant understandings of modernism that situate it both in terms of writerly technique (self-conscious, anti- or at least post-realist, etc.) and as a Western European phenomenon, whose claims to being the literature of modernity are underscored precisely by this geo-political provenance." WReC, *Combined and Uneven Development*, 18.
43 The case of China within the socialist world-system deserves a more detailed consideration than space allows here. For the development of the parallel Afro-Asian Writers Associations supported by China and the USSR, respectively, see Yoon, "Our Forces Have Redoubled."
44 Cleary, "Realism after Modernism," 258.
45 WReC, *Combined and Uneven Development*, 57. Referring to the Adorno-Lukács

polemic around the middle of the twentieth century, the WReC reminds us that Adorno proclaimed modernism as resistant to incorporation (58). This claim has been debunked by the recent research on the CCF and the hijacking of abstract modernism by the U.S. government's cultural politics.

46  La Guma, "Alexander Solzhenitsyn," 76.
47  See Armah, *Eloquence of Scribes*, especially chs. 20–22.
48  Mphahlele, *Afrika My Music*, loc. 443 of 3723, Kindle.
49  Mukoma, *Rise of the African Novel*, 105, 10.
50  Arenberg, "Tanzanian *Ujamaa*."
51  For evaluations of this debate, see also Gugelberger, "Marxist Literary Debates," 11–14; and Lazarus, "Modernism and African Literature," 229–32.
52  Chinweizu, Jemie, and Madubuike, *Decolonization of African Literature*, 149.
53  Chinweizu, Jemie, and Madubuike, *Decolonization of African Literature*, 149.
54  Chinweizu, Jemie, and Madubuike, *Decolonization of African Literature*, 157.
55  J. P. Clark, "Another Kind of Poetry," *Transition* 25 (1966): 17.
56  Clark, "Another Kind of Poetry," 18.
57  Brennan, *Wars of Position*, 43.
58  See Kalliney, "Modernism"; A. Rogers, "*Black Orpheus*"; Rubin, *Archives of Authority*; and Bulson, "Little Magazine, World Form."
59  P. Benson, *Black Orpheus*, 24.
60  P. Benson, *Black Orpheus*, 95.
61  P. Benson, *Black Orpheus*, 66.
62  Julian Beinart, "Malangatana," *Black Orpheus* 10 (1961): viii.
63  Janheinz Jahn, "Aime Cesaire," *Black Orpheus* 2 (January 1958): 34.
64  Jahn, "Aime Cesaire," 35.
65  Jahn, "Aime Cesaire," 35.
66  Starting in 1976, *Transition* briefly circulated as *Ch'indaba*, edited by Wole Soyinka and produced in Ghana. The cover of the double issue was "designed by Ampofo Anti, an Art Fellow at the Institute of African Studies, University of Ghana" based "on the motif of the original cover (Nos. 1–9)." *Transition* 50/*Ch'indaba* 1, inside front cover.
67  "Culture in Transition," *Transition* 1 (November 1961): 2.
68  "Culture in Transition," 2.
69  Rajat Neogy, "Poems," *Transition* 1 (November 1961): 37.
70  Rajat Neogy, "7T ONE == 7E TON," *Transition* 1 (November 1961): 10.
71  Dennis Duerden, "Mbari Writers' Conference in Uganda," 3–4, TC Records, series I, box 1, folder 3.
72  Ulli Beier, "Contemporary African Poetry in English," 4, TC Records, series I, box 1, folder 3. According to TC files, Beier did not read the paper at the conference owing to ill health; however, its presence among the key conference documents speaks to Beier's influence in literary circles.
73  G. Moore, "Language of Poetry," 100.
74  Mphahlele, "Postscript on Dakar," 80–82.
75  Eldred Jones, discussion section in Mphahlele, "Postscript on Dakar," 83.

76 Gugelberger, "Introduction," vii, viii.
77 Although Rubin rather ungenerously presents Soyinka as a willing beneficiary of the CCF, the situation is more complex. Rubin, *Archives of Authority*, 66. When he understood that his friends at the Transcription Centre and the CCF were likely funded by the U.S. government, Soyinka distanced himself from them. TC Records, series II, box 18, folder 1. Biodun Jeyifo urges us to take a more nuanced approach to Soyinka's work, in all its "contradictory determinateness," concluding that the Nigerian writer's oeuvre is "the elaboration of a distinctly African literary modernity through a poetics of culture and a revolutionary tragic mythopoesis which is also neo-modernist." Jeyifo, *Wole Soyinka*, 45.
78 Gugelberger, "Marxist Literary Debates," 1.
79 See also Onoge, "Crisis of Consciousness," 21.
80 Nkosi, "Postmodernism and Black Writing," 81.
81 Wanjala, "Lewis Nkosi's Early Literary Criticism," 32.
82 Hardt and Negri, *Empire*, 137–39.
83 Lazarus, "Modernism and African Literature," 239.
84 Lazarus, "Modernism and African Literature," 239. Lazarus's analysis of modernism is a stepping-stone toward the more complex analysis the WReC laid out later.
85 Kalliney, "Modernism," 337.
86 Rubin, *Archives of Authority*, 19–21.
87 Editorial, *Black Orpheus* 1 (1957): 4.
88 Adeboye Babalola, "Ijala: The Poetry of Yoruba Hunters," *Black Orpheus* 1 (September 1957): 7.
89 Esty and Lye, "Peripheral Realisms Now," 270.
90 Esty and Lye, "Peripheral Realisms Now," 270. See also Lazarus: "African writers sought to cast their 'modernism' instead as an articulatory form of practice . . . mediating between their wider communities and the colonial order beyond. This form of practice could only be symbolic. The resort to aesthetics involved no necessary 'ideology of the aesthetic': instead, it registered their commitment to social self-determination." Lazarus, "Modernism and African Literature," 239.
91 Cleary, "Realism after Modernism," 262–63.
92 According to Esty and Lye, "Colin McCabe's 1974 criticism that 'classical realism' fixes 'the subject in a point of view from which everything becomes obvious' is usually cited as an inaugural moment for postmodernism's dismissal of realism." Esty and Lye, "Peripheral Realisms Now," 271.
93 Mazisi Kunene, "Background to African Literature," *Afro-Asian Writings* 1, no. 1 (1968): 37.
94 Helgesson, *Transnationalism in Southern African Literature*, 103.
95 Dipoko, "Cultural Diplomacy in African Literature," 69–70.
96 "Literature and Resistance in South Africa: Report of the South African Delegation to the 3rd Afro-Asian Writers Conference," *Lotus: Afro-Asian Writings* 1, nos. 2–3 (Summer 1968): 93.
97 Balutansky, *Novels of Alex La Guma*, 14, 19.

98   M. Shafeek Faind, "Modern African Stories," *Lotus: Afro-Asian Writings* 1, nos. 2–3 (Summer 1968): 176–77.
99   Alex La Guma, "What I Learned from Maxim Gorky," *Lotus: Afro-Asian Writings* 34, no. 4 (October-December 1977): 167.
100  Quoted in Woll, "Russian Connection," 225.
101  The cover of *Lotus: Afro-Asian Writings* 10, no. 4 (October 1971), features an armrest, described on the inside of the front cover: "The Luba tribe, in the Congo, often carve motifs in wood similar to this arm-rest destined for the dance. The carving represents a man and wife in fanshape unit adorned with leads. The man and woman appear as one bosit [sic] unit of life, as twins, the whole expressing their deep attachment." However, the very first issue of the journal sports a cover of abstract lines and circles, while the inside of the front cover reproduces a painting by Sudanese artist Ibrahim Salahi, whose modernist work was much admired by the art critics associated with *Black Orpheus*.
102  Mugo, "Culture and Imperialism," 4.
103  Inside back cover of *Afro-Asian Writings* no. 5 (April 1970).
104  Mirza Ibrahimov, "The Problem of Innovation and Tradition," *Lotus: Afro-Asian Writings* 1, no. 4 (January 1970): 248.
105  Dobrenko, "Socialist Realism," 100. Caute notes, "Early in 1936 *Pravda* launched a series of articles attacking formalism, fully ten years before the same campaign was renewed at the onset of the cold war." Caute, *Dancer Defects*, 510.
106  Clark, *Soviet Novel*, ix.
107  Sarvar Azimov, "Inaugural Address," *Lotus: Afro-Asian Writings* 1, no. 4 (January 1970): 229.
108  *La Conférence des Écrivains*, 6, 10.
109  La Guma refers to Gorky in "Literature and Life," *Lotus: Afro-Asian Writings* 1, no. 4 (1970): 237, and El-Sebai invokes Sholokhov in "The Role of Afro-Asian Literature and the National Liberation Movements," *Lotus: Afro-Asian Writings* 1, no. 1 (March 1968): 11.
110  La Guma, "Alexander Solzhenitsyn," 75.
111  Gikandi, *Ngugi wa Thiong'o*, 148, 144. For a discussion of diverging trends in Ngũgĩ's aesthetics, see also Amoko, *Postcolonialism*, 2, 71–72; and Sharma, "Socialism and Civilization," 22.
112  J. T. Ngugi, "A Kenyan at the Conference," *Transition* 5 (July–August 1962): 7.
113  Ngugi, "Kenyan at the Conference," 7.
114  Gikandi, *Ngugi wa Thiong'o*, 105.
115  Ngugi, "Kenyan at the Conference," 7.
116  Gikandi, *Ngugi wa Thiong'o*, 104.
117  See, for instance, Caminero-Santangelo, "Neocolonialism." Ngũgĩ wrote his honors thesis at Makerere on Conrad's oeuvre, hence his fascination with the Polish writer.
118  Mwangi, *Africa Writes Back to Self*, 151–63. Mwangi's focus is on the gendered features of the changes between the 1967 and the 1986 editions.
119  For the socialist realist label, see Gikandi, *Ngugi wa Thiong'o*, 135.

120 Robson, *Ngũgĩ wa Thiong'o*; and Asong, *Detective Fiction*.
121 Ngũgĩ, *Petals of Blood*, 45.
122 Gikandi speaks of Ngũgĩ's continuous reevaluation and reinvention of the novel genre to address the demands of postindependence Kenya. Gikandi, *Ngugi wa Thiong'o*, 13. For the social background, see Branch, *Kenya*.
123 Robson, quoted in Asong, *Detective Fiction*, 22.
124 His first literary attempt "was an imitation of the American thriller writer Edgar Wallace." Ngũgĩ, *Ngũgĩ wa Thiong'o Speaks*, 103.
125 Asong, *Detective Fiction*, 54, 53.
126 Ngũgĩ, *Ngũgĩ wa Thiong'o Speaks*, 371.
127 Ngũgĩ, *Ngũgĩ wa Thiong'o Speaks*, 371.
128 Gikandi, *Ngugi wa Thiong'o*, 278.
129 Gikandi and Apollo Obonyo Amoko point out that Ngũgĩ challenges the ideology of the novel as a bourgeois genre and that of Western literature in general. Gikandi, *Ngugi wa Thiong'o*, 143; and Amoko, *Postcolonialism*, 12–13.
130 See Gikandi, *Ngugi wa Thiong'o*; and Balogun, *Ngugi*.
131 Ngũgĩ is not the only African writer to express admiration for Russian literature. For the role of Russia in the South African literary imaginary, see Popescu, *South African Literature*.
132 Booker and Juraga, "Reds and the Blacks," 276, 277–80.
133 Ngũgĩ makes repeated references to his admiration for nineteenth-century Russian novelists. *Ngũgĩ wa Thiong'o Speaks*, 50, 220. See also P. Williams, *Ngugi wa Thiong'o*, 5–6. For South African writers' fascination with Russian and Soviet writers, see Popescu, *South African Literature beyond the Cold War*; and Jeanne-Marie Jackson, *South African Literature's Russian Soul*.
134 Ngũgĩ, *Ngũgĩ wa Thiong'o Speaks*, 221.
135 Ngũgĩ, *Writers in Politics*, 81.
136 In the preface to *Detained*, Ngũgĩ distances himself from direct Soviet or Chinese influences that could be reductively understood as forms of ideological indoctrination (xvi–xvii).
137 Clark, *Soviet Novel*, 46. Despite official narratives that subsumed socialist realist fiction to direct filiations to Gorky's *Mother*, the authors' practices and views were quite divergent. Clark, *Soviet Novel*, 28.
138 Ngũgĩ, *Petals of Blood*, 345.
139 Irele, "Orality, Literacy, and African Literature," 79.
140 Ngũgĩ, *Decolonising the Mind*, 83.
141 See, for instance, his accounts of the reception of *Devil on the Cross* and *Matigari*. Ngũgĩ, *Decolonising the Mind*, 68.
142 Balogun, *Ngugi*, 146. Balogun uses *Matigari* as a case study to show the numerous perspectives and aesthetic lenses through which it can be read, from oral performance to hagiography, and from mythology to reconceptualized realism.
143 I have used the title of a special issue edited by Jed Esty and Colleen Lye and that of a collection of essays edited by Kobena Mercer to signal the current worlding of these modes of writing.

## Chapter 3: Creating Futures, Producing Theory

1. Albie Sachs made these remarks at the thirty-year commemoration of Ruth First's assassination. See Sachs, "General View."
2. Wicomb, *David's Story*, 133.
3. Popescu, *South African Literature*, 50.
4. The most poignant representation of this process appears in Ousmane Sembène's novella and film *Xala*.
5. Byrne, "Africa's Cold War," 104. Frederick Cooper also explores the possibilities opened and foreclosed by the 1958 referendum that gave French Africans the choice of immediate independence or a status within a "French Community." Sembène's idea of revolution as discussed in this chapter clashed with what a large section of the Senegalese political class desired: "Senghor hoped to transform French rule into a layered form of sovereignty: each African territory would choose a government with authority over local affairs; French West Africa as a whole would constitute an African federation with a legislature and executive; and that federation would in turn associate with other territories and federations in a reformed French Union in which all would be rights-bearing citizens." F. Cooper, "Possibility and Constraint," 175.
6. Fraser, "Decolonization," 470.
7. Fanon, *Wretched of the Earth*, 2.
8. Fanon, *Wretched of the Earth*, 55. For Fanon's attention to the context of the Cold War, see Shringarpure, *Cold War Assemblages*, especially ch. 1; and Lee, *Frantz Fanon*, 175.
9. Fanon, *Wretched of the Earth*, 5, 55.
10. Fanon, *Wretched of the Earth*, 2.
11. While arranging the three literary works chronologically would have made lots of sense in terms of establishing causal relations, I have preferred to move from strike (*God's Bits of Wood*), to revolution (*To Every Birth Its Blood*), to the morning after (*The Beautiful Ones Are Not Yet Born*), in order to emphasize a gradation of affective temporal structures. I am grateful to Dan Magaziner for pointing out the merits of a possible chronological arrangement.
12. R. Williams, *Marxism and Literature*, 133.
13. See Hardt, "Foreword," and the collection of essays *The Affective Turn*, edited by Patricia Ticineto Clough and Jean Halley.
14. Hardt argues that affects signal "both our power to affect the world around us and our power to be affected by it, along with the relationship between these two powers." Hardt, "Foreword," ix.
15. Berlant, *Cruel Optimism*, 3.
16. Like Williams, Berlant perceives the idiom of feelings and affects as appropriate for developing "an architecture for apprehending the perturbed world with all the kinds of knowing to which one has access, from the neuro-affective to the rationally processed." Berlant, "Thinking about Feeling Historical," 6.
17. Julie-Françoise Tolliver, analyzing Aimé Césaire's play *A Season in the Congo*,

identifies "an anti-imperialist ethics of 'what could have been,' but it is not a gesture of longing or nostalgia; rather, it represents an active engagement with ... contemporary politics." J.-F. Tolliver, "Césaire/Lumumba," 399.

18   Scott, *Omens of Adversity*, 20, 9–10. The defeat of the Grenada Revolution, Scott argues, contributes to "a wider critical discussion of the ethical-political experience of the temporal 'afterness' of our postcolonial, postsocialist time" (20).

19   Sembène's name was originally printed on books as Sembène Ousmane, with the family name first; unless rendering titles of older publications, I follow the current first-name-first convention. While I draw on the French original, for consistency with the other works discussed, all quotations are from the 1995 Heinemann African Writers Series edition, translated by Francis Price, unless otherwise indicated.

20   Case, "Workers Movements," 283, 284.

21   See also Jones, "Fact and Fiction," 119–20, for connections between the strike and the decolonization struggle in French West Africa.

22   See, for instance, Jones, "Fact and Fiction"; Case, "Workers Movements"; and McDonald, "(Third World) Women." By contrast, Yénoukoumé Enagnon highlights some of the points of Marxist-Leninist theory we can find refracted in *Vehi-Ciosane (White Genesis*, 1966). See Enagnon, "Sembene Ousmane."

23   See especially Gadjigo, *Ousmane Sembène*, ch. 12, "The Docker."

24   Quoted in Gadjigo, *Ousmane Sembène*, 112.

25   Quoted in Gadjigo, *Ousmane Sembène*, 116.

26   Luxemburg, *Mass Strike*, ch. 6.

27   Sembène, *God's Bits of Wood*, 210.

28   "The embryonic urban proletariat is relatively privileged. In the capitalist countries, the proletariat has nothing to lose and possibly everything to gain. In the colonized countries, the proletariat has everything to lose." Fanon, *Wretched of the Earth*, 64. James Jones confirms the disunity among workers' unions in 1947 West Africa. Jones, "Fact and Fiction," 122.

29   Gadjigo identifies the works and ideas of Mongo Beti, Ferdinand Oyono, Césaire, Fanon, and Mario de Andrade as interlocutors for Sembène during his time in France. Gadjigo, *Ousmane Sembène*, 143.

30   See Gadjigo, *Ousmane Sembène*, 144, for Sembène's admiration for and relationship with *Présence Africaine*.

31   See Fanon, *Wretched of the Earth*, especially the chapters "The Trials and Tribulations of National Consciousness" and "On National Culture."

32   Harlow, *Resistance Literature*, 11.

33   Fanon, "Algeria Unveiled," 60n14.

34   Andrade, *Nation Writ Small*, 11.

35   Andrade, *Nation Writ Small*, 6.

36   Numerous articles analyzing *God's Bits of Wood* focus on the women's determining role. See, for instance, Case, "Workers Movements"; and McDonald, "(Third World) Women."

37 Sembène, *God's Bits of Wood*, 34.
38 Sembène, *God's Bits of Wood*, 205.
39 Sembène, *God's Bits of Wood*, 248. For the role of orature in the novel, see also Lavatori, "Alienation or Empowerment?"
40 Case points out a couple of instances when nature prefigures the hopefulness embodied by Bakayoko. Case, "Workers Movements," 279.
41 Sembène, *God's Bits of Wood*, 1.
42 Sembène, *God's Bits of Wood*, 18. This mastery of perceptions of temporality is even more evident when we consider that Sembène condensed fourteen years of labor history into a year. Jones, "Fact and Fiction," 117.
43 Sembène, *God's Bits of Wood*, 21.
44 Sembène, *God's Bits of Wood*, 22.
45 Onoge, "Crisis of Consciousness," 38.
46 Sembène, *God's Bits of Wood*, 94.
47 Sembène, *God's Bits of Wood*, 62.
48 Roman, *Opposing Jim Crow*, 132–33. For the complex ties between black intellectuals and the USSR until the 1950s, see also Baldwin, *Beyond the Color Line*, especially the chapter on Paul Robeson.
49 Bianchini, "Une autre aventure ambigüe," n.p.
50 Katsakioris, "Creating a Socialist Intelligentsia," 259.
51 Josephine Woll traces the aesthetic networks that shaped Sembène's style, from the revolutionary Soviet directors of the 1920s and the 1960s to the Italian neorealists of the 1950s. According to Woll, Sembène never learned Russian, and the instruction took place through an interpreter. Woll, "Russian Connection," 227–28.
52 Quoted in Woll, "Russian Connection," 228.
53 According to Rossen Djagalov and Masha Salazkina, from 1968 throughout the 1970s Sembène frequently took part in the Tashkent Film Festival. Djagalov and Salazkina, "Tashkent '68," 283.
54 Peary and McGilligan, "Ousmane Sembene: An Interview," 19.
55 The same reserved attitude and an almost outright refusal to name the USSR and Marxist-Leninist thinkers as sources of intellectual sustenance can be identified in other interviews as well. There are only sparse references to Marx, Lenin, and socialism in *Ousmane Sembène: Dialogues with Critics and Writers*, edited by Samba Gadjigo et al. and *Ousmane Sembène: Interviews*, edited by Annett Busch and Max Annas, even if they begin to make an appearance in the 1970s.
56 R. Williams, *Marxism and Literature*, 132.
57 Biographical evidence supports this sense of trepidation: Serote seems to have started writing the novel in exile in the United States, a few months before the Soweto Uprising, and the dramatic events forced him to change narrative gears. Visser, "Fictional Projects," 69. Relocating to Botswana in 1977, where he became involved with the Medu Ensemble, he moved geographically closer to the struggle and received military training as an Umkhonto wa Sizwe (MK) member. Ngũgĩ and Serote, "Role of Culture," 42.

58  For debates on the significance of the two-part form, see Titlestad, "Serote's *To Every Birth*"; Bethlehem, "'A Primary Need'"; Visser, "Fictional Projects"; and Sole, "'This Time Set Again.'"
59  Serote emphasizes the importance of representing a collective character in his works and is critical of Hollywood movies that focus on individual achievement. Serote, interview with Solberg, 82.
60  Serote, *To Every Birth*, 179.
61  Titlestad, "Serote's *To Every Birth*," 110–11.
62  Green, "Nadine Gordimer's 'Future Histories,'" 15.
63  Douglas, "Periodizing the American Century," 84.
64  Yet not all novels conform to this pattern (as Hope's and Coetzee's works suggest), and even within the same literary work, not all narrative strands convey the same affect.
65  Miles, "Word and Image," 29.
66  Miles, "Word and Image," 29.
67  Serote, interview with Solberg, 182.
68  See Barboure, "Mongane Serote"; and Villa-Vicencio and Soko, *Conversations in Transition*.
69  See his 1988 discussion with Kenyan writer Ngũgĩ wa Thiong'o: Ngũgĩ and Serote, "Role of Culture," 33, 40–41. Also, in his interview with Solberg, Serote emphasized the interconnection between his political activity and his writing. Serote, interview with Solberg, 180.
70  Serote, in Ngũgĩ and Serote, "Role of Culture," 35.
71  Patel, "Literary Profile," 187.
72  R. Williams, *Marxism and Literature*, 130.
73  Serote, *To Every Birth*, 185.
74  Byrne, "Africa's Cold War," 103–4.
75  Ellis, *External Mission*, 281–93.
76  Sole, "Days of Power," 65.
77  Umkhonto we Sizwe, sometimes spelled uMkhonto we Sizwe (MK), a name that means "Spear of the Nation," was the armed branch of the ANC. For Serote's military training, see Villa-Vicencio and Soko, *Conversations in Transition*, 244.
78  Ellis, *External Mission*, 60–64.
79  See Ellis, *External Mission*, 62–63, on the ill-fated Wankie campaign, when insufficiently equipped MK cadres were sent to infiltrate Rhodesia, with the hope that they would eventually reach South Africa. On the clash between the ANC-SACP leadership's long-term planning and the impatience of guerrillas, see also Serote's rendering of this conflict in his novel *Scatter the Ashes and Go*.
80  For instance, the poem "What's in This Black 'Shit,'" from the volume *Yakhal'inkomo*, weaponizes language, as the expletive *shit* changes from reflection on township life, to insult, to a form of linguistic resistance.
81  Serote, "The Seed and Saints," in *Tsetlo*, 34.
82  Serote, *To Every Birth*, 132.
83  Fanon, *Wretched of the Earth*, 2.

84 Quoted in Villa-Vicencio and Soko, *Conversations in Transition*, 244.
85 Ellis, *External Mission*, 281–83.
86 Quoted in Villa-Vicencio and Soko, *Conversations in Transition*, 244.
87 Serote, *To Every Birth*, 142.
88 Yaone's estrangement and personal crisis in the United States are reflections of Serote's own views on the isolation of exile. In 1974 Serote received a Fulbright scholarship that enabled him to complete a master of fine arts at Columbia University. Villa-Vicencio and Soko, *Conversations in Transition*, 242; Patel, "Mongane Wally Serote," 190.
89 Serote, *To Every Birth*, 106 (emphasis in original).
90 See Nkrumah, *Neo-colonialism*; and First, Steele, and Gurney, *South African Connection*.
91 Serote, *To Every Birth*, 107 (emphasis mine).
92 Serote, *To Every Birth*, 110.
93 For such indirect relations, see also Borstelmann, *Apartheid's Reluctant Uncle*.
94 Ellis, *External Mission*, 76–80.
95 Serote, *To Every Birth*, 133.
96 Serote, *To Every Birth*, 108.
97 The ideological unity and similarities between these two guiding policy documents arise not only from the increasingly tighter links between the ANC and the SACP but also from SACP and ANC leader Joe Slovo's significant role in the formulation of both documents. Ellis, *External Mission*, 77.
98 Serote, *To Every Birth*, 143.
99 A compelling example is Gordimer's *A Sport of Nature* (1987): the author is able to envisage the inauguration of a black president in South Africa who closely resembles Nelson Mandela, yet she is unable to envision the collapse of the Soviet Union and the end of the Cold War.
100 Serote, *To Every Birth*, 163.
101 Serote, *To Every Birth*, 139–40.
102 Serote, *To Every Birth*, 133.
103 Ngũgĩ and Serote, "Role of Culture," 40.
104 Ngũgĩ and Serote, "Role of Culture," 42.
105 Serote, *To Every Birth*, 206.
106 Titlestad, "Mongane Serote's *To Every Birth Its Blood*," 108.
107 Popescu, "Aesthetic Solidarities," 398.
108 See also Saunders, *Cultural Cold War*; and Caute, *The Dancer Defects*.
109 Shringarpure, *Cold War Assemblages*, 15, 63–66. Shringarpure defines the three binds of time as the burden of colonialism and deliberate underdevelopment; the revolutionary leaders' plea to the masses that they "put on hold their immediate identitarian or particularly political concerns for the collective good of the nation" (15); and the assassinations and coups manufactured in Western capitals.
110 Lazarus, *Resistance*, 1.
111 Lazarus, *Resistance*, 8 (emphasis in original).

112 See Ali Mazrui, "Nkrumah: The Leninist Czar," *Transition* 26 (1966): 8–17; Boateng, *Political Legacy*; Biney, *Political and Social Thought*; and Rooney, *Kwame Nkrumah*. Rooney's problematic analysis presents the image of a well-intentioned leader swindled by the Soviet Union (310–12). According to the U.S. ambassador to Ghana, William P. Mahoney, in a report to President John F. Kennedy in 1963, "Nkrumah often serv[ed] the purposes of Mao and Khrushchev but he is too much of an egotist to be their pawn" (313).

113 Nkrumah, *Axioms of Kwame Nkrumah*, 113.

114 Biney, *Political and Social Thought*, 91.

115 Boateng, *Political Legacy*, i–ii. As Boateng points out, Nkrumah had a lasting impact as the leader of the first country on the continent to shake off the colonial yoke; as a political figure who argued for Pan-Africanism; as a voice representing the continent on the world stage, especially as one of the initiators of the Non-Aligned Movement; and as a philosopher, a theorist of neocolonialism, and a "precursor of the structuralist and dependency perspectives" (ii).

116 Nkrumah, speech at the Positive Action Conference.

117 Nkrumah, *Neo-colonialism*, ix.

118 Rooney assesses the impact of the Eastern Bloc as ephemeral: "Nkrumah made flamboyant pro-Soviet remarks, and surrounded himself with left-wing advisers, but apart from fairly wide suspicion of neocolonialism there was little real support in Ghana for the Eastern bloc. The bloc had many opportunities through trade links and special agencies, but muffed every chance it had. Most goods from the East were of poor quality, credits had very difficult conditions attached, Hungarian buses proved hopelessly unreliable, and Nkrumah had personally to intervene over a shipment of Russian cars which were sold as new but proved to be old cars resprayed." Rooney, *Kwame Nkrumah*, 310.

119 The Ministry of Information and Broadcasting, *Osagyefo in the East*, 9.

120 The Ministry of Information and Broadcasting, *Osagyefo in the East*, 9, 13.

121 "Nonalignment, as practiced in Ghana and many other countries, is based on cooperation with all States, whether they be capitalist, socialist or have a mixed economy. Such a policy, therefore, involves foreign investment from capitalist countries, but it must be invested in accordance with a national plan drawn up by the government of the nonaligned State with its own interests in mind." Nkrumah, *Neo-colonialism*, x.

122 Nkrumah, "African Socialism Revisited," 87, 91.

123 Nkrumah, "African Socialism Revisited," 92.

124 Nkrumah, "African Socialism Revisited," 87.

125 The novel's indebtedness to existentialism is signaled by the protagonist's namelessness, the sense of entrapment that permeates his outlook, and the unsolvable moral dilemma he faces: to give in to the cycle of corruption in order to feed his family and provide a more stable social position for them or to self-centeredly cling to his ethical principles, disregarding the effects his decisions have on his family.

126 See D. Wright, "Totalitarian Rhetoric"; and Griffith, "Structure and Image."

127  John Lutz summarizes these criticisms. Lutz, "Pessimism," 94–95; see also Kibera, "Pessimism," 92–93.
128  Nnolim, "Dialectic as Form," 209.
129  Armah, *Beautyful Ones*, 183.
130  Armah, "African Socialism," 30.
131  Armah, "African Socialism," 27. In "Masks and Marx" (originally published in 1985), he addresses the imperialist fashion in which Marxism-Leninism has been aggressively presented as the only correct way of bringing about revolution. There he is much closer to the position he criticizes in Nkrumah's works.
132  Armah, *Beautyful Ones*, 56.
133  Armah, *Beautyful Ones*, 135, 136. Ama Biney remarks on the cynical transformation of Nkrumah's mottos and aphorisms into criticisms of his regime, so that instead of agreeing with their leader that neocolonialism was the highest stage of imperialism, Ghanaians saw Nkrumahism as "the highest stage of opportunism." Biney, *Political and Social Thought*, 91.
134  Armah, *Beautyful Ones*, 136.
135  Armah, *Beautyful Ones*, 56, 7, 89, 136, 95.
136  McGovern, *Socialist Peace?*, 12–13.
137  Lazarus, *Resistance*, 36.
138  Lazarus, *Resistance*, 37.
139  Koselleck, *Futures Past*, 43–45.
140  Armah, *Beautyful Ones*, 81.
141  Armah, *Beautyful Ones*, 106. According to Edmund Bamiro, the phrase stands for "Socialism Means That You Eat and Let Others Eat." Bamiro, "The Pragmatics of English in African Literature," 17.
142  Lazarus, *Resistance*, 48.
143  Armah, *Beautyful Ones*, 91.
144  Armah, *Beautyful Ones*, 157.
145  Armah, "African Socialism," 26.
146  Shringarpure, *Cold War Assemblages*, 15.
147  Koselleck, *Futures Past*, 44.
148  Arendt quoted in Koselleck, *Futures Past*, 48.

## Chapter 4: The Hot Cold War

1  Ractliffe, *As Terras*, 115.
2  The title *As Terras do Fim do Mundo*, or *The Lands of the End of the World*, points to the Portuguese colonizers' disdainful attitude toward Angola, a distant colony they exploited yet never regarded as part of the world truly worth knowing. See also Ractliffe, *As Terras*, 7. For an overview of Ractliffe's work, see Bystrom, "Ideological Disorientation," 69–71.
3  As numerous historians have pointed out, the war in Angola was fueled from the outside, making the civil war label an insufficient descriptor. In fact, even the superpowers described the country as an ideological battlefield. See Gleijeses, *Visions of Freedom*, 299; and Guimarães, *Angolan Civil War*, 175.

4   On Jamba's interstitial position as a Portuguese-speaking Angolan in exile who writes in English, see Rogers and Hofmeyr, "'Papa AK47,'" 35.
5   South West Africa (today Namibia) was a League of Nations mandate of South Africa (1919–1966) and remained under South African control until its independence in 1990. The South African general Edward McGill Alexander wrote exultingly about the Cassinga attack as "a finely coordinated movement, delivering an awesome total of 1,200 antipersonnel bombs, 20,000 pounds ... of high-explosive bombs and a devastating two-aircraft strafing run with 30mm high-explosive fragmentation shells.... [It] sowed death, destruction and terror amongst the occupants of Cassinga." Quoted in Gleijeses, *Visions of Freedom*, 60. For detailed descriptions of the Cassinga attack, see the accounts in Gleijeses, *Visions of Freedom*; Baines, *South Africa's "Border War"*; and C. Williams, "'Remember Cassinga?'"
6   In a detailed account about the Cassinga camp, Christian Williams complicates both sides of the argument, showing that Cassinga was not a military camp as the SADF claimed yet was nonetheless run by PLAN officers and soldiers. The camp started as a military camp for PLAN forces hosted within Angola, yet it developed into a refugee camp. It was overcrowded with Namibians seeking to escape South African abuses by crossing the border into Angola; at the time of the South African raid, these refugees had not been sent farther inland to the Jamba camp owing to lack of space. Williams refuses to fall into the trap of Cold War binarism: "But may we oppose only the story of 'authentic' refugees with the one of 'authentic' soldiers ...? Or are there other histories which may be told, histories which honour the many, diverse victims of Cassinga; histories which include both those who were laid to rest in Cassinga's graves and those whose lives have been shaped by the national history of it?" C. Williams, "'Remember Cassinga?,'" 241. See also Baines, *South Africa's "Border War,"* especially ch. 5, "The Battle *for* Cassinga: Competing and Complicating Histories."
7   According to Williams, the caption was written by Jane Bergerol for the *Guardian*. C. Williams, "'Remember Cassinga?,'" 240–41.
8   Akerman, *Somewhere on the Border*, 1.
9   Akerman, *Somewhere on the Border*, 1.
10  Ractliffe, *As Terras*, 5.
11  Trouillot, *Silencing the Past*, 26.
12  The title of this chapter, with the emphasis on armed conflict, is indebted to the title of Vladimir Shubin's *The Hot "Cold War": The USSR in Southern Africa*. For a discussion of hot Cold War conflicts elsewhere, see Kwon, *Other Cold War*, especially the conclusion; and Rastogi, *Postcolonial Disaster*, especially ch. 4 on Kashmir.
13  Although one of the first liberation movements in Angola, the FNLA folded in the years immediately following the country's independence. Gleijeses, *Visions of Freedom*, 68.
14  For instance, even in Baines and Vale's pathbreaking collection of essays *Beyond the Border War*, the majority of the individual essays focus on national (South African, Namibian, or Angolan) aspects.

15  R. Hamilton, "African Literature in Portuguese," 610.
16  R. Hamilton, "African Literature in Portuguese," 611.
17  A political leader, poet, and Marxist thinker, Neto (1922–1979) led Angola from its independence in 1975 until his death, while also profoundly influencing southern African anticolonial literary traditions.
18  R. Hamilton, "African Literature in Portuguese," 609.
19  *Lotus: Afro-Asian Writings* 13 (July 1972): 148–79.
20  R. Hamilton, "African Literature in Portuguese," 607.
21  Coundouriotis, *People's Right*, 264.
22  For the two opposing views, see Gordon, "Marginalia on 'Grensliteratuur,'" 91; and Roos, "Writing from Within," 141–42.
23  See Barnard, "*Smell of Apples*"; and Heyns, "Fathers and Sons," on the workings of ideology in Behr's *The Smell of Apples*. See also Behr's confession ("South Africa: Living in the Fault Lines") about his co-optation as an informer during his student years.
24  Henriette Roos offers several reasons for the predominance of Afrikaans as the chosen language in which Border War narratives were printed. They range from publication policies (books in Afrikaans were encouraged for cultural reasons and texts critical of the status quo slipped by censors' desks more easily than their counterparts in English) to psychological reasons (given the strong anti-conscription sentiment among the English-speaking population, ex-servicemen might have considered their war stories to be politically incorrect) and literary history explanations. Thus, she observes that the more radical of these writers, like Etienne Van Heerden, Opperman, Behr, Prinsloo, and Weideman can be seen as the harbingers of postmodernist Afrikaans literature. Roos, "Writing from Within," 147.
25  Conway, "'Somewhere on the Border,'" 77.
26  Baines (*South Africa's "Border War"*) and Roos ("Writing from Within") are among the few scholars who have inventoried and evaluated the texts reflecting directly on South Africa's participation in the Border War. However, memoirs and popular-culture accounts of the conflict are not always critical of the aimless loss of lives, political blunders, and human rights abuses committed by the Pretoria government. Nostalgia for the military might of the apartheid state is visible in some publications and especially on right-wing websites.
27  RUTV Journalism Rhodes University, "Somewhere on the Border." For the participation of MK soldiers in Angola, see also the following Mayibuye Archives interviews: "Joe Slovo Interview in London on MK," Mayibuye Center Archives (MCA) 12 – 1304; "Interview with Ayanda Ntsawba, April 20, 1993," MCA 6 – 344; "Oral History Interview with Mandla Langa Conducted by Wolfie Kodesh, 16 September 1993," MCA 6 – 302; "Oral History Interview with Abraham Lentsoane Conducted by Wolfie Kodesh, 5 April 1993," MCA 6 – 305.
28  Akerman, *Somewhere on the Border*, 11.
29  Daniel Conway discusses the psychological proximity of the Border War

30. Akerman, *Somewhere on the Border*, 48. *Bosbefok*, in literal English translation "bush befucked," combines the appellation "bush war" and its "going native" colonial undertones with the recognition of posttraumatic stress disorder as a real hazard for conscripts.
31. Akerman, *Somewhere on the Border*, 27.
32. Akerman, *Somewhere on the Border*, 26.
33. *Swart gevaar* (Afrikaans) means "black threat."
34. Gordimer, *July's People*, 93, 88.
35. "Total onslaught" and "total defense" were governmental terminology to justify the militarization of the country in order to withstand an allegedly imminent communist invasion.
36. Rogez, "Borderline Cases," 131.
37. Delivered at an international congress on the dangers of communism, this statement by the head of the Security Branch was intended as an explanation for the high number of Jewish people attracted by the South African Communist Party. What it demonstrated, in fact, is the kinship between German Nazi ideology and apartheid politics. See Bunting, *South African Reich*, 412.
38. Sparks, *Beyond the Miracle*, 170.
39. Behr, *Smell of Apples*, 81.
40. Behr, *Smell of Apples*, 12–13.
41. Rothwell, "Unmasking Structures," 122.
42. Pepetela, *Mayombe*, 5.
43. Pepetela, *Mayombe*, 2.
44. Pepetela, *Mayombe*, 84.
45. Daniel, "Pepetela," 78, 77; Rothwell, "Unmasking Structures," 125; and Phyllis Peres, quoted in Rothwell, "Unmasking Structures," 125.
46. Some of these theoretical and practical questions can be found in pages 76–86 of *Mayombe*.
47. Pepetela, *Mayombe*, 184.
48. Fanon, *Wretched of the Earth*, 175.
49. Ngũgĩ, *Decolonising the Mind*, 22.
50. See Cabral, "National Liberation and Culture."
51. Jamba, *Patriots*, 12.
52. Jamba, *Patriots*, 175, 195.
53. Jamba, *Patriots*, 195.
54. Jamba, *Patriots*, 136–37.
55. Jamba, *Patriots*, 137–38.
56. Jamba, *Patriots*, 292.
57. Jamba, *Patriots*, 114.
58. Jamba, *Patriots*, 125.
59. Fanon, *Wretched of the Earth*, 175; and Ngũgĩ, *Decolonising the Mind*, 22.

Note: Item 29 continues at top: "through propaganda and militarization of white gender identities. Conway, "'Somewhere on the Border,'" 77."

60 Jamba, *Patriots*, 116.
61 See Hepburn, *Intrigue*.
62 Douglas, "Periodizing the American Century," 76.
63 The archived radio recordings of the South African Broadcast Corporation (SABC), located at the SABC headquarters in Johannesburg, illuminate the silences, denial, and downplaying of the extent to which South Africa was involved in Angola.
64 Windrich, *Cold War Guerrilla*, 67–68.
65 Sanders, *South Africa*, 143.
66 Mikki van Zyl and Leandra Elion have analyzed the content of two radio soap operas, *Die vrou van Shangetti* and *Dr. Louisa Maritz* and have noted the high number of references to the Border War. See also SABC Archives news items, for example, 19750122 (December 1975), 19751128 (November 1975), 19760130 (January 1976), 19760201 (n.d.), 19761231 (December 1977).
67 Behr, *Smell of Apples*, 83.
68 The novel's climax is reached when Marnus peeps through the chinks in his floor and witnesses his father sexually assaulting Frikkie, the boy's trusted friend and playmate. Far from bringing the expected rebellion, this shocking revelation leads to a collusion between the father's values and the son's goals for the future. Barnard, "Smell of Apples," 215.
69 Bystrom, "South Africa," 127.
70 Gordimer, *Essential Gesture*, 282.
71 The thesis of "colonialism of a special type" was developed in the SACP's 1962 program *The Road to South African Freedom: The Programme of the South African Communist Party*.
72 La Guma, "Africa and the USSR," n.p.
73 See Shubin, *Hot "Cold War,"* 240–46, 252–53. For interviews with ANC and SACP cadres who received military training in the USSR, see also "Oral History Interview with James (Loots H.G.) Stuart, NEC Member and Former ANC Rep in Madagascar, Conducted by Wolfie Kodesh, 25/3/93," MCA 6 - 375; and "Oral History Interview with William (General) Twala, MK Veteran and Expert Plumber, Conducted by Wolfie Kodesh, 26/3/93," MCA 6 - 380, Mayibuye Archives.
74 Matusevich, "Journeys of Hope," 55.
75 Westad, *The Global Cold War*; Matusevich, "Journeys of Hope"; Quist-Adade, "From Paternalism to Ethnocentrism."
76 Quoted in Sanders, *South Africa*, 4. For additional news items that promoted this view of Soviet and Cuban imperialism, see the following items in the SABC Archives: "New Year's Message for 1977 by the Prime Minister Mr. BJ Vorster," T 76/187, 19761231; "Douglas McClure Reported on the Release of the British Hostages Held in Unita Controlled Angola," T 84/341, 19840514; "Interview by Mario Crespo with Foreign Affairs Minister Pik Botha about the Withdrawal of Cuban Troops from Angola," T 87/524, 19871013; and "Andre Le Roux in Conversation with Gen. Magnus Malan, the South African Minis-

77 Botha, "R. F. Botha Addresses the American Security Council," *News at Nine*, April 8, 1976, item 7, SABC Archives.
78 Serote, *Scatter the Ashes*, 202.
79 Jacob Dlamini proposes rethinking the history of apartheid through "collaboration and complicity." "How different would the history of apartheid sound if told, not as a history of a racial war, but of what we might call, after Njabulo Ndebele, a 'fatal intimacy' between black and white South Africans?" Dlamini, *Askari*, 2.
80 See Douglas, "Periodizing the American Century"; Piette *The Literary Cold War*; and Hepburn, *Intrigue*.
81 Serote, *Scatter the Ashes*, 3.
82 Serote, *Scatter the Ashes*, 112–13.
83 See Gleijeses, *Visions of Freedom*.
84 R. Young, *Postcolonialism*, 247.
85 Stephen Ellis and Tsepo Sechaba consider the "Strategy and Tactics" document adopted at Morogoro to be "the single most authoritative statement of ANC strategy in the war fought over the next two decades with the South African state." Ellis and Sechaba, *Comrades against Apartheid*, 58.
86 The two-stage transformation was the official view proposed by the ANC and the SACP, and it had its roots in the "colonialism of a special type" thesis. See *Road to South African Freedom*.
87 For the forms of material support given by the USSR to the ANC-SACP movement, see Shubin, *Hot "Cold War."*
88 For tensions between the Soviet and Cuban perspectives on southern Africa, see Gleijeses, *Visions of Freedom*.
89 Serote, *Scatter the Ashes*, 113.
90 Serote, *Scatter the Ashes*, 100–101.
91 Timothy Garton Ash, "True Confessions," *New York Review of Books*, July 17, 1997, 2.
92 Bauman, "Living without an Alternative," 35.
93 Nixon, *Homelands*, 213.
94 See also Popescu, *South African Literature*, 50, for a discussion of temporal inversions in Mandla Langa's *The Memory of Stones*.
95 Sachs, "General View."
96 Born in 1973 in Soweto, Mhlongo is the author of three novels—*Dog Eat Dog* (2003), *After Tears* (2007), and *Way Back Home* (2013)—as well as a collection of short stories, *Affluenza* (2016). For further information on his background and formation, see Moreillon and Stiebel, "Speaking Out."
97 See The South African Truth and Reconciliation Commission, The TRC Final Report, vol. 2, ch. 4, "The Liberation Movements from 1960 to 1990," 348–66.
98 *Tenderpreneur* refers to the new class of black South African business persons who made their fortune through access to government tenders. See also Moreillon and Stiebel, "Speaking Out," 262–63.

99  As Mhlongo pointed out, the novel "is about the implications of the past on the present." In Moreillon and Stiebel, "Speaking Out," 257.
100 For Mhlongo's account of the formative role of the story of "Vera the ghost," an oral tale familiar to numerous Sowetans, see Moreillon and Stiebel, "Speaking Out," 263, 266.
101 Mhlongo, *Way Back Home*, 194.
102 Okri, *Incidents at the Shrine* and *Stars of the New Curfew*.
103 For the representation of Princess Mkabayi as an important political figure who was both revered and reviled for assuming male political attributes, see Masuku, "Depiction of Mkabayi."
104 Mhlongo, *Way Back Home*, 7, 9.
105 According to Mhlongo, his novel "talks about how the ANC government has betrayed the people in post-apartheid South Africa, but also about betrayal within the anti-apartheid movement during the height of the apartheid regime." In Moreillon and Stiebel, "Speaking Out," 260.
106 Mbembe, "Necropolitics," 31. For Mhlongo's discussion of the repeated forms of displacement inflicted by various forms of imperialism in South Africa, see Moreillon and Stiebel, "Speaking Out," 258–59.
107 Mbembe, "Necropolitics," 32.
108 Mhlongo, *Way Back Home*, 53, 114.
109 Ondjaki is the pen name of Ndalu de Almeida, born in Angola in 1977. He studied in Portugal (writing a thesis on Angolan writer José Luandino Vieira) and currently lives in Brazil. He has published several volumes of poetry and novels, several of them (including *Good Morning, Comrades* and *Granma Nineteen and the Soviet's Secret*) focusing on socialist Angola and the (after)effects of the Cold War. For further information on Ondjaki's literary formation, see Bystrom, "Ideological Disorientation," 76–77.
110 Quoted in Leick, *Tombs*, 246.
111 Bystrom draws attention to the conflicting narratives about what happened to Neto's body and the implicit mythologization of the Angolan leader. Bystrom, "Ideological Disorientation," 76. See also Mercedes Sayagues, "Father of Angola Rots in a Grey Mausoleum," Mail & Guardian Online, October 10, 1997, https://mg.co.za/article/1997-10-10-father-of-angola-rots-in-a-grey-mausoleum.
112 Bystrom, "Ideological Disorientation," 79.
113 Bystrom, "Ideological Disorientation," 68.
114 Bystrom points out that the children shout, "Long live the revolution!" before beginning their plan to destroy the mausoleum, thereby repurposing a vocabulary of socialist solidarity against its Soviet initiators. Bystrom, "Ideological Disorientation," 80.
115 For a similarly bivalent view of Russia as colonizer and inferior culture, see Popescu, "Lewis Nkosi in Warsaw."
116 Ondjaki, *Granma Nineteen*, 114.
117 Ondjaki, *Granma Nineteen*, 14, 34, 14.
118 Ondjaki, *Granma Nineteen*, 24.

119  Ondjaki, *Granma Nineteen*, 143.
120  George, *Cuban Intervention in Angola*, 159. Gleijeses explains the singularity of Cuba's intervention in Angola: "No other Third World Country has projected its military power beyond its immediate neighborhood." Gleijeses, *Visions of Freedom*, 9.
121  Mahler, *From the Tricontinental*, 35.
122  Ondjaki, *Granma Nineteen*, 166.
123  Bystrom, "Ideological Disorientation," 80.
124  Bhabha, "Introduction," 7.
125  Ahmad, *In Theory*, 135.
126  Franco, *Decline and Fall*, 159.
127  B. Cooper, *Magical Realism*, 17.
128  "On the negative side, magical realism was a form of cultural incorporation that collapsed literature into anthropology or made it into something of a raid on the rain forests in search of genetic samples." Franco, *Decline and Fall*, 159.
129  Ngũgĩ wa Thiong'o, "Ngugi wa Thiong'o Interviewed on His New Novel, *Wizard of the Crow*," interview by Ken Olende, *Socialist Worker*, November 4, 2006, https://socialistworker.co.uk/art/9867/Ngugi+wa+Thiongo+interviewed+on+his+new+novel,+Wizard+of+the+Crow.
130  Armillas-Tiseyra, "Marvelous Autocrats," 193.
131  Ondjaki, *Granma Nineteen*, 167.

## Conclusion: From Postcolonial to World Literature Studies

1  I am grateful to my friend Andrew McGregor, who, during our time at the University of Pennsylvania, always asked the most insightful and probing questions.
2  Jameson, *Postmodernism*, 45–46.
3  In chapter 2 I developed a theory of two Cold War aesthetic world-systems.
4  See also Shringarpure, *Cold War Assemblages*, ch. 4, for the long arm of the Cold War in digital publishing.
5  In a 1989 article Fukuyama celebrated "the triumph of the West, of the Western idea" as evidenced by "the total exhaustion of viable systematic alternatives to Western liberalism." Fukuyama, "The End of History," 3.
6  Siebers, *Cold War Criticism*, viii.
7  Brennan, *Wars of Position*, 9.
8  Brennan, *Wars of Position*, 24–25; and Scott, *Refashioning Futures*, 14.
9  Scott, *Refashioning Futures*, 12.
10  R. Young, *Postcolonialism*, 270; and Scott, *Refashioning Futures*, 14.
11  Scott, *Refashioning Futures*, 200.
12  Mugo, "Culture and Imperialism," 1.
13  Mugo, "Culture and Imperialism," 2.
14  A number of anthologies that defined the contours of the field came during the 1990s, e.g., Bill Ashcroft, Gareth Griffith, and Helen Tiffin's *The Post-colonial Studies Reader* (1995); Patrick Williams and Laura Chrisman's *Colonial Discourse and Postcolonial Theory* (1994); and Homi K. Bhabha's *Nation and Narration* (1990).

15 Bauman, "Living without an Alternative," 35. Bauman observes that "the world without an alternative needs self-criticism as a condition of survival and decency. But it does not make the life of criticism easy" (44).

16 Brennan, "Postcolonial Studies," 186. Antonio Negri and Michael Hardt present this form of postcolonial scholarship as encircled and overtaken by empire. Hardt and Negri, *Empire*, 137–39.

17 This poststructuralist vocabulary became mainstream in postcolonial studies after the publication of Bhabha's *The Location of Culture* (1994).

18 Shringarpure, *Cold War Assemblages*, 100, 107–28.

19 Misleading parallels and the generalization of statements about a specific site or text to other areas from the Global South further increased the abstraction of postcolonial studies. This is particularly true of "hybridity" and "in-betweenness"—concepts popularized by Bhabha's work—which were then indiscriminately applied to a whole array of postcolonial contexts.

20 Shringarpure, *Cold War Assemblages*, 128.

21 Bartolovich, "Introduction," 1.

22 Armah, "Masks and Marx," 498.

23 See also Nimtz and Jani in Bartolovich and Lazarus, who dismantle the claims that Karl Marx's approach is Eurocentric.

24 Moretti, "Conjectures on World Literature."

25 Khotimsky, "World Literature, Soviet Style," 120; and Djagalov, *From Internationalism to Postcolonialism*, 4.

26 Youssef El-Sebai, "The Role of Afro-Asian Literature and the National Liberation Movements," *Afro-Asian Writings* 1, no. 1 (March 1968): 11.

27 Halim, "Lotus," 565, 572.

28 Rubin, *Archives of Authority*, 12.

29 WReC, *Combined and Uneven Development*, 56.

30 Ngũgĩ, *Globalectics*, 53.

31 Ngũgĩ, *Globalectics*, 8.

32 Ngũgĩ, *Globalectics*, 6, 53.

# BIBLIOGRAPHY

## Archival Sources
Chemchemi Cultural Centre, Kenya National Archives, Nairobi, Kenya
International Association for Cultural Freedom (IACF) Records, Special Collections Research Center, University of Chicago
Mayibuye Center Archives (MCA), University of the Western Cape, South Africa
South African Broadcasting Corporation (SABC) Radio Archives, Johannesburg, South Africa
The Transcription Centre (TC) Records, Harry Ransom Center, University of Texas at Austin

## Periodicals
*Black Orpheus*
*Lotus: Afro-Asian Writings*
*Présence Africaine*
*Transition*

## Primary and Secondary Sources
Adesokan, Akin. "Retelling a Forgettable Tale: *Black Orpheus* and *Transition* Revisited." *African Quarterly on the Arts* 1, no. 3 (1996): 49–57.
Adorno, Theodor. *Minima Moralia: Reflections on a Damaged Life*. Translated by E. F. N. Jephcott. London: Verso, 2005.
Adorno, Theodor, Walter Benjamin, Ernst Bloch, Bertold Brecht, and Georg Lukács. *Aesthetics and Politics*. London: Verso, 2007.
Afro-Asian Writers' Bureau. *The Struggle between the Two Lines in the Afro-Asian Writers' Movement*. N.p.: Afro-Asian Writers' Bureau, 1968.
Ahmad, Aijaz. *In Theory: Classes, Nations, Literatures*. London: Verso, 1992.
Akerman, Anthony. *Somewhere on the Border*. In *South Africa Plays*, edited with an introduction by Stephen Gray, 1–58. 1982. London: Nick Hern, 1993.
Amoko, Apollo Obonyo. *Postcolonialism in the Wake of the Nairobi Revolution*. New York: Palgrave, 2010.
Amuzu, Koku. *Beyond Ideology: Literary Technique in Ngugi's "Petals of Blood" and "Devil on the Cross."* London: Minerva, 1997.
Andrade, Susan. *The Nation Writ Small: African Fictions and Feminisms, 1958–1988*. Durham, NC: Duke University Press, 2011.

Andrade, Susan. "Realism, Reception, 1968, and West Africa." *Modern Language Quarterly* 73, no. 3 (2012): 289–308.

Andrew, Rick. *Buried in the Sky*. London: Penguin, 2001.

Apter, Andrew. *Oil, Blood and Money: Culture and Power in Nigeria*. Chicago: University of Chicago Press, 2005.

Arenberg, Meg. "Tanzanian *Ujamaa* and the Shifting Politics of Swahili Poetic Form." In "African Literary History and the Cold War," edited by Monica Popescu and Bhakti Shringarpure. Special issue, *Research in African Literatures* 50, no. 3 (Fall 2019): 7–28.

Armah, Ayi Kwei. "African Socialism: Utopian or Scientific?" *Présence Africaine* 64 (1967): 6–30.

Armah, Ayi Kwei. *The Beautyful Ones Are Not Yet Born*. London: Heinemann, 1968.

Armah, Ayi Kwei. *The Eloquence of Scribes: A Memoir on the Sources and Resources of African Literature*. Popenguine, Senegal: Per Ankh, 2006.

Armah, Ayi Kwei. *Fragments*. Boston: Houghton Mifflin, 1970.

Armah, Ayi Kwei. "Masks and Marx: The Marxist Ethos vis-à-vis African Revolutionary Theory and Praxis." In *African Literature: An Anthology of Criticism and Theory*, edited by Tejumola Olaniyan and Ato Quayson, 496–503. Malden, MA: Blackwell, 2007.

Armah, Ayi Kwei. *Remembering the Dismembered Continent*. Popenguine, Senegal: Per Ankh, 2010.

Armah, Ayi Kwei. *Why Are We So Blest?* Garden City, NY: Doubleday, 1972.

Armillas-Tiseyra, Magalí. "Marvelous Autocrats: Disrupted Realisms in the Dictator Novel of the South Atlantic." In *The Global South Atlantic*, edited by Kerry Bystrom and Joseph R. Slaughter, 186–204. New York: Fordham University Press, 2017.

Asein, Samuel Omo. "Las ideas de Alex La Guma viven en nuestros pueblos." *Tricontinental* 105 (May–June 1986): 3–10.

Ashcroft, Bill, Gareth Griffiths, and Helen Tiffin. *Key Concepts in Post-Colonial Studies*. London: Routledge, 1998.

Ashcroft, Bill, Gareth Griffiths, and Helen Tiffin, eds. *The Post-Colonial Studies Reader*. London: Routledge, 1995.

Asong, Linus T. *Detective Fiction and the African Scene: From the "Whodunit?" to the "Whydunit?"* Mankon, Cameroon: Langaa Research and Publishing 2012.

Baines, Gary. *South Africa's "Border War": Contested Narratives and Conflicting Memories*. London: Bloomsbury, 2014.

Baines, Gary, and Peter Vale, eds. *Beyond the Border War: New Perspectives on Southern Africa's Late-Cold War Conflicts*. Pretoria: UNISA, 2008.

Baldwin, Kate. *Beyond the Color Line and the Iron Curtain: Reading Encounters between Black and Red, 1922–1963*. Durham, NC: Duke University Press, 2002.

Balogun, F. Odun. *Ngugi and African Post-colonial Narrative: The Novel as Oral Narrative in Multi-genre Performance*. St Hyacinthe, QC: World Heritage, 1997.

Balutansky, Kathleen M. *The Novels of Alex La Guma: The Representation of a Political Conflict*. Washington, DC: Three Continents, 1990.

Bamiro, Edmund. "The Pragmatics of English in African Literature." *Revista de Lenguas para Fines Específicos* 3 (1996): 14–37.

Barboure, Dorian. "Mongane Serote: Humanist and Revolutionary." In *Momentum: On Recent South African Writing*, edited by M. J. Daymond, J. U. Jacobs, and Margaret Lenta, 171–81. Pietermaritzburg: University of Natal Press, 1984.

Barnard, Rita. "*The Smell of Apples, Moby-Dick* and Apartheid Ideology." *Modern Fiction Studies* 46, no. 1 (2000): 207–26.

Barnhisel, Greg. *Cold War Modernists: Art, Literature, and American Cultural Diplomacy.* New York: Columbia University Press, 2015.

Bartolovich, Crystal. "Introduction: Marxism, Modernity and Postcolonial Studies." In *Marxism, Modernity and Postcolonial Studies*, edited by Crystal Bartolovich and Neil Lazarus, 1–17. Cambridge: Cambridge University Press, 2002.

Bartolovich, Crystal, and Neil Lazarus, eds. *Marxism, Modernity and Postcolonial Studies.* Cambridge: Cambridge University Press, 2002.

Bauman, Zygmunt. "Living without an Alternative." *The Political Quarterly* 62, no. 1 (January 1991): 35–44.

Behr, Mark. *The Smell of Apples.* New York: Picador, 1995.

Behr, Mark. "South Africa: Living in the Fault Lines." *Common Sense* 11, no. 1 (October 1996). Accessed March 5, 2014. http://www.nd.edu/~com_sens/issues/old/vii/vii_n1.html#fault.

Benson, Peter. *Black Orpheus, Transition, and Modern Cultural Awakening in Africa.* Berkeley: University of California Press, 1986.

Benson, Peter. "'Border Operators': *Black Orpheus* and the Genesis of Modern Art and Literature." *Research in African Literatures* 14, no. 4 (Winter 1983): 431–73.

Benson, T. G., ed. *Kikuyu-English Dictionary.* London: Oxford University Press, 1964.

Berlant, Lauren. *Cruel Optimism.* Durham, NC: Duke University Press, 2011.

Berlant, Lauren. "Thinking about Feeling Historical." *Emotion, Space and Society* 1 (2008): 4–9.

Bethlehem, Louise. "'A Primary Need as Strong as Hunger': The Rhetoric of Urgency in South African Literary Culture under Apartheid." *Poetics Today* 22, no. 2 (Summer 2001): 365–89.

Bhabha, Homi K. "Introduction: Narrating the Nation." In *Nation and Narration*, edited by Homi K. Bhabha. 1–7. Oxon, UK: Routledge, 1990.

Bhabha, Homi K. *The Location of Culture.* London: Routledge, 1994.

Bianchini, Pascal. "Une autre aventure ambigüe: Les étudiants sénégalais de l'autre coté du « rideau de fer ». Un aperçu de la variabilité de l'expérience du « socialisme réel » à travers quelques trajectoires biographiques." Colloques, Mohammedia. Carnets du Réseau International Afrique-Monde. Posted October 26, 2013. https://riae.hypotheses.org/321.

Biney, Ama. *The Political and Social Thought of Kwame Nkrumah.* New York: Palgrave, 2011.

Boateng, Charles Adom. *The Political Legacy of Kwame Nkrumah of Ghana.* Lewiston, NY: Edwin Mellen, 2003.

Booker, M. Keith, and Dubravka Juraga. "The Reds and the Blacks: The Historical

Novel in the Soviet Union and in Postcolonial Africa." *Studies in the Novel* 29, no. 3 (1997): 275–96.

Borstelmann, Thomas. *Apartheid's Reluctant Uncle: The United States and South Africa in the Early Cold War*. Oxford: Oxford University Press, 1993.

Branch, Daniel. *Kenya: Between Hope and Despair, 1963–2011*. New Haven, CT: Yale University Press, 2011.

Brennan, Timothy. "The Cuts of Language: The East/West of North/South." *Public Culture* 13, no. 1 (2001): 39–63.

Brennan, Timothy. "Postcolonial Studies between the European Wars: An Intellectual History." In *Marxism, Modernity and Postcolonial Studies*, edited by Crystal Bartolovich and Neil Lazarus, 185–203. Cambridge: Cambridge University Press, 2002.

Brennan, Timothy. *Wars of Position: The Cultural Politics of Left and Right*. New York: Columbia University Press, 2006.

Breytenbach, Jan. *Forged in Battle*. Cape Town: Saayman and Weber, 1986.

Brouillette, Sarah. "UNESCO and the Book in the Developing World." *Representations* 127, no. 1 (Summer 2014): 33–54.

Brouillette, Sarah. "US-Soviet Antagonism and the 'Indirect Propaganda' of Book Schemes in India in the 1950s." *University of Toronto Quarterly* 84, no. 4 (Fall 2015): 170–88.

Brown, Nicholas. *Utopian Generations: The Political Horizon of Twentieth-Century Literature*. Princeton, NJ: Princeton University Press, 2005.

Brutus, Dennis. *Poetry and Protest: A Dennis Brutus Reader*. Edited by Lee Sustar and Aisha Karim. Chicago: Haymarket, 2006.

Buck-Morss, Susan. *Dreamworld and Catastrophe: The Passing of Mass Utopia in East and West*. Cambridge, MA: MIT Press, 2000.

Bulson, Eric. "Little Magazine, World Form." In *The Oxford Handbook of Global Modernisms*, edited by Mark Wollaeger and Matthew Eatough, 267–87. Oxford: Oxford University Press, 2013.

Bunting, Brian Percy. *The Rise of the South African Reich*. London: Penguin, 1969.

Burton, Antoinette. *Brown over Black: Race and the Politics of Postcolonial Citation*. Delhi: Three Essays Collective, 2012.

Burton, Antoinette. "The Sodalities of Bandung: Toward a Critical 21st-century History." In *Making a World after Empire: The Bandung Moment and Its Political Afterlives*, edited by Christopher J. Lee, 351–61. Athens: Ohio University Press, 2010.

Busch, Annett, and Max Annas, eds. *Ousmane Sembène: Interviews*. Jackson: University Press of Mississippi, 2008.

Byrne, Jeffrey James. "Africa's Cold War." In *The Cold War in the Third World*, edited by Robert J. McMahon, 101–23. New York: Oxford University Press, 2013.

Bystrom, Kerry. "Ideological Disorientation and Urban Struggle in Postwar Luanda: Notes on Neto's Mausoleum." In *South and North: Contemporary Urban Orientations*, edited by Kerry Bystrom, Ashleigh Harris, and Andrew J. Webber, 65–86. Oxon, UK: Routledge, 2018.

Bystrom, Kerry. "South Africa, Chile and the Cold War: Reading the South Atlantic in Mark Behr's *The Smell of Apples*." In *The Global South Atlantic*, edited by Kerry

Bystrom and Joseph R. Slaughter, 124–43. New York: Fordham University Press, 2017.

Bystrom, Kerry, and Joseph R. Slaughter, eds. *The Global South Atlantic*. New York: Fordham University Press, 2017.

Cabral, Amílcar. "National Liberation and Culture." In *African Literature: An Anthology of Criticism and Theory*, edited by Tejumola Olaniyan and Ato Quayson, 484–91. Malden, MA: Blackwell, 2007.

Caminero-Santangelo, Byron. "Neocolonialism and the Betrayal Plot in *A Grain of Wheat*: Ngũgĩ wa Thiong'o's Re-Vision of *Under Western Eyes*." *Research in African Literatures* 29, no. 1 (Spring 1998): 139–52.

Casanova, Pascale. *The World Republic of Letters*. Translated by M. B. DeBevoise. Cambridge, MA: Harvard University Press, 2004.

Case, F. "Workers Movements: Revolution and Women's Consciousness in *God's Bits of Wood*." *Canadian Journal of African Studies* 15, no. 2 (1981): 277–92.

Caute, David. *The Dancer Defects: The Struggle for Cultural Supremacy during the Cold War*. Oxford: Oxford University Press, 2003.

Caute, David. *Politics and the Novel during the Cold War*. New Brunswick, NJ: Transaction, 2010.

Cazenave, Odile, and Patricia Célérier. *Contemporary Francophone African Writers and the Burden of Commitment*. Charlottesville: University of Virginia Press, 2011.

Césaire, Aimé. "Discourse on Colonialism." In *Postcolonialisms: Critical Concepts in Literary and Cultural Studies*, edited by Diana Brydon, 1: 310–39. London: Routledge, 2000.

Césaire, Aimé. *Discours sur le colonialisme*. Paris: Éditions Présence Africaine, 1955.

Césaire, Aimé. "Letter to Maurice Thorez." *Social Text* 28, no. 2 (Summer 2010): 145–52.

Césaire, Aimé. *Lettre à Maurice Thorez*. Paris: Éditions Présence Africaine, 1956.

Chinweizu, Onwuchekwa Jemie, and Ihechukwu Madubuike. *Toward the Decolonization of African Literature: African Fiction and Poetry and Their Critics*. London: KPI, 1985.

Clark, Katerina. *Moscow, the Fourth Rome: Stalinism, Cosmopolitanism, and the Evolution of Soviet Culture, 1931–1941*. Cambridge, MA: Harvard University Press, 2011.

Clark, Katerina. *The Soviet Novel: History as Ritual*. Bloomington: Indiana University Press, 1981.

Cleary, Joe. "Realism after Modernism and the Literary World-System." *Modern Language Quarterly* 73, no. 3 (September 2012): 255–68.

Clough, Patricia Ticineto, and Jean Halley, eds. *The Affective Turn: Theorizing the Social*. Durham, NC: Duke University Press, 2007.

Coetzee, J. M. *Waiting for the Barbarians*. New York: Penguin, 2010.

Coleman, Peter. *The Liberal Conspiracy: The Congress for Cultural Freedom and the Struggle for the Mind of Postwar Europe*. New York: Free Press, 1989.

Comaroff, Jean, and John Comaroff. "Naturing the Nation: Aliens, Apocalypse and the Postcolonial State." *Journal of Southern African Studies* 27, no. 3 (September 2001): 627–52.

Comaroff, Jean, and John Comaroff. *Theory from the South: Or, How Euro-America Is Evolving toward Africa*. Boulder, CO: Paradigm, 2011.

*La Conférence des Écrivains d'Asie et d'Afrique à Tachkent*. Paris: Traveaux et Recherches, 1960.

Conway, Daniel. "'Somewhere on the Border—of Credibility': The Cultural Construction and Contestation of 'the Border' in White South African Society." In *Beyond the Border War: New Perspectives on Southern Africa's Late-Cold War Conflicts*, edited by Gary Baines and Peter Vale, 75–93. Pretoria: UNISA, 2008.

Cooper, Brenda. *Magical Realism in West African Fiction: Seeing with a Third Eye*. London: Routledge, 1998.

Cooper, Frederick. "Possibility and Constraint: African Independence in Historical Perspective." *Journal of African History* 49 (2008): 167–96.

Coundouriotis, Eleni. *The People's Right to the Novel: War in the Postcolony*. New York: Fordham University Press, 2014.

Damrosch, David. *What Is World Literature?* Princeton: Princeton University Press, 2003.

Daniel, Mary L. "Pepetela and the New Angolan Mythology." In *Homenagem a Alexandrino Severino*, edited by Margo Milleret and Marshall Eakin, 77–85. Austin, TX: Host, 1993.

Dipoko, Mbella Sonne. "Cultural Diplomacy in African Writing." In *The Writer in Modern Africa: African-Scandinavian Writers' Conference, Stockholm, 1967*, edited by Per Wästberg, 59–70. Uppsala: Scandinavian Institute of African Studies, 1968.

Dirlik, Arif. "Global South: Predicament and Promise." *Global South* 1, nos. 1–2 (2007): 12–23.

Djagalov, Rossen. *From Internationalism to Postcolonialism: Literature and Cinema between the Second and the Third World*. Montreal: McGill-Queen's University Press, 2020.

Djagalov, Rossen, and Masha Salazkina. "Tashkent '68: A Cinematic 'Contact Zone.'" *Slavic Review* 75, no. 2 (Summer 2016): 279–98.

Dlamini, Jacob. *Askari: A Story of Collaboration and Betrayal in the Anti-apartheid Struggle*. Auckland Park, South Africa: Jacana Media, 2014.

Dobrenko, Evgeny. *The Making of the State Reader: Social and Aesthetic Contexts of the Reception of Soviet Literature*. Translated by Jesse M. Savage. Stanford, CA: Stanford University Press, 1997.

Dobrenko, Evgeny. "Socialist Realism." In *The Cambridge Companion to Twentieth-Century Russian Literature*, edited by Evgeny Dobrenko and Marina Balina, 97–113. Cambridge: Cambridge University Press, 2011.

Doherty, Megan. "PEN International and Its Republic of Letters, 1921–1970." PhD diss., Columbia University, 2011. https://academiccommons.columbia.edu/doi/10.7916/D8KW5PDT.

Dorn, Charles, and Kristen Ghodsee. "The Cold War Politicization of Literacy: Communism, UNESCO, and the World Bank." *Diplomatic History: The Journal of the Society for Historians of American Foreign Relations* 36, no. 2 (April 2012): 373–98.

Douglas, Ann. "Periodizing the American Century: Modernism, Postmodernism, and

Postcolonialism in the Cold War Context." *Modernism/Modernity* 5, no. 3 (1998): 71–98.

Duerden, Dennis, and Cosmo Pieterse, eds. *African Writers Talking: A Collection of Interviews.* London: Heinemann, 1972.

Eatough, Matthew. "The Critic as Modernist: Es'kia Mphahlele's Cold War Literary Criticism." In "African Literary History and the Cold War," edited by Monica Popescu and Bhakti Shringarpure. Special issue, *Research in African Literatures* 50, no. 3 (Fall 2019): 136–56.

Edwards, Brent Hayes. "The Uses of Diaspora." *Social Text* 19, no. 1 (Spring 2001): 45–73.

Eikhenbaum, Boris. "Literary Environment." In *Readings in Russian Poetics: Formalist and Structuralist Views*, edited by Ladislaw Matejka and Krystyna Pomorska, 56–60. Cambridge, MA: MIT Press, 1971.

Ellis, Stephen. *External Mission: The ANC in Exile, 1960–1990.* New York: Oxford University Press, 2013.

Ellis, Stephen, and Tsepo Sechaba. *Comrades against Apartheid: The ANC and the South African Communist Party in Exile.* London: Currey, 1992.

Enagnon, Yénoukoumé. "Sembene Ousmane, la theorie Marxiste et le roman." *Peuples Noirs Peuples Africaines* 11 (1979): 92–127.

Esty, Jed, and Colleen Lye. "Peripheral Realisms." Special issue, *Modern Language Quarterly* 73, no. 3 (September 2012): 269–87.

Esty, Jed, and Colleen Lye. "Peripheral Realisms Now." *Modern Language Quarterly* 73, no. 3 (September 2012): 269–96.

Fanon, Frantz. "Algeria Unveiled." *A Dying Colonialism.* 35–67. Translated by Haakon Chevalier. Introduction by Adolfo Gilly. New York: Grove, 1965.

Fanon, Frantz. *The Wretched of the Earth.* 1963. Translated by Richard Philcox. Introduction by Homi K. Bhabha. New York: Grove, 2004.

Field, Roger. *Alex La Guma: A Literary and Political Biography.* Woodbridge, UK: James, Currey, 2010.

First, Ruth, Jonathan Steele, and Christabel Gurney. *The South African Connection: Western Investment in Apartheid.* New York: Harper and Row, 1973.

Fischer, Louis. "Louis Fischer." In *The God That Failed*, edited by Richard Crossman, 196–228. New York: Harper, 1949.

Fox, Michael David. *Showcasing the Great Experiment: Cultural Diplomacy and Western Visitors to the Soviet Union, 1921–1941.* Oxford: Oxford University Press, 2012.

Franco, Jean. *The Decline and Fall of the Lettered City: Latin America in the Cold War.* Cambridge, MA: Harvard University Press, 2002.

Fraser, Cary. "Decolonization and the Cold War." In *The Oxford Handbook of the Cold War*, edited by Richard H. Immerman and Petra Goedde, 469–85. Oxford: Oxford University Press.

Fukuyama, Francis. "The End of History?" *The National Interest* 16 (Summer 1989): 3–18.

Gaddis, John. *We Now Know: Rethinking Cold War History.* Oxford: Oxford University Press, 1997.

Gadjigo, Samba. *Ousmane Sembène: The Making of a Militant Artist*. Bloomington: Indiana University Press, 2010.

Gadjigo, Samba, Ralph Faulkingham, Thomas Cassirer, and Reinhard Sander, eds. *Ousmane Sembène: Dialogues with Critics and Writers*. Amherst: University of Massachusetts Press, 1993.

Galgut, Damon. *The Beautiful Screaming of Pigs*. 1991. London: Atlantic, 2005.

George, Edward. *The Cuban Intervention in Angola, 1965–1991: From Che Guevara to Cuito Cuanavale*. Abingdon, UK: Frank Cass, 2005.

Ghosh, Amitav. *In an Antique Land*. London: Granta, 2012.

Ghouse, Nida. "Lotus Notes." *Mada Masr*, May 14–August 20, 2014. http://www.madamasr.com/en/2014/05/14/feature/culture/lotus-notes-part-one/.

Gikandi, Simon. *Ngugi wa Thiong'o*. Cambridge: Cambridge University Press, 2000.

Gleijeses, Piero. *Conflicting Missions: Havana, Washington, and Africa, 1959–1976*. Chapel Hill: University of North Carolina Press, 2002.

Gleijeses, Piero. *Visions of Freedom: Havana, Washington, Pretoria and the Struggle for Southern Africa, 1976–1991*. Chapel Hill: University of North Carolina Press, 2013.

Gonzales, David. "Alex La Guma: Twenty Years in Cuban Memories." *Review of African Political Economy* 32, no. 106 (December 2005): 646–51.

Goodlad, Lauren M. E. "Introduction: Worlding Realisms Now." *Novel: A Forum on Fiction* 49, no. 2 (August 2016): 183–201.

Gordimer, Nadine. *The Essential Gesture: Writings, Politics, and Places*. Edited by Stephen Clingman. London: Penguin, 1989.

Gordimer, Nadine. *July's People*. London: Penguin, 1988.

Gordimer, Nadine. *A Sport of Nature*. New York: Knopf, 1987.

Gordon, Robert J. "Marginalia on 'Grensliteratuur': Or How/Why Is Terror Culturally Constructed in Northern Namibia?" *Critical Arts: A Journal for Cultural Studies* 5, no. 3 (1991): 79–93.

Gorin, Zeev. "Socialist Societies and World System Theory: A Critical Survey." *Science and Society* 49, no. 3 (Fall 1985): 332–66.

Gould-Davies, Nigel. "The Logic of Soviet Cultural Diplomacy." *Diplomatic History* 27, no. 2 (Apr. 2003): 193–214.

Green, Michael. "Nadine Gordimer's 'Future Histories': Two Senses of an Ending." *Wasafiri* 19 (Summer 1994): 14–18.

Griffith, Gareth. "Structure and Image in Kwei Armah's *The Beautyful Ones Are Not Yet Born*." In *Critical Perspectives on Ayi Kwei Armah*, edited by Derek Wright, 75–91. Washington, DC: Three Continents, 1992.

Gugelberger, Georg M. "Introduction." In *Marxism and African Literature*, edited by Georg M. Gugelberger, v–xiv. Trenton, NJ: Africa World, 1985.

Gugelberger, Georg M. "Marxist Literary Debates and Their Continuity in African Literary Criticism." In *Marxism and African Literature*, edited by Georg M. Gugelberger, 1–20. Trenton, NJ: Africa World, 1985.

Guimarães, Fernando Andresen. *The Origins of the Angolan Civil War: Foreign Intervention and Domestic Political Conflict*. London: Palgrave, 2001.

Gupta, Pamila, Isabel Hofmeyr, and Michael Pearson, eds. *Eyes across the Water: Navigating the Indian Ocean*. Pretoria: UNISA, 2010.

Halim, Hala. "Lotus, the Afro-Asian Nexus, and Global South Comparatism." *Comparative Studies of South Asia, Africa and the Middle East* 32, no. 3 (2012): 563–83.

Hamilton, Guy, dir. *Diamonds Are Forever*. 1971; London: Eon Productions. DVD.

Hamilton, Russell G. "African Literature in Portuguese." In *The Cambridge History of African and Caribbean Literature*, edited by Abiola Irele and Simon Gikandi, 2:603–25. Cambridge: Cambridge University Press, 2004.

Hammond, Andrew, ed. *Cold War Literature: Writing the Global Conflict*. London: Routledge, 2006.

Hammond, Andrew, ed. *Global Cold War Literature: Western, Eastern and Postcolonial Perspectives*. New York: Routledge, 2012.

Hammond, Andrew. "On the Frontlines of Writing: Introducing the Literary Cold War." In *Global Cold War Literature: Western, Eastern and Postcolonial Perspectives*, edited by Andrew Hammond, 1–16. New York: Routledge, 2012.

Hanhimäki, Jussi M., and Odd Arne Westad, eds. *The Cold War: A History in Documents and Eyewitness Accounts*. Oxford: Oxford University Press, 2003.

Hardt, Michael. "Foreword: What Affects Are Good For." In *The Affective Turn: Theorizing the Social*, edited by Patricia Ticineto Clough and Jean Halley, ix–xiii. Durham, NC: Duke University Press, 2007.

Hardt, Michael, and Antonio Negri. *Empire*. Cambridge, MA: Harvard University Press, 2000.

Harlow, Barbara. *Resistance Literature*. New York: Methuen, 1987.

Helgesson, Stefan. *Transnationalism in Southern African Literature: Modernists, Realists, and the Inequality of Print Culture*. New York: Routledge, 2009.

Hepburn, Allan. *Intrigue: Espionage and Culture*. New Haven, CT: Yale University Press, 2005.

Heyns, Michiel. "Fathers and Sons: Structures of Erotic Patriarchy in Afrikaans Writing of the Emergency." *Ariel* 27 (January 1996): 81–103.

"Historical News." *Journal of Negro History* 45, no. 4 (October 1960): 285–88.

Hofmeyr, Isabel. "The Black Atlantic Meets the Indian Ocean: Forging New Paradigms of Transnationalism for the Global South—Literary and Cultural Perspectives." *Social Dynamics* 33, no. 2 (2007): 2–33.

Holt, Clive. *At Thy Call We Did Not Falter*. Cape Town: Zebra, 2005.

Holt, Elizabeth. "Cold War in the Arabic Press: *Hiwār* (Beirut, 1962–67) and the Congress for Cultural Freedom." In *Campaigning Culture and the Global Cold War: The Journals of the Congress for Cultural Freedom*, edited by Giles Scott-Smith and Charlotte A. Lerg, 227–42. London: Palgrave, 2017.

Hope, Christopher. *Kruger's Alp*. London: Heinemann, 1984.

Indangasi, Henry. "Ngugi's Ideal Reader and the Postcolonial Reality." *The Yearbook of English Studies* 27 (1997): 193–200.

Irele, Abiola. "Orality, Literacy and African Literature." In *African Literature: An*

*Anthology of Criticism and Theory*, edited by Tejumola Olaniyan and Ato Quayson, 74–82. Malden, MA: Blackwell, 2007.

Ivaska, Andrew. "Movement Youth in a Global Sixties Hub: The Everyday Lives of Transnational Activists in Postcolonial Dar es Salaam." In *Transnational Histories of Youth in the Twentieth Century*, edited by Richard Ivan Jobs and David M. Pomfret, 188–210. New York: Palgrave, 2015.

Iwara, A. U., and E. Mveng, eds. *Colloquium on Black Civilization and Education: Colloquium Proceedings*. Second World Black and African Festival of Arts and Culture, Nigeria. Lagos: Federal Military Government of Nigeria, 1977.

Jackson, Jeanne-Marie. *South African Literature's Russian Soul: Narrative Forms of Global Isolation*. London: Bloomsbury Academic, 2015.

Jamba, Sousa. *Patriots*. London: Penguin, 1992.

Jameson, Fredric. *The Antinomies of Realism*. London: Verso, 2013.

Jameson, Fredric. "Culture and Finance Capital." *Critical Inquiry* 24, no. 1 (Autumn 1997): 246–65.

Jameson, Fredric. *Postmodernism, or The Cultural Logic of Late Capitalism*. Durham, NC: Duke University Press, 2003.

Jameson, Fredric. "Third-World Literature in the Era of Multinational Capitalism." *Social Text* 15 (Fall 1986): 65–88.

Jani, Pranav. "Karl Marx, Eurocentrism, and the 1857 Revolt in British India." In *Marxism, Modernity and Postcolonial Studies*, edited by Crystal Bartolovich and Neil Lazarus, 81–97. Cambridge: Cambridge University Press, 2002.

Jeyifo, Biodun. "Ayan Contra *Ujamaa*: Soyinka and Ngũgĩ as Theatre Theorists." In *African Theatre 13: Ngũgĩ wa Thiong'o and Wole Soyinka*, edited by Martin Banham, Femi Osofisan, and Kimani Njogu, 8–14. Woodbridge, UK: Boydell and Brewer, 2014.

Jeyifo, Biodun. *Wole Soyinka: Politics, Poetics and Postcolonialism*. Cambridge: Cambridge University Press, 2004.

Jones, James. "Fact and Fiction in *God's Bits of Wood*." *Research in African Literatures* 31, no. 2 (Summer 2000): 117–31.

Kalliney, Peter. "Modernism, African Literature, and the Cold War." *Modern Language Quarterly* 76, no. 3 (September 2015): 333–67.

Kamenju, Grant. "*Petals of Blood* as a Mirror of the African Revolution." In *Marxism and African Literature*, edited by Georg M. Gugelberger, 130–35. Trenton, NJ: Africa World, 1985.

Katsakioris, Constantin. "Creating a Socialist Intelligentsia: Soviet Educational Aid and Its Impact on Africa (1960–1991)." *Cahiers d'études africaines* 57, no. 2 (2017): 259–88.

Kellerman, Gawie. *Wie de hel het jou vertel?* Cape Town: Tafelberg, 1988.

Kemedjio, Cilas. "When the Detour Leads Home: The Urgency of Memory and the Liberation Imperative from Aimé Césaire to Frantz Fanon." Translated by R. H. Mitsch. *Research in African Literatures* 29, no. 3 (Autumn 1998): 191–202.

Khotimsky, Maria. "World Literature, Soviet Style: A Forgotten Episode in the History of the Idea." *Ab Imperio* 3 (2013): 119–54.

Khrushchev, Nikita. "Nikita Khrushchev's Secret Speech, 1956." In *The Cold War: A History in Documents and Eyewitness Accounts*, edited by Jussi M. Hanhimäki and Odd Arne Westad, 247–49. Oxford: Oxford University Press, 2003.

Kibera, Leonard. "Pessimism and the African Novelist: Ayi Kwei Armah's *The Beautyful Ones Are Not Yet Born*." In *Critical Perspectives on Ayi Kwei Armah*, edited by Derek Wright, 92–101. Washington, DC: Three Continents, 1992.

Koselleck, Reinhart. *Futures Past: On the Semantics of Historical Time*. Translated by Keith Tribe. New York: Columbia University Press, 2004.

Kruger, Louis. *'n Basis oorkant die grens*. Cape Town: Tafelberg, 1984.

Kwon, Heonik. *The Other Cold War*. New York: Columbia University Press, 2010.

La Guma, Alex. "Africa and the USSR: A Friendly Handshake." *Moscow News* 15 (1977): n.p.

La Guma, Alex. "Alexander Solzhenitsyn: Life through a Crooked Eye." *African Communist* 56 (1974): 69–79.

La Guma, Alex. *In the Fog of the Season's End*. Oxford: Heinemann, 1992.

La Guma, Alex. *A Soviet Journey: A Critical Annotated Edition*. Edited by Christopher J. Lee. Lanham, MD: Lexington, 2017.

La Guma, Alex. *Time of the Butcherbird*. London: Heinemann, 1986.

La Guma, Alex. *A Walk in the Night*. Ibadan, Nigeria: Mbari Publications, 1962.

Langa, Mandla. *The Memory of Stones*. Boulder, CO: Rienner, 2000.

Lavatori, Gerard. "Alienation or Empowerment? Reading, Writing and Orature in *God's Bits of Wood*." *Neohelicon* 41 (2014): 175–84.

Lazarus, Neil. "Modernism and African Literature." In *The Oxford Handbook of Global Modernisms*, edited by Mark Wollaeger and Matt Eatough, 228–45. New York: Oxford University Press, 2012.

Lazarus, Neil. *The Postcolonial Unconscious*. Cambridge: Cambridge University Press, 2011.

Lazarus, Neil. *Resistance in Postcolonial African Fiction*. New Haven, CT: Yale University Press, 1990.

Lee, Christopher J. *Frantz Fanon: Toward a Revolutionary Humanism*. Ohio Short Histories of Africa. Athens: Ohio University Press, 2015.

Lee, Christopher J. "Introduction: Anti-Imperial Eyes." In *A Soviet Journey: A Critical Annotated Edition*, by Alex La Guma, edited by Christopher J. Lee, 1–61. London: Lexington, 2017.

Lee, Christopher J., ed. *Making a World after Empire: The Bandung Moment and Its Political Afterlives*. Athens: Ohio University Press, 2010.

Lee, Christopher J., and Alex La Guma. "Addressing an Afro-Asian Public: Alex La Guma's Report to the 25th Anniversary Conference of the Afro-Asian Writers Association Conference in 1983." *Safundi: The Journal of South African and American Studies* 19, no. 3 (2018): 269–83.

Leick, Gwendolyn. *Tombs of the Great Leaders*. London: Reaktion, 2013.

Lenin, V. I. *Imperialism: The Highest Stage of Capitalism*. London: Penguin Books, 2010.

Lenin, Vladimir. *"Left-Wing" Communism: An Infantile Disorder*. Translated by Julius Katzer. 1920. Marxists Internet Archive. 1999. https://www.marxists.org/archive/lenin/works/1920/lwc/.

Lenin, Vladimir Ilyich. *What Is to Be Done?: Burning Questions of Our Movement*. Translated by Joe Fineberg and George Hanna. 1902. Marxists Internet Archive. 2008. https://www.marxists.org/archive/lenin/works/1901/witbd/.

Lindfors, Bernth. "*Petals of Blood* as a Popular Novel." In *Contemporary African Literature*, edited by Hal Wylie, Eileen Julien, and Russell J. Linnemann, 49–55. Washington, DC: Three Continents, 1983.

Lombardozzi, Litzi. "An Introduction to the Poetry of Lewis Nkosi." In *Still Beating the Drum: Critical Perspectives on Lewis Nkosi*, edited by Lindy Stiebel and Liz Gunner, 127–41. Amsterdam: Rodopi, 2005.

López, Alfred J. "Introduction: The (Post) Global South." *Global South* 1, no. 1 (Winter 2007): 1–11.

Lukács, Georg. *Writer and Critic and Other Essays*. Translated by Arthur D. Kahn. New York: Grosset and Dunlap, 1970.

Lutz, John. "Pessimism, Autonomy and Commodity Fetishism in Ayi Kwei Armah's *The Beautyful Ones Are Not Yet Born*." *Research in African Literatures* 34, no. 2 (Summer 2003): 94–111.

Luxemburg, Rosa. *The Mass Strike, the Political Party and the Trade Unions*. 1906. Translated by Patrick Lavin. Marxists Internet Archive. Rosa Luxemburg Internet Archive, 1999. https://www.marxists.org/archive/luxemburg/1906/mass-strike/index.htm.

Mahler, Anne Garland. *From the Tricontinental to the Global South: Race, Radicalism and Transnational Solidarity*. Durham, NC: Duke University Press, 2018.

Masuku, Norma. "The Depiction of Mkabayi: A Review of Her Praise Poem." *South African Journal of African Languages* 29, no. 1 (2009): 121–30.

Matusevich, Maxim, ed. *Africa in Russia, Russia in Africa: Three Centuries of Encounters*. Trenton, NJ: Africa World, 2007.

Matusevich, Maxim. "Journeys of Hope: African Diaspora and the Soviet Society." *African Diaspora* 1 (2008): 53–85.

Matusevich, Maxim. *No Easy Row for a Russian Hoe: Ideology and Pragmatism in Nigerian-Soviet Relations, 1960–1991*. Trenton, NJ: Africa World, 2003.

Mbembe, Achille. "Necropolitics." Translated by Libby Meintjes. *Public Culture* 15, no. 1 (2003): 11–40.

McDonald, Patrick. "The Power of (Third World) Women: Liberation and Limits in *God's Bits of Wood*." *Research in African Literatures* 46, no. 3 (Fall 2015): 146–64.

McGovern, Mike. *A Socialist Peace? Explaining the Absence of War in an African Country*. Chicago: University of Chicago Press, 2017.

Mercer, Kobena, ed. *Cosmopolitan Modernisms*. Cambridge, MA: MIT Press, 2005.

Mhlongo, Niq. *Affluenza*. Cape Town: Kwela, 2016.

Mhlongo, Niq. *After Tears*. Cape Town, Kwela, 2013.

Mhlongo, Niq. *Dog Eat Dog*. Cape Town: Kwela, 2013.

Mhlongo, Niq. *Way Back Home*. Cape Town: Kwela, 2013.

Miles, Elza. "Word and Image: A Dialogue—the Art of Thami Mnyele." *Thami Mnyele and the MEDU Art Ensemble*, edited by Clive Kellner and Sergio-Albio Gonzales, 29–35. Auckland Park, South Africa: Jacana Media, 2009.

The Ministry of Information and Broadcasting. *Osagyefo in the East: Speeches, Communiques, and Pictures of Osagyefo's Tour of the USSR, Eastern Europe and China in 1961*. Accra: Ministry of Information and Broadcasting, 1961.

Moore, David Chioni. "Is the Post- in Postcolonial the Post- in Post-Soviet? Toward a Global Postcolonial Critique." *PMLA* 116, no. 1 (January 2001): 111–28.

Moore, Gerald, ed. *African Literature and the Universities*. Ibadan, Nigeria: Ibadan University Press, 1965.

Moore, Gerald. "The Language of Poetry." In *African Literature and the Universities*, edited by Gerald Moore, 96–114. Ibadan, Nigeria: Ibadan University Press, 1965.

Moore, Gerald. "The Transcription Centre in the Sixties: Navigating in Narrow Seas." *Research in African Literatures* 33, no. 3 (Fall 2002): 167–81.

Moreillon, Olivier, and Lindy Stiebel. "Speaking Out: In Conversation with Niq Mhlongo." *Alternation* 22, no. 2 (2015): 255–69.

Moretti, Franco. "Conjectures on World Literature." *New Left Review* 1 (2000): 54–68.

Mphahlele, Es'kia. *Afrika My Music: An Autobiography, 1957–1983*. Johannesburg: Ravan, 1986.

Mphahlele, Es'kia. "Postscript on Dakar." In *African Literature and the Universities*, edited by Gerald Moore, 80–83. Ibadan, Nigeria: Ibadan University Press, 1965.

Mphahlele, Es'kia. *Voices in the Whirlwind and Other Essays*. London: Macmillan, 1972.

Mugo, Micere Githae. "Culture and Imperialism." International Seminar Series, Seminar on Intellectuals, the State and Imperialism: Towards Intellectual Decolonisation. University of Zimbabwe, Harare, 1987. Harare: University of Zimbabwe Departments of Economics, Law, Political and Administrative Studies, 1987.

Mukoma wa Ngugi. *The Rise of the African Novel: Politics of Language, Identity, and Ownership*. Ann Arbor: University of Michigan Press, 2018.

Mwangi, Evan Maina. *Africa Writes Back to Self: Metafiction, Gender, Sexuality*. Albany: State University of New York Press, 2009.

Neto, António Agostinho. *Sacred Hope*. Translated by Marga Holness. Luanda, Angola: Endiama, 1989.

Newell, Stephanie. "Articulating Empire: Newspaper Readerships in Colonial West Africa." *New Formations* 73 (2011): 26–42.

Ngũgĩ wa Thiong'o. "In Chekhov's House: The Writing of *Petals of Blood* (In Memory of the Late Victor Ramzes)." In *The East Was Read: Socialist Culture in the Third World*, edited by Vijay Prashad, 21–38. New Delhi: LeftWord Books, 2019.

Ngũgĩ wa Thiong'o. *Decolonising the Mind: The Politics of Language in African Literature*. London: James Currey, 1986.

Ngũgĩ wa Thiong'o. *Detained: A Writer's Prison Diary*. Nairobi: East African Educational Publishers, 1981.

Ngũgĩ wa Thiong'o. *Devil on the Cross*. Johannesburg: Heinemann, 1987.

Ngũgĩ wa Thiong'o. *Globalectics: Theory and the Politics of Knowing*. New York: Columbia University Press, 2012.

Ngũgĩ wa Thiong'o. *A Grain of Wheat*. London: Heinemann, 1967.

Ngũgĩ wa Thiong'o. *Matigari*. Translated by Wangũi wa Goro. London: Heinemann, 1989.

Ngũgĩ wa Thiong'o. *Moving the Centre: The Struggle for Cultural Freedoms*. Nairobi: East African Educational Publishers, 1993.

Ngũgĩ wa Thiong'o. *Ngũgĩ wa Thiong'o Speaks: Interviews with the Kenyan Writer*. Edited by Reinhard Sander and Bernth Lindfors. Trenton, NJ: Africa World, 2006.

Ngũgĩ wa Thiong'o. *Penpoints, Gunpoints and Dreams: Towards a Critical Theory of the Arts and the State in Africa*. Oxford: Oxford University Press, 1998.

Ngũgĩ wa Thiong'o. *Petals of Blood*. New York: Penguin, 1991.

Ngũgĩ wa Thiong'o. *Wizard of the Crow*. New York: Pantheon Books, 2006.

Ngũgĩ wa Thiong'o. *Writers in Politics*. London: Heinemann, 1981.

Ngũgĩ wa Thiong'o and Mongane Wally Serote. "The Role of Culture in the African Revolution: Ngugi wa Thiong'o and Mongane Wally Serote in a Round-Table Discussion." *African Communist* 113 (Second Quarter 1988): 31–48.

Ngũgĩ wa Thiong'o and Ngũgĩ wa Mĩriĩ. *I Will Marry When I Want*. Translated by Ngũgĩ wa Thiong'o and Ngũgĩ wa Mĩriĩ. Oxford: Heinemann, 1982.

Nimtz, August. "The Eurocentric Marx and Engels and Other Related Myths." In *Marxism, Modernity and Postcolonial Studies*, edited by Crystal Bartolovich and Neil Lazarus, 65–80. Cambridge: Cambridge University Press, 2002.

Nixon, Rob. *Homelands, Harlem, and Hollywood: South African Culture and the World Beyond*. New York: Routledge, 1994.

Nkosi, Lewis. *Mating Birds*. New York: Harper and Row, 1987.

Nkosi, Lewis. "Postmodernism and Black Writing in South Africa." In *Writing South Africa: Literature, Apartheid and Democracy, 1970-1995*, edited by Derek Attridge and Rosemary Jolly, 75–90. Cambridge: Cambridge University Press, 1998.

Nkosi, Lewis. *Tasks and Masks: Themes and Styles of African Literature*. Harlow, UK: Longman, 1981.

Nkrumah, Kwame. "African Socialism Revisited." In *Africa: National and Social Revolution; Collection of Papers Read at the Cairo Seminar*, 86–92. Prague: Peace and Socialism, 1967.

Nkrumah, Kwame. *Axioms of Kwame Nkrumah*. Freedom Fighters' Edition. London: Panaf, 1967.

Nkrumah, Kwame. *Neo-colonialism: The Last Stage of Imperialism*. New York: International Publishers, 1996.

Nkrumah, Kwame. Speech at the Positive Action Conference for Peace and Security in Africa, Accra, April 7, 1960. Accessed March 15, 2018. http://www.nkrumahinfobank.org/article.php?id=354&c=46.

Nnolim, Charles. "Dialectic as Form: Pejorism in the Novels of Armah." In *African Literature Today: No. 10, Retrospect and Prospects*, edited by Eldred Jones, 207–23. London: Heinemann, 1979.

Okri, Ben. *Incidents at the Shrine*. London: Vintage, 1993.

Okri, Ben. *Stars of the New Curfew*. London: Vintage, 1999.

Ondjaki. *Good Morning Comrades*. Translated by Stephen Henighan. Emeryville, ON: Biblioasis, 2008.

Ondjaki. *Granma Nineteen and the Soviet's Secret*. Translated by Stephen Henighan. Windsor, ON: Biblioasis, 2014.

Onoge, Omafume F. "The Crisis of Consciousness in Modern African Literature: A Survey." In *Marxism and African Literature*, edited by Georg M. Gugelberger, 21–49. Trenton, NJ: Africa World, 1985.

Onslow, Sue, ed. *Cold War in Southern Africa: White Power, Black Liberation*. London: Routledge, 2009.

Patel, Essop. "Literary Profile: Mongane Wally Serote; Poet of Revolution." *Third World Quarterly* 12, no. 1 (January 1990): 187–93.

Peary, G. M., and Patrick McGilligan. "Ousmane Sembène: An Interview." In *Ousmane Sembène: Writer, Filmmaker, Revolutionary Artist*, edited by Ernest Cole and Oumar Chérif Diop, 13–22. Trenton, NJ: Africa World Press, 2016.

Pepetela. *A Gloriosa Família*. Lisbon: Dom Quixote, 2009.

Pepetela. *Mayombe*. Translated by Michael Wolfers. London: Heinemann, 1983.

Pepetela. *Ngunga's Adventures: A Story of Angola*. Harare, Zimbabwe: Anvil, 1988.

Piette, Adam. *The Literary Cold War, 1945 to Vietnam*. Edinburgh: Edinburgh University Press, 2009.

Pietz, William. "The 'Post-colonialism' of Cold War Discourse." *Social Text* 19–20 (1988): 55–75.

Platt, Kevin, M. F. "Global Exchange, Aesthetics, Arbitrage." Paper presented at the Soviet Literature as World Literature Conference, New York University, November 21–22, 2019.

Popescu, Monica. "Aesthetic Solidarities: Ngũgĩ wa Thiong'o and the Cold War." In "Alternative Solidarities: Black Diasporas and Cultural Alliances during the Cold War," edited by Monica Popescu, Cedric Tolliver, and Julie Tolliver. Special issue, *Journal of Postcolonial Writing* 50, no. 4 (2014): 384–97.

Popescu, Monica. "Lewis Nkosi in Warsaw: Translating Eastern European Experiences for an African Audience." *Journal of Postcolonial Writing* 48, no. 2 (2012): 176–87.

Popescu, Monica. "Reading through a Cold War Lens: Apartheid Era Literature and the Global Conflict." *Current Writing: Text and Reception in Southern Africa* 24, no. 1 (2012): 37–49.

Popescu, Monica. *South African Literature beyond the Cold War*. New York: Palgrave, 2010.

Prashad, Vijay. *The Darker Nations: A People's History of the Third World*. New York: New Press, 2007.

Prashad, Vijay. *The Poorer Nations: A Possible History of the Global South*. London: Verso, 2012.

Prinsloo, Koos. "Grensverhaal." In *Forces Favorites*. Johannesburg: Taurus, 1987.

Quayson, Ato. *Postcolonialism: Theory, Practice or Process?* Cambridge, UK: Polity, 2000.

Quist-Adade, Charles. "From Paternalism to Ethnocentrism: Images of Africa in Gorbachev's Russia." *Race and Class* 46, no. 4 (2005): 79–89.

Ractliffe, Jo. *As Terras do fim do mundo: The Lands of the End of the World*. Cape Town: Michael Stevenson, 2010.

Ractliffe, Jo. *Terreno ocupado*. Johannesburg: Warren Siebrits, 2008.

Ram, Harsha. *The Imperial Sublime: A Russian Poetics of Empire*. Madison: University of Wisconsin Press, 2003.

Rastogi, Pallavi. *Postcolonial Disaster: Narrating Catastrophe in the Twenty-First Century.* Evanston, IL: Northwestern University Press, 2020.

Roberts, Brian Russell. *Artistic Ambassadors: Literary and International Representation of the New Negro Era.* Charlottesville: University of Virginia Press, 2013.

Robson, Clifford B. *Ngũgĩ wa Thiong'o.* New York: St. Martin's, 1979.

Rogers, Asha. "*Black Orpheus* and the African Magazines of the Congress for Cultural Freedom." In *Campaigning Culture and the Global Cold War: The Journals of the Congress for Cultural Freedom*, edited by Giles Scott-Smith and Charlotte A. Lerg, 243–59. London: Palgrave, 2017.

Rogers, Sean, and Isabel Hofmeyr. "'Papa AK 47' or Lolita in Africa." *Scrutiny2: Issues in English Studies in Southern Africa* 10, no. 2 (2005): 35–45.

Rogez, Mathilde. "Borderline Cases: Madness and Silence in the Representation of the Border War in the Works of Select South African Novelists." In *Beyond the Border War: New Perspectives on Southern Africa's Late–Cold War Conflicts*, edited by Gary Baines and Peter Vale, 120–36. Pretoria: UNISA, 2008.

Roman, Meredith. *Opposing Jim Crow: African Americans and the Soviet Indictment of U.S. Racism, 1928–37.* Lincoln: University of Nebraska Press, 2012.

Rooney, David. *Kwame Nkrumah: Vision and Tragedy.* Accra: Sub-Saharan Publishers, 2007.

Roos, Henriette. "Writing from Within: Representations of the Border War in South African Literature." In *Beyond the Border War: New Perspectives on Southern Africa's Late–Cold War Conflicts*, edited by Gary Baines and Peter Vale, 137–57. Pretoria: UNISA, 2008.

Rothwell, Phillip. "Unmasking Structures: The Dynamics of Power in Pepetela's *Mayombe*." *Luso-Brazilian Review* 39, no. 1 (2002): 121–28.

Rubin, Andrew N. *Archives of Authority: Empire, Culture, and the Cold War.* Princeton, NJ: Princeton University Press, 2012.

Rui, Manuel. *Quem me dera ser onda.* Rio de Janeiro: Gryphus, 2018.

RUTV Journalism Rhodes University. "Somewhere on the Border." Interview with Anthony Akerman. YouTube video. Accessed September 15, 2017. https://www.youtube.com/watch?time_continue=13&v=gBfjvoBz6Wg&feature=emb_logo.

Sachs, Albie. "A General View." Presentation at A Revolutionary Life: Ruth First 1925–1982 conference, The Institute of Commonwealth Studies, University of London, June 7, 2012. http://www.sas.ac.uk/videos-and-podcasts/politics-development-human-rights/ruth-first-revolutionary-life-1925-1982-justic.

Said, Edward. *Culture and Imperialism.* New York: Vintage, 1993.

Said, Edward. *Humanism and Democratic Criticism.* New York: Columbia University Press, 2004.

Said, Edward. *Orientalism.* New York: Vintage, 1979.

Said, Edward. *Representations of the Intellectual: The 1993 Reith Lectures.* New York: Pantheon, 1994.

Sanders, James. *South Africa and the International Media, 1972–1979: A Struggle for Representation.* London: Frank Cass, 2000.

Șandru, Cristina. *Worlds Apart? A Postcolonial Reading of Post-1945 East-Central European Cultures.* Newcastle upon Tyne, UK: Cambridge Scholars, 2012.

Sartre, Jean-Paul. *What Is Literature? And Other Essays*. Introduction by Steven Ungar. Cambridge, MA: Harvard University Press, 1988.

Saunders, Frances Stonor. *The Cultural Cold War: The CIA and the World of Arts and Letters*. New York: New Press, 2013.

Scott, David. *Omens of Adversity: Tragedy, Time, Memory, Justice*. Durham, NC: Duke University Press, 2014.

Scott, David. *Refashioning Futures: Criticism after Postcoloniality*. Princeton, NJ: Princeton University Press, 1999.

Scott-Smith, Giles. *The Politics of Apolitical Culture: The Congress for Cultural Freedom, the CIA, and Post-war American Hegemony*. London: Routledge, 2002.

Sembène, Ousmane. *God's Bits of Wood*. Translated by Francis Price. Oxford: Heinemann, 1995.

Sembène, Ousmane. *Xala*. Westport, CT: Lawrence Hill, 1976.

Sembène, Ousmane, dir. *Xala*. 2005; New York: New Yorker Films.

Serote, Mongane Wally. Interview with Rolf Solberg. In *Writing South Africa: Literature, Apartheid, and Democracy, 1970–1995*, edited by Derek Attridge and Rosemary Jolly, 180–86. Cambridge: Cambridge University Press, 1998.

Serote, Mongane Wally. *Rumours*. Auckland Park, South Africa: Jacana Media, 2013.

Serote, Mongane Wally. *Scatter the Ashes and Go*. Braamfontein, South Africa: Ravan, 2002.

Serote, Mongane Wally. *To Every Birth Its Blood*. London: Heinemann, 1983.

Serote, Mongane Wally. *Tsetlo*. Johannesburg: Ad Donker, 1974.

Serote, Mongane Wally. *Yakhal'inkomo*. Johannesburg: Renoster, 1972.

Sharma, Govind Narain. "Socialism and Civilization: The Revolutionary Traditionalism of Ngugi wa Thiong'o." *Ariel* 19, no. 2 (1988): 21–30.

Shringarpure, Bhakti. "The Afterlives of Frantz Fanon and the Reconstruction of Postcolonial Studies." *Journal of French and Francophone Philosophy* 23, no. 1 (2015): 113–28.

Shringarpure, Bhakti. *Cold War Assemblages: Decolonization to Digital*. New York: Routledge, 2019.

Shubin, Vladimir. *The Hot "Cold War": The USSR in Southern Africa*. London: Pluto, 2008.

Siebers, Tobin. *Cold War Criticism and the Politics of Skepticism*. New York: Oxford University Press, 1993.

Solanas, Fernando, and Octavio Getino. "Toward a Third Cinema." *Cinéaste* 4, no. 3 (Winter 1970–1971): 1–10.

Sole, Kelwyn. "The Days of Power: Depictions of Politics and Community in Four Recent South African Novels." *Research in African Literatures* 19, no. 1 (Spring 1988): 65–88.

Sole, Kelwyn. "'This Time Set Again': The Temporal and Political Conceptions of Serote's *To Every Birth Its Blood*." *English in Africa* 18, no. 1 (May 1991): 51–80.

The South African Communist Party. *The Road to South African Freedom: The Programme of the South African Communist Party*. London: Bowles, n.d.

The South African Truth and Reconciliation Commission. *The TRC Report*. Department of Justice and Constitutional Development. Accessed October 20, 2018. https://www.justice.gov.za/trc/report/.

Soyinka, Wole. "The Critic and Society: Barthes, Leftocracy and Other Mythologies." *Black American Literature Forum* 15, no. 4 (Winter 1981): 133–46.

Soyinka, Wole. "The Writer in a Modern African State." *The Writer in Modern Africa: African-Scandinavian Writers' Conference, Stockholm, 1967*, edited by Per Wästberg, 14–21. Uppsala: Scandinavian Institute of African Studies, 1968.

Sparks, Allister. *Beyond the Miracle: Inside the New South Africa*. Chicago: University of Chicago Press, 2003.

Spender, Stephen. "Stephen Spender." In *The God That Failed*, edited by Richard Crossman, 229–73. New York: Harper, 1949.

Stiebel, Lindy, and Liz Gunner, eds. *Still Beating the Drum: Critical Perspectives on Lewis Nkosi*. Amsterdam: Rodopi, 2005.

Strachan, Alexander. *'n Wêreld sonder grense*. Cape Town: Tafelberg, 1983.

Thomson, J. H., ed. *An Unpopular War: From Afkak to Bosbefok; Voices of South African National Servicemen*. Cape Town: Zebra, 2006.

Tihanov, Galin. "The Location of World Literature." *Canadian Review of Comparative Literature* 44, no. 3 (September 2017): 468–81.

Titlestad, Michael. "Mongane Serote's *To Every Birth Its Blood*: History and the Limits of Improvisation." *Journal of Literary Studies* 19, no. 2 (2003): 108–24.

Todorova, Maria. *Imagining the Balkans*. New York: Oxford University Press, 1997.

Tolliver, Cedric. "Making Culture Capital: *Présence Africaine* and Diasporic Modernity in Post–World War II Paris." In *Paris, Capital of the Black Atlantic: Literature, Modernity and Diaspora*, edited by Jeremy Braddock and Jonathan P. Eburne, 200–22. Baltimore: Johns Hopkins University Press, 2013.

Tolliver, Cedric. *Of Vagabonds and Fellow Travelers: African Diaspora Literary Culture and the Cultural Cold War*. Ann Arbor: University of Michigan Press, 2019.

Tolliver, Julie-Françoise. "Césaire/Lumumba: A Season of Solidarity." In "Alternative Solidarities: Black Diasporas and Cultural Alliances during the Cold War," edited by Monica Popescu, Cedric Tolliver, and Julie Tolliver. Special issue, *Journal of Postcolonial Writing* 50, no. 4 (2014): 398–409.

Trouillot, Michel-Rolph. *Silencing the Past: Power and the Production of History*. Boston: Beacon, 1995.

Van den Bergh, Regardt, dir. *Boetie gaan border toe*. 1984; South Africa: Philo Pieterse Production. YouTube. Accessed September 15, 2017. https://www.youtube.com/watch?v=7338S_8CaGs.

Van den Bergh, Regardt, dir. *Boetie op manoeuvers*. 1985; South Africa: Philo Pieterse Production. YouTube. Accessed September 15, 2017. No longer available.

Vieira, José Luandino. *Luuanda: Short Stories of Angola*. Translated by Tamara L. Bender and Donna S. Hill. London: Heinemann, 1980.

Villa-Vicencio, Charles, and Mills Soko. *Conversations in Transition: Leading South African Voices*. Cape Town: David Phillip, 2012.

Visser, Nick. "Fictional Projects and the Irruptions of History: Mongane Serote's *To Every Birth Its Blood*." *English Academy Review* 4, no. 1 (1987): 67–76.

Von Eschen, Penny. *Satchmo Blows Up the World: Jazz Ambassadors Play the Cold War.* Cambridge, MA: Harvard University Press, 2006.

Wainaina, Binyavanga. *One Day I Will Write about This Place: A Memoir.* Minneapolis: Graywolf, 2011.

Wallerstein, Immanuel. *The Capitalist World-Economy.* Cambridge: Cambridge University Press, 1979.

Wanjala, Chris. "Lewis Nkosi's Early Literary Criticism." In *Still Beating the Drum: Critical Perspectives on Lewis Nkosi*, edited by Lindy Stiebel and Liz Gunner, 27–38. Amsterdam: Rodopi, 2005.

Warwick Research Collective (WReC). *Combined and Uneven Development: Towards a New Theory of World-Literature.* Liverpool: Liverpool University Press, 2015.

Wästberg, Per, ed. *The Writer in Modern Africa: African-Scandinavian Writers' Conference, Stockholm, 1967.* Uppsala: Scandinavian Institute of African Studies, 1968.

Watson, Jini Kim, and Gary Wilder. "Introduction: Thinking the Postcolonial Contemporary." In *The Postcolonial Contemporary: Political Imaginaries for the Global Present*, edited by Jini Kim Watson and Gary Wilder, 1–29. New York: Fordham University Press, 2018.

Weideman, George. *Tuin van klip en vuur.* Cape Town: Tafelberg, 1983.

Westad, Odd Arne. *The Global Cold War: Third World Interventions and the Making of Our Times.* Cambridge: Cambridge University Press, 2005.

Wicomb, Zoë. *David's Story.* New York: Feminist, 2001.

Wilford, Hugh. *The Mighty Wurlitzer: How the CIA Played America.* Cambridge, MA: Harvard University Press, 2009.

Wilhelm, Peter. *At the End of a War.* Johannesburg: Ravan, 1981.

Wilhelm, Peter. *LM and Other Stories.* Johannesburg: Ravan, 1975.

Williams, Christian. "'Remember Cassinga?' An Exhibition of Photographs and Histories." *Kronos* 36, no. 1 (November 2010): 213–50.

Williams, Patrick. *Ngugi wa Thiong'o.* Manchester: Manchester University Press, 1999.

Williams, Patrick, and Laura Chrisman, eds. *Colonial Discourse and Post-colonial Theory: A Reader.* New York: Columbia University Press, 1994.

Williams, Raymond. *Marxism and Literature.* Oxford: Oxford University Press, 1977.

Williams, Raymond. *The Politics of Modernism: Against the New Conformists.* Edited by Tony Pinkney. London: Verso, 1989.

Windrich, Elaine. *The Cold War Guerrilla: Jonas Savimbi, the U.S. Media, and the Angolan War.* New York: Greenwood, 1992.

Winkler, Allan M. *The Cold War: A History in Documents.* Oxford: Oxford University Press, 2000.

Wolff, Larry. *Inventing Eastern Europe: The Map of Civilization on the Mind of the Enlightenment.* Stanford, CA: Stanford University Press, 1994.

Woll, Josephine. "The Russian Connection: Soviet Cinema and the Cinema of Francophone West Africa." In *Focus on African Films*, edited by Françoise Pfaff, 223–40. Bloomington: Indiana University Press, 2004.

Worsley, Peter. "One World or Three? A Critique of the World-System Theory of Immanuel Wallerstein." *The Socialist Register 1980: A Survey of Movements and Ideas* 17 (1980): 282–338.

Wright, Derek. "Totalitarian Rhetoric: Some Aspects of Metaphor in *The Beautyful Ones Are Not Yet Born*." *Critique: Studies in Contemporary Fiction* 30, no. 3 (1989): 210–20.

Wright, Richard. *The Color Curtain: A Report on the Bandung Conference*. Cleveland: World, 1956.

Yoon, Duncan. "Our Forces Have Redoubled: World Literature, Postcolonialism and the Afro-Asian Writers' Bureau." *Cambridge Journal of Postcolonial Literary Inquiry* 2, no. 2 (September 2015): 233–52.

Young, Robert J. C. "Ideologies of the Postcolonial." *Interventions: International Journal of Postcolonial Studies* 1, no. 1 (October 1998): 4–8.

Young, Robert J. C. *Postcolonialism: An Historical Introduction*. Malden, MA: Blackwell, 2001.

Young, Trence, dir. *Dr. No*. 1962; London: Eon Productions. DVD.

Zien, Katherine. *Sovereign Acts: Performing Race, Space, and Belonging in Panama and the Canal Zone*. New Brunswick, NJ: Rutgers University Press, 2017.

# INDEX

Abrahams, Peter, 47
Achebe, Chinua, 35, 39, 47, 49, 95, 164; *Things Fall Apart*, 47, 95
Adorno, Theodor, 44, 207n12, 209n45
aesthetic world-systems, 25–6, 65–103, 186, 190–1
affective temporal structures, 110–26, 131–5, 139, 141, 143–4, 214n11
African feminism, 113
African literature and literary studies, 2–4, 11, 13–16, 18–20, 25–6, 31–2 35, 36, 38, 39, 44, 47, 54–5, 57, 64, 67, 70, 77–8, 81, 83, 85–6, 88, 95, 103, 108, 135, 144, 187, 190, 194n11, 194–5n16, 197n60
African National Congress (ANC), 11, 61, 125–33, 157, 162, 168–74, 176, 184, 217n77, 217n79, 218n97, 225n85, 225n86, 226n105; alliance with SACP, 125–32, 162, 168, 171–2, 174, 184, 217n79, 218n97; armed wing (*see* Umkhonto we Sizwe); "Strategy and Tactics" (1969), 131, 132, 172, 225n85
African socialism, 5, 26, 108, 110, 135–41; Armah, Ayi Kwei, 26, 138–41; Nkrumah, Kwame, 110, 135–41; Nyerere, Julius, 172; Senghor, Léopold Sédar, 137, 139
African-Scandinavian Writers' Conference (1967) Stockholm, 31
Afro-Asian People's Solidarity Organization (AAPSO), 23–24
Afro-Asian Writers Association (AAWA), 6, 17, 22–25, 33, 48–29, 51–2, 59, 61, 71, 74, 76, 89–90, 93, 101, 120, 152, 186, 191, 198n77, 199n83, 204n74; 1958 Conference, Tashkent, 17, 22, 48, 51, 59, 93, 120; 1962 Conference, Cairo, 51; 1967 Conference, Beirut, 49, 51, 53, 89; 1968 Tashkent International Symposium on "Literature and the Modern Art," 53, 90, 93; 1970 Conference, Delhi, 51; 1973 Conference, Alma-Ata, 26, 51–2, 61, 101; 1979 Conference, Luanda, 51, 152; 1983 Conference, Tashkent, 51; 1988 Conference, Tunis, 24, 51; El-Sebai, Youssef (*see* El-Sebai); Faiz, Faiz Ahmed (*see* Faiz); La Guma, Alex (*see* La Guma); *Lotus* magazine and prize (*see Lotus: Afro-Asian Writings*); Permanent Bureau, 23–4, 49, 198n77
Akerman, Anthony, 146, 148, 154–6; *Somewhere on the Border*, 146, 148, 154–6
Alexis, Jacques Stephen, 56
American Security Council Foundation, 168
Anand, Mulk Raj, 22
Andrade, Fernando Costa, 152
Andrade, Mário Pinto de, 152, 215n29
Andrew, Rick, 153
Angola, 4, 18, 24, 27, 49, 109, 123–4, 127–8, 133, 145–84, 193n3, 199n85, 220n2, 220n3, 221n6, 222n17, 222n27, 224n63, 226n109, 226n111; border with Namibia, 147–8, 150, 154–5, 165, 221n6; and Cuba, 149, 162, 171, 178, 180–182. *See also* Border War (also: Angolan Civil War); National Front for the Liberation of Angola (FNLA); National Union for the Total Independence of Angola (UNITA); People's Movement for the Liberation of Angola (MPLA)

anti-imperialism, 22, 23, 59–60, 108, 151–2, 214n17
antiapartheid struggle, 61, 107, 122–3, 125, 127, 132–3, 153, 155, 167, 169–73, 226n105. *See also* African National Congress (ANC); Soweto Uprising
anticolonialism, 9–11, 14, 17, 35, 51, 56–7, 72, 87, 95–6, 109, 113–4, 117–20, 123, 135, 144, 151, 160, 167, 184, 186, 187, 222n17
Arendt, Hannah, 144
Armah, Ayi Kwei, 3, 26, 76, 78, 111, 124–5, 135, 137–43, 189–90, 214n11; and socialism, 26, 138–41; *Fragments*, 141; *The Beautyful Ones Are Not Yet Born*, 26, 111, 124–5, 135, 138–44, 214n11; *Why Are We So Blest?*, 141
Azimov, Sarvar, 93

Baldwin, James, 58
Bandung Conference (1955), 2, 5, 6, 12, 22, 23, 48, 55–6, 58–9, 62, 75, 93
Behr, Mark, 27, 146, 153, 157–9, 165, 166, 222n24; *The Smell of Apples*, 27, 146, 153, 157–9, 166
Beier, Ulli, 35, 38, 39, 43, 79, 84, 201n29, 210–11n72
Beirut, 24, 49, 51, 54, 89, 199n83, 204n74
Berlin International Literature Festival (2003), 71
Berlin Wall, 3, 13, 16, 71, 170, 186, 188. *See also* Cold War
Beti, Mongo, 47–8, 215n29
Biafra War, 34, 199n8
Biko, Steve, 26, 128
Black Consciousness (BC), 125, 128
*Black Orpheus* magazine, 20, 21, 25, 38–9, 42–4, 61, 76, 79–81, 84–7
Bolshevik Revolution (also: October Revolution; Revolution of 1917), 100, 109, 120, 168
Bolshevism, 63
Booker Prize, 44
Border War (also: Angolan Civil War), 27, 109, 123, 145–7, 150–6, 158, 162, 165–6, 174–5, 177, 181, 184, 220n3, 222n24, 222n26, 222n29, 224n66; Border War literature (*see grensliteratuur*); Caprivi Strip, 154; Operation Savannah, 166; Operational Zone, 153–4
Botha, Roelof Frederik "Pik," 168–9, 224–5n76
Botswana, 123, 127, 133, 169, 216–7n57
Breton, André, 81
Breytenbach, Jan, 152
Brezhnev, Leonid, 109–10
British Colonial Office, 59
brotherhood of nations, 11, 47
Brutus, Dennis, 31, 34–5, 43, 203n57

Cabral, Amílcar, 9, 26, 116, 117, 125, 143, 161–2, 176–7, 189
*Cadernos Brasileiros* magazine, 21
Cairo, 23–24, 26, 51, 137, 198n77, 199n83
capitalism, 5, 8, 9, 11–13, 16, 22, 32, 35, 36, 63, 68, 69, 70, 72–5, 78, 85, 93, 98, 99, 102, 109, 113, 118, 121, 124, 135, 137, 141, 149, 156–8, 162, 163, 167–8, 173, 177–8, 180, 184–6, 189–91, 209n34, 209n39; and colonialism, 9, 36, 69, 70, 75, 99, 109, 113, 118, 121, 135, 141, 168; and communism, 5, 11, 12, 73, 78, 156–8, 163; late capitalism, 70, 186; neoliberal capitalism, 13, 32, 85, 124, 184, 186, 189–91; Western capitalism, 9, 13, 16, 156, 158, 167
Cărtărescu, Mircea, 183
Cassinga massacre, 145–8, 221n5, 221n6
Castro, Fidel, 60, 109–10, 142
Castro Soromenho, Fernando Monteiro de, 88, 152
censorship, 34, 44, 47, 147–54, 164, 187, 222n24
Césaire, Aimé, 8, 9–11, 13, 16, 56, 58, 64, 74, 81, 116, 180, 196n36, 215n29; "Discourse on Colonialism," 9; "Letter to Maurice Thorez," 10, 58, 196n36
Chemchemi Centre (Nairobi), 38, 43, 59, 202n43, 203n50

China, 13, 17, 23, 56, 61, 74, 108, 150, 196n36, 207n123, 209–10n43
Chinese Great Leap Forward, 109
Chinweizu (also: Chinweizu Ibekwe), 77–8, 86
Churchill, Winston, 156, 193n2
Cini Foundation, Venice, 43
Clark, John Pepper, 35, 39, 78, 84
Coetzee, J. M., 124, 155, 186, 217n64; *Waiting for the Barbarians*, 124, 155
Cold War: Eastern Bloc (see also: Second World), 2–3, 5–6, 10, 11, 16, 17, 20, 26, 32, 37, 46, 47–55, 64, 67, 69, 71, 73–5, 78, 99–100, 102–3, 108–9, 132, 136–7, 140–2, 148, 151, 156, 167–74, 185, 187, 190, 191, 204n75, 205n87, 219n118; global Cold War, 2, 4, 12, 26, 65, 145, 150, 193n2, 199n85; hot Cold War, 4–5, 12, 20, 27, 37, 145–84; Iron Curtain, 2–3, 6–7, 11, 16, 18, 22, 24, 37, 59, 76, 103, 156, 172, 209n39; and postcolonial scholarship, 2, 5–8, 13–16, 28, 187–90; superpowers, 1–5, 7, 10–12, 15–20, 25–6, 32, 37, 46, 51, 54–5, 57, 59, 62–3, 66–7, 71, 76–8, 87, 108, 130, 136, 149–50, 171, 177, 179, 186, 192, 194n8, 220n3. See also Soviet Union; United States
colonialism, 5, 7, 10–11, 15–16, 23, 55, 57–9, 61, 66, 69, 81, 86, 89, 95–6, 100, 108–9, 113–4, 118–9, 128, 135–6, 140, 143, 167, 169, 177, 189, 195n19, 224n71, 225n86; Fanon, Frantz, 6, 109–10, 118, 128, 135, 189; and capitalism, 9, 36, 69, 70, 75, 99, 109, 113, 118, 121, 135, 141, 168; cultural colonialism, 66, 81, 189; neocolonialism, 6–7, 10–11, 15–6, 26, 36, 55, 61–2, 71, 77, 94, 97, 99–100, 102, 121, 124, 127, 130, 135–8, 141, 151, 172, 187, 189, 219n115, 219n118, 220n133; Russian colonialism, 7, 10, 12–13, 51; Soviet colonialism, 4–13, 15–24, 36, 58, 135, 162, 167–8, 184, 195n24, 224n76; Western colonialism, 15–16, 58–9, 96, 100, 108, 119, 135–6, 140, 143, 169. See *also* anticolonialism; decolonization; imperialism
communism, 5, 7, 10–12, 17, 19, 23, 41, 46, 48, 56, 58, 73, 75, 78, 121, 137, 143, 153, 155–9, 162–3, 165–6, 168, 170, 173–4, 178, 180, 188–9, 196n36, 205n96, 223n35, 223n37; Soviet-style communism, 23, 75, 121, 156, 178, 180, 188. See *also* French Communist Party; Marxism; Negro Bureau of the Communist International of Trade Unions; South African Communist Party (SACP); Soviet Union: Central Committee of the Communist Party
comprador, 62, 114, 116
Congress for Cultural Freedom (CCF), 20–2, 25, 32–3, 37–49, 55, 57–9, 61, 63, 67, 71, 76, 79, 83–7, 186, 191, 197n60, 201n30, 201n32, 202n39, 202n42, 202–3n49, 203n52, 203n53, 205n95, 207n129, 209n45, 211n77; Africa Program, 39, 43, 45–6, 58; *Black Orpheus* magazine (*see Black Orpheus*); Dakar Conference on African Literature in French and the University Curriculum (1963) (*see* Dakar conference); Duerden, Dennis (*see* Duerden); *Encounter* Magazine (*see Encounter*); funding by the CIA, 21, 37–8, 40–4, 46, 55, 63, 67, 85, 87, 191, 201n30, 202n39, 202n42, 202n43, 203n52, 205n95, 207n129; Freetown Conference on African Literature and the University Curriculum (1963) (*see* Freetown conference); Hunt, John (*see* Hunt); International Association for Cultural Freedom, 21, 201n30; Makerere Conference (*see* Makerere College Conference); Mphahlele, Ezekiel (*see* Mphahlele); Neogy, Rajat (*see* Neogy); Thompson, John (*see* Thompson); Transcription Centre (London) (*see* Transcription Centre); *Transition* magazine (*see Transition*)
Conrad, Joseph, 96, 213

Cook, Mercer, 38, 58
Couto, Mia, 186
Craveirinha, Jose, 49
*Cuadernos del Congreso por la Libertad de la Cultura* magazine, 21
Cuba, 5, 6, 15, 60, 61, 108, 109, 133, 147, 149, 151, 162, 166, 171, 173, 177, 178, 180–2; Cuban Missile Crisis (1962), 15; Cuban Revolution, 60, 109; and Angola, 149, 162, 171, 178, 180–2
cultural diplomacy, 2, 19, 25, 37, 48, 67, 203n53

Dakar conference on the teaching of African literature (1963), 14, 26, 38, 39, 57, 83–4, 197n60
Dakar-Niger railway workers' strike (1947–1948), 26, 113–20
Daniel, Yuli, 44
decolonization, 1–2, 4, 7, 12–14, 17, 21, 25–7, 31, 33, 36, 47–8, 51, 55, 61, 66, 75, 78, 85–6, 88, 90, 92–6, 108–12, 114, 119, 122, 124–5, 127, 132, 134–5, 146–8, 157, 161, 168, 187–9
*Der Monat* magazine, 21
Dickens, Charles, 89, 98
Diop, Alioune, 57–9, 152, 192
Dipoko, Mbella Sonne, 88
Djumblatt, Kamal, 54
Dostoevsky, Fyodor, 100
*Drum* magazine, 38
Duerden, Dennis, 38, 40, 43, 55
Duodu, Cameron, 48

Egypt, 23, 49, 120
Ekwensi, Cyprian, 47, 204n70
El-Sebai, Youssef, 13–14, 23–4, 49, 52–4, 191, 205n86
Eliot, T. S., 70, 72, 77, 79, 83–4
Empire. *See* imperialism
*Encounter* magazine, 21, 43, 63, 202n49

Faiz, Faiz Ahmed, 24, 53
Fanon, Frantz, 6, 8, 9, 26, 31, 56, 59, 61, 109–10, 112, 116–18, 125, 128–9, 135, 139, 141–3, 161–2, 164, 189, 215n29; "Algeria Unveiled," 117; and colonization, 6, 109–10, 118, 128, 135, 189; and Marxism, 9, 26; and revolution, 26, 31, 116–17, 128–9, 139, 141, 161, 164; *The Wretched of the Earth*, 31, 59, 61, 112, 119, 141–2
Farfield Foundation, 21, 37, 42, 44, 202n42
Festac '77 (Second World Festival of Negro Arts, 1977), Lagos, Nigeria, 1, 193n4
First Congress of the Union of Soviet Writers (1934), 47, 92
First, Ruth, 107, 130, 214n1
First World, 8, 72, 74
First World Congress of Black Writers and Artists (1956), Paris, France, 58
First World Festival of Negro Arts (1966), Dakar, Senegal, 1
Ford Foundation, 44
*Forum* magazine, 21
Freetown conference on the teaching of African literature (1963), 14, 38, 39, 83, 84
French Communist Party, 9–10, 58, 114

Galgut, Damon, 153
Garvey, Marcus, 125
General Confederation of Labor (CGT), France, 114–15
Germany, 115; Nazi Germany, 15, 21, 223n37
German Democratic Republic (GDR), 61, 170, 173, 181, 203n50
Ghana, 24, 39, 48, 49, 64, 76, 110, 112, 135–43, 192, 193n3, 201n30, 202n40, 210n66, 219n112, 219n118, 219n121, 220n133; independence (1957), 112, 135–6, 139, 143; Ghanaian Ministry of Information and Broadcasting, 137
Ghosh, Amitav, 61–2
Gide, André, 56
Gĩkũyũ, 15–16, 99, 102
Global South, 2, 59, 102, 151, 191, 194n8, 206n112, 228n19

Gordimer, Nadine, 6, 11, 27, 88, 123, 125, 146, 155, 167, 186, 218n99; *July's People*, 27, 123, 146, 155; *A Sport of Nature*, 125, 218n99
Gorky, Maxim, 22, 89, 92-3, 100-1, 120, 190-1, 213n137; *Mother*, 213n137; and socialist realism, 89, 92-3, 100-1, 191; Speech at the First Congress of the Union of Soviet Writers (1934), 92-3; Vsemirnaia Literatura (World Literature) Press, 22, 190
Gorky Studios (Moscow), 120, 121
Grenada Revolution (1979), 112, 124, 215n18
*grensliteratuur* (also: border literature), 153, 155
Gugelberger, Georg, 70, 72, 77, 85

Haitian Revolution, 109
Havana, 24, 59-60, 62, 150
Heinemann, 40, 48, 215n19; African Writers Series, 215n19
*Hiwar* magazine, 21
Holt, Clive, 153
Honwana, Luís Bernardo, 64, 88
Hope, Christopher, 123, 124, 217n64
Horn of Africa, 4-5, 149
Hughes, Langston, 39
Hunt, John, 43, 46, 59, 203n52

Ibrahimov, Mirza, 90
imperialism, 2-17, 19-21, 103, 108, 128, 143, 160, 186, 23, 36, 42, 57-8, 60-1, 63, 72, 74-6, 81, 90, 93, 108, 115, 124, 135-7, 140, 151, 162, 167-8, 177, 180, 184, 187-9, 195n24, 197n47, 220n133, 224n76, 226n106; cultural imperialism, 2, 5, 7, 13-14, 19, 72, 75-6, 187; French, 11, 13, 110, 113-4, 119, 169, 214n5; Habsburg, 7, 13; Japanese, 7; Ottoman, 7, 13; new forms of imperialism, 7, 10, 12, 14, 17, 75, 108, 115, 124, 140; Portuguese, 61, 128, 151-2, 159-60, 178, 220n2; Soviet, 4-13, 15-24, 36, 58, 135, 162, 167-8, 184, 195n24, 224n76; Western, 4-13, 15-24, 23, 36, 42, 60, 63, 67, 81, 85-6, 93, 135, 167, 188. *See also* anti-imperialism
International Association for Cultural Freedom. *See* Congress for Cultural Freedom
International Emergency Conference on Korea (1976) Tokyo, Japan, 62, 207n127
internationalism, 9, 11, 12, 47, 51, 59, 92, 109, 152, 162, 174-84
Irele, Abiola, 39, 102, 207n1

Jahn, Janheinz, 35, 81
Jamba, Sousa, 27, 146, 151, 159, 162-5; *Patriots*, 27, 146, 151, 159, 162-5
James Bond franchise, 4, 165; *Diamonds are Forever*, 4; *Dr. No*, 4
James, C. L. R., 8, 9

Kafka, Franz, 74
Kant, Immanuel, 85
Katz, Ivan, 46, 59, 202n43
Kazakh Soviet Socialist Republic, 51
Kellerman, Gawie, 153
Kenya, 1, 6, 16, 24, 49, 52, 59, 61-3, 71, 90, 95-102, 176, 207n123
Kenya Land and Freedom Army (also: the Mau Mau), 96-98, 100, 102, 176
Khrushchev, Nikita, 10, 219n112
Kipling, Rudyard, 7
Koestler, Arthur, 41
Kruger, Louis, 153
Kunene, Mazisi, 88

La Guma, Alex, 6, 24, 31, 33-5, 39, 43-4, 47-9, 51-2, 54-5, 60-1, 70, 76, 89-90, 94, 125, 167-8, 186, 191, 203n66; AAWA, 6, 24; *Black Orpheus* Prize, 39, 44, 76; in Cuba, 6, 24; in the Eastern Bloc, 6, 48, 203n66; *In the Fog of the Season's End*, 125; *Lotus* Prize, 49, 76, 191; *A Soviet Journey*, 61, 203n66; *Time of the Butcherbird*, 125; *A Walk in the Night*, 43, 44, 47, 61, 89

Index  253

Langa, Mandla, 107, 154; *The Memory of Stones*, 107, 154
Lebanon, 21, 24, 49, 89; civil war, 24, 49
Lenin, Vladimir, 19, 115–16, 132, 136, 178, 189, 208n18, 216n55; *"Left-Wing" Communism: An Infantile Disorder*, 12; *Imperialism: The Highest Stage of Capitalism*, 189; *What Is to Be Done?*, 115–16, 132
London, 2, 21, 24, 33, 38, 40, 43, 55, 50
*Lotus: Afro-Asian Writings*, 13–14, 20, 23–5, 48–54, 61, 71, 76, 87–93, 101, 152, 191–2, 198–9n80, 199n83, 204n77, 212n101; Lotus Prize 49, 52, 61, 76, 101, 191
Luanda, 24, 51, 60, 151, 152, 164, 178–82
Lukács, Georg, 69, 207n12, 209n45
Lumumba, Patrice, 143
Lusaka, 60
Luxemburg, Rosa, 115

Makerere College Conference of African Writers of English Expression (1962), Kampala, Uganda, 1, 18, 38–40, 45, 71, 77, 84, 202n42
Malangatana (also: Malangatana Valente Ngwenya), 79
Malcolm X, 125, 128
Mandela, Nelson, 127, 128, 169, 180, 218n99
Mao Zedong, 23, 34, 74, 142, 219n112
Marseille, 114–15
Martinique, 81, 117, 128
Marx, Karl, 116, 192, 216n55, 228n23
Marxism, 6, 9, 11, 14, 16, 26, 34, 37, 41, 51, 54, 61, 63, 66, 69, 70, 77, 85, 94, 99, 102, 109, 111, 113, 115, 116, 118, 121–37, 139, 157, 161–3, 167, 174, 177, 184, 187–90, 194n9, 207n12, 215n2, 216n55, 220n131; Marxism-Leninism, 26, 61, 113, 115, 116, 118, 121–36, 161, 215n22, 216n55, 220n131; Marxism in Africa, 70, 77, 85, 109, 139, 157, 167, 189
Mazrui, Ali, 192, 202n40
Mbari Press, 39, 43, 48, 61

Mbari Writers and Artists Club, Nigeria, 38, 39, 84, 201n29, 202n43, 202n49
McCarthy, Joseph, 41
Mhlongo, Niq, 27, 147, 154, 174–8, 180, 182–4, 225n96, 226n99, 226n100, 226n105; *Way Back Home*, 27, 147, 154, 174–8, 225n96
Mihloti Black Theatre, 125
Mnyele, Thami, 125
modernism, 3, 6, 25–26, 32, 38, 66–71, 74–9, 83–8, 90, 92, 94–6, 103, 182, 200n19, 207n12, 208n18, 209n41, 209n42, 209n45, 211n90; African modernism, 78–97; Euro-American modernism, 34, 69, 79, 81, 83–4, 96; and realism, 6, 8, 26, 65–72, 75–8, 90, 103, 207n12, 207n12
Modisane, Bloke, 39, 88
Moore, Gerald, 35, 84
Morogoro Conference (1969), 128, 131, 172
Moscow, 2, 8, 24, 42, 48, 60, 61, 63, 120, 121, 137, 173, 178, 190, 195–6n29, 204n77
Movement against Racism and for Friendship between Peoples, 114
Mozambique, 49, 124, 128, 133
Mphahlele, Es'kia (also: Ezekiel), 14, 18–19, 26, 31, 35, 38–41, 43–6, 48, 57, 59, 64, 77, 84, 88, 89, 197n60, 201n29, 201n30, 202n42, 202n43, 203n53; *Afrika My Music*, 44, 201n29, 201n30; *Black Orpheus*, 39, 44; CCF Africa Program, 39, 43, 45–6; *Down Second Avenue*, 48; and Négritude, 18, 59, 77, 197n60. *See also* Chemchemi Cultural Centre; Makerere College Conference of African Writers of English Expression
Mugo, Micere, 26, 90, 188

Namibia (also: South West Africa), 61, 124, 128, 147–8, 150, 154–5, 165, 171, 221n5, 221n6, 221n14; border with Angola, 147–8, 150, 154–5, 165, 221n6

National Front for the Liberation of Angola (FNLA), 150–1, 162, 177, 221n13
National Union for the Total Independence of Angola (UNITA), 150–1, 159, 162–4, 166, 168, 171, 177, 180
nationalism 5, 9, 19, 94, 117, 135, 137, 155, 158, 161, 168–9, 180
Nazareth, Peter, 192
Négritude, 18–19, 33, 56, 58, 59, 77, 197n60
Negro Bureau of the Communist International of Trade Unions, 120
*Negro Worker* journal, 120
neocolonialism. *See* colonialism
Neogy, Rajat, 38, 39, 41–42, 43, 83, 191–92, 201n30, 202n39, 202n40, 202n42, 202n43, 203–4n67
neoliberalism, 13, 32, 85, 124, 184, 186, 189–91, 206n112; neoliberal capitalism, 13, 32, 85, 124, 184, 186, 189–91
Neto, Agostinho, 18, 49, 109–10, 125, 152, 159, 163, 178–80, 193n3, 222n17, 226n111; mausoleum, 178–80, 182, 226n111, 226n114; *Sacred Hope*, 152
New York, 24, 33, 44
Ngũgĩ wa Thiong'o, 1, 14–16, 26, 31, 35, 39, 49, 51–2, 61–3, 65–6, 70–1, 77, 94–103, 116, 126, 161, 164, 183, 186, 189, 191, 193n1, 193n2; *Decolonising the Mind*, 15, 61, 66, 95; *Devil on the Cross*, 65, 94, 102; *A Grain of Wheat*, 94–6, 100; Lotus Prize, 49, 52, 101; *Matigari*, 94, 102, 103, 213n142; and Marxism, 6, 16, 63, 66, 94, 99; *Petals of Blood*, 1, 62, 66, 94–8, 100–102, 193n2, 207n123; and the call for abolition of the English Department (1968), 14, 39, 192; *Wizard of the Crow*, 94, 102
Nigeria, 24, 34, 38, 39, 44, 49, 55, 77, 84, 176, 193n3, 193n4, 199n8, 201n29, 202n49, 204n70, 211n77; Nigerian Civil War (*see* Biafra War)
Nkosi, Lewis, 25, 26, 31, 33, 35, 39, 71–2, 76–7, 85, 88; *Mating Birds*, 71–2

Nkrumah, Kwame, 64, 130, 135–43, 193n3, 202n40, 219n115, 219n118, 220n133; and socialism, 110, 135–41
Nobel Prize for Literature, 44
Non-Aligned Movement, 5, 6, 27, 56, 62, 219n115
nonalignment, 2, 5, 23, 24, 25, 36, 48, 55–64, 87, 93, 137, 219n121
North Atlantic Treaty Organization (NATO), 17, 19, 22; 1958 confidential report, 17, 22
Northern Hemisphere, 4–5, 20
Nsukka group, 77
Nwoko, Demas, 39
Nyerere, Julius, 172

Okigbo, Christopher, 39, 43, 84
Okri, Ben, 176, 186
Ondjaki (also: Ndalu de Almeida), 27, 146–7, 178–84, 226n109; *Granma Nineteen and the Soviet's Secret*, 27, 146–7, 178–84, 226n109
Onoge, Omafume F., 35–36, 77, 119
Opperman, Deon, 153, 222n24
oral literature, 34, 65, 66, 78, 86–7, 94, 99, 102, 103, 183, 194n11, 207n1, 213n142, 226n100
Organization of the Solidarity of the Peoples of Africa, Asia, and Latin America (OSPAAAL), 59

p'Bitek, Okot, 70
Padmore, George, 120
Pan-Africanism, 25, 27, 32, 56, 59, 76, 119, 129, 136, 152, 172, 202n40, 219n115
Paris, 2, 20, 24, 33, 38–40, 56, 58, 81, 192, 205n96
*partynost*, 8
Pelevin, Victor, 183
PEN International, 44, 45; 1966 Congress, 44
People's Liberation Army of Namibia (PLAN), 148, 150, 165, 177, 221n6

People's Movement for the Liberation of Angola (MPLA), 109, 148, 149, 151, 152, 157, 159–64, 168, 173, 177–8, 180, 184

Peoples' Friendship University, 120

Pepetela (also: Artur Pestana dos Santos), 27, 146, 151, 159–62, 165, 186; *Mayombe*, 27, 146, 151, 159–62

Per Ankh press, 76

Picasso, Pablo, 79, 81

Pinochet, Augusto, 166

postcolonial studies, 2, 5–8, 13–16, 28, 94, 187–90, 194n9, 228n17, 228n19; and Cold War scholarship, 2, 5–8, 13–16, 28, 187–90; postcolonial literature, 3, 11, 13, 24, 28, 94, 110, 113, 124, 146, 191

postmodernism, 27, 32, 66, 68–70, 75, 79, 85, 90, 97, 147, 165, 182, 185–6, 208n18, 211n92, 222n24

Pound, Ezra, 70, 72, 77, 79, 84

*Présence Africaine* journal, 25, 56–9, 116, 152, 192

*Preuves* magazine, 21

Prinsloo, Koos, 153, 222n24

*Quadrant* magazine, 21

*Quest* magazine, 21

Ractliffe, Jo, 109–10, 145–9, 180; *As Terras do Fim do Mundo*, 145; *Terreno Ocupado*, 180

*Ramparts* magazine, 48

realism, 6, 25–7, 32, 35, 47, 65–72, 75–97, 99–103, 119, 145–7, 151, 165, 176, 182–4, 186, 207n12, 209n42, 211n92, 213n137, 213n142, 216n51; critical realism, 35–6, 69, 74, 88; magical realism, 27, 97, 145–6, 176, 182–4, 186, 227n128; and modernism, 6, 8, 26, 65–72, 75–8, 90, 103, 207n12, 207n12; socialist realism, 8, 25, 35–6, 47, 52, 68–9, 75, 87–94, 97, 99–103, 119, 151, 203n65, 213n137

revolution, 26, 31, 100, 107–44, 159–64, 172, 174, 176, 214n5, 214n11, 220n131, 226n114; Fanon, Frantz, 26, 31, 116–17, 128–9, 139, 141, 161, 164; temporality of revolution, 26, 107–8, 122. *See also* Bolshevik Revolution; Cuba: Cuban Revolution; Grenada Revolution; Haitian Revolution

Rhodesia, 128, 158, 217n79

Rivonia trial (1963–1964), 127

Rodney, Walter, 189

Rui, Manuel, 151

Rushdie, Salman, 44, 182

Sachs, Albie, 107, 174, 177, 214n1

Sadat, Anwar, 23

Sahni, Bhisham, 54

Said, Edward, 5–6, 13–14, 44, 46, 186, 189, 195n19; *Culture and Imperialism*, 6; *Orientalism*, 5–6, 13–14

Sankara, Thomas, 143

Santos, Marcelino dos, 49

Saroukhan, Alexander, 49–50

Sartre, Jean-Paul, 35, 56

Savimbi, Jonas, 152, 163

Scramble for Africa, 5, 169

Second World, 3, 8, 33, 36, 75, 157, 193n4. *See also* Cold War: Eastern Bloc

Sembène, Ousmane, 6, 8, 26, 35, 49, 51–2, 70, 88, 90, 102–3, 110, 113–21, 124, 144, 151, 214n4, 214n5, 215n19, 215n29; *God's Bits of Wood*, 26, 110, 113–120, 214n11; *Le Mandat*, 88; *Lotus* Prize, 51–2; in Marseilles, 114–16, 215n29; training in film in Moscow, 6, 8, 120–1; *Xala*, 124, 214n4

Senegal, 1, 18, 24, 33, 39, 49, 52, 114, 117, 120, 121, 192, 193n3, 214n5

Senghor, Léopold Sédar, 18, 33, 56–9, 121, 137–8, 139, 193n3, 214n5; and African socialism, 137, 139

Serote, Mongane Wally, 26, 110–11, 121–34, 144, 146, 154, 167, 169–74, 216–17n57, 217n59, 217–18n80, 218n88; and exile, 127–9, 153, 169, 172, 216–17n57, 218n88; *Scatter the Ashes and Go*, 146, 154, 169–71, 174, 217n79; *To*

256    Index

*Every Birth Its Blood*, 26, 110–11, 121–43, 214n11; *Tsetlo*, 128; *Yakhal'inkomo*, 128, 217–18n80
Seven Seas Press, 61, 203n50
Sholokhov, Mikhail, 92, 93, 100, 101; *And Quiet Flows the Don*, 100
Sinyavsky, Andrei, 44
Sissako, Abderrahmane, 8
Sisulu, Walter, 128
Sobukwe, Robert, 128
socialism, 7–8, 10, 16, 31, 33, 35–6, 64, 69, 73–5, 93, 108–10, 115, 121, 124, 126, 132, 135–44, 149, 157, 162–3, 167–8, 170, 172–3, 178, 180–1, 183, 185, 189, 195–6n29, 196n36, 204n70, 209n39, 209–10n43, 219n121, 226n109, 226n114, 216n55; African socialism, 5, 26, 108, 110, 135–44, 172. *See also* realism: socialist realism
Solzhenitsyn, Alexander, 76, 177; *Gulag Archipelago*, 177
South Africa, 11, 18, 24, 27, 31, 38–9, 45, 49, 60–1, 71–2, 77, 88–9, 110, 121, 123–34, 144, 145–58, 162, 165–70, 173–7, 191, 195n24, 202n48, 217n79, 218n99, 221n5, 221n6, 222n26, 223n37, 224n63, 225n79, 225n85, 226n105; National Party (South Africa), 88, 157; South African Security Branch, 156, 223n37. *See also* Border War; South African Broadcast Corporation (SABC); South African Communist Party (SACP); South African Defence Force (SADF)
South African Broadcast Corporation (SABC), 166, 224n63
South African Communist Party (SACP), 11, 61, 125–32, 132, 157, 162, 167–8, 170–4, 184, 217n79, 218n97, 223n37, 224n71, 224n73, 225n86; alliance with ANC 125–32, 162, 168, 171–2, 174, 184, 217n79, 218n97; *The Road to South African Freedom: The Programme of the South African Communist Party*, 132, 224n71
South African Defence Force (SADF), 123, 147–50, 153, 154, 158, 171, 221n6

South West Africa People's Organization, 148
Southern Hemisphere, 5, 11, 168
Soviet Union (also: USSR), 1, 3–12, 16–23, 25, 27, 33–4, 43, 47–8, 51–2, 54–5, 57, 67, 69–70, 73–6, 87, 92–3, 99, 101–2, 108–9, 120–1, 127, 136, 142, 147, 150–1, 157, 167–8, 171–3, 177, 179–81, 186, 189–90, 195n19, 195n24, 195n28, 196n36, 203n66, 204n70, 216n55, 218n99, 219n112; Central Committee of the Communist Party, 19; Kremlin, 8, 11, 157, 168; Soviet imperialism, 4–13, 15–24, 36, 58, 135, 162, 167–8, 184, 195n24, 224n76; Soviet paternalism/fraternalism, 10, 33, 73, 120, 137, 143, 170, 178, 180; Soviet-style communism, 23, 75, 121, 156, 178, 180, 188; State Committee for Cultural Ties, 19. *See also* Cold War: superpowers; Union of Soviet Societies of Friendship and Cultural Relations with Foreign Countries; Union of Soviet Writers
Soweto Uprising (1976), 121–3, 127, 130, 131, 216–17n57, 225n96
Soyinka, Wole, 14–15, 31, 33–4, 35, 39–40, 70, 77–8, 84–5, 192, 201n30, 202n49, 204n70, 208n20, 210n66, 211n77; imprisonment, 34, 44; Nobel Prize, 44
space race, 12, 179
Spender, Stephen, 63, 207n129
Stalin, Joseph, 10, 19, 20, 41, 44, 120, 193n2
Strachan, Alexander, 153
Suez Canal, 120, 194n15
Sutherland, Efua, 47, 48

Tanzania, 131, 172, 176
*Tempo Presente* magazine, 21
temporality, 26, 107–8, 110–12, 118, 121–4, 131, 134, 139, 141–3, 174–5, 216n42; of revolution, 26, 107–8, 122. *See also* affective temporal structures

Index  **257**

Third World, 2–8, 11–12, 17, 19–20, 23, 25, 27, 32–3, 37, 47–8, 51, 55–62, 67, 72, 74–5, 86, 87, 92, 109, 143–4, 147, 168, 190, 193n2, 194n8, 195n19
Thompson, John, 42, 202n42, 202n43
Thu Bon, 51–2
Tolstoy, Leo, 98, 100
Transcription Centre (London), 33, 38, 40, 43, 55, 201n32, 202n43, 211n77; Africa Abroad radio program, 40; Commonwealth Arts Festival (1965), 40; Cultural Events in Africa newsletter, 40, 43
*Transition* magazine, 20–1, 25, 38, 39, 41–3, 47–8, 71, 77–9, 82–3, 85–6, 95, 191–2, 201n30, 202n40, 202n49, 210n66
*Tricontinental* journal, 60
tricontinentalism, 60, 62, 93–4, 152
Trotsky, Leon, 73
Turgenev, Ivan, 100

Uganda, 1, 18, 24, 38, 39, 41, 176, 191, 193n3
*Ujamaa*, 172, 208n20
Umkhonto we Sizwe (MK), 107, 127, 131, 146, 150, 154, 165, 169–71, 173–7, 216–17n57, 217n77, 217n79, 222n27
UNESCO, 20, 44
Union of Soviet Societies of Friendship and Cultural Relations with Foreign Countries, 19, 198n64
Union of Soviet Writers, 1, 6, 47, 90, 92–3, 99, 193n1
United Nations (UN), 34, 195n19; United Nations High Commissioner for Refugees 147
United States (also: U.S., America), 1, 3–17, 19–21, 23, 25, 27, 32–4, 36–39, 41–43, 46–8, 51, 55, 58, 60, 63, 66–7, 69, 74, 76, 79, 81, 83–89, 93, 94, 96, 108, 119–21, 128, 130, 133, 135–6, 140–1, 150, 151, 157–8, 165–70, 177, 185–8, 192, 195n19, 198n67, 201n30, 202n39, 208n21, 209n45, 211n77, 216–17n57, 218n88; Black Power Movement, 128; Civil Rights Movement, 12, 128; Red Scare (United States), 165; space program, 4, 12, 179. *See also* imperialism: Western
Uzbek Soviet Socialist Republic, 17, 22, 48, 51

Van den Bergh, Hendrik, 156
Vieira, José Luandino, 151, 226n109
Vietnam, 5, 13, 52, 133, 149, 158, 198n67
*Voprosy Literatury*, 18

Wallerstein, Immanuel, 72–4, 209n34
Warwick Research Collective (WReC), 22, 72–5, 190, 191, 209n41, 209n45
Weideman, George, 153, 222n24
Wicomb, Zoë, 107; *David's Story*, 107
Wilhelm, Peter, 153
Williams, Raymond, 111, 121, 126
Woolf, Virginia, 79
World Health Organization, 147
world literature, 2–3, 21–2, 26, 28, 73, 185–92. *See also* postcolonial literature
World War I, 22
World War II (also: Second World War), 4, 5, 7, 9, 13, 15, 21, 31, 37, 44, 45, 56, 67, 68, 74, 84, 87, 88, 92, 108, 114, 119, 124, 145, 193n2, 194n8
Wright, Richard, 56, 205n96

Yacine, Kateb, 31, 49
Yoruba poetry, 87

Zimbabwe, 124, 128

www.ingramcontent.com/pod-product-compliance
Lightning Source LLC
Chambersburg PA
CBHW070758230426
43665CB00017B/2401